THE AGONY OF THE G.O.P. 1964

Robert D. Novak

THE AGONY
OF THE G.O.P. 1964

THE MACMILLAN COMPANY, NEW YORK
COLLIER-MACMILLAN LIMITED, LONDON

Contents

This book could not have been written without an enormous amount of help from its cast of characters: the leaders and followers of the Republican Party. Scores of them supplied suggestions, opinions and—most important—information to me in the preparation of this book. I shall not embarrass any of them by singling them out, but they have my thanks.

Specifically, my thanks also go to Peter Ritner of The Macmillan Company, who back in 1962 came up with the idea for this book, and to Rowland Evans, Jr., my partner in the column-writing business, whose perceptive reporting has been utilized time and again in collecting information for the book.

Most of all, thanks are due to my wife Geraldine, whose research work, secretarial work, and patience were absolutely essential.

R. D. N.

November 11, 1964
Washington, D.C.

THE AGONY OF THE G.O.P. 1964

I

★ ★

"Extremism . . . Is No Vice"

On Friday morning, July 17, 1964, Tom Stagg, Jr., of Shreveport, Louisiana, just couldn't keep himself from bursting out in smiles as he waited for the start of a meeting of the Republican National Committee in the rococo Colonial Room of the St. Francis Hotel in San Francisco.

National Committeeman Stagg had in his hands a press copy of Senator Barry Goldwater's speech at the Cow Palace the night before, when the latter had formally accepted the Republican Party's nomination for President of the United States. What had Tom Stagg's attention and what was causing those smiles were these two sentences in the text (underscored in the press copy at Goldwater's express direction):

I would remind you that extremism in the defense of liberty is no vice.

And let me remind you also that moderation in the pursuit of justice is no virtue!

In a convention where the victor's supporters had been constantly accused of "extremism" and the vanquished had raised high the banner of "moderation," the Senator's words were loaded with political meaning. They were no less than

1

a slap in the face of the long dominant and now defeated progressive wing of the Republican Party.

That's one reason why Tom Stagg—young, Southern, segregationist, and militantly conservative—was so delighted by the two sentences. "I sure like that," Stagg said, mostly to himself, "I sure like that."

Others didn't, among them Governor Nelson A. Rockefeller of New York and Governor William W. Scranton of Pennsylvania. General of the Army Dwight David Eisenhower told friends that he was concerned about Goldwater's language. But July 17, 1964, was not a day for the Rockefellers or the Scrantons or the Eisenhowers. This was a day for the Tom Staggs, the new leaders of the Republican Party.

At the meeting soon to begin, the National Committee would pick as its chairman Goldwater's choice: a young Arizona lawyer named Dean Burch (recognized on sight by few national committeemen). In turn, Burch would name as his chief aide and staff director of the National Committee a young Alabama lawyer named John Grenier. Arizona and Alabama were taking over the inner sanctum of the Grand Old Party, once ruled by the kingmakers of New York and Pennsylvania.

That Friday morning in San Francisco was the morning after a revolution.

In some small part, the revolution was a vindication for the futility of the Old Guard of Robert Alfonso Taft in twenty-nine years of defeat at the hands of the Eastern Establishment.

But the Dean Burches and John Greniers and Tom Staggs were not the lineal heirs of Bob Taft. Rather, they were a new breed of conservative, and they had just crushed the party's Eastern masters.

And what of the general-election campaign against Lyndon Baines Johnson? This didn't seem to concern the new breed of conservatives on July 17 in San Francisco. In fact, the nomination was in itself the fulfillment of their ambitions. The dismal campaign against Johnson was an anticlimax.

The unhappy aftermath of those buoyant July days in San Francisco came on Wednesday morning, November 4, in the Peace Pipe Room of the Camelback Inn in Phoenix, Arizona.

The night before, reporters from Washington and New York had waited in the Peace Pipe Room for Goldwater to concede his overwhelming defeat and to congratulate the victor—as tradition demands. Instead, the Senator remained at his house on the mountain, sending down word that he had gone to bed at 11 P.M. Inexplicably, he had broken a graceful and useful tradition.

He did come down from the mountain on Wednesday morning, but his words of concession were bereft of grace and courtesy. In his telegram of congratulations to the President, he reminded Johnson of all the problems facing him. In the face of overwhelming defeat, he boasted that "twenty-five million votes is a lot of votes." He grumbled that criticisms of him by newspaper columnists and radio-television commentators "have made the fourth estate a rather sad, sorry mess." His mood was truculent and defiant.

That night, at a postelection cocktail party in Washington's National Press Club, a faithful Goldwater staffer whispered to a friend: "I know Barry could have conceded better than he did today at Phoenix. I *know* he could have. If I didn't think so, I couldn't look myself in the mirror."

In his column from Phoenix for the *New York Herald Tribune*, Jimmy Breslin was not so charitable. He wrote:

> Among the many things Barry Goldwater knows nothing of is the way men are supposed to act when they lose the Presidency of the United States.

But this was not the Barry Goldwater who had charmed the Washington press corps, excited the rank and file of the

Republican Party, and served as the inspiration for one of the few spontaneous political movements in American history. The long journey of the past four years had taken much from him. It also left a bitterness that had not existed before. Worst of all had been the meaningless, dull eight-week campaign of September and October.

For one thing, Goldwater never was able to escape his ghost-written words at San Francisco that Tom Stagg enjoyed so much. He never repeated them, but neither did he repudiate them. Moreover, Democrats had plenty of help in reminding the general electorate of those words—help from the most ardent Goldwaterites themselves.

A week before the election, Goldwater forces went to the considerable expense of purchasing a full-page advertisement in the *New York Times* of October 28 listing the names of famous fighter pilots (headed by Captain Eddie Rickenbacker) who were supporting Goldwater. The advertisement's bold type read:

FIGHTING ACES FOR GOLDWATER
". . . extremism in the defense of
liberty is no vice. Moderation
in the pursuit of justice is no virtue."
Senator Barry Goldwater, San Francisco,
July 16, 1964.

WE   WERE
    E   X   T   R   E   M   I   S   T   S

We are civilians who served our country in wartime.

This was the tone of the entire campaign: Goldwater's friends supplying the Democrats with their best ammunition, both sides quibbling about definitions, the great American middle being driven into Lyndon Johnson's arms. Indeed, it often seemed as though Goldwater's general staff and the Goldwater Movement generally were more concerned about proving a point than in winning an election. Aside from an abortive Republican "summit" meeting in Hershey, Pennsylvania, shortly after the convention, there was no real effort made to achieve party unity.

Consider Goldwater's monster rally in Pittsburgh the Thursday night before the election. Governor William Scranton of Pennsylvania, Goldwater's last foe for the nomination, was there to introduce him. As a party regular, Scranton had been crisscrossing the country with remarkably warm speeches in Goldwater's behalf. Now, as the disastrous campaign neared an end, he presumably was prepared to say the same kind words to Goldwater's face.

But early in his introduction, Scranton remarked in passing that he did not always agree with Goldwater. The fanatically devoted Goldwaterites in the auditorium were incensed and immediately—as a reflex action—started booing Scranton. Booed in his own state in front of Barry Goldwater, Bill Scranton stiffened. He hurried through the rest of the speech, coolly introducing Goldwater as "the Republican candidate for President of the United States" instead of as "the next President of the United States" as custom dictates.

In such an atmosphere of mutual distrust and suspicion across the country, rank-and-file Republican moderates and liberals stayed away on election day or voted for Johnson by the millions. The result was one of the great landslides of American political history, raising ominous question marks for the future of the Republican Party.

More than 61 percent of the voters supported Johnson. Goldwater's Southern strategy of writing off the Eastern industrialist states, holding the traditional Republican states of the Midwest and West, and cutting into the South had backfired. He did win in the sections of the South where racist sentiment was strongest (Alabama, Mississippi, Louisiana, South Carolina, Georgia) and in his native Arizona— but nowhere else, not even the more industrialized and urbanized areas of the South (Virgina, Florida, Tennessee,

Texas) that had been going Republican in recent elections.

The result was a Johnson win in forty-four out of fifty states, an electoral margin of 486 votes to 52 votes. Democrats maintained their two-to-one edge in the Senate and among Governorships, and they gained forty seats in the House, pushing their edge to two-to-one there. State Legislatures fell to the Democrats in New York, Michigan, Iowa, and elsewhere.

By and large, the most impressive Republican winners were those who kept clear of the Goldwater campaign. Governor George Romney of Michigan and Representative John V. Lindsay of New York City, neither of whom endorsed Goldwater, were landslide winners in the face of the Johnson tide. But Republican victories were rare on November 3. Such promising figures as Charles Percy (running for Governor in Illinois), Robert Taft, Jr. (running for the Senate from Ohio), and Bud Wilkinson (running for the Senate from Oklahoma) were cut down.

And the debacle was followed quickly by a cacophony of Republican bickering and fault finding that pointed toward another four years of party chaos.

Yet, it was all predictable back in July in San Francisco. The long, dreary general-election campaign really had changed nothing. The disastrous conclusion was foredoomed by the events of the Cow Palace. And those events were the product of a struggle stretching back four years—to the campaign of 1960.

II

★ ★

The View from 1960

Although history probably shall best remember the 1960 Presidential election between John F. Kennedy and Richard M. Nixon for the closeness of the final vote, this was one campaign that found the supporters of one of the candidates conducting a post-mortem on the cause of his defeat nearly a month before election day. The fact that Republicans were explaining the "defeat" of Richard Milhous Nixon so far in advance tells much about the Republican Party and the internal power struggle that was to preoccupy it the next four years.

The business of Republican politicians talking in guarded tones among themselves and to the press about how Nixon was kicking away the election reached its peak during his dismal whistle-stop tour through the Republican heartland of Ohio, Michigan, and Illinois on October 26-27-28, two weeks before the election. Willard Edwards of the *Chicago Tribune,* an old friend of Nixon dating back to his career as a Red-hunter in the House, wrote that the sour smell of defeat on the Nixon train reminded him of the atmosphere on the Herbert Hoover campaign train in 1932. The Nixon campaign's morale picked up a bit the next week when the Republican candidate opened up with some give-'em-hell speeches against Kennedy, but before-the-fact analyses of

7

why Nixon might be defeated continued right up to election day.

Much of the reason for this premature burial can be laid to Nixon himself. Because Nixon and his immediate staff maintained an iron curtain of seclusion around the candidate, an abnormally high number of Republican politicians were offended during the course of the long campaign. It was easier to gain an audience with the Pope than to see Nixon privately during the 1960 campaign. Even Leonard Hall, a former national party chairman and senior member of Nixon's five-man "strategy board," found it difficult to confer with Nixon. Since Nixon didn't even listen to the advice of most of the party functionaries, it's quite natural that they were singing a lament of how Nixon was booting away the campaign through improper tactics. As a lifelong practicing politician, Nixon should have known that the surest way to alienate a politician is to refuse to listen to him.

Yet the Republican dirge about Nixon's tactics had roots deeper than mere personal pique. From beginning to end of his carefully prepared Presidential campaign, Nixon attempted to appeal to both the left and the right wings in a party that is more deeply divided than it dares to admit. Nixon made a bad job of it. He failed to satisfy either faction.

This ideological dissatisfaction was voiced almost from the moment of Nixon's nomination at the Chicago convention in July. The Republican left complained that Nixon was killing his chances for victory by moving too far to the right and thereby alienating the necessary independent and Republican voters. The Republican right contended he was defeating himself by moving too far to the left as another me-too candidate, thereby alienating the Republican faithful as well as Southern conservative Democrats. Of course, both the left and the right Republicans were really betraying their own ideological bias in what was supposed to be objective, non-ideological criticism of Nixon's tactics. At any rate, Nixon gave both camps of critics plenty of ammunition. In his effort personally to bridge the schism in his party, Nixon would flop first one way and then the other trying to maintain himself in the middle of the Republican road.

It must be stressed that this criticism was subdued rather than virulent, private rather than public. Nobody publicly attacks his party's candidate before the returns are in. But behind-the-back criticism was the order of the day in the Republican Party. Everybody was doing it, including the two leaders who symbolized the opposite poles of the Republican Party: Governor Nelson A. Rockefeller of New York on the Republican left and Senator Barry Goldwater of Arizona on the Republican right.

As Nelson Aldrich Rockefeller's family-owned Convair flew the short hop from Dutchess County, New York, into New York City on Saturday night, October 22, 1960, he was strangely ebullient. Strangely, because the 1960 Presidential campaign was scarcely an invigorating experience for the Governor of New York.

The Nixon high command regarded Rockefeller as a campaigner of limited and extremely specialized value. By assigning him to campaign only in overwhelmingly Democratic areas, the Nixon high command was saying in effect: "Governor, you may appeal to just enough Democratic and independent voters to help us in these areas. But your Republicanism is entirely too suspect for you to go off into the Republican heartland." From the standpoint of Rockefeller's own political career, it might have helped him in the troubled years ahead if he had been permitted during the fall of 1960 to show the rock-ribbed Republicans of the Midwest and Far West that he really was a bona fide Republican. Instead, he was assigned out-of-state speaking assignments in spots that could best be described as political disaster areas from the Republican point of view: the Mexican section of Los Angeles, the Mesabi iron range in northern Minnesota, and—right across the river from New York City—Newark, New Jersey. Rockefeller probably couldn't have run too well in these areas himself. It was absurd to think that he could help Nixon here.

Actually, Rockefeller's major assignment for the 1960 campaign was New York. This was a triply frustrating task for Rockefeller.

The least important of these frustrations was the lack of satisfaction Rockefeller derived in barnstorming through his own state singing Richard Nixon's praises. The Governor could not then or ever have been called a special admirer of the Vice-President. Consequently, it could hardly have been a pleasant chore to trot about the New York countryside declaring: "We need Dick Nixon for our leader for the next four years."

Far more important, it was quite clear by late October that Kennedy was going to win New York and its forty-five electoral votes. In fact, the usually reliable *New York Daily News* poll pointed to a Kennedy landslide in the state. Thus, Rockefeller could not really save Nixon in New York no matter how many testimonials he delivered. The real purpose of his trip was to save himself, to prove to regular Republicans for future reference that he was fighting to elect Nixon as President despite their past differences.

This was where Rockefeller's third and most galling frustration came in. Some party workers in the Governor's own state were so convinced of his deep-seated enmity to Nixon that they refused to believe their ears when they heard him endorse the Nixon-Lodge ticket without qualifications.

On October 21 in Amsterdam, New York, a youthful Republican lawyer had just listened to Rockefeller's praise of Nixon. "Sure I heard him," said the lawyer, "but I don't believe him. I think he wants Kennedy to win." The disbelief was understandably stronger among party workers outside New York. Whether Rockefeller foresaw it or not, an enduring postelection myth was to begin among party workers that Rockefeller deliberately sabotaged Nixon in New York to ensure that he would not be elected (and that Rockefeller could then seek the office in 1964).

Nevertheless, campaigning can carry with it a joyous intoxication that drives away all rational cares—particularly campaigning through New York's Mohawk Valley in the golden days of late October. Just completing his second year in elective politics, Rockefeller had learned by this time how to draw a response from a partisan audience. And, like any good campaigner, he was elated by the response. It had been a good day for cheers and applause as Rockefeller concluded two weeks of upstate campaigning and prepared for one week of speeches and handshaking in New York City.

So, despite his unpleasant political position in the campaign, he was in a rare mood this Saturday night. As a light-drinking descendant of teetotaling Baptists, he usually stuck to Dubonnet on the rocks. However, he surprised his aides by asking for a bottle of beer on the plane. His conversation also seemed less inhibited than usual.

He immediately launched into the then popular party game of "How's Nixon's kicking away the campaign." His version, delivered without venom, ran like this:

It looks very much as though Nixon is going to lose the election for failing to pick up enough electoral votes in the big industrialized states. He's losing the big industrialized states, because he's chasing a will-o'-the-wisp trying to capture Southern states. No matter how hard he tries, Nixon can't win the South. But he can alienate the North, which is attainable—and absolutely necessary.

Rockefeller was particularly aroused by Nixon's failure to come into New York often enough. At that point, Nixon had made only two campaign visits each to upstate New York and New York City—all of them quite brief—and had completely neglected the massive Negro vote in Harlem and Brooklyn. Rockefeller disclosed that he had tried—without any success at all—to try to talk Nixon into canceling some of his Southern expeditions and concentrating on the big Northern urban vote and particularly the Negro vote.

Rockefeller was pleased that Nixon was making an eleventh-hour New York swing—upstate on November 1, in the city on November 2. But the Governor considered this too little, too late. Furthermore, he feared that whatever good Nixon did himself by the New York City visit would be wiped out the next day when he addressed a rally at one of the citadels of racial segregation: the Statehouse at Columbia, South Carolina.[1]

Two weeks later on the other side of the country, Barry Goldwater was resting at his home in Phoenix, waiting for election day. In truth, he hadn't really worked that hard during the campaign to require much rest. In many ways, the 1960 campaign was even more unpleasant for Goldwater than for Rockefeller.

After the July convention in Chicago, when the nation suddenly found that a spontaneous mass movement was growing for Goldwater, the leaders of the Republican Party —including Nixon—realized they had a phenomenon on their hands. But they still couldn't take Goldwater seriously as a national party leader. To the contrary, they feared that wide exposure of Goldwater's harshly conservative votes might lose votes for Nixon.

Yet Goldwater could not be exiled to Phoenix and forgotten. In his way, he was incomparably more important to the

---

[1] Democratic politicians tend to agree with Rockefeller on this point. After the election, Democrats declared that the turning point in the fight for the Negro vote was reached at the Columbia rally. In the closing days of the campaign, Democrats distributed a news photo at the Columbia rally showing Nixon with Dixiecrat Jimmy Byrnes, an archsegregationist. Furthermore, news stories told of how Attorney General William Rogers, a staunch civil rights advocate, had stayed aboard the plane during the Columbia visit. However, the point is debatable. Polls taken well before the Columbia rally indicated that Kennedy had the Negro vote wrapped up anyway.

Republican campaign effort than Rockefeller. Many ultra-conservative businessmen, particularly west of the Alleghe-nies, were tightening up on their purse strings because of what they regarded as Nixon's flirtation with me-too liber-alism. Goldwater was the only man who could unloosen them and get the needed money flowing.

The problem in Southern California was typical. The busi-nessmen there, a rabidly conservative lot, once were Nixon's most enthusiastic patrons but were souring on their boy. They were particularly incensed over what would seem a most esoteric issue: Nixon's support of repeal of the Con-nally Reservation limiting United States acceptance of World Court jurisdiction. Whether these businessmen understood the Connally Reservation or not is unimportant. They were undeniably exercised over it. Goldwater, a steadfast cham-pion of the Connally Reservation, was needed to mollify them. But the Los Angeles County Republican Committee, then squarely under Nixon's control, had no desire to see Goldwater address a major rally in the Hollywood Bowl with a conservative exhortation that might scare independent and wavering Democratic voters into the Kennedy camp. The answer was for Goldwater to address a little-publicized, in-vitation-only meeting of fat cats. It was that kind of cam-paign for Goldwater all over the country.

As a loyal party man, Goldwater did his part to tone down his own statements. But back home in Phoenix on Saturday night, November 5, he was ready to talk frankly but privately about Nixon and deliver his autopsy of Nixon's defeat two days before the election.

Nixon had appeared side by side with Goldwater on Oc-tober 15 for two speeches in Phoenix. Goldwater wasn't particularly impressed. Nor were his friends around the country who heard Nixon and reported back to him. More-over, Goldwater and his allies couldn't have disagreed more with Nixon's overall strategy (or at least what they conceived his strategy to be). What makes the Goldwater position particularly fascinating is the fact that it was the exact reverse of Rockefeller's.

Goldwater believed that Nixon made his basic mistake by moving to the left to woo an urban Democratic vote and particularly a Negro vote that was irrevocably Democratic. In Goldwater's opinion, the electoral votes of New York and probably a good many other industrialized states were locked up for the Democrats when they nominated Kennedy and drafted a liberal platform in Los Angeles back in July.

Therefore, Goldwater was aghast at Nixon's gestures toward the left: capitulation to Rockefeller's demands for a strong civil rights plank in the national platform, selection of Henry Cabot Lodge as nominee for Vice-President in an effort to pick up Eastern votes, sporadic statements suggesting a strong civil rights stand.[2]

These moves, Goldwater felt, had not only lost Nixon his golden opportunity to become the first Republican in a generation to bring out the full conservative vote but also had botched up the chance to sweep all or most of the segregationist South. Four days before the election, Goldwater felt a Nixon victory would be more the product of an unseen and benevolent hand than Nixon's skill and wisdom.

Unfortunately from the standpoint of internal Republican harmony, the election results could be interpreted to prove both Goldwater and Rockefeller correct. As Rockefeller had feared, Nixon *did* lose all the Northeastern industrial states. As Goldwater had feared, Nixon *did* fare worse in the South than expected (failing to win South Carolina, North Carolina, and Texas, all of which were considered favorable to

---

[2] It ought to go without saying that Goldwater was furious when Lodge pledged that Nixon would appoint a Negro to the Cabinet. This was not a matter of racial prejudice on Goldwater's part. He simply felt that Lodge was alienating Southern voters, with no real prospect of gains among Negroes.

Nixon). The razor-thin margin of the Kennedy win only enhanced the possibility for tactical debate within the party. If Nixon had won the Northeastern states, he could have been elected President, Rockefeller could say. Nixon could have been elected President had he swept the South, Goldwater could say.

Actually, both the Goldwater and Rockefeller tactical arguments are oversimplifications. But that doesn't really matter. They weren't really talking about political tactics at all. They were talking political ideology with a veneer of political tactics to make it more acceptable. Furthermore, this ideological debate between Goldwater and Rockefeller descends directly from the great schism that devitalized the Republican Party in 1912 and has been debilitating it ever since.

From the end of the Civil War to the turn of the century, the Republican Party was the nation's dominant party. Its internal differences were the strivings for power between opposing factions (Stalwarts versus Half-Breeds) or battling between reform-minded Mugwumps and the machine politicians. There were no serious problems of ideological division. This state of high Republican health reached a climax in 1896 when William McKinley defeated William Jennings Bryan with the biggest plurality ever recorded by a Republican Presidential candidate up to that time. The Republican Party of McKinley was a broad-based party of the businessman, the laborer, the more prosperous farmer. The Democratic Party of Bryan was a minority party of the solid and sullen South, with support from discontented Western farmers and some immigrant elements (mainly the Irish) in the East.

But in the Republican Party's very political prosperity were the seeds for dissolution. As a broad-based majority party, it contained inherently antagonistic elements that had to be kept in careful balance. Moreover, its left wing was growing. The traumatic experience of three Bryan candidacies in four elections made the Democratic Party something less than attractive for intelligent progressives. The Democratic Party really was, as Theodore Roosevelt was to say later, the party of "rural toryism." It was natural that progressives flocked under the wide Republican tent, building an ever stronger left wing within the Republican Party between 1900 and 1912.

A facade of party harmony persisted mainly because Colonel Roosevelt was a master at reconciling the irreconcilable. Basically a progressive (even a radical progressive), Roosevelt as President distributed his favors evenly among the party's left and right wings. He even managed an amiable and fruitful relationship with Speaker Joseph (Uncle Joe) Cannon, the crusty old reactionary from Illinois. Indeed, the one great error Roosevelt committed during the Presidency was the designation of William Howard Taft as his successor. But it was a fatal error.

Taft, who was a lawyer's lawyer but a politician's nightmare, had no taste for a political juggling act. Though he considered himself a progressive, his basically conservative nature pushed him more and more to the party's right wing. He had no skill whatever in reconciling the irreconcilable. Still worse, Colonel Roosevelt returned from big game hunting in Africa midway through the Taft Administration. With Roosevelt looking over his shoulder, Taft's political record grew worse and worse.

Actually, the party's conservative wing was not markedly superior in numbers to the progressive wing in 1912. On the contrary, Roosevelt was so much more clearly popular than President Taft within the party that the progressive wing was probably stronger under Roosevelt's leadership than the conservative wing under Taft's. At that fateful Chicago convention in June, 1912, Taft was nominated only because he controlled the rotten borough delegations from the South.

However, the conservatives' use of pressure not only nominated Taft but provoked the schism from which the Republican Party never has recovered. When the defeated Roosevelt and his progressive followers bolted the Republican Party to form the Progressive (or Bull Moose) Party, the results in November were predictable. Roosevelt easily outran Taft, and the two Republican candidates divided 55 percent of the vote. But Democrat Woodrow Wilson was elected President with 45 percent of the vote.

After this debacle, it would seem sensible for the Republican Party to forego ideological hairsplitting and instead effect a grand reunion of the party. But here is where the Republican Party begins to show a taint, an aberration, a sort of political masochism that plagues it to this day. The conservatives who had stayed with Taft and the Republican Party actually were delighted that the party's left wing was no longer there to bother them. They rejoiced that Senator William Beveridge of Indiana and other Bull Moose members of the Senate and House were beaten in 1912, thereby removing progressive influences from Congressional caucuses of the Republicans.[3] Joseph B. Foraker, an Old Guard Republican leader from Ohio, made it clear that the Bull Moosers could return to the party only on the conservatives' conditions. According to Foraker, those conditions required belief "in the protective tariff policies" and belief in "our representative form of government, without any of the socialistic vagaries that are being put forward in the name of progressiveness to first modify, then ultimately destroy our Institutions." When a band of ex-Bull Moosers, including Gifford Pinchot and Harold Ickes, did try to return to the party in 1916, the Republican National Committee imposed humiliating terms for reentry.

[3] Beveridge, the brilliant biographer of Abraham Lincoln, later returned to the Grand Old Party but on the party's own terms. Indiana's greatest progressive ended his political career as an embittered reactionary.

All this, predictably enough, led to the permanent loss of the party's left wing with a cry of "good riddance" from the conservatives. What the Old Guard didn't realize was that the Republican Party was descending into minority status, a party that could go to its right but not its left. That rightward movement was adequate for survival during the post-World War I reaction. But when the nation demanded a leftward movement in the Depression, the party of Theodore Roosevelt was immobile. It was similarly paralyzed when the political revolution of Franklin Roosevelt's New Deal in 1932 turned the Democratic Party into the nation's majority party for the first time since the Civil War.[4] While the rejuvenated Democratic Party extended its base as never before, the Republicans were transfixed—embedded in a stance of monolithic conservatism in no way appropriate to the 1930's.

By 1940, the Republican situation was clear enough for realistic party leaders to see. Eight years of the New Deal had confirmed the Democratic Party, now clearly identified with a left-of-center ideology, as the nation's dominant party. This put the Republicans approximately in the unhappy straits faced by the Democrats from the time of the Civil War until the Republican schism of 1912. Because the Democrats were so clearly the minority party in that Republican golden era, they could pose a serious Presidential election challenge only by offering a candidate—such as Grover Cleveland—who would appeal not only to Democrats but to a substantial number of Republicans. When the Democrats instead picked a candidate—such as William Jennings Bryan—who clearly reflected the desires of the Democratic Party but repelled Republicans, the result was electoral disaster. In 1940, just twenty-eight years after the great Republican schism, the tables were turned. Just as political necessity required the pre-1912 Democrats to turn to Cleveland-type

[4] A few of the old Bull Moosers, notably Ickes, actually became New Deal stalwarts.

candidates who stood to the right of the party's true power balance, realistic Republicans now believed they must endorse national candidates and platforms to the left of the party consensus.

This type of reasoning, rather than some miraculous conversion to progressivism, was the reason for the party's turn to the left in 1940. It was relatively easy. Senator Robert A. Taft of Ohio, making his first serious bid for President in 1940, was then a freshman Senator with only two years' experience in the Capital and hardly the charismatic figure for the Republican right he was to become within the next decade. Besides, the big business Republicans of the eastern seaboard felt action was absolutely necessary for the survival of the party. If 1940 duplicated the Republican debacle of 1936, the party might go the way of the Whigs and Federalists. The answer was the nomination of the antithesis of the Old Guard Republican: public utilities executive Wendell Willkie, a reconstructed ex-Democrat with mildly liberal views regarding both domestic and foreign policy issues.

But it wasn't that easy. The nomination of Willkie in 1940 was to many of the party regulars a solution imposed from without by the moneyed interests of Wall Street. Unquestionably, Willkie's internationalist and reformist views were alien to the majority of tried-and-true Republicans. Thus, Republican liberalism of the mid-twentieth century was alien and frail and essentially expediential. It was in no way kin to the sturdy Republican progressivism before 1912. Indeed, it is an open question whether progressives or conservatives really dominated the party in 1912. Only the power of the White House (and Federal patronage in the South) really decided the nomination for William Howard Taft against Roosevelt. But in 1940, there was no question where the party's true ideological leanings belonged. The new Republican liberalism of 1940 was a hothouse creature openly despised by the party faithful.

The fact that Willkie's losing campaign against Franklin

Roosevelt in 1940 did succeed in luring some strays of 1932 and 1936 back to the Republican fold in no way convinced the party that his nomination was a wise one. On the contrary, the nomination of moderately liberal Governor Thomas E. Dewey of New York in 1944 and 1948 (against Senator John Bricker of Ohio in 1944 and against Taft in 1948) contributed to the growing tension within the party. This repeated knuckling under by the party faithful to the dictates of a few leaders was building up intolerable pressure. It was ready to explode after the supposedly sure Dewey win in 1948 turned into Harry Truman's famous upset victory. Although it is scarcely provable that a more conservative Dewey in 1948 would have been the winner, it became an article of faith among rank-and-file workers after 1948—and remains one to this day—that Dewey kicked away the election by turning away from Republican orthodoxy and dispensing a tepid brand of me-too liberalism. There was no question that the explosion was due at the next convention in 1952. The party workers were dead set upon regaining control of their own party by finally nominating Robert Alfonso Taft, by now unchallenged as Mr. Republican.

That they failed is in part testament to the political skill of Governor Dewey and the other Eastern professional politicians who so skillfully engineered the one-year campaign that for the last time derailed Taft and nominated General of the Army Dwight D. Eisenhower. But the reasons for Eisenhower's nomination transcend professional skill. With a supposed mess in Washington and the tragic Korean War in progress, Republicans quite correctly caught the long-denied scent of victory in 1952 far more clearly than in 1948. This was no year for gambling. Even unwashed Republicans accepted the theory that Taft, as an unwashed Republican, simply could not be elected President.

Even more than Willkie in 1940, Eisenhower—seriously considered by anti-Truman Democrats as their candidate in

1948—was an outsider enlisted to broaden artificially the party's base. If he had been upset by Adlai Stevenson in 1952, there is little doubt that an enraged party rank and file would have rebelled at long last in 1956, and picked a true-blue Republican in a mood of damn-the-consequences.

But the fact that Eisenhower proved to possess the broad-based voter appeal that really did lure away Democratic votes by the millions didn't solve the party's internal problems. It merely postponed them for the eight-year Eisenhower era. In fact, that strange tendency of the post-1912 Republican Party to distrust its own winners was never more in evidence than during the Eisenhower regime. There was a bitter resentment of Eisenhower's very success at the polls —a resentment heightened when the General registered another landslide in 1956 while Democrats were winning control of Congress.

Of course, a political genius in the White House might have used those eight years to bring together the party's divergent elements and—more important—try to break out of its minority status by broadening its base. Not even the General's most extravagant admirers would call him a political genius. With Eisenhower ignorant of and not really interested in party affairs, he didn't really try. No wonder that a growing number of party leaders began checking off the days until Richard M. Nixon would assume party leadership.

Considering the intraparty sniping aimed at Nixon during the 1960 campaign and after, it is hard to imagine the extent of his immense popularity within the party during the second Eisenhower term. Filling the void left by Eisenhower's disinterest in party affairs, Nixon carefully tended the problems of party workers all the way down to the county chairman level as he slowly and meticulously laid the groundwork for the 1960 nomination. Although Nixon's credentials as an internationalist and a moderate were entirely acceptable to the party's dominant minority who had dictated the nomination since 1940, Nixon was—unlike Willkie, Dewey, and Eisenhower—the great favorite of the party workers. There can be no question that he would have won the 1960 nomination without dictation from above. Thus, Nixon seemed to be the one man who could weld together the party's leadership and rank-and-file workers into true unity.

It was illusory. Nixon's popularity with both wings of the party could not last, because these wings remained basically antagonistic. In fact, Nixon never really got to grips with the overall Republican problem. All he really achieved was the superficial unanimity that comes from an uncontested nomination.

The Chicago convention in July, 1960, proved that Nixon had not been able to shut off the internal party pressure building up within the Republican Party for twenty years. Governor Rockefeller, representing not the old Eastern money forces who engineered the Willkie-Dewey-Eisenhower nominations (they were now quite content with Nixon) but only himself and his New York State delegation, started the trouble by demanding a more liberal platform than the convention was apt to accept in a free vote. Although Rockefeller would have been able to muster little more than the New York delegation's votes in an open floor fight over the platform, Nixon was eager to avoid even the impression of internal dissension. What followed was Nixon's telephone call from Washington to Rockefeller in New York City and their impromptu dinner meeting at the Governor's Fifth Avenue apartment. After dinner, they pounded out agreement on the most potentially divisive sections of the platform: civil rights, medical care, national defense.

That was enough to provoke a conservative outburst, which showed that Nixon really had not pacified the party's downtrodden but numerically superior conservatives. The conservatives—with a new and vocal leader, Barry Goldwater of Arizona—were incensed by the "sellout of Fifth Avenue" and "dictation from Rockefeller." Their discontent lacked the poignancy of the conservative heartbreak of 1952, but there was something of the same feeling among rank-and-file delegates, the feeling that they were again being taken for a ride by the Eastern me-too Republicans. Now, the threat of rebellion over the platform was coming not from the Governor of New York and his delegation but from the mighty Republican right wing.

This was to prove to be Nixon's high-water mark as a political technician. Never again was he quite so masterful. Flying to Chicago, he skillfully soothed down ruffled feelings of the right. The Nixon-Rockefeller platform was accepted without a murmur, that is, without an audible murmur, Nixon easily dictated the choice of Henry Cabot Lodge, a liberal Easterner, as Vice-Presidential nominee. Except for ten diehard Louisiana delegates who cast their votes for Goldwater, Nixon's nomination was unanimous.

It seemed that the momentary conservative outburst at Chicago was only an aberration. Or was it?

Of course, by the time the convention met, it was too late for the party even to think about anybody except Nixon for the nomination. Only some Southern delegations and squadrons of youth-for-Goldwater postadolescents were halfway serious about drafting Goldwater.[5] But the pro-Goldwater flurry at Chicago was concerned with more than the identity of the 1960 candidate. The conservative rank and file never again could look upon Nixon with the feeling that "he is one of us." Nixon had sold out to "them"—those misty, unnamed Machiavellians who had thwarted the wishes of the party

[5] The bright young men and women beating the drums for Goldwater at Chicago reconvened after the convention at Sharon, Connecticut, to form the Young Americans for Freedom. The YAF was to be the principal youth organization boosting Goldwater for President until fanatically fervent Goldwater forces took over the regular Young Republicans national organization in June, 1963.

faithful for a generation. Really then, Nixon's "uniting" of the party's two wings was but a fantasy.

Even when defeat is expected, there usually is no organized preparation for its aftermath. This was the case of the Republican Party on November 9, 1960, the day after the election. Although almost any Republican politician was willing to tell how Nixon could have won the election, none could say exactly what the party would or should do now.

Goldwater's following was intense and devoted but small. Rockefeller's following was microscopic.

The handful of new party figures brought to power in the 1960 election—Governor Elmer Anderson of Minnesota and Governor John Volpe of Massachusetts, most notably—were obviously not of national stature.

What about Nixon? Hadn't he just lost the Presidency by a wafer-thin margin? For the same reasons that party politicians were conducting post-mortems on his "defeat" a month before election day, they were unwilling to give him another chance in 1964.

Not even his friends were willing to throw their support to Nixon-in-1964 on an unqualified basis. Typical was Lawrence Lindemer, the able and articulate Republican state chairman of Michigan—a nondoctrinaire, moderately liberal Republican and a Nixon man all the way.[6] "I've been a real strong Nixon man," Lindemer told a reporter, "but I believe that there's a real difficulty—I can't put my finger on it—that he has trouble making people like him, getting them ecstatic over him."

As for Eisenhower, nobody expected leadership from the General after he left the White House.

As it had been many times before, the Republican Party was leaderless—and ready for internal bloodletting.

[6] Lindemer eventually wound up as a Rockefeller man. He was named Midwestern coordinator for Rockefeller in January, 1964.

III

★ ★

A New Goldwater?

If there is any time for a pause in the incessant whirlings of partisan politics, it is during those three months immediately following an election whose results decree that a new party shall assume the reins of government. Partisan political activity suspends during the transition. Exhausted from the grueling campaign, party leaders head during November and December for Florida, Puerto Rico, Acapulco, and other watering spots. The next January is a festive time, brightened by parties and preparations for the Inauguration. Not until the day after the new President's Inauguration does the pause really end.

Yet, it was this transition period after the 1960 election that saw the creation of a most remarkable document. Prepared by Senator Barry Goldwater and a few of his closest aides, it was an unusually bold and imaginative attempt to set forth a new doctrine of political tactics for the Republican Party by appealing to "The Forgotten American." Implicit in the doctrine—which soon became known as the Goldwater Manifesto (though Goldwater never gave it any name)— was the superiority of Goldwater as the party leader to preach the new doctrine. Indeed, the purpose of the Goldwater Manifesto was not only to broaden the Republican Party's base but to widen Goldwater's support enough to win the nomination.

Shortly after the Manifesto was published in the *Wall Street Journal,* Goldwater buried it—without fanfare but with finality—for reasons we shall discuss later. It never again figured in intra-Republican maneuverings over the next four years. Yet, it is worth recounting the brief history of the Goldwater Manifesto for two reasons. First, it was the opening shot—albeit an errant shot—in the Goldwater-for-President campaign. Second, the formula prescribed by the Manifesto might well have shown the way to widen public support for the Republican Party in a way that might have satisfied both its liberal and its conservative wings. Indeed, it might have been a blueprint for unity.

Barry Goldwater, a Phoenix, Arizona, department-store executive and the grandson of a Russian-Jewish immigrant peddler, entered the Senate in January, 1953, after unseating Senator Ernest McFarland, the Democratic leader of the Senate, in the 1952 elections.[1] Just six months later, Robert A. Taft was dead of cancer—his burning dream to enter the White House forever stilled.

However, it would be absurd to say that Goldwater, then forty-four years old, quickly picked up the mantle of conservative Republican leadership as it fell from Taft's dying grasp. William S. White, Taft's biographer, has written that Taft was recognized by his peers as a leader on the first day that he entered the Senate in 1939. Not so with Goldwater in 1953. He was just another conservative Republican. True, he soon began to make his mark—but not in the Senate. Goldwater became one of the more popular regulars of the rubber chicken and buckshot pea circuit, addressing the cosmeticians, the lumbermen, the accountants—in fact, almost any business or trade group. There was nothing extraordinary about his message: a return to the old Republican

[1] It is worth noting that Goldwater's upset election victory in 1952 paved the way for Lyndon B. Johnson to become President eleven years later. Johnson was elected Democratic leader to succeed McFarland, permitting him to begin his brilliant career as a legislative leader.

virtues of States' Rights, limited government, a balanced budget, and a tough line against communism. The same message was being carried in those days by the likes of Senator William E. Jenner of Indiana and Senator Karl Mundt of South Dakota with a good deal more venom. It was precisely this lack of venom and his infectious charm that made Goldwater the choice of the cosmeticians' convention over the Jenners and the Mundts. Here was a conservative who smiled, who laughed, who was young and dynamic. But to become the champion of the banquet circuit was a good deal less than assuming—or even trying to assume—leadership of the Republican Party.

Goldwater's first real national attention came in 1958 when he decisively won a second term against an attempted comeback by McFarland in a year that conservative Republicans —William Knowland of California and John Bricker of Ohio most prominently—were falling like flies. Returning to the Senate in 1959 as senior Republican member of the Labor Committee, he gained increasing national attention as a principal foe of Senator John F. Kennedy's labor reform and minimum wage bills and as the principal Congressional antagonist of President Walter Reuther of the United Auto Workers. Yet, it came as a surprise to many within the Republican Party that the hysteria for Goldwater—limited though it was—was the most fervent emotion exhibited by anybody at the 1960 convention in Chicago.

The support behind Goldwater in January, 1961, was both wider and weaker than the Taft following. If Taft was Mr. Republican, Goldwater was Mr. Conservative. Taft never had matched Goldwater in the fanatical support outside party ranks—the conservative independents who had lost faith in the Republican Party, the bright young conservative intellectuals in button-down collars and horn-rimmed glasses, the disenchanted conservative Democrats of the South who had begun to look upon Goldwater as the only national politician sympathetic to their problems. Although Goldwater was even then the most popular Republican among rank-and-file workers, he did not approach Taft's phenomenal popularity within the party (which, of course, was never enough by itself to give him the nomination). Moreover, the party leaders, including such old Taft stalwarts as Ohio State Chairman Ray Bliss and Senator Everett McKinley Dirksen of Illinois, were in no way behind Goldwater. Rather, they found it difficult to think seriously of him in terms of the White House.

In short, Goldwater was not a great deal more than a very strong factional leader in January, 1961. Even those party workers who agreed with Goldwater that Nixon had kicked away chances for victory by adopting me-too liberalism, and were absolutely determined to keep the 1964 nomination away from Rockefeller were uncertain whether Goldwater might just be a little too conservative. There was no uncertainty among a sizable majority of party leaders. They believed Goldwater could not begin to pick up enough Democratic and independent votes in a Presidential election to give him a chance to keep Kennedy from a second term.

Consequently, many of Goldwater's friends and aides believed he most needed to prove himself flexible enough to attract support beyond the confines of the Republican Party's conservative wing. The result was the Goldwater Manifesto.

The originator and principal author of the Manifesto was Michael J. Bernstein, at that time one of Goldwater's most important advisers. A labor lawyer by trade, Bernstein was chief minority (Republican) counsel on the Senate Labor Committee (where Goldwater was the senior Republican member). But as an imaginative intellectual, Bernstein's influence on Goldwater went far beyond the fields covered by the Labor Committee. At the Senator's side during the protracted legislative struggles over labor and education in the late 1950's and early 1960's, Bernstein came to advise him on broad areas of public policy—and even party politics.

Bernstein contrasted sharply with most of Goldwater's advisers, who tended to be backslapping congratulators who reinforced the Senator's beliefs in his own set of nostrums. Bernstein was perhaps the only true innovator to get a toe inside the Goldwater inner circle. It was Bernstein who conceived the Manifesto's master plan of a popular Republicanism that would neither reiterate Old Guard mouthings nor slavishly imitate New Deal axioms. Although Bernstein himself later realized that the Manifesto was far from perfect, at least it pointed a possible way to the future for the party.

But issuance of the Manifesto was Mike Bernstein's apogee as a Goldwater adviser. He was gradually shunted aside to routine tasks and took only a peripheral part in the long campaign ahead. His name shall not appear in this account again. The reason is central to Barry Goldwater's failing as a politician. As a political innovator, Bernstein demanded new, often difficult departures of Goldwater—breaking away from the comfortable conservative shibboleths. So did the Manifesto. Unable to make this departure and embarrassed by the demands of Bernstein and the Manifesto, Goldwater withdrew from both of them.

The implicit political reasoning behind the Manifesto contained these four basic assumptions:

Assumption No. 1: The landslide election victories by Eisenhower in 1952 and 1956 were no real answer to the Republican plight. They proved only that a once-in-a-lifetime war hero can become a devastating political candidate.

Assumption No. 2: Efforts such as Nixon's in 1960 to synthesize the party's liberal and conservative views can end only in a tasteless hash that finds no enthusiastic support among voters.

Assumption No. 3: Attempts to preempt the Democrats' own ground by advocating a liberal policy cannot woo Democrats and independents in any great numbers but can alienate Republicans.

Assumption No. 4: Unwashed Republican doctrine—what

was becoming known as Goldwater Republicanism—might
in its pristine form excite the Republican faithful but could
not possibly draw away enough Democratic votes to bring
victory.

The Goldwater Manifesto's answer: a new kind of conservatism, stripped of the more doctrinaire and hackneyed
elements of conservative Republicanism. The new doctrine's
aim would be to wrest enough of the Democratic voters
away from the Democratic candidate slowly to return the
Grand Old Party to majority status.

Just who is going to be added to the ranks of Republican
voters? "That dragooned and ignored individual, 'The Forgotten American,'" says the Goldwater Manifesto. The Manifesto sees a huge, faceless, voiceless mass not identified with
any political pressure group, and stifled amid the competing
pressures of big business, big labor, and big government.

Contending that "America has become a society of competing pressure groups" during the past twenty-five years,
the Manifesto goes on to describe the political relevance of
this development:

> Americans largely fall into one of four categories with re-
> spect to pressure group organizations: (1) they may be truly
> voluntary members agreeing with all or most of the policies
> enunciated by their leaders; or (2) they may be pressured and
> forced by economic necessity into joining the pressure organi-
> zations; or (3) they may successfully resist joining such organi-
> zations; or (4) finally, as members of the most numerous ethnic
> or religious groupings of the nation, they may consider it un-
> necessary and even humiliating to organize themselves as do
> the minority of so-called "under-dog" groups.

> All of which means that there are literally scores of millions
> of Americans who are either outside the organized pressure
> groups or find themselves represented by organizations with
> whose policies they disagree in whole or in part. These millions
> are the silent Americans who, thus isolated, cannot find voice
> against the mammoth organizations which mercilessly pressure

their own membership, the Congress, and society as a whole, for objectives which these silent ones do not want. They thereby have become "The Forgotten Americans" despite the fact that they constitute the majority of our people.

The Republican Party in this era in which so many pressure groups are seeking to dominate the total man is the vehicle and the voice for that dragooned and ignored individual, "The Forgotten American." It too recognizes that those private activities which are essential to the successful functioning of a modern society have tended to become institutionalized in huge organizational units which, themselves growing larger with each passing year, continuously narrow the area in which the individual may act freely, decisively, and effectively. . . .

This is not fuzzy political declamation but a specific action program. The Manifesto goes on, directly and indirectly, to pinpoint "The Forgotten American." He is the labor union member who mistrusts and resents his leaders. He is the old-age pensioner who feels he is neglected by present political leaders. He is the Catholic ("members of the most numerous ethnic or religious groupings") who resents special preference for smaller minority groups.

The Manifesto's program for satisfying the needs of these "Forgotten Americans" is scarcely revolutionary. Tough labor control legislation for the dissident union members, militant anticommunism for the Catholic. A stable dollar (which, according to Goldwater, means a balanced budget) for the pensioner. This is the normal Goldwater diet.

What was revolutionary about the Manifesto from the conservative standpoint is the concept that the Federal Government need not be dismantled but should be put to work for conservative ends. The Manifesto declared:

> Inasmuch as the Federal Government has by its actions, often at the cost of weakening state and local government as well as private and community life, contributed substantially to the growth and development not only of its own power, but to the expansion of and strength of private organizational

power, the Republican Party believes that the Federal Government must begin to consider and adopt measures designed to halt this dehumanizing trend in our society.

This suggests a pragmatism that had been wholly lacking in Goldwater conservatism previously. Indeed, at the time the Manifesto was first issued, Goldwater and his aides had in the drafting stage conservative-oriented bills providing Federal aid to education, medical care for the aged, aid to economically depressed areas, and a new minimum wage law. Previously, Goldwater had dismissed out of hand any such program as an improper role for the Federal Government. Now, he was trying to devise his own alternative to the Democratic proposals.

Yet, the most significant feature of the Manifesto may have been its omissions. Gone were the catchwords and slogans of Goldwater and the Republican Party's right wing —words that clearly had failed to ignite the nation. There was no mention of "right to work" laws or applying the antitrust laws to organized labor or States' Rights or even budget deficits. The old shibboleths were to be forgotten. Even opposition to foreign aid and the United Nations were toned down.

The unstated goals of the Manifesto were threefold.

1. To attract enough dissident Democrats—the "Forgotten Americans"—to turn the Republican Party into the majority party.

2. To establish a new conservatism that would be sufficiently broad-based in its appeal to unite the Republican Party or at least unite the vast majority of the party.

3. To establish Goldwater as more than a factional leader but as the leader of the entire party, considerably more flexible and progressive than his old image.

Whether the Manifesto ever could have been put into action to achieve these goals is debatable. Nobody shall ever know, however, for Goldwater backed away from the Manifesto almost as soon as he released it.

On Sunday, January 15, shortly after the publication of the Manifesto in the *Wall Street Journal*, Goldwater appeared on "Issues and Answers," an ABC Radio and Television interview program. In answer to the first question, he promptly—perhaps instinctively—discarded the Manifesto's concept of the Government being put to conservative uses.

"My personal feeling is that man being the creature he is, a creature of God, that he works best when he has the least interference with his life from any central government such as Washington, and I think we could serve as an example to the rest of the world with the type of freedom we have been able to maintain for nearly two hundred years," Goldwater said. "To me, this is one of the miracles of the ages and I would not think that we need direction from Washington. Certainly Americans need inspirations from the leaders of their government, but this is more of the moral inspiration than it is a material inspiration."

This was the old Goldwater. In fact, when David Nichols of ABC asked the Senator whether the issuance of the Manifesto meant he was changing his views, Goldwater replied, "I am not changing one bit."

Only once during the program did Goldwater refer to the Manifesto's revolutionary doctrine of turning big government to conservative ends. "We are going to explore all of the fields where principle will allow us to inject the Federal Government and see what we can do about it, and we have some interesting approaches coming up in all these fields," Goldwater said.

But the only "interesting approach" that actually was written into a bill and introduced in the Senate was a conservative styled Federal aid to education measure, permitting a Federal tax deduction for all local school taxes. Introduced almost sheepishly without fanfare, it was never really pro-

moted by the Senator.[2] The promised Goldwater proposals
for medical care, depressed areas, and the minimum wage
never materialized. From time to time the "Forgotten American" slogan popped up in Goldwater's speeches and offhand
remarks. It was the last vestige of the Goldwater Manifesto.
Otherwise, the brave new doctrine of conservatism was a
dead letter.

Why? Jack Bell, the astute political writer for the Associated Press and Goldwater's friend and biographer, had one
answer. In *Mr. Conservative: Barry Goldwater*, Bell conceded that Goldwater was trying "to make conservatism
more palatable to more people."[3]

> But [Bell added] he could not afford to exchange his own
> peculiar Jacob's coat of conservative leadership for the somber
> garments of the moderates by changing any fundamental po-
> sition.
> Furthermore, Goldwater always encountered his conscience
> when he was tempted to change his stance on some issue. For
> him the sea of expediency never quite engulfed the rock of
> what he regarded as the fundamental and traditional truths.
> Here and there a few pebbles fell in the water but they de-
> noted minor erosion.

There is considerable truth in this reasoning. Yet Goldwater's inflexibility has another and more important source.
Self-conscious of his position as Mr. Conservative, he was
extremely sensitive—really oversensitive—about the feeling
in conservative ranks that he might be selling out. Mixed in
with the overwhelmingly favorable mail response to the
Manifesto (and the surprising demand for reprints) were a
few vitriolic letters from outraged diehards accusing Gold-

---

[2] Because the explanation of this bill was not delivered by Goldwater as a
speech on the Senate floor but was inserted in the *Congressional Record* by a
fellow Senator at Goldwater's request, it appeared in the *Record* in nearly
illegible italic type and went generally unnoticed.

[3] Jack Bell, *Mr. Conservative: Barry Goldwater*, Garden City, N. Y.:
Doubleday & Company, Inc., 1962.

water of selling the conservative cause down the river to further his own career. It was this minority criticism that hurt and worried Goldwater. It might have been the principal reason for his failure to carry through the program of "The Forgotten American."

Moreover, it is questionable whether Goldwater was emotionally and psychologically prepared to forego using the old conservative shibboleths. In conversation with friends, he could agree intellectually that "deficit spending" and "States' Rights" and "the right to work" were battle cries that would titillate the party faithful without converting the infidel. Still, these were the slogans that had brought the frenzied cheers and applause from the businessmen, housewives, and college students who compose the conservative movement. In a sense, it was expecting too much for Goldwater suddenly to discard them just as his political career was reaching its zenith.

The incident of the Goldwater Manifesto is but a forgotten footnote to history. It is interesting to speculate whether its program could have simultaneously broadened the base of Republican support and inhibited the perpetual and exhausting struggle between the party's conservative and progressive wings. That is only speculation.

But the incident told much about Goldwater that goes beyond speculation. It pointed up the fact that he was an instinctive and natural politician, not a studied one. His rise to prominence from obscurity had been unplanned and accidental. It was clear now that he was not going to follow any plan to move from prominence to the Presidency. Apart from revealing Goldwater's extreme sensitivity to charges of betraying conservatism, the incident revealed a certain stubbornness regarding the White House. He would do so much —no more—to become President. That "so much" clearly did not include making over his political personality.

IV

★ ★

1961: The First Maneuvers

Actually, the first intraparty sniping began even before Goldwater issued his Manifesto. The first week of the first session of the Eighty-seventh Congress, three weeks before John F. Kennedy's Inauguration as President, saw the first blood spilled. It wasn't much blood, but it served as an omen of things to come.

Mostly in private conversations, but occasionally in public, the leaders of the Republican Party had been playing the game of interpreting Nixon's defeat almost continuously since election day (with time out, of course, for vacations). Rockefeller men were saying that the Governor would win back to the Republican fold the independent votes that had gone for Eisenhower in 1952 and 1956 but had been snared by Kennedy in 1960. Goldwater men—and Goldwater himself—expressed the opinion that Rockefeller would do even worse than Nixon. This long-distance duel exploded at short range in the Republican Conference Room of the New Senate Office Building on January 3, 1961.

Republican Senators were holding their routine first-of-the-year caucus, going through the dull ritual of reelecting their officers without opposition. Benign and dignified Senator Leverett Saltonstall of Massachusetts, presiding over the caucus, turned to the matter of reelecting Goldwater as chairman of the Senate Campaign Committee. Unexpectedly, without prior warning, Senator Jacob Javits of New York jumped up. Javits—abrupt, intense, and far more liberal than his colleagues believed a Republican should be—urged the caucus to think over Goldwater's reelection. Javits's argument: Goldwater was too rigidly conservative to continue in a job where he would be distributing campaign funds to 1962 Senatorial candidates (including Javits) of widely varying ideologies. Hence, Javits argued, a more moderate Senator should replace Goldwater as the campaign chief. Upset at the unexpected development, Saltonstall hastily adjourned the caucus.

Goldwater was furious. He was absolutely certain that the voice was the voice of Javits in Washington but the hand was the hand of Rockefeller—or at least Rockefeller's staff —back in Albany. Goldwater contended to friends that Rockefeller was worried about the 1962 campaign. Seeking a second term as Governor, Rockefeller would be pretty much confined to New York State for that campaign. But Goldwater would be traveling across every portion of the country as campaign chairman, trying to get Senatorial candidates elected. According to Goldwater's own reasoning, the Rockefeller camp was afraid Goldwater would get a big head start in the Presidential sweepstakes. One way to prevent it was purging Goldwater as campaign chief.

When the caucus reconvened two days later, Goldwater was loaded for bear. He even took the unusual step of distributing to the press copies of his remarks to the closed-door caucus. Those remarks were blunt enough.

"In light of the 1960 election results in New York," Goldwater declared, "I think it is particularly inappropriate that a member of the Republican leadership of that state should seek to prescribe the pattern of political conduct of the party nationally." Goldwater's punch intentionally sailed over Javits's head all the way up to Albany. This was another slap at Rockefeller for failing to carry New York State for Nixon.

Moreover, Goldwater was just getting warmed up. He was scheduled the next day to address a closed session of the Republican National Committee, its first meeting since Nixon's defeat. Senator Thruston Morton of Kentucky, the party's national chairman, wanted to keep this postdefeat conclave as harmonious as possible, and asked Goldwater to stay away from controversy in his address to the Committee. But Goldwater was in a fighting mood. He had prepared a speech, accompanied by charts, that spelled out the failure of liberal Republicanism in the 1960 elections and particularly the Rockefeller failure in New York. "I don't think that Morton and his friends want any realism at the meeting," Goldwater grumbled to a friend.

Actually, both Rockefeller and Javits pulled their punches in this first skirmish. Otherwise, the carnage would have been awesome to behold.

When Rockefeller heard about Javits's unexpected purge attempt, he telephoned Washington to personally ask Javits to please drop his opposition to Goldwater's reelection.[1] When the caucus reconvened, Javits did drop his opposition following a token concession by Goldwater. The concession: Goldwater agreed not to enter any state where he wasn't wanted or where his presence might hurt Republican candidates in 1962—a pledge that did not inhibit his subsequent traveling noticeably, and certainly did not keep him from making numerous flights to New York City to address trade organizations. But the pledge was enough to produce Goldwater's unanimous reelection by the thirty-five Republican Senators.

For his part, Goldwater took a relatively soft line in his address to the National Committee. He did blast away at a proposal by New York's other Republican Senator, Kenneth B. Keating, to form a national Republican policy board that

[1] However, Goldwater always nursed the belief that Rockefeller tried to purge him.

presumably would be more liberal in tone than the National Committee itself, and would closely parallel the liberal Democratic Advisory Council that the Democrats maintained during the Eisenhower Administration. "We do not need a fancy advisory group such as the Democrats have," Goldwater argued.[2] But he did not tee off against Rockefeller and the New York Republican Party as he had planned.

The fact that both Rockefeller and Goldwater steered away from party conflict could have indicated a new sweet reasonableness permeating the leaders of the Grand Old Party. In fact, their restraint was for two widely different reasons—neither of them really permanent. It wasn't clear then, but Rockefeller and Goldwater were entering a two-and-a-half-year truce that was to last until its unpleasant end in the summer of 1963.

From his personal standpoint, Rockefeller had plenty of reason to desire a truce. This was no time for him to be riding off on crusades against fellow Republicans. His brief career in party politics had marked him in the minds of many fellow Republicans as a party splitter. By 1961, he had a bad reputation to live down.

Actually, the heir of a family that had contributed so much money to Republican campaigns got off to a pretty good start with the Grand Old Party. His surprisingly easy victory over Governor Averell Harriman in New York was by far the brightest Republican performance in a landslide Democratic year (easily outshining Goldwater's reelection in Arizona). From the moment he was elected Governor, Rockefeller was eyeing the Presidency. But he avoided any direct clash with Vice-President Nixon, whom most party leaders accorded a proprietary right to the 1960 nomination by virtue of his tireless campaigning as Vice-President. Al-

---

[2] Goldwater won this fight. Despite support from Chairman Morton, the Keating proposal was pigeonholed.

though Rockefeller's experience as a middle-level appointed official under Eisenhower was an unhappy one and, in fact, convinced him that he could affect national policy only by entering elective politics, he wisely restrained from criticizing the first Republican President in a generation. There were implications that he might want faster progress in civil rights, defense preparedness, and economic growth than Eisenhower and Nixon, but these were only implications—not attacks. Rockefeller's aides tried their best to stave off the party's anti-Nixon and anti-Eisenhower elements that were looking for a port to weather the storm, and naturally looked toward Rockefeller.[3]

So, the impression created by Rockefeller in two sentiment-testing trips late in 1959—one to the Far West, the other to the Midwest, Southwest, and Florida—was generally favorable. Before these trips, local party leaders weren't quite sure that they were going to like the liberal Republican multimillionaire who once was Franklin D. Roosevelt's coordinator for Latin American affairs. They weren't even sure whether he was a bonafide Republican. What they found was no polished campaigner but a bright new face with the kind of latent dynamism and crowd appeal that Nixon demonstrably lacked. But even more important, they found a self-professed party regular who went out of his way to enunciate his respect for party organization and his dislike for mavericks. He made sure to clear all his travels through the local party organization, not some rump opposition group, no matter how committed to Nixon the regulars were.

The regular party leaders in some states—Wisconsin, Oklahoma, Florida—were so enthusiastically committed to Nixon that they met Rockefeller with a frigid reception (despite specific requests from Nixon's office in Washington that he be treated warmly). By and large, however, party leaders

---

[3] When Rockefeller visited Wisconsin in October, 1959, he found it particularly difficult to stave off the bear hugs of the late Senator Joseph McCarthy's followers.

and party workers were both curious and courteous. What's more, they were favorably impressed by Rockefeller—particularly so in Minnesota. Ed Viehmann, Minnesota's young state chairman (who was to die tragically the next year), put it this way after meeting Rockefeller in Minneapolis' Leamington Hotel: "I'm 99 percent for Rockefeller, but I'm 100 percent for Nixon."

Viehmann's arithmetic may have been faulty, but his meaning was clear. It was far too late for anyone to challenge Nixon successfully in 1960. But if Nixon should lose the 1960 election, Rockefeller would have the option on the nomination for 1964. This was a widespread sentiment in Republican circles late in 1959. It must be remembered that this was a period of relative harmony within the party as a result of Nixon's exertions for party peace the previous seven years. Certainly, there were times ahead when Rockefeller's strength within the party would be far greater than it was in December, 1959. But never again would he be troubled by less mistrust and suspicion directed against Rockefeller.

Of course, there were very few pledges of support for the Presidency in 1960 received by Rockefeller during those late 1959 excursions. It was understandable, but this apparently was distressing and humiliating to the Governor. It had been generally expected by most Republicans, including Nixon, that Rockefeller would try his hand against Nixon in the primary elections. Instead, Rockefeller made one of those surprising and inexplicable moves that were to characterize his long, unhappy quest for the Presidency.

During the last week of December, 1959, he announced he would not seek the Presidential nomination because the party managers apparently had already made up their minds for Nixon. The astringency of the statement did much to wipe away the aura of good feeling Rockefeller had inspired during his barnstorming a few weeks earlier.

There was more of the same to come. From time to time, Rockefeller would drop a barb about the bosses of the

Republican Party barring him from any chance at the nomination. Then, without warning, he exploded his biggest bombshell yet in June, 1960.

He opened fire on the foreign and domestic policies of the Eisenhower Administration. He challenged Nixon to talk sense to the American people about defense and civil rights. He demanded tough defense and tough civil rights planks in the platform. He threatened to get back into the Presidential race against Nixon.

Party leaders were furious. It wasn't just a case of Nixon men fearing that an eleventh-hour challenge would defeat their man. It was obvious to everybody that Rockefeller would have to utilize all the mighty patronage power of the Governor's office to keep even the New York delegation in line, and would have no chance to pick up appreciable strength outside his own state. That was just the point. Why unleash such a fearsome blast against an incumbent Administration if there's no chance to be nominated anyway? Why worry that much about a platform nobody reads? And, why wait until this late hour when Democrats can easily pick up the anti-Nixon statements for use in the fall campaign.

These were the questions asked at Washington's Statler-Hilton Hotel as the Republican National Committee held its last session before the national convention in Chicago the next month. There was scarcely a good word to be said for Rockefeller. The sentiment was best summed up by Meade Alcorn, national committeeman from Connecticut and a former national chairman. Alcorn asserted that Rockefeller had been sitting in a party position second only to Nixon's. If Nixon lost in 1960, Rockefeller was the obvious choice for 1964. In fact, Alcorn added, Rockefeller would have been his own choice for 1964 under those circumstances. "But now," Alcorn commented bitterly, "he'll never be the nominee. Never."

Rockefeller's reputation as a party wrecker was enhanced

by his rigid insistence at the Chicago convention that civil rights and defense planks be changed to his liking. To the party's conservatives, he became Nixon's seducer at their infamous Fifth Avenue confrontation. His flat refusal of Nixon's offer of the Vice-Presidential nomination did not enhance his reputation as a self-sacrificing party man. As we have seen, Rockefeller's genuinely energetic campaigning for Nixon in the autumn of 1960 failed to raise his prestige among the party faithful.

By January, 1961, Rockefeller was seasoned enough in the ways of the national Republican politics to realize that, at all costs, he should avoid a knock-down, drag-out fight with Goldwater (particularly since few Republican leaders regarded Goldwater as a serious Republican contender at that stage). Rockefeller most certainly did not want Jack Javits tilting against Senate windmills in a suicidal effort to purge Goldwater from a secondary party position.

What Rockefeller did need for 1961 was slowly, painfully to rebuild his reputation as a good party man.

Goldwater's reasons for pulling away from intraparty feuding in January, 1961, were less clear and less consciously arrived at.

He had always been ambivalent on the question of party harmony. At times, he sounded as though he would exile the liberal minority from the Republican Party, transforming it into a monolithic conservative party where Rockefeller-Javits liberals would be replaced by Byrd-style Dixiecrats from the Democratic Party. On other occasions, he was the ever-loyal party regular who would die even for Javits against any Democrat, even a Harry Byrd. His most eloquent declamation as a party harmonizer came at the 1960 convention in Chicago in his memorable speech withdrawing his name from nomination for the Presidency. Attempting to quell right-wing furor over the Nixon-Rockefeller platform, Goldwater declared:

> We are conservatives. This great Republican Party is our historical house. This is our home. Now some of us don't agree with every statement in the official platform of our party, but I might remind you that this is always true in every platform of an American political party.
>
> Both of the great historical parties represent a broad spectrum of views spread over a variety of individual and group convictions. Never are all of these views expressed totally and exclusively in the platform of either party.

But perhaps more important than the two conflicting patterns in Goldwater's political nature—his desire for a Republican Party of pure conservatism and his understanding of a broad-based Republican Party containing more than strictly conservative views—is the fact that Goldwater basically is not a political infighter by instinct or desire. If the other man backs off a bit, it's doubtful that Goldwater will pursue him to keep at the fight. "I didn't even want that campaign chairman's job," Goldwater would tell friends later. "It's just that Rockefeller got me mad when he tried to take it away from me."

Moreover, it was obvious in January, 1961, that Goldwater clearly did not want to be President of the United States. Even less did he want to engage himself in a four-year test of brains, money, and physical stamina against a Rockefeller who made little effort to hide his yearning to sit in the White House.

After the 1960 election, Goldwater made only one change in his free-and-easy method of operation. At long last and after much urging, he hired a press secretary: Tony Smith, a former Washington and Philadelphia newspaperman and more recently a Republican publicity man. Goldwater had been his own press secretary in past years. But the Chicago convention had made him a national figure. He couldn't handle the flow of requests for interviews or the growing pile of requests for magazine articles with Goldwater's by-line. Hiring Smith was a necessity, not a step on the road to the White House. Otherwise, his staff remained the typically small and unspecialized staff of a Senator from a small Western state.

Nor was there really much change in the way Goldwater spent his time: at colleges, at businessmen's conventions, at political rallies. There was no attempt whatever to sort out the requests in an effort to give him the most effective exposure to build him into a serious Presidential candidate.

Nevertheless, it was sinking home to party leaders that Goldwater was by far the most sought-after speaker at party functions across the country. With Eisenhower gone from the White House, the Republican Party had taken a predictable but sharp turn to the right. The party's Congressional wing has been dominated by conservatives for at least a generation, and was moderated only by the hard necessities of responsible leadership under the eight-year Eisenhower rule. Rough and tough Representative Charles Halleck of Indiana, Republican floor leader in the House, now could revert to hard-line conservatism against Kennedy's New Frontier. Indeed, the very return to opposition accentuated the rightward drift. Goldwater, now firmly established as Mr. Conservative, was much more comfortable in the Republican Party of 1961 than the Republican Party of 1960. Besides, even his political enemies were appreciating him as an attractive political personality for the first time. "He's made it respectable to be a conservative again," Javits mused one day later in the summer of 1961, not without a touch of sadness.

All this was duly noted by veteran party chieftains. Their prognosis of Goldwater's chances was changing from "impossible" to "possible but not likely." But if the improbable were to be attained, they added, Goldwater would have to seek the nomination. He clearly wasn't going to be drafted.

And Goldwater wasn't in the mood to go after the nomination. A man who enjoys privacy and tinkering around gadgets
and his sport car, Goldwater wasn't about to change his life
to one of dedicated effort for the Presidency. The months of
the Congressional recess in autumn and early winter were
not spent in any frantic preparation for the Presidential campaigning but in the pleasant way Goldwater always spent his
Congressional recesses. He and his wife Peggy joined thirteen
other vacationers on a freighter leisurely winding its way
from San Francisco to Liverpool via the Panama Canal. He
fulfilled two or three routine speaking engagements after
returning from this vacation but then divorced himself from
politics for the balance of the year: two weeks on active duty
as an Air Force brigadier general and then home to Phoenix
for the Christmas holidays. This scarcely seemed the way a
Presidential candidate spent his time.

There was no question about the intentions of Nelson A.
Rockefeller. He had spent 1961 cautiously trying to build his
stock within the party. There were no direct challenges to
Goldwater or conservatives. There was no attempt to build
up a national organization or sign supporters on the dotted
line. Instead, the Rockefeller campaign moved forward in
two ways:

First, the missionary work of George Hinman, the party's
national committeeman from New York State and one of
Rockefeller's closest political advisers. Although he is a native and resident of Binghamton, New York, Hinman's poise
and polish are of Manhattan, not upstate New York. During
the abortive Presidential bid in 1959–1960, Hinman had
been at sea in his attempts to pick up national support for
Rockefeller. But by the end of 1961, he was well on his way
to becoming an accomplished national politician. Traveling
unobtrusively about the country, Hinman was Rockefeller's
suave and never-ruffled prophet. He asked for no commit-

ments. He sought only good will. Even conservative diehards who could not abide Nelson Rockefeller had a good word for George Hinman.

Second, Rockefeller's own travels. On a slower and more subdued scale, it was a repeat of late 1959 when Rockefeller showed himself around the country for the first time. He was careful not to violate Republican orthodoxies, intent upon describing himself as a regular Republican born and raised within the party. But in 1961, Rockefeller was more cautious than he had been two years earlier. There were no frantic, week-long safaris with a planeload of newsmen accompanying him. Rockefeller and Hinman picked the spots where the Governor was to appear, striving for occasional appearances with maximum impact.

Much to the pleasure of the Rockefeller camp, there was curiosity about him from the Republican faithful and a minimum of outward lingering resentment over the Governor's antics of 1960. One incident is illustrative.

With a big fund-raising dinner scheduled for the fall of 1961, Republicans in Minneapolis, Minnesota, were anxious to get the most attractive speaker possible in order to attract a sellout. Eisenhower was their first choice, but he was unavailable. Nixon, their second choice, couldn't make it either. It turned out that just about everybody Minneapolis requested was occupied elsewhere that night. Finally, Representative William Miller of New York, who had replaced Senator Morton as national chairman, suggested Rockefeller (though Miller and Rockefeller were far from political allies). The planners of the Minneapolis dinner were reluctant at first, fearful that Rockefeller would depress ticket sales. But without any real alternative, they decided to ask Rockefeller —and received a favorable response. What happened next amazed them. Ticket sales surpassed all expectations. The party faithful were eager to fork over cold cash to see this

dynamic, multimillionaire politician. It was a reaction repeated elsewhere in the country.

As 1961 neared an end, there were signs of a gentle upswing in Rockefeller sentiment. Then the Governor exploded
another of his periodic bombshells. This time it was the
divorce.

Anyone who had ever seen Rockefeller campaign with his
wife recognized that austere and aristocratic Mary Todhunter
Rockefeller was less than comfortable in the hurly-burly
world of partisan politics. While Nelson Rockefeller seemed
revitalized by personal—indeed, physical—contact with
grasping, autograph-seeking admirers, Tod Rockefeller
seemed repelled and embarrassed. Nor was she an asset on
the campaign trail. Taller and appearing much older than
her husband, she was unable to unbend. Beyond these surface appearances, insiders in Albany had been saying ever
since the gubernatorial campaign of 1958 that all was not
well between the Rockefellers. There had been much talk of
"another woman."

But most party leaders and workers around the country
were shocked and surprised by the divorce—and puzzled
about how to assess its impact. Their consensus: Although
the divorce certainly wouldn't help Rockefeller, it wasn't
likely to cause him appreciable political damage.

The American public was growing tolerant of divorce. It
was the exceptional American family that had not been
touched by divorce. It was perfectly understandable that
Nelson and Tod Rockefeller, after a lifetime together, and
with their family grown, should find it necessary to part in
late middle age. And from a strictly political point of view,
most politicians doubted that Adlai Stevenson's divorce really
had much to do with his failures in the 1952 and 1956 elections.

This analysis proved to be essentially correct—until it was
overtaken by events some eighteen months later.

Even in 1961, the contest for the Republican Presidential nomination was nothing so simple as a two-man race between Goldwater and Rockefeller. The third man talked about then was none other than Richard M. Nixon.

Although the defeated candidate for President is supposed to become his party's "titular leader," the role is pretty nearly an impossible one for anybody to fill. He usually runs into grousing and complaints over the way he conducted the losing campaign. In most cases, he has no public office or other political base. His personal organization tends to drift away after the defeat. All these afflictions made Dick Nixon's brief stint as titular leader a miserable one.

Worst of all, as we have seen, was the insistent chant—from both his left and his right—that Nixon had kicked away the victory in 1960. Regardless of ideology, Republican politicians complained that Nixon had superimposed his personal staff, headed by urbane Los Angeles lawyer Robert Finch, over the regular National Committee staff. At the January 6, 1961, closed-door session of the National Committee, Goldwater drew heavy applause when he declared that the National Committee should be supreme in future campaigns. Nixon received a more direct rebuff that night at a private party he gave for National Committee members at the Columbia Country Club in suburban Chevy Chase, just outside Washington. At such parties during the past eight years, Nixon had been mobbed by Republican politicians once he finished his duties on the reception line. But this time, no more than three or four at a time stopped to talk with the lame-duck Vice-President of the United States. Politicians, ever alert for the slightest snub, perceived the contrast—and so did Nixon.

Nor was there any solace to be found by Nixon in returning to his native Southern California to "practice law." He had scarcely lived there since college days. There had been law school on the other side of the continent at Duke Uni-

versity, a very brief stint as a Washington bureaucrat, his
World War II hitch in the Navy, and then—after a short
spell back in California following the war—fourteen years in
Washington as Congressman, Senator, and Vice-President.
Almost a generation had passed since California and Dick
Nixon had last been together. Both had changed.

It was clear from the start that Nixon was unhappy as a
Los Angeles suburbanite. One of the first weekends back in
California, Nixon called up an old friend. "My God," Nixon
complained, "what do you do out here? There's nothing to
do, nobody to talk to. What am I supposed to do? Go out
and garden in the yard? I can't take this."

Moreover, Nixon's everyday work was less than satisfying.
Primarily a political activist rather than a theorist, he is not
a natural or an accomplished writer. But to try to build up a
financial nest egg for his family, he had been commissioned
at a fat fee to write a series of newspaper articles and an
autobiographical book (which became the best-selling *Six
Crises*). The book was sheer torture for Nixon. After groping
over words and constant rewriting, he called on Earl Mazo of
the *New York Herald Tribune*, his friend and biographer, to
come West to help put the book in shape.

It was natural that, in such an unhappy year, Nixon began
dabbling in California politics—as a relief from the miserable
chores of writing, if for no other reasons. In a series of private
conferences with Bob Finch and other close California political associates, Nixon saw that the Republican picture in
the state was deteriorating badly.

As Vice-President, Nixon had filled the Republican leadership void in the state created in 1958 when Senator William
F. Knowland and Governor Goodwin Knight tried to change
jobs, and both were defeated by Democrats. But now, in
1961, California's aggressive and ambitious right-wing Republicans were rolling into the void. The conclusion by
Nixon and Finch: Unless a moderate Republican were nomi-

nated for Governor in 1961 and elected, the radical right would take over the California Republican Party of Hiram Johnson, Earl Warren, and Richard Nixon.

There was desultory talk about some essentially nonpolitical figure—perhaps a college president—to run for Governor. But the talk at these meetings always got back to one man uniquely fitted to save the California Republican Party: Nixon.

There were, of course, less unselfish reasons why Nixon was eyeing the Governor's Mansion in Sacramento. Although close personal friends believed Nixon would like to sit out the 1964 Presidential election and try again in 1968 when Kennedy wouldn't be running, Nixon was enough of a political realist to know that a politician can't always pick his spots. Who could foresee what rising young figure might capture the imagination of the party by 1968? Nixon might be washed up by then. Thus, it could be 1964 or never for another chance. And, if it were to be 1964, Nixon would be in a much stronger position at the nominating convention as Governor of California and head of its delegation than merely "titular leader" of his party with no political base.

Naturally, this was something of a gamble. Should he lose to California's Democratic Governor Edmund G. (Pat) Brown in 1962, something close to a political miracle would be needed to nominate him for President in 1964 or ever. Yet, running against fumbling, bumbling, good-natured Pat Brown didn't really seem that much of a gamble.[4] Statewide polls conducted late in 1961 indicated that Nixon versus Brown would be no contest. It was Nixon all the way.

It was to nobody's great surprise that Nixon announced his candidacy for Governor, opening the way for the most frustrating and dismal experience in his life. In answer to a

[4] Brown's popularity had reached an all-time low in 1961, after his inept and unsuccessful efforts to save murderer-author Caryl Chessman from the electric chair by abolishing capital punishment for all Californians and his refusal to save Chessman alone by giving him a personal reprieve.

question at a press conference in Newark, New Jersey, in October, 1961, General Eisenhower expressed the opinion that Nixon, as a candidate for Governor, no longer was "titular leader" of the party. He never really had been.

When the Republican National Committee held its winter meeting at Oklahoma City, Oklahoma, in January, 1962, the party's conservative and progressive wings were maintaining an edgy and uneasy truce after one year of John F. Kennedy's New Frontier. The meeting had a decidedly conservative flavor. The liberal minority on the National Committee complained in private conversation that all three major addresses —by National Chairman Miller, by Representative Bob Wilson of California, and by Barry Goldwater—were strictly give-Kennedy-hell polemics with no positive aspect. Miller even went to the point of comparing Kennedy's request for standby powers from Congress with Hitler's assumption of dictatorial power in Germany. Conservatives retorted in private that this was the only way to tear down the Kennedy image.

In truth, neither faction was really optimistic over the prospects of winning in 1964. Nor was there any candidate that could be considered a front-runner at this stage. It was clear now that Rockefeller's divorce had not been fatal or even overly damaging. But the party leaders were less than enthusiastic for Rockefeller or for Goldwater or for Nixon.

Instead, there seemed to be a search for a new face. The more sophisticated politicians were talking about George Romney, the dynamic boss of American Motors Company, who was expected to run for Governor of Michigan. None of them knew much about Romney. Some hadn't even seen his picture. They talked about Romney because they were looking for somebody (unlike Rockefeller or Goldwater) who was not identified with factional strife and who (unlike Nixon) was not associated with disasters of the past.

V

* *

Two Battle Plans

Not all Republicans wanted to explain Richard Nixon's loss to John F. Kennedy in ideological terms. A small band of party professionals, eager to prevent another intraparty bloodletting, hunted for a nonideological explanation of Nixon's defeat. They noted that Nixon had run very poorly in the great cities of the North. They noted that Nixon had run only a hair behind Kennedy in both popular and electoral vote. Their simplistic conclusion was that the next Republican candidate could beat Kennedy the next time around, if only he picked up a better vote in the cities.

This became the battle cry of Senator Thruston Morton, the national chairman, and other professionals in the weeks following the election. In more detailed form, their reasoning went something like this: Nixon lost such states as Illinois, Pennsylvania, and Michigan only because he lost such cities as Chicago, Philadelphia, and Detroit. If he had cut his losses in these cities enough to carry the states, he would have been elected President. How could he have done better in the cities? By better organization, of course. Hence, spruce up your big city organizations, and the White House is yours in 1964.

This argument did have the merit of avoiding ideological factionalism. It implied that policies and issues were unimportant, that Nixon or Rockefeller or Goldwater could have won in 1960 if only there had been better organization in the cities. Apart from this virtue of pacification, however, the argument didn't make a great deal of sense.

It ignored too many facts. It ignored the fact that Dwight Eisenhower had run remarkably well in Chicago and even New York City in 1956 with less organizational effort behind him than Nixon had in 1960. It ignored the fact that good organization is very nearly impossible to achieve where there is no basic support for the party. It ignored the fact that a good candidate with good issues can and does often triumph over superior organization.

Nevertheless, building up the Republican organizations in the big cities was the watchword when the Republican National Committee held its first postelection meeting at Washington in January, 1961. Morton named Ray Bliss, the energetic and highly respected Ohio state chairman, to head a committee on the big city vote. Morton told Bliss to report back and "tell us what steps have to be taken everywhere to erode the monolithic Democratic big city vote."

The selection of Bliss as committee chairman was indicative of an aura of unreality surrounding the entire project. True enough, Ohio and most of its cities were bright spots in 1960. Not only did Nixon carry this vote-rich state by a comfortable margin, but he also won handsome victories in Cincinnati and Columbus, two of Ohio's largest cities. However, Cincinnati and Columbus were, are, and probably always will be essentially Republican cities with essentially homogeneous white Protestant populations. Cleveland, Ohio's only city with the polyglot population found in Chicago, Detroit, and Philadelphia, was another matter in 1960. Kennedy won a greater percentage of the vote there than in any other city in the country. Based on the experience of 1960, Bliss's credentials for lecturing the rest of the party on corraling the big city vote were less than sufficient.

But his credentials for the job as envisioned by Morton

were impeccable. Morton could depend on Ray Bliss not to lead the party down some dangerous side alley of ideological strife. High-strung, chain-smoking Ray Bliss is the epitome of the professional political technician who wants to stay as far away from the party-splitting issues as possible—a type much more prevalent among Democrats than Republicans. Although of a conservative nature, Bliss is obsessed by the specter of emotion-generating conservative issues that can drive votes away from the Republicans. This obsession, it must be added, was spawned by the hard facts of 1958 when Bliss's masterful organization could not prevent ill-advised Republican sponsorship of a state "right to work" referendum from causing a Democratic landslide.[1]

The Bliss Committee's report was made to the National Committee a year later in January, 1962, at the Skirvin Hotel in Oklahoma City. "Senator Morton stressed that our committee should not get involved in issues or political principles," Bliss told the National Committee. "Our committee was established only to examine and report on the mechanics and techniques of campaigning in the cities." Because political issues never can really be severed from political techniques, the report that followed was 99 percent eyewash. National Committee members yawned through a dismal winter afternoon of oral presentations by Bliss's subcommittee chairmen and then stuck the printed copies of the 102-page report in their briefcases with some good intentions to look it over when they returned home. It's doubtful many of them ever did. If they had, they would have found some how-to-do-it ABC's of precinct organization in a big city.

But in January, 1962, others in the party, not nearly so

---

[1] In this respect, Bliss is typical of the pragmatic Republicans who for twenty-four years have sublimated their own conservative preferences in quest of victory. But Bliss is no liberal. He was thought of so highly by the Goldwater camp that Stephen Shadegg, then Arizona state chairman and a Goldwater ghost writer, tried in January, 1961, to promote the immediate replacement of Morton as national chairman by Bliss.

circumspect as Thruston Morton and Ray Bliss about fomenting intraparty warfare, were concocting more imaginative
battle plans for 1964. Two of them, the antithesis of each
other, typify the basic cleavage in the Republican Party. One
was drafted by a group of Goldwater supporters, whose identity still cannot be revealed. The other was drafted by L.
Judson Morhouse, the Republican state chairman of New
York and then a key Rockefeller supporter.

About the only real mistake Morton and Bliss made in
insulating the big city committee from any nonconformist
notions was to name big, crew-cut Jud Morhouse to its membership. Morhouse, irrepressible and outgoing, quickly argued in closed-door sessions that the urban voting problem
could not be handled in any satisfactory manner unless issues
were indeed discussed. Bliss and his committee's majority
promptly slapped down Morhouse. Apparently to suppress
Morhouse's zeal, Bliss exiled the New York state chairman
to head a subcommittee on public opinion polling—the least
important of the subcommittees.

But Morhouse was not discouraged. He produced a fire-
snorting subcommittee report with passages such as this:
"Those who disagree with Republicans may be 'stupid' in
the minds of some arch-Republicans, but they still have
enough votes to win elections. And it is not enough for Republicans to know what they think of themselves—they must
know what the housewife, the truck driver, the farmer and
the Democrats think of them. . . . Until the Republican Party
listens to the people, talks to the people, and helps to solve
the problems of the people, it will remain a minority party."

As might be expected, this and other incendiary passages
were stricken from the subcommittee report by the full Bliss
Committee. Still, the sanitized version of Morhouse's subcommittee report comes closer to the forbidden country of
ideology than any other part of the Bliss Report.

Even after the Bliss Report was presented to the National Committee in Oklahoma City, Morhouse was still brooding about it. So, on February 27, 1962, he fired off an outspoken confidential memorandum to Governor Rockefeller (with copies to Hinman and to Harry O'Donnell, publicity man for the Republican State Committee). The subject of the memorandum was "Big City Politics." But the document really went much further, suggesting the outlines of an over-all battle plan for the Republican Party. After explaining the origin of the Bliss Committee, Morhouse started teeing off:

> . . . Following its [the Bliss Committee's] organization, we had a somewhat bitter battle over whether the committee should analyze what the Republican Party should stand for in order to obtain the confidence—and the votes—of people who live in urban areas.
>
> Most other members of the committee were determined that we should not discuss "issues." (Representatives of minority groups and labor stood with me.) We were overcome, however, and the committee ultimately made a report which talked about practically nothing but organization—the same subject on which Republican chieftains have concentrated for the past twenty years without any noticeable improvement for the Republican Party. The only exception was the report of a sub-committee on "Public Opinion Polls, Television and Public Relations" which tried to recognize the need to face up to the people's problems, but the parent committee tore up two-thirds of that.
>
> . . . In addition, Republicans in Congress (whether justifiably or not) managed to achieve the blame for opposing a Department of Urban Affairs at the same time that the National Committee was alerting the party to the necessity to pay more attention to the urban areas—a fact which President Kennedy commented upon.

Then Morhouse began to move toward his plan for revamping the Grand Old Party.

The points that I have been attempting to make for a long time seem to me of all the greater consequence now. They are as follows.

1. The Republican Party nationally (and the Republican National Committee) should be dominated by people from the states which have the big cities—which is not now the case.

2. The Republican Party, its National Committee and its elected members must recognize the problems which face people who live in big cities—which it does not now do.

3. The Republican Party must run a candidate for President with whose philosophy the people in big cities can agree and in whose honesty of purpose they have confidence—which it is not now inclined to do.

Somewhere along the line, someone who understands these facts and who is determined to make the rest of the party understand them must break with the existing party structure so that those who want to win can rise out of the lethargic and amorphous slough of defeat and despair to which the Republican Party has fallen.

Morhouse spelled out these views more completely a few weeks later in his Albany hotel suite in an interview with a reporter. Morhouse contended that the grasp of the conservatives over the National Committee should be broken by ending the near-equality of representation for all states, big and little, on the Committee. The present system, which gives every state two seats and awards one bonus seat for good Republican performances in recent elections, naturally favors the small, conservative states.[2] Morhouse wanted to allocate National Committee seats on a strict population basis, just like the House of Representatives. Acknowledging

[2] The bonus seat is awarded to any state which either delivers its electoral votes to the Republican candidate in the last Presidential election, has a Republican governor, or has a Republican majority in its Congressional delegation. On that basis, New York and Arizona each had three National Committee seats in 1961–1964. The bonus seat always goes to the state party chairman.

that the National Committee's conservative majority wasn't
about to repeal its own power, Morhouse had an alternative.
Republicans from big city states would boycott the National
Committee and establish an informal council of their own as
a sounding board for liberal Republican views.

It is these views which really are important in Morhouse's
battle plan. It must be said that his proposals for reorganiz-
ing or boycotting the National Committee were far removed
from reality. But these proposals were only his way of trying
to promote the policies that he believed would bring Republican victories.

To broaden its base and become the nation's majority
party, Morhouse argued, the Republican Party must start
promoting ideas with a broad base of support.

"The party will never be successful until we start considering what concerns the people," Morhouse said. "The party's
leaders all make the same central mistake. They say: 'We're
going to tell you what to do. We don't care what you want.'"

In Morhouse's view, it was plain enough what concerned
the people in the winter of 1962: medical care for the aged,
the education of their children and the problem of crowded
schools, unemployment and the fear of more unemployment
caused by automation. The people, he contended, were not
really at all worried about the orthodox Republican ideals of
balanced budgets and fiscal responsibility.

With utter candor, Morhouse admitted that Republican
plans for the Government to assault the problems of medical
care, education, and automation would not differ greatly
from New Frontier schemes. But me-tooism was the least of
Morhouse's worries. He was bothered by Republican nega-
tivism. "The Republican Party is the party that says 'no'
before it hears the question," Morhouse said. In fact, he believed that Nixon's opposition to medical care for the aged
financed through the Social Security system was the final
factor that cost him the election.

But why would city voters suddenly start voting in greater numbers for Republican candidates who were espousing essentially the same social welfare programs as Democrats? Morhouse's answer here was the weakest part of his argument: "I think Republicans can do a better job than the Democrats and the public can see it."

On balance, there was not much new in the Morhouse battle plan (apart from his quixotic plans for reforming or boycotting the National Committee). But his public airing of these views did clarify what really had been the grand strategy of the Republican Party since 1940—a grand strategy that Barry Goldwater and his followers wanted to dispense with in 1964. What was revolutionary about Morhouse was not his battle plan but the fact that he talked about it in public. This was regarded as totally improper by most Republicans, including Morhouse's chief, Nelson A. Rockefeller, as we shall soon see.

If the Morhouse plan was dynamite, a more detailed plan and presentation worked up by some of Goldwater's friends and supporters constituted a political atom bomb.

For more than two decades, the Republican Party's conservatives hadn't been able to come up with any rational formula for winning a national election—a failure that had helped cost Robert A. Taft the shot at the White House that he so much wanted. About the only theory the conservatives could concoct was their hoary maxim that millions upon millions of conservatives who hadn't bothered to vote since the days when the Republicans were nominating the likes of Calvin Coolidge and Herbert Hoover for President would suddenly emerge from the woodwork and march to the polling places if only the Grand Old Party were courageous enough to nominate a true-blue conservative for President. It was a mythological sort of political theory that all conservatives—even Goldwater, usually the most practical of men in matters pertaining to party politics—echoed on occasion. But hardly anybody could accept the woodwork theory of hidden conservatives, probably not even the conservatives mouthing it.

It was essential for Republican conservatism in 1961–1962 to devise some rational blueprint for victory. This was the intended function of the battle plan drafted for Goldwater by his friends. But in seeking and—at least on paper—finding a route to victory for a conservative candidate, the battle plan employed concepts and language so harsh that they were unfit for the day-to-day operations or dialogue of American politics.

In greatly condensed form, the detailed and documented battle plan went something like this:

In the first place, American voters would have to be considered for the first time in realistic ethnic groupings —not meaningless geographical (Northerner, Southerner, Westerner, et cetera), occupational (bricklayers, truck drivers, physicians, et cetera), or even unrealistic ethnic (Greek American, Polish American, Serbian American, et cetera) groupings. Instead, all voters could be most meaningfully placed in one of four great ethnic groups with distinctive political characteristics.

Group A. White Protestants, almost all of Anglo-Saxon or Germanic origin. This is the American "native stock." More important, it is the bedrock of Republican strength. Among white Protestants, the Republican Party is the majority party.

Group B. The Northern Negroes.[3] As an economically depressed minority group, they are really far more interested

[3] The Southern Negro is not listed because he has so much difficulty registering and voting under white supremacist voting procedures in the South that his political importance is nominal. The Southern Negro who has managed to vote is more likely to vote Republican than the Northern Negro, mainly because the Democratic Party in the South still carries the image of James O. Eastland. This pattern is changing, however, as a lily-white, segregationist Republican Party grows in the South.

in economic bread-and-butter issues than in civil rights.[4]
Consequently, since the inception of the New Deal in 1934,
when the Northern Negro deserted the party of Lincoln, he
has been a steadfast Democrat. No amount of Republican
crusading for Negro rights could outweigh the magnetic
attraction of the Democratic Party's social welfare programs.
Anyway, the Northern Negro has come to think of the Democratic Party in terms of the Northern integrationist, not the
Southern segregationist. Thus, it would be extremely difficult
for the Republicans to outdo the Democrats in championing
civil rights, even if they tried.

Group C. The Jews. They adhere to the Democratic Party
as closely as the Northern Negroes but for entirely different
reasons. When Franklin Roosevelt was condemning Hitler's
persecution of the Jews in the 1930's and urging aid for Bri-
tain against the Nazis after 1939, prominent Republican
leaders were adhering to a policy of isolation and noninter-
vention. Robert A. Taft put the punctuation mark on the
estrangement of the Jews from the Republican Party when
he denounced the Nazi war crimes trials at Nuremberg.[5]

Group D. The White Catholics. This is by far the least
predictable—and hence, most important—of the four groups.
Although all of the various Catholic ethnic groups once were
firmly attached to the Democratic Party, there was a cumula-
tive defection to the Republicans since 1940, climaxing in
the Eisenhower campaigns of 1952 and 1956. These Catholic
defectors tend to be members of early immigrant groups, such
as the Irish and Germans, who were most successful in as-
similating with white Protestant "native stock." The Italians
and later Catholic immigrant groups had shown more loyalty
to the Democrats in 1952 and 1956. All of these Catholic
ethnic groups returned to the Democratic fold in 1960 to

[4] This battle plan was devised before the 1963 Negro rights revolution,
which has made even the lowest-income Negro aware of the close correlation
between civil rights and economic well-being.

[5] But this act by Taft was included by John F. Kennedy among his *Profiles
in Courage.*

make John F. Kennedy the first Catholic to sit in the White House. But once the point was made that a Catholic *could* be elected President, then there was the chance that their defections to the Republicans would resume in 1964—even against Kennedy.

In addition to these ethnic groupings, two facts and one assumption are integral parts of the conservative blueprint.

Fact No. 1: The white Protestants are dominant in upper New England, the nonurban Midwest, the Great Plains, the Rocky Mountains—and the South and Southwest. Except for the traditionally Democratic South and Southwest, this area comprises the Republican heartland and the starting point for any Republican Presidential nominee, be he Rockefeller or Goldwater.

Fact No. 2: The Catholics, including the politically volatile early immigrant groups, are found in the big cities that provided the needed Democratic votes in victorious Democratic years, such as 1960.

Assumption: The Catholics are particularly susceptible to a strong anti-Communist line. It was anger by rank-and-file Catholics over what they felt was a soft-on-Communists failing among Democrats that triggered the big Catholic defection to Eisenhower in 1952.[6]

On the basis of all this, the conservative battle plan calls for these policies to win the next election:

Policy A: Soft-pedal civil rights. While stopping short of actually endorsing racial segregation, forget all the sentimental tradition of the party of Lincoln. Because the Negro and Jewish votes are irrevocably tied to the Democrats anyway, this agnostic racial policy won't lose votes among the groups most sensitive to Negro rights. But it might work wonders in attracting white Southerners into the Republican Party, joining white Protestants in other sections of the country as hard-core Republicans.

Policy B: Assume a vigorously strong anti-Communist

[6] This sidesteps the impact on Catholics of Adlai Stevenson's divorce.

line. Return the party's stance on foreign affairs to a twentieth century version of Teddy Roosevelt's Big Stick policy. This wouldn't lose many votes among white Protestants and might snatch enough Catholic voters away from the Democrats to cut down Democratic margins in the big cities.

Policy C: Except for the civil rights question, stick to orthodox Republicanism on domestic issues. Don't retreat from economic conservatism. Avoid the slightest hint of metooism. This will make sure the vital Republican heartland neither defects nor stays at home on election day. Remember: The industrialized states are to be won by a vigorous anti-Communist line, not by liberal social welfare plans.

The final ingredient is a conservative candidate who can follow these policies. In terms of 1964, who else but Barry Goldwater? His Republican orthodoxy would ensure the basic Republican heartland states. His agnosticism on Negro rights would pick up a considerably fatter bundle of electoral votes from the South and Southwest than Nixon won in 1960. His anti-communism would pick up enough Catholic votes to carry some of the big industrialized states. The sum total: Victory over Kennedy in 1964.

Whatever its logical defects, this conservative battle plan was something new. The Negro revolution of 1963 was to make it all more tempting in Republican eyes by turning white Protestants—North and South—against Kennedy. Cut down the plan's reliance on anti-Communism to pick up some electoral votes in the high population states, and the plan is not much different from the victory formula concocted by Goldwater's supporters in 1963.

Although both the Morhouse plan and the conservative plan represented wide segments of opinion and power within the party and fairly reflected the true tactical policy of the two great factions, neither plan as such ever was embraced by working politicians. Each plan was too harsh in its language, too plainspoken for the euphemistic world of practical politics.

When first shown the conservative battle plan, Goldwater was shocked over the blunt way sensitive ethnic questions were handled. Rockefeller was more than just shocked when Jud Morhouse's memorandum and views were published in the *Wall Street Journal*. He was furious at Morhouse. That's because early 1962 was the precise period when Rockefeller was making a determined effort to mend his fences with party conservatives.

VI

* *

Rockefeller Moving Up

Some events of the night of February 2, 1962, reveal the basic problem faced that winter by Nelson Rockefeller in his drive for the Presidential nomination and the basic tactic he was using to solve the problem.

The Republican National Committee had selected February 2 as the fund-raising kickoff for the 1962 campaign. It was using the closed-circuit television technique that had become so popular with Republicans during the Eisenhower Administration. Tickets were sold to some three hundred thousand of the party faithful for dinners in seventeen cities. Each dinner would have its own speaker, but all would see the party's most renowned celebrities through closed-circuit television: Eisenhower from the Los Angeles dinner; Goldwater from Cleveland; Nixon from Fresno, California; Rockefeller from Des Moines, Iowa; Representative William Miller of New York, the party's national chairman, from the Washington dinner; and a few others.

The Republicans who forked over one hundred dollars a plate for filet mignon and red wine at the Mayflower Hotel's ballroom in Washington were representative of the typical middle-level contributors to Republican campaign funds. Staunchly conservative and deeply suspicious of the party's progressive wing, most were suburbanites from just over the District of Columbia border in Maryland and Virginia who

66

were so little affected by living next door to the nation's capital that they might just as well have been from Dallas, Texas.

They were determined to have a good time for their hundred dollars. After fortifying themselves for the massive onslaught of oratory with a massive dose of predinner cocktails, the diners were in a jovial but rambunctious mood. When wine and dinner were completed, they were ready to cheer. And cheer they did as the Republican celebrities flashed on the giant screen. (Because Nixon was struck down at the last minute with a virus infection, his speech was read by actor George Murphy.)

But the good-fellowship at the Mayflower Hotel came to a jarring end when Nelson Rockefeller's gleaming face was flashed on the television screen from Des Moines. The cheers of the Iowans assembled to hear the Governor of New York were drowned out in Washington by booing and hissing from the slightly tipsy diners at the Mayflower. After a moment or two the booing turned into self-conscious laughter, but the deed was done. A typical segment of hard-core Republican conservatives had demonstrated vividly enough that they did not accept Rockefeller now, and weren't ever likely to accept him. Their cheers and applause for Goldwater, markedly more enthusiastic than the reception for any other televised speaker, including Eisenhower, showed their preference for President.

But really more significant than Rockefeller's reception in Washington was the content of his speech from Des Moines.

The most burning political issue in February, 1962, was President Kennedy's proposal to establish a Cabinet-level Department of Urban Affairs. Democrats and a good many Republicans saw this proposal as one way for Kennedy to clinch the city vote. Nevertheless, Republicans and conservative Southern Democrats zeroed in on the proposal as a further movement toward centralized government and heavy

Federal spending. A Republican–Southern Democratic coalition had stopped the bill by jamming it up in the House Rules Committee, whose clearance is necessary in order for major legislation to reach the House floor.

But Kennedy wasn't willing to let his Urban Affairs Department die a quiet death in the recesses of the House Rules Committee. He resubmitted the proposal as a reorganization plan, which—unlike a bill—automatically goes into effect unless either the House or Senate votes *against* it. In other words, the Urban Affairs Department would become reality unless brought to the floor of Congress and voted down. That wasn't all. Kennedy next took the extraordinary step of announcing that Dr. Robert Weaver, head of the Housing and Home Finance Agency, would become Secretary of Urban Affairs if Congress permitted establishment of the new department. Weaver would be the first Negro ever to serve in the Cabinet. Democratic politicians were pounding themselves on the back in self-congratulation for what they regarded as a Kennedy masterstroke. They felt they now had a tails-I-win-heads-you-lose proposition. If Republicans killed the Urban Affairs proposal, they would bear the stigma of preventing racial integration at the Cabinet level. If the plan cleared Congress, then Kennedy would go down in history for another milestone in Negro rights.[1] Some Republicans agreed that Kennedy had maneuvered them into a box.[2] It was surmised in party circles that Rockefeller, as chief representative of Republicans who look to gains among Negroes and urban voters as the formula for victory, would be greatly embarrassed by the opposition of Republicans in Congress to the Urban Affairs Department and Dr. Weaver.

---

[1] As is so often the case, the politicians were wrong. The struggle over the Urban Affairs Department was all but forgotten by election day in 1962 even though near-solid Republican votes helped defeat the plan on both the House and Senate floors.

[2] It will be remembered that Jud Morhouse's February 27 memorandum to Rockefeller took this position.

Rockefeller proved in Des Moines on February 2 that this surmise was absolutely unfounded. He shocked and surprised almost everybody by his biggest swing to the right in order to please party conservatives: an attack against Kennedy's Urban Affairs Department scheme that could have come from the mouth of Barry Goldwater.

He did not ignore the proposed Weaver appointment but used it to accuse Kennedy of racial demagoguery. "The Democratic Administration is afraid to let its Department of Urban Affairs proposal, in its present form, stand on its merits," said Rockefeller. "That is why they have brought in the completely unrelated race issue. What is this but political fakery?"

But Rockefeller was not content with attacking the President's tactics. He went after the substance of the proposal, charging that the Urban Affairs Department "might well be used, in the form proposed, as a subterfuge to bypass the Constitutional sovereignty of the states and to gain direct political control over the nation's cities."

Even the hostile hundred-dollar-a-plate diners at the Mayflower applauded quietly at this restatement of Republican orthodoxy by the man they believed guilty of New Deal and New Frontier heresies. And in Des Moines, some three thousand Republicans who had jammed into the city's biggest movie theater to see Rockefeller loved it. They paid three dollars apiece for a fried chicken box supper, not one hundred dollars for filet mignon. They had come to be convinced by Rockefeller, not to hiss and boo. The hard core of conservatives were fully committed to Goldwater and opposed to Rockefeller, but a good many less dedicated conservatives in Iowa and elsewhere were trying to keep an open mind.

During his one-day visit to Des Moines, Rockefeller didn't make a wrong move. He never deviated from Republican orthodoxy. In this citadel of the conservative American Farm Bureau Federation, he told a news conference that the Kennedy farm program would have a "tremendous impact on the loss of freedom by farmers."

Moreover, Iowa Republican leaders helped Rockefeller play the game. George Nagle, the state party chairman, told Leo Egan of the *New York Times* that Rockefeller "has been tagged as a liberal, but I know better; he is a good businessman." In introducing Rockefeller at the movie theater, Governor Norman A. Erbe spoke of the New Yorker's devotion to "sound Republican principles." When Rockefeller was getting this kind of reaction from two conservative Republicans in the old Taft heartland, his campaign was indeed moving along nicely—boos or no boos at the Mayflower.

The Des Moines speech was not really a new departure for Rockefeller but rather the beginning of a new intensification. Aware that he must break down the animosity among the conservative rank and file if he was to win the Presidential nomination, Rockefeller had been trying ever since the 1960 election to show off his conservative side. But there had been spills and fumbles—plus what appeared to be some occasional backsliding toward liberalism.

One instance of this came late during the 1961 session just as President Kennedy's proposal for long-term financing of foreign aid through "backdoor spending," a scheme bitterly opposed by the vast majority of Republicans in Congress, was coming up for a vote in the House. In letters to Republican Congressmen, Rockefeller appeared to be urging approval of the Kennedy plan. Representative Charles Halleck of Indiana, the House Republican leader, angrily told the Governor of New York to stick to his own business up in Albany. Rockefeller compounded rather than relieved the damage the next day by wiring each of the Republican Congressmen that he wasn't really in favor of the "backdoor spending" plan after all.

But coming out against the Urban Affairs Department and

the announcement of the prospective Weaver appointment proved that Rockefeller meant business. He and his closest aides were absolutely determined to prevent anything that might once again depict the Governor as a party splitter or a heretic.

One small incident points up this determination. The word was passed in New York and Washington during the summer of 1962 about the planned publication of an inflammatory book of memoirs by Emmett Hughes, a White House speech writer during the early days of the Eisenhower Administration and a speech writer and foreign policy adviser on Rockefeller's payroll since 1959. It was understood that Hughes, who had become bitterly disillusioned with Eisenhower, used his book as a launching pad for missiles against his old chief as well as other sacrosanct Republicans, including the late John Foster Dulles. A link between the Rockefeller camp and Hughes's heresy could be damaging to the Governor. That was the appraisal of one Republican politician when he telephoned George Hinman in New York City to tell him about the Hughes book. Hinman replied that the news about the book came as a complete surprise to him. But Hinman assured his caller of one certainty: If such a book were published over Emmett Hughes's byline, it would come at a time when Emmett Hughes was no longer on Nelson Rockefeller's payroll. Hinman may not have had anything to do with it, but the fact is that Hughes *did* leave the Rockefeller staff before publication of his book.

Sometimes this careful presentation of Rockefeller as a conservative was a bit clumsy. The clumsiest was a secret memorandum of August 14, 1962, sent to Republican county chairmen and vice-chairmen in New York by State Chairman L. Judson Morhouse (the same Jud Morhouse who back in February was proposing that Rockefeller lead the way in forming a new, liberal Republican Party). Morhouse sent the local leaders twenty-eight "items" of information intended to

show Rockefeller as a fiscal conservative and accompanied it
with this memorandum:

> A number of you have requested some basic information on
> Rockefeller Record which would show his "Conservative" side.
> The items listed on the attached sheets do show this and
> is being sent to you for your use in talking to people who feel
> the Governor is strictly a liberal.
>
> It must be used cautiously and should not be published be-
> cause we do not want to emphasize the conservative side so
> much that we lose some other votes.

Because not all of the county chairmen and vice-chairmen
in New York were staunch Rockefeller supporters, it was
natural that one of them turned it over to the enemy—in this
case David H. Jaquith, then state chairman and later gubernatorial candidate of the fledgling Conservative Party of
New York. Jacquith promptly released the memorandum to
the press. Rockefeller immediately denied any prior knowledge of it. The entire incident was most embarrassing.

When it came to Presidential politics, Jud Morhouse often
was a bull in a china shop. But most of Rockefeller Presidential politicking in 1961 was not Morhouse's business at all
but the chief occupation of suave and debonair George Hinman. Moving quietly and gracefully around the country,
Hinman was giving the Rockefeller soft sell, and getting a
better response than ever. Congressmen, state chairmen,
and national committeemen were beginning to believe Hinman when he talked about Rockefeller's belief in fiscal integrity, states' responsibilities, and private enterprise.

By the summer of 1962, Representative Frank Bow of
Ohio seemed convinced. As representative of William Mc-
Kinley's old district, Bow is the epitome of the Old Guard
Republican. He is a vigorous champion of balanced budgets
and the protective effort and made his biggest splash nation-
ally during the Eisenhower Administration by trying to pre-

vent allied governments from prosecuting United States servicemen for crimes. But Bow believed that Rockefeller was proving himself conservative enough for even an Ohio Old Guardsman. He was telling friends in the Speaker's Lobby just off the House floor that Rockefeller probably would be the man for him.

Frank Bow was not alone. As Rockefeller's campaign for reelection as Governor opened in the autumn of 1962, it was clear that his national position had improved amazingly over the past nine months. Of course, he had no pledged support or active state organizations. It was much too early for that. But by Labor Day of 1962, Nelson Rockefeller was in front for the Republican nomination and moving steadily farther in front. And one reason for Rockefeller's bright outlook at that time was the strange but valuable friendship that was growing between him and Barry Goldwater.

Most Republican politicians were aghast when they first noticed the Rockefeller-Goldwater friendship. It just didn't make sense, they complained. Besides, they added, it was against the natural laws of politics—or at least of Republican politics.

There was a natural affinity of a sort between the two men. Both were extroverted, dynamic figures. They liked each other's company. Furthermore, they *did* agree about a good many things. Neither could be classed as Eisenhower admirers, and Goldwater agreed with Rockefeller that Eisenhower's "bigger bang for a buck program" was dangerous to national security. Neither had much use for Richard Nixon as a politician. From a superficial point of view, they were on common ground in supporting fiscal responsibility and private enterprise as well as a tough anti-Communist line. In party affairs, they found agreement on the desirability of the regular party organization maintaining the upper hand over volunteer groups and on the absolute need for Republican unity. Rockefeller's move to the right in 1962–1963 made it all the easier for Goldwater to like him.

In truth, however, a few amicable conversations and superficial agreements between Rockefeller and Goldwater had not solved the Republican Party's habitual and debilitating problem of fratricidal warfare over ideology. The two men —and thousands behind them in the party—were worlds apart on such basic issues as foreign policy, civil rights, and the role of the Federal Government in a modern society. Natural affinity or not, the Rockefeller-Goldwater friendship started and flourished because Nelson Rockefeller wanted it that way. Rockefeller was the suitor in this love affair.

A Rockefeller-Goldwater alliance was far more to Rockefeller's interests than Goldwater's. What better way to gain the confidence of the party's rank and file than by getting Goldwater's approval? Even if Rockefeller were to win the nomination without Goldwater's actual help, the prize wouldn't be worth much if Goldwater and his millions of devoted followers refused to back the Rockefeller ticket. It was absolutely imperative for Rockefeller at least to neutralize Goldwater.

And Goldwater was indeed less pugnacious as the months went by. The personal accord between him and Rockefeller became obvious by the summer of 1961 and in sharp contrast to the Senator's sarcastic slighting remarks—mostly in private but sometimes in public—about Nixon. By the beginning of 1962, Goldwater was telling his conservative friends that "Rocky's really not such a bad fellow. He's more conservative than you would imagine. You ought to talk to him someday."

The two leaders also were pulled together by what they considered a common enemy. Neither trusted Eisenhower and Nixon or the businessmen and politicians close to them. Rockefeller and Goldwater believed they saw the fine hand of the Eisenhower-Nixon crowd at work when an "All-Republican Conference" held the last weekend of June, 1962, on General Eisenhower's farm at Gettysburg, Pennsylvania, unveiled the formation of a new National Republican Citizens Committee with headquarters in Washington. It was to provide an outlet for the funds and energies of citizens who preferred not to work with the Republican National Committee or the regular Republican organizations at the state and local levels.

Never a man to hold his fire, Goldwater exploded in a July 2 letter to Representative Miller, the national chairman. He wrote:

> We already have a National Committee. Where is there unity in two groups working in the same field? How can unity exist when this outside organization competes with the functions of the National Committee? This can lead to the same kind of confusion and distrust which cost us the Presidency in 1960, and it should be resisted by you and all Republican leaders.

But Goldwater was really thinking about more than just party unity and the prerogatives of the National Committee. So was Rockefeller. Goldwater discussed the situation over the long-distance telephone with both Rockefeller and George Hinman. They were suspicious about the part played in the formation of the Citizens Committee by Walter Thayer, president of the *New York Herald Tribune* and a friend of Nixon's. Could it be a holding operation for Nixon until (after his presumed election as Governor of California) he decides to run for President? Then there was the active role in the Citizens Committee by David Kendall of Michigan, a White House aide under Eisenhower. This brought suspicion that the Citizens Committee might be a front not for Nixon but for George Romney, the supersalesman from Detroit who now was running for Governor of Michigan. In the summer of 1962, there was no question in Goldwater's mind whom he preferred for President in a three-way race between Rockefeller, Nixon, and Romney. It was Rockefeller all the way.

But the one great service Goldwater could perform for Rockefeller was outright withdrawal from Presidential consideration. Indeed, Goldwater was coming closer and closer to eliminating himself from consideration.

As we shall see in Chapter IX, Goldwater was honestly and eagerly trying to dissuade the politicians and businessmen who later formed the National Draft Goldwater Committee. He was making it clear to them, to friends, and to his staff that he had no desire whatever to be President and was repelled at the very thought of a grueling Presidential campaign.

It was in September, 1962, that Goldwater stopped just short of a Sherman-style disclaimer in trying to eliminate himself from consideration. He told a newspaper reporter that the barnstorming Goldwater of the banquet circuit was no more. He had been averaging between 200 and 250 separate speaking engagements outside Arizona each year. Now he planned to curtail this schedule drastically. In the 1962 Congressional campaign, he would speak outside Arizona only nine times. His cutdown for 1963 was even more shocking. He hoped to accept only ten out-of-state speaking engagements for the entire year. Obviously, a man who has any serious interest in the White House increases rather than decreases his barnstorming activities as the nominating convention nears.

Goldwater's avowed reasons for the big cutdown in traveling had nothing to do with Presidential politics. Facing a 1964 campaign for a third term in the Senate, Goldwater wanted more time to mend his fences back in Arizona. He also wanted more time to spend in Washington as an active Senator. Finally, he claimed he was weary of the one-night stands of the banquet circuit. "I believe I deserve a letup," he said.

But Goldwater also had been thinking about the connection between the Republican Presidential nomination and the conservative movement inside and outside the Republican Party.

He believed that a Republican could not win his party's nomination without support from what Nixon used to call the "Big Six" states: New York, California, Pennsylvania, Ohio, Illinois, and Michigan. In the autumn of 1962, Goldwater believed that Ohio was the only one of these six where he had a chance of winning a majority of the convention delegation. On the other hand, he was convinced that Rockefeller had a good chance to wrap up the delegations from all six states. Moreover, if he tried for the Presidential nomination and failed, Goldwater feared this would be interpreted as a defeat for conservatism generally.

Goldwater was by no means about to abdicate from national politics. He knew that delegations from the South and Southwest and perhaps the Great Plains and Rocky Mountain states as well would come to the National Convention pledged to him whether he was a candidate or not. He planned to use these delegates, probably hundreds of them, as leverage to force through as conservative a platform as possible and to shape the national ticket (perhaps with a conservative Vice-Presidential running mate for Rockefeller). "I think you're going to find the entire convention more conservative than it was the last time, and it was pretty conservative then," he said.

Most of all, Goldwater was willing to fade out of the Presidential picture because of his newfound faith in Rockefeller. He believed the Governor had really and sincerely moved to the right. In fact, Goldwater did not then think a Rockefeller-Goldwater ticket—Rockefeller for President and Goldwater for Vice-President—was at all absurd. Goldwater had no intention whatever of giving up his Senate seat to run for Vice-President. Nor did he relish running for Senator and Vice-President simultaneously after having mercilessly broiled Lyndon B. Johnson for doing the same thing in

1960.[3] It was this special problem—not a lack of philosophical or personal compatibility—that made a Rockefeller-Goldwater ticket unlikely, in Goldwater's opinion.

The news of Goldwater's cutdown in speaking engagements was greeted by shock and dismay by hard-core conservatives around the country. One such group gathered for dinner at the home of a well-known newspaper corre pondent in Washington. They were just about convinced that Goldwater really meant it. They began searching their minds for the names of other conservatives to oppose Rockefeller. Senator John Tower of Texas was articulate and attractive, but not the Presidential type. The old-line conservatives in the Senate such as Karl Mundt of South Dakota or Carl Curtis of Nebraska just weren't attractive enough. Anyway, the diners decided, it might be impossible for any Republican to beat Kennedy in 1964. It might be just as well for Rockefeller to serve as a sacrificial lamb, getting the nomination only to be destroyed by Kennedy in November. That would leave the way open for Goldwater to run against a new Democratic candidate in 1968. Backhanded though it was, this dinner-table conversation reflected wide acquiescence— if not always approval—to Rockefeller as the party's nominee.

As Rockefeller suspended national politicking in September to seek a second term as Governor against a nondescript Democratic candidate, the sun was shining on Rockefeller's march to the nomination. But there were two storm clouds that worried some of Rockefeller's friends.

One storm cloud—an ever-present storm cloud—was that primordial, basic split in the party. At the slightest provocation, Goldwater diehards and conservatives were ready to turn on Rockefeller. In fact, the Governor couldn't really count too much on the friendship with Goldwater that he had

[3] However, Goldwater satisfied himself as early as September, 1962, that the Arizona Constitution permitted the same man to run for two offices simultaneously.

cultivated so assiduously. One incident during the 1962 campaign shows that their relationship was on a foundation of less than complete trust.

Rockefeller had invited Goldwater to appear with him before a select group of well-heeled New York businessmen. Goldwater accepted. But his acceptance was followed by a series of strange and not entirely cogent long-distance telephone calls to Tony Smith, Goldwater's press secretary in Washington, from two of Rockefeller's aides in New York— speech writer Hugh Morrow and press secretary Robert McManus. The Rockefeller men wanted to make sure the meeting with the fat cats was kept secret. But then, apparently fearful that Goldwater might say something in New York that would embarrass Rockefeller during the height of a gubernatorial campaign, they suggested the Senator make a statement at the airport—a statement carefully prepared at Rockefeller Headquarters in New York. Smith reported this procedure to Goldwater with the comment that the entire business looked fishy. Goldwater promptly canceled the trip to New York. The incident was not a sterling example of mutual faith.

But the much more ominous storm cloud concerned Rockefeller's personal life. Ever since Rockefeller's divorce it had been common knowledge—though unpublished knowledge— in Washington, New York, and elsewhere that there was "another woman" in the case. She was a youthful matron and mother of four small children: Margaretta Fitler (Happy) Murphy, the wife of Dr. James Murphy, a Philadelphia physician. Attractive, vivacious, and highly intelligent, Happy Murphy had met Nelson Rockefeller during the 1958 campaign for Governor and had served on his staff. It was well known that Rockefeller wanted to marry her as soon as she could obtain a divorce.

Republican politicians in New York were terrified. The reaction to Rockefeller's divorce had been surprisingly mild.

But how would the average housewife react to his marrying the other woman—a young and pretty other woman? The politicians didn't know and weren't interested in finding out for sure. Nor were they content to sit in suspenseful agony while waiting for the other shoe to drop.

The state's Republican Congressmen, all of them seeking reelection in 1962, were particularly upset by the prospect that a Rockefeller remarriage not only would cause Rockefeller's defeat in the gubernatorial race but would hurt the entire Republican ticket enough to force the involuntary retirement from Congress for some of them. Consequently, they dispatched Representative William Miller to talk things over with the Rockefeller camp. Miller reported back to them that he had been pledged that Rockefeller would not remarry before the 1962 election. Nothing was said about the future.

* *

VII

1962: Four Campaigns

Robert Morgenthau, a pleasant young man of forty-three who seemed to be doing a workmanlike job as United States District Attorney for the Southern District of New York, was an absolutely incredible choice as the Democratic nominee to oppose Governor Nelson Rockefeller's reelection bid in 1962. Never was there a more inept campaigner. Tall, thin, and self-effacing (with a vague resemblance to "Mr. Peepers" of television fame a decade earlier), Morgenthau was one candidate who actually got lost in his own crowds. Unknown to the voters of New York when nominated in September, he was scarcely better known on election day in November. His speeches and handshaking techniques were so inhibited and colorless that they may have done him more harm than good. But quite apart from Morgenthau's personal limitations, his campaign itself was a marvel of disorganization. The hired limousines in his entourage would get lost on the way to a campaign date. Morgenthau would arrive at a county fair at precisely the moment when the crowds were home for the supper break. It was a standing but grim joke at Democratic Headquarters in Manhattan's Commodore Hotel that Morgenthau was going to turn up one Sunday afternoon all by himself for a rally at the silent, empty corner of Wall and Broad streets.

The tortuous maneuverings that finally flushed Morgenthau as the nominee for Governor aren't worth pursuing here. But a major factor in the amazing decision of the Democratic bosses to tap Morgenthau was a survey conducted for the party by pollster Louis Harris of New York. He found that the only Democrat with a fighting chance of scoring an upset over Rockefeller would be somebody in the mold of Herbert Lehman, former Senator and four times Governor—aristocratic, liberal, wealthy, Jewish, and blessed with a famous name. Octogenarian Lehman couldn't run himself, unfortunately. Harris concluded the nearest available substitute was Robert Morgenthau, the son of Henry Morgenthau, Franklin Roosevelt's Secretary of the Treasury.

The logic was brilliant save for one small point. Bob Morgenthau was no Lehman. He resembled him in no important way—not even in ethnic appeal. Far from rallying Jewish community leaders around the Democratic ticket, Morgenthau at the head of the ticket irritated them. Morgenthau had never been closely associated with Jewish community affairs and had married a Protestant. Moreover, as Rockefeller's indefatigable researchers soon discovered, Morgenthau was an officer in the Christian Association, actually an interfaith non-sectarian group, while an undergraduate at Amherst. Rockefeller gleefully relayed this information to Mayor Robert Wagner, who was a major force in maneuvering Morgenthau toward the nomination, as they reviewed the 1962 Columbus Day Parade in New York City.

But neither the Governor nor his aides were going to do much more laughing about the Democrats' horrible mistake. For it was to become apparent that Morgenthau was the one Democratic candidate who could hurt Rockefeller.

Rockefeller was then thought of by President Kennedy and his political advisers as the Republican who would be toughest to run against in 1964. Therefore, the real desire of the White House was to find a Democrat who could defeat Rockefeller in New York in 1962 and save Kennedy the trouble in 1964. No New York Democrat was that strong in

1962. Failing that, Kennedy would have liked a Democratic candidate who could at least tarnish Rockefeller's prestige. By sheer accident, they had unveiled in Morgenthau the most difficult candidate Rockefeller could possibly face.[1]

In the first place, Morgenthau was so anonymous to his fellow New Yorkers that any attack upon him would be self-defeating for the Governor. It would merely serve to build up Morgenthau. Thus, Rockefeller could not criticize Morgenthau, could not debate with Morgenthau, could not mention Morgenthau. "This isn't at all the kind of campaign we would have liked to have," Bob McManus, Rockefeller's press secretary, mentioned glumly to a reporter during the campaign. He meant that they would have preferred a better-known opponent—somebody like Mayor Wagner—whom Rockefeller would have been free to attack.

There was another and more important reason why the Rockefeller camp would have preferred Wagner to Morgenthau. If Rockefeller had defeated Wagner by a fairly comfortable margin (as probably would have been the case), Rockefeller could have claimed a victory over a major political figure and added prestige on his pathway to the nomination. This was really why Morgenthau was so difficult an opponent. He was so lightly regarded that a landslide victory would count for nothing. But Rockefeller's national prestige could be hurt badly if Morgenthau made it fairly close in a closing effort. The Governor's aides lived in dread of the possibility that Rockefeller's margin over Morgenthau would fall below the 570,000 vote margin by which Rockefeller drove Averell Harriman out of the Governor's Mansion in 1958. Right up to election day, they would only predict a victory margin anywhere between 350,000 and 700,000 votes and hope for the best.

Why couldn't Rockefeller count on a million-vote edge

[1] Some Democratic politicians insist the Kennedy brothers were shrewd enough to see the way Morgenthau could hurt Rockefeller and picked him for that reason. This seems extremely doubtful.

against an unknown and maladroit campaigner? Because Rockefeller had made enemies over the previous four years. He was no longer the bright and shining new face of 1958. Some New Yorkers hadn't forgiven him for the tax increase of 1959. Others feared (with some justification, as it turned out) that Rockefeller would call for still higher taxes if given a second term. Right-wing Republicans were going to vote for the new Conservative Party's candidate as an anti-Rockefeller protest. Add to these dissenters the solid party-line Democrats who would vote for any Democratic candidate —even Morgenthau—and a one-million vote margin would seem out of reach.

Nevertheless, Joseph Bachelder, Rockefeller's usually reliable pollster from Princeton, New Jersey, who had called the 1958 victory over Harriman right on the nose, came up with glad tidings on election eve. His surveys showed Rockefeller a million votes ahead of Morgenthau. State Chairman Jud Morhouse duly issued a statement predicting a million-vote victory.

There was precious little election night frolicking in Rockefeller's campaign headquarters at the Roosevelt Hotel in Manhattan. Out of 5,750,000 votes cast, Rockefeller won by 529,000—about 40,000 below his 1958 win. What made this win all the less impressive was the fact that Senator Jacob Javits had won reelection to the Senate by the one-million-vote margin that Bachelder had predicted for Rockefeller.[2] This was no disaster for Rockefeller, but it was nothing to brag about.

It had been a hot, long, enervating day for Richard M. Nixon as he sought votes for Governor in the Southern California desert around Palm Springs. The worst part came at Indio, where Nixon stood shaking hands for better than an

---

[2] The Javits campaign, operating on a vastly smaller budget than Rockefeller's, had no pollsters and consequently no election eve forecasts.

hour under a 100-degree sun. A tall young man in cowboy boots and cowboy hat quickly made it clear he wanted more than a handshake when he finally got to Nixon. Introducing himself as a member of the local Young Republicans organization, he asked Nixon what he thought of the Air Force putting out a manual with the United Nations flag on the cover—a manual that right-wingers were displaying as proof that Kennedy was trying to turn our military might over to the United Nations. Nixon, the man who had served eight years as Vice-President of the United States and was very nearly elected President, told his questioner that he was seeking state office—not Federal office—and was not qualified to answer these kinds of questions. Nixon didn't seem to enjoy this kind of exchange and he faced months and months more of it. This was May, 1962.

That night, Nixon chatted about himself and the future with a reporter. As usual when removed from the ordeal of campaign hustings, Nixon was frank, realistic—and more than a little fatalistic. "I realize, of course, that I have to win this election," Nixon said. "If I lose, I'm through in politics. I can never run for public office again."

From the tone of his voice, Nixon seemed regretful that he was risking everything in this race for Governor. By May, it was clear enough that bumbling, fumbling Governor Pat Brown was not going to be the pushover he was thought to be a year earlier. Brown, his weight down and his confidence restored, had rebounded from the Caryl Chessman affair. The Field Poll, published in California newspapers, showed Brown passing Nixon for the first time in May.

But much worse than Brown's resurgence was the lack of Republican unanimity behind Nixon. It was a rude shock for Nixon to find that after coming within an eyelash of the Presidency he had to fight for his own party's nomination for Governor in his own state. Once again, Nixon was bombarded within his own party from both left and right. The attack from the left was led by former Governor Goodwin J. Knight, who planned a vituperative primary election campaign against Nixon but was forced to withdraw because of hepatitis. The attack from the right was led by former Southern California football star Joe Shell, now a wealthy oil executive and leader of the Republicans in the State Assembly.

The attack from the right was infinitely the more dangerous for Nixon. He found some of his old political supporters —particularly his old sources for campaign funds—defecting to Shell. He was shocked to discover A. C. (Cy) Rubel, former president of Union Oil Company and a staunch Nixon man, was raising funds for Shell. The Los Angeles County Committee, once a preserve for Nixon, now was dominated by Shell men. A right-wing faction in the Young Republicans, headed by a fanatically rightist Los Angeles lawyer named Robert Gaston, was solidly for Shell.

This was partly a reflection of the vigorous Republican conservative movement spawned in California after the 1960 election defeat. But it also showed that Dick Nixon was something less than campaign magic in his own ball park. It was no surprise that he defeated Shell. But the difficulty he experienced in doing so was an omen of evil to come in the fall campaign against Brown and a California Democratic Party far better unified than in 1960 when Nixon carried his home state narrowly against Kennedy.

The fall campaign was a dismal case of Nixon trying to get the best of both worlds and ending up with the worst of both. He infuriated the Republican right by denouncing the rightist John Birch Society. He inflamed a good many independents and Republican liberals by suggesting that the Brown Administration was soft on communism.

But Nixon's nastiest problem was one that could trouble only a California politician. Through all that long campaign, he was forced to repeat over and over that he was not— absolutely not under any conditions—going to run for President again in 1964. In New York, Morgenthau had interested nobody by demanding that Rockefeller pledge that he would serve out his full term until 1966, and forego the election for President in 1964.[3] New Yorkers were accustomed to their governors eyeing the White House. The citizens of Pennsylvania and Michigan weren't, but they seemed more flattered than annoyed in 1962 when the Republican candidates for Governor in those states—William Scranton and George Romney—were mentioned as Presidential timber. But California was another matter.

Perhaps it is a lingering parochialism or self-conscious provincialism in California, which now has passed New York as the nation's most populous state. Perhaps it is insularity that makes Californians feel that being Governor of California ought to be just as desirable as being President of the United States. Whatever the cause, Californians of both parties were genuinely upset by the notion that Nixon was running for Governor in 1962 strictly as a springboard to try again for President in 1964.

And Nixon never could really disabuse Californians of this notion. Sometimes he was whipsawed by newsmen, who would ask him about national or international affairs and then criticize him for not talking about state matters. But Nixon never really did seem to have his heart and soul in California's water problem and the momentous question of parking fees for students at state universities the way that Pat Brown did. Nixon seemed far more interested in Cuba, Viet Nam, and Moscow. It was something that Californians perceived and resented, and it may have been the most important reason why Brown breezed home as the victor.

This loss seemed to be enough to destroy Nixon's Presidential hopes for all time. But he reinforced the damaging impact of the loss itself in an amazing display of political masochism. This was the remarkable nationally televised

[3] Naturally, Rockefeller ignored the demand.

"last press conference" by Nixon before reporters in Los
Angeles on November 7, 1962, the day after the election.

It was a rambling, disorganized soliloquy by a defeated,
demoralized, and obviously worn-out man who once was
almost President. He opened by commenting how "all the
members of the press are so delighted that I have lost,"
thrashed around embarrassingly, and ended with a peroration that included:

> The last play. I leave you gentlemen now and you will now
> write it. You will interpret it. That's your right. But as I leave
> you I want you to know—just think how much you're going to
> be missing. You won't have Nixon to kick around any more
> because, gentlemen, this is my last press conference. . . .

To many shocked politicians who heard him, Nixon seemed
to be saying goodbye to politics.

On an October evening in 1962, about fifty Republican
business executives and professional men pushed their chairs
away from coffee and apple pie after finishing a dinner cost-
ing a hundred dollars apiece. The scene was a motel dining
room near the General Motors Technical Center in Warren,
Michigan, an industrial suburb just outside Detroit. The
diners were ready to listen to George Romney, their party's
nominee for Governor and the man charged with the mission
of ending fourteen years of Democratic domination over the
Governor's office in Lansing. Romney was an odds-on favorite to defeat Governor John B. Swainson. And so the Republican diners were content and happy, awaiting a rousing
speech by their champion after a good meal.

Romney's disposition that night was stormy. He was
bitterly opposed to the idea of the hundred-dollar-a-plate
dinner, that tried-and-true fund gimmick of both political
parties. To put his idea of broad-based citizens' parties into
effect, Romney wanted fund-raising broadened so that small

contributions of up to ten dollars from millions of people would eliminate the need for the hundred-dollar-a-plate dinner or the big campaign contributor. What's more, he told the diners so that night. He almost made it appear that they'd committed some kind of crime because they had forked over one hundred dollars just to hear him speak.

This was unorthodox. But George Wilcken Romney's campaign for Governor of Michigan in 1962 was filled with surprises. That very day he had got off to a wild start by arguing politics for the better part of a half hour with a young bookkeeper who was trying to grab a cup of coffee at a lunch counter in Center Line, Michigan. Unlike most candidates, Romney wasn't content to merely shake hands but quite often asked the voter's preference. The young bookkeeper made the fatal error of admitting he was a Democrat who intended to vote for Swainson. That was enough to set Romney off on a long and energetic, though futile, attempt to convert the bookkeeper. Later in the day when heckled by some low-level United Auto Workers Union officials in front of the Dodge truck plant in Warren, Romney carried on a shouting, angry debate with the UAW porkchoppers over the right of free speech. Campaigning with jet-jawed George Romney, his coat off and his sleeves rolled up, was an electric experience. He was the most exciting political personality to come along in years.

Romney has always been placed with the Republican progressives (or "moderates" as they are called in Michigan) rather than the conservatives, because he is more flexible on key economic questions than the typical conservative Michigan Republican, and because of his strong stand in favor of Negro rights. But Romney cannot be conveniently placed in a pigeonhole. He is a follower of something of his own creation called Romneyism more than any conventional ideology.

Economic Romneyism was best spelled out on February 7, 1958, when Romney testified in Washington before the Senate Antitrust Subcommittee as president of American Motors Corp. The subcommittee, conducting an investigation of competition and monopolistic practices in the auto industry, had heard pallid, conventional economic conservatism from representatives of Detroit's Big Three—General Motors, Ford, and Chrysler. They heard something quite different from Romney. He asked the Senators to break up the automotive giants.

> To promote competition, economic progress, individual opportunity and to enlarge benefits to consumers generally, economic power in the automobile industry should be limited and divided. Limitations should be placed on firms whose size, integration and financial strength make possible the domination of a national market. . . .
>
> To achieve the desired ends, the antitrust laws should provide that when any one firm in a basic industry, such as the automobile business, exceeds a specific percentage of total industry sales over a specified period of time, it shall be required by law to propose to an administrative agency a plan of divestiture that will bring its percentage of sales below the specified level. . . .

Romney next proceeded to open fire on Walter Reuther's United Auto Workers.

> By removing limitations on the concentration of union power, the labor laws have created union monopoly. The inherent economic conflict between the antitrust laws and the labor laws must be resolved if America is to survive. In the face of our international challenge, America cannot survive half-competitive and half-monopolistic.

Romney concluded his statement by firing a few shots at "a centralized planned economy" and "excess concentration of government power."

This constitutes the unholy trinity for Romney: big business, big labor, and big government. Economic Romneyism ordains all must be cut down.

Political Romneyism amounts to cutting down existing political parties. Contending that both parties were ruled from above, Romney spent years calling for broad-based citizens' participation in parties. Before he affiliated with the Republican Party, there were some who thought Romney was trying to start a third party when he formed the Citizens for Michigan.[4]

Conservative Michigan Republicans, puzzled and confused over both Economic Romneyism and Political Romneyism, have thought at times that Romney himself was stark raving mad. Even the moderates and liberals within the Michigan party who are his strong supporters have admitted that they don't always know what their leader is talking about.

Actually, Romney became a top political figure in spite of his unique political doctrine. It was his personality, not his ideas, that attracted the public. Here was the virile super-salesman (who sold his country on the compact car) with more than a dash of righteous Mormon evangelism tossed in. The polls showed early in 1962 that he was unbelievably strong for somebody who never before had engaged in party politics. Conservative Republicans saw the polls too. They were so eager for a winner in Michigan after the long drought that they were willing to swallow Romney, strange doctrines and all.

Romney entered the campaign with everything in his favor. Swainson, a legless veteran of World War II, had been elected in 1960 after six two-year terms by G. Mennen (Soapy) Williams as Governor but inherited little of Williams's personal appeal or prestige. Swainson was still an unfamiliar face in Michigan. This was one campaign where the challenger, his face familiar from exposure on television screens and the covers of national news magazines, was more easily recognizable by the voters than the incumbent.

---

[4] Actually, the association served only the purpose of launching Romney's idea of a new state constitution for Michigan. It then disbanded.

Moreover, a good many Michiganders were ready for a change in the Governor's office after fourteen years of nothing but Democrats. Soapy Williams probably would have been strong enough to continue the Democratic dynasty, but Swainson was vulnerable against Romney. Beneath the surface, in the low-to-middle-income white suburbs around Detroit which always had produced preponderantly Democratic votes, there was a growing resentment against the part played by the Democrats in fostering equal job opportunity and equal housing for Negroes—a resentment now to be directed against Swainson.[5] One specific factor also was working against Swainson in the pivotal suburbs around Detroit. By vetoing a bill earlier in the year, he had authorized the city of Detroit to deduct income taxes from the paychecks of suburbanites who worked in Detroit but lived outside the city limits. On this sensitive pocketbook issue, Swainson—not the Democratic Party at large—was held responsible by the suburban voters. Finally, the monolithic Michigan Democratic Party of Soapy Williams and Walter Reuther was now racked by dissension.[6]

In mid-October, polls showed Romney to be a sure winner over Swainson, perhaps in a runaway. There is no question that Romney would have won easily in a short campaign and might have pulled into office a few other Republicans on the state ticket. But American political campaigns are long, not short.

As the final weeks of the Michigan campaign droned on, it was becoming clear to many Republican politicians that Romney did not wear too well with the voters. What had first been admired as dynamism and energy was now being

[5] It is unlikely that the Negrophobia in the Mormon Church either helped Romney with these anti-Negro voters or hurt him with the Negroes.

[6] Democratic Party leaders had tapped James Hare, Michigan's Secretary of State, to succeed Williams as Governor. But Swainson, with important support from Reuther's UAW, beat Hare in the 1960 primary election. The scars from that primary contest were still to be seen hampering the general election campaign against Romney.

labeled as egotism and a Napoleonic complex. The voters were growing tired of Romney's temper outbursts, whether feigned or genuine. Although Romney had expected to out-point the easygoing Swainson handily in a series of televised debates, it was generally agreed that the Governor came out ahead of his more famous challenger in these encounters. Swainson was closing the gap rapidly in the final weeks of the campaign.

The election results showed less than a rousing Republican success. The Democrats captured all the statewide races (including a hotly contested Congressman-at-large seat) except Governor. That contest was in doubt all evening until Romney finally pulled ahead in the wee hours of the morning and won by 75,000 votes. Michigan Republicans were thrilled to have the Governor's office once more but weren't cheering too lustily about the nip-and-tuck finish.

However, there was plenty of cheering from Republicans beyond Michigan's borders. To these Republicans, Michigan's Democratic Party was still the monolithic party of the 1950's when Soapy Williams swept to victory after victory. For any Republican to win in Michigan against the evil legions of the UAW was a historic feat (no matter how small the margin might be). Romney was a giant-killer. Increasing numbers of Republicans around the country were now viewing him as a Presidential possibility.

On a balmy August night in 1962, Thacher Longstreth, a Philadelphia advertising man (and a teetotaler), sipped a Coca-Cola in the Harrisburger Hotel bar at Harrisburg, Pennsylvania, and rhapsodized about his party's candidate for Governor. "I can't tell you what it means to some of us to have somebody right here in Pennsylvania being mentioned seriously as a possibility for President," enthused Longstreth, a Republican activist who had run a vigorous but losing campaign for Mayor of Philadelphia in 1955. "I mean, after all the typical potbellied Pennsylvania politicians, it's really something to have somebody like Scranton right here—whether he ever really runs for President or not."

Representative William Warren Scranton of Scranton, Pennsylvania, forty-five, slim, articulate, and patrician, liberal but not too liberal, was indeed the antithesis of the archetype Republican boss in Pennsylvania. But there wasn't really any logical reason in the summer of 1962 to class him with Rockefeller, Goldwater, Nixon, and Romney as a Presidential possibility. A freshman Congressman who never had run for public office before 1960, he had no public record of accomplishment. Nor was there any carefully devised propaganda campaign to put him in the national limelight. Perhaps it was merely the fact that Scranton looked like a Presidential candidate when he first arrived in the House at Washington in January, 1961. Perhaps the superficial similarities to John F. Kennedy—the diffidence, the aristocratic manner, the boyishness—intrigued the party leaders. Whatever the reason, politicians and journalists were talking about Scranton as a Presidential dark horse even before he made up his mind to run for Governor.

But Scranton was neither a papier-mâché creation of the press nor a willing puppet of the Pennsylvania Manufacturers Association and the Pennsylvania Republican Party's Old Guard. There was no question of Scranton's side in the Republican struggle of progressive against conservative. On economic affairs, he was perhaps a shade to the right of Rockefeller, but far left of Goldwater. He was about as far left as anybody in the Republican Party on civil rights and foreign policy questions.

In fact, his brief career in the House before he virtually vacated Washington to run for Governor in the spring of 1962 carries a pattern of party irregularity. During his first week as a Congressman, Scranton was one of a handful of Republicans to support Kennedy on a key vote to enlarge the

House Rules Committee, thereby giving Kennedy a clear majority over that key unit. One House Republican major domo telephoned Scranton to plead with him—and then threaten. His threat: Scranton might be deprived of campaign funds in some future political battle, perhaps the 1962 race for Governor. Multimillionaire Scranton, whose family had been contributing to the Republican Party since the days of Abraham Lincoln, was more amused than worried. After the Rules Committee fight, Scranton voted with his party most of the time, but never hesitated to defect on matters of great interest to his unemployment-plagued Congressional district in the Pennsylvania hard coal country, such as Kennedy's bill to provide Federal economic aid to economically depressed areas.

Yet, for all this tendency to stray from Republican orthodoxy, Scranton managed to avoid the stigma of party splitter that had fallen on Rockefeller in 1960 and was to fall on him again. Unlike Rockefeller, Scranton was wise enough to keep his mouth shut when committing heresy. In addition, he was blessed with an apparently instinctive talent for ingratiating himself with the conservative party chieftains—both in the House and back in Pennsylvania. The party's crusty conservatives in the House were quick to explain away Scranton's lapses into liberalism on the grounds that he never could have been elected to Congress in 1960 from a Democrat-dominated district that Kennedy carried with ease if he had adhered to Old Guard copybook maxims. This very untypical tolerance by the party leaders in Congress is no small tribute to Scranton. But much more remarkable was his record of smoothing the waters of Pennsylvania's turbulent Republican Party.

Defying normal political logic, Scranton had refused to run for either Congress in 1960 or Governor in 1962 until he was assured of unanimous support from party leaders—a totally unrealistic condition in a state party badly split be-

tween conservative Old Guardsmen and liberal-leaning independents. Nevertheless, Scranton got what he demanded in
both 1960 and 1962. Moreover, he managed to go his own
way after the nomination while helping keep the Old Guardsmen relatively happy. Typical was his retention of George
Bloom, an aging and moustachioed Old Guardsman, as
figurehead state Republican chairman through the 1962
campaign while boosting up his own bright young men to
positions of real authority in the party. During these early
tests in partisan politics, Scranton proved to be that rare
commodity in the Republican Party: the progressive who can
keep conservatives happy.

This was apparent to the Pennsylvania party leaders and
Republican chieftains from elsewhere who cared to look.
What was less apparent was Scranton's skill as campaigner.
He showed in that long 1962 campaign that he was no
Romney. Using the measurement of dynamism, he wasn't a
Rockefeller or Goldwater either—or even a Nixon. A little
sleepy-looking, he sometimes seemed to be boring himself on
the stump. He was urbane, unruffled, unelectrifying.

It was easy enough then to underestimate Scranton's face-
to-face prowess against his Democratic opponent. Richardson
Dilworth, tough, handsome, and bloodied in political wars
many years before, had resigned as Mayor of Philadelphia to
try to realize his old ambition of becoming Governor. But
the early polls showed both a great public desire for a change
in party at Harrisburg and an ennui with Dilworth after so
many years. Dilworth was running behind Scranton. To close
the gap, he wanted to use the face-to-face debate against the
untried Scranton—as many debates as possible, in fact.

Scranton agreed to appear in just one debate, but this was
one debate too many in the opinion of State Chairman
George Bloom and other old-line party leaders. "A hard-
bitten trial lawyer like Dick Dilworth can make mincemeat
out of Scranton," a worried Bloom told friends.

Both Dilworth and Bloom had a surprise coming. Scranton was the clear winner in their televised debate at Philadelphia. Dilworth, the great hatchet man of Pennsylvania Democratic politics, was kept on the defensive by Scranton —forced to defend the unpopular Democratic administration of Governor David Lawrence. Furious that he had muffed his chance to gain ground, Dilworth demanded a second debate. Scranton refused. Dilworth retorted that he would debate an empty chair, if need be, on television. What's more, the one-way debate would originate right in Scranton's home town of Scranton, Pennsylvania. Then came a flurry of newspaper advertisements questioning whether Scranton had enough courage to debate Dilworth a second time.

But Dilworth was in for the shock of his long political life when Scranton walked away from a fifty-dollar-a-plate Lackawanna County Republican dinner at the Masonic Temple in Scranton and into the studios of television station WNEP three blocks away to sit in Dilworth's empty chair. It was a stroke of melodrama that threw Dilworth badly off balance. He never really recovered during the raucous debate.

In a state of rage over his second failure, Dilworth ran up to Scranton as soon as the thirty-minute program ended. After some extemporaneous exchanges of insults between the two candidates for Governor, Dilworth opened up in full vituperation.

"They're trying to use you," he told Scranton. "You couldn't possibly do any good in Harrisburg. They're using you up and down. Don't be a fool."

Dilworth's face was only inches from Scranton's.[7] But Scranton smiled weakly and retorted: "What a desperate man we have here. It's his guilt complex."

The quiet goad was enough to unleash new fury in Dil-

[7] One of Scranton's aides thought that Dilworth was about to strike the younger man. The aide later recalled that he thought about physically restraining Dilworth for a moment.

worth. "You're a phony," he shouted at Scranton. "Nothing but a phony."

After some more of the same, Scranton decided to call a halt. "We're not getting anywhere here," he said. "This man is desperate."

As Scranton left the studio to return to the fifty-dollar-a-plate dinner at the Masonic Temple, a frenzied Dilworth had the last word: "I knew you wouldn't have the nerve to stick around."

Dilworth knew he had lost his last desperate shot at becoming Governor. But for Scranton, it was a cool and calculated performance under the kind of fire a politician seldom encounters.

In fact, however, Scranton had about everything running for him. After eight years of Democrats in Harrisburg, the time-for-a-change sentiment was strong. Governor Lawrence's laudable crackdown on highway speeders was particularly unpopular and damaging to Dilworth. Reports from Philadelphia of corruption during Dilworth's mayoralty didn't help. The Democrats were blamed for the chronic unemployment around so much of the state. Polls showed that Scranton had failed to impress his face and personality on Pennsylvania, but would ride the anti-Democratic tide to an easy victory anyway.

Scranton's winning margin over Dilworth of 486,000 votes was stunning even for Republican politicians. It was an important enough win to mark Scranton as a dark horse possibility. But on the day-after-election skull sessions among Republicans in 1962, Bill Scranton was a poor second to George Romney in the dark horse stable.

VIII

★ ★

Rockefeller's Sputtering Bandwagon

An accurate situation report on the state of the race for the Republican Presidential nomination immediately following the 1962 elections was included in a Washington dispatch by Paul Duke in the December 10, 1962, edition of the *Wall Street Journal*. Duke wrote:

> Gov. Nelson Rockefeller of New York is running so far ahead for the Republican Presidential nomination in 1964 that he may have an unbreakable hammerlock on the prize even at this early date.
>
> Support for him appears stronger than ever among the party's top leaders. It is even beginning to embrace some party stalwarts from Midwest and Rocky Mountain regions who are closer to the conservatism of Sen. Barry Goldwater of Arizona.
>
> Mr. Rockefeller's narrower-than-expected re-election over a weak Democratic foe hasn't dampened enthusiasm for him. His divorce is no longer causing deep worries. And while there is much speculation about possible challenges from Govs. William Scranton of Pennsylvania and George Romney of Michigan, there is astonishingly little talk about either among party professionals.

Duke was reporting the consensus at the postelection session of the Republican National Committee in Washington December 7–8. There was at that meeting a sense that nothing short of a miracle would keep the nomination from

99

Rockefeller. Jean Tool, the young and highly effective Colorado state chairman, told Duke: "There are people [in Colorado] enthusiastically working for him now who bitterly opposed him before."

Clearly, Rockefeller had snapped back quickly from the slight slump in his fortunes following the unimpressive win against Morgenthau for the New York Governorship in 1962. On the day after that election, some party leaders were entertaining the thought that Romney might make a more attractive candidate than Rockefeller. But errant musing constituted no groundswell for Romney. Indeed, Romney-for-President talk faded away shortly after the election when it became clear that Romney—like Scranton—was going to devote himself for the time being to being Governor of his state.

As for Goldwater, there was no sign whatever after the election that he was any more interested in becoming President than he was before the election. It is true that some of his supporters, particularly his zealous Southern supporters, were cheered by the victories of conservative Republican Congressional candidates in Texas, North Carolina, Tennessee, Florida, and Kentucky; two wafer-thin misses of Congressional candidates in Virginia; and the near upset of Democratic Senator Lister Hill in Alabama—bright spots for the Republicans in otherwise glum election returns.[1] But the first overt efforts by Goldwater activists after the election were so inept as to be almost laughable.

The most active of these Goldwater activists was good-looking, personable Wirt Yerger, a fire-breathing young segregationist from Jackson, Mississippi. Yerger, Mississippi's Republican state chairman, had been elected chairman of all Southern Republican state chairmen. Hailing the muddy

[1] The 1962 election results were ambivalent enough to bring joy to Republican liberals because of the election of Rockefeller, Romney, and Scranton, the easy reelection of Governor Mark Hatfield in Oregon, and landslide reelection victories by Senator Jacob Javits of New York and Senator Thomas Kuchel of California.

results of the November election as conclusive proof that the South was the key to national victory for the party, Yerger called a meeting of Southern Republican chairmen to be held in Dallas shortly after the election. There was little doubt about the proposed conference's true purposes: a Goldwater-for-President pep rally. Representative William Miller, the national chairman, immediately quashed Yerger's plans for a separate Dallas meeting and decreed that the Southern chairmen, along with all the other regional group-ings of state chairmen, would meet at Washington the first weekend of December in conjunction with the Republican National Committee's winter meeting. Miller, upstate New York conservative, was no particular ally of Rockefeller, but wasn't going to permit any Southern separatist movement within the party.

Furious that the Dallas meeting had been forestalled, Yerger and a few other Southern firebrands met in secret session in Washington on the eve of the National Committee meeting. Their purpose: to purge Miller. They proposed that he be replaced by State Chairman Ray Bliss as a full-time, paid national chairman. Bliss, ever anxious to ward off party-splitting fights, wanted no part of it. National Committeeman George Hinman put the Rockefeller camp solidly behind Miller. The attempt to purge Miller was a fiasco.

These frenetic maneuvers by Yerger were not officially supported by what was soon to become the National Draft Goldwater Committee and certainly had no backing from Goldwater himself. Yet, the unintended impact of Yerger's failures was to make it appear that Goldwater's only support within the party came from a few wild-eyed Southerners and that the party's mainstream—conservatives and progres-sives alike—was behind Rockefeller. In effect then, Yerger was playing into Rockefeller's hands. For this illusion of the party uniting behind Rockefeller was precisely the effect the Governor wanted.

From the time that Rockefeller propelled himself into national politics in 1959, there had been two basic schools of tactics within his camp. At the risk of oversimplification, they can be called the Morhouse and Hinman schools. State Chairman L. Judson Morhouse wanted the Governor to mount a crusade for the liberalization of the Republican Party, grappling for party control with the old-line conservative leaders. National Committeeman George Hinman wanted Rockefeller to gain party leadership by coming to terms with and converting the Old Guardsmen, not by fighting them.[2] The dizzy swings of Rockefeller's career in national politics can be best explained as following first the Morhouse school, then the Hinman school, then back to the Morhouse school, and so on.

At no time was Rockefeller following the tactics of the Hinman school more closely than in those early months of 1963 when Rockefeller seemed to be wrapping up the nomination fully eighteen months in advance of the National Convention. In countless conversations with party leaders from one end of the country to the other, Hinman stated and restated the assurance that Rockefeller was no liberal crusader out to remake the Grand Old Party in his own image. Rockefeller's public utterances reinforced Hinman's missionary work. The Governor avoided potentially divisive issues, and concentrated on flailing away at Kennedy—for blundering in the international fight against communism, for failing to speed up the economic growth rate and cut down unemployment, for lagging in the fight for civil rights, for failing to balance the budget, for discouraging private enterprise. Both Rockefeller and Hinman kept chanting their thesis that "liberal" and "conservative" had become outmoded themes

---

[2] Typically, Morhouse was one of the few political advisers in the Rockefeller camp to urge the Governor to make a slam-bang race against Nixon for the 1960 nomination. Hinman and the others advised him to sit it out and wait for 1964. Rockefeller later came to believe he could have taken the nomination from Nixon and gone on to defeat Kennedy in the general election.

with no validity in the real world. This blurring of ideological lines was convincing to many, including Gould Lincoln, septuagenarian political columnist for the Washington *Evening Star* and a devoted promoter of Republican unity. In one column entitled "Rocky No 'New Frontiersman,'" Lincoln concluded:

> Gov. Rockefeller's views on . . . major issues run almost on all fours with those of Senator Barry Goldwater of Arizona, darling of the G.O.P. conservatives, and those recently expressed here by former Vice President Nixon. The wings of the Republican Party—progressive and conservative—are drawing closer and closer together, if these party leaders are to be believed.

Of course, Lincoln was premature in heralding the end of more than fifty years of devitalizing internal warfare. But on a personal basis at least, Rockefeller and Goldwater *were* "drawing closer and closer together." Their carefully nurtured friendship was ripening.

The principal mutual bond for the two leaders had become a desire for party unity. Party unity, and how to achieve it, was the chief topic in a series of unpublicized breakfast meetings between Goldwater and Rockefeller during the winter and early spring of 1963 at Rockefeller's Washington mansion on Foxhall Road. Only two others attended these meetings. One was Hinman. The other was Victor Johnston, a professional politician who for two decades had been associated with the party's conservative wing, and had become one of Goldwater's chief political advisers as staff director for the Senate Republican Campaign Committee.[3]

The need for Republican unity was stressed endlessly during these pleasant and amiable chats over the breakfast table. Rockefeller and Goldwater agreed that they were

[3] Hinman and Johnston often met together without their chiefs being present. On each of his many visits to Washington, Hinman would phone Johnston, and sometimes lunch with him.

much closer to each other than either was to John F. Kennedy's New Frontier. Each talked of the need to emphasize their points of agreement, not their areas of disagreement. Each declared that the only way the party would have a ghost of a chance to beat Kennedy in 1964 would be through absolute unity. And they agreed that the party effort should be made through the Republican National Committee and the various state committees, not through the National Republican Citizens Committee (which for some time had been functioning from a Washington headquarters). Goldwater and Rockefeller were more certain than ever that the Citizens Committee was an Eisenhower-Nixon front to keep the nomination away from both Goldwater and Rockefeller and give it instead to Romney.

As a result of this frequent contact with Rockefeller, Goldwater was becoming assured that a Rockefeller nomination would not really be a setback for Republican conservatism. He tried again and again to soft-pedal consideration of himself as a candidate for President. ". . . I think our party ought to think more about building up its strength in Congress in 1964 than wasting a lot of time and energy on the White House," he told Cabell Phillips of the *New York Times*. "We can do more to advance the cause of conservatism in Congress than with the Presidency." It was a message that Goldwater had been delivering to fellow conservatives for months.

Moreover, Goldwater was supplying Rockefeller with fairly substantial help on occasion. Before Rockefeller's March 9 speech in Milwaukee, where he had suffered through a frigid reception in 1959, Goldwater telephoned Wisconsin State Chairman Claude Jasper to urge a cordial reception for the Governor.[4] Goldwater's help was even more important in smoothing the way for Rockefeller's one-night stand in the conservative stronghold of Omaha, Nebraska, on April 5.

[4] Jasper was also state chairman when Rockefeller was given the cold shoulder during his 1959 visits to Madison and Milwaukee.

Some zealous Goldwater supporters started organizing a boycott of Rockefeller's appearance that night at a testimonial
banquet for Senator Roman Hruska of Nebraska. Goldwater
got on the long-distance telephone to Omaha to convince his
adherents to call off the boycott. He even enlisted the help
of Senator Carl Curtis of Nebraska, one of the Senate's most
tenacious conservatives and a devoted friend and admirer of
Goldwater. The boycott was prevented, and one thousand
diners who had paid fifty dollars for each plate at Omaha's
Municipal Auditorium heard Rockefeller give his "I am a
Republican" speech. Goldwater received a thank-you call
from Rockefeller the next day.

With Goldwater neutralized, the Rockefeller camp's big
worry was some "third-force" candidate who would be de-
picted as a compromise candidate midway between Goldwater the conservative and Rockefeller the liberal. But there
was no "third-force" candidate readily available in the winter of 1963. The California election and Nixon's nightmarish
press conference that followed it were too recent for anyone
to consider Nixon as a serious Presidential possibility. Scranton was then cloistered at his state capital of Harrisburg,
trying to push a sales tax increase through the Pennsylvania
Legislature. The logical "third-force" candidate then seemed
to be neither Nixon nor Scranton but Romney.

For all of his bizarre economic ideology, Romney seemed
to be more the orthodox Republican than Rockefeller on such
issues as Federal health insurance, Federal aid to education,
and labor policy. In fact, however, Romney was far less
acceptable to the Old Guard than Rockefeller for reasons
quite apart from economic policy or national issues. Romney
was not a party regular. While both Rockefeller and Goldwater were swallowing their misgivings about Nixon during
the 1960 campaign and hitting the hustings for the party's
Presidential nominee, Romney maintained a splendid isolation from the partisan struggle—firing off gratuitous letters

to both Nixon and Kennedy in which he slapped each of the two candidates smartly across the cheek for failing to talk issues to the American people. Far worse in the minds of party leaders outside Michigan was Romney's record in the 1962 campaign. While winning himself, he completely disassociated himself from the rest of the state Republican ticket. Refusing to share speaking platforms with his fellow Republican candidates (and sometimes even refusing to permit their posters in the storefront windows of various local Romney Headquarters in the state), Romney was campaigning as an independent. Finally, he made no friends in the party by constantly scolding Republican chieftains for not converting the Grand Old Party into a "citizens' party."

Thus, in the winter of 1963 there was not even a close challenger to front-running Nelson Rockefeller. Here's the way it seemed to shape up then in the Big Six states:

New York: Rockefeller's delegation, of course.

Pennsylvania: Rockefeller men were confident that Governor Scranton and Senator Hugh Scott would throw this big delegation to Rockefeller. A token first-ballot favorite-son vote for Scranton was considered possible though not certain by any means.

Ohio: Hinman and the rest of the Rockefeller camp had tried with a large degree of success to develop a warm relationship with State Chairman Ray Bliss. Rockefeller also had struck up a friendship with Governor James Rhodes, the most conservative of the new Republican governors elected in 1962. Representative John Ashbrook of Ohio, a militant young conservative and devoted Goldwater man, feared that Bliss and Rhodes were at least halfway within the Rockefeller orbit.

Michigan: Despite the conversations between Rockefeller and Goldwater over the Romney threat, Rockefeller's advisers believed Romney and Michigan probably would climb aboard the Rockefeller bandwagon by convention time. The

Rockefeller men were counting on John B. Martin, Jr., a liberal and Michigan's Republican national committeeman, to promote Rockefeller there.

Illinois: Senator Everett McKinley Dirksen, that shrewd practitioner of Illinois Republican politics, believed that Rockefeller would wind up with the entire delegation to the National Convention. It seemed likely that Rockefeller would have the support of Dirksen. It seemed certain that he would have the support of Charles Percy, boy wonder boss of Bell & Howell camera makers and a probable candidate for the Republican gubernatorial nomination in Illinois.

California: Nobody could tell the Presidential preference of California's party leaders or even the identity of these leaders in the chaos following Nixon's defeat for Governor. But it really didn't seem to matter much. Rockefeller men were certain that he could win California's Presidential primary in June, 1964, against any possible contender, thereby capturing the entire delegation.

If all of the Big Six states really did wind up with Rockefeller, the nomination would be assured.

But Rockefeller's support was by no means confined to these highly industrialized, thickly populated states.

Rockefeller was the front runner in the lesser Great Lakes states. He could boast substantial backing from party leaders in Minnesota, Wisconsin, and even Indiana, the most conservative state in the Great Lakes region. Because of probable support from State Chairman H. Dale Brown, the wily Republican boss of Indianapolis, Rockefeller seemed slightly ahead of Goldwater in Indiana. Rockefeller was slowly picking up support in the Rocky Mountain states, with State Chairmen Jean Tool of Colorado and John Wold of Wyoming regarded as particularly sympathetic. It was no surprise that Rockefeller was way ahead in the East.

That meant that a conservative movement to draft Goldwater probably would go into the convention with support from only the Great Plains states, the Border states, and the South. However, there were cracks showing in Goldwater's Solid South. There was scattered Rockefeller support in Virginia, Georgia, and Florida—perhaps not enough to take the states away from Goldwater but enough to give Rockefeller a few more delegates.

No adding machine was needed to show that this pointed to a first-ballot nomination for Rockefeller. The Rockefeller bandwagon was rolling. Everybody could see it. But only a few seasoned politicians could detect some wheezings and sputterings in the engine that drove the bandwagon.

The worst engine failure was to be found right at home. A smooth-running home front had been expected to be one of Rockefeller's principal advantages in 1963 against potential rivals. While the newly elected Romney and Scranton would have to stick close to home to handle tax crises and other pressing state problems, Rockefeller would be free to romp around the countryside in search of Presidential support. It was assumed that Rockefeller had taken care of his most pressing fiscal problems back in 1959 and that the state bureaucracy in New York, justly famed for its efficiency, was self-functioning anyway. Nothing could have been further from the truth. The first six months of 1963 marked Nelson Rockefeller's most unhappy governmental experience in a lifetime of public service. It was far worse than the first half of 1959, when Rockefeller rammed a tax increase through a balky State Legislature and then weathered the public indignation.

Rockefeller was the beneficiary of one lucky break in 1963, however. A strike had quieted New York City's newspapers all winter. Not until the worst of Rockefeller's woes were over did the newspapers resume publication in April. Had they been publishing all that year, their meticulous reporting of Rockefeller's problems might well have triggered similar reports in newspapers and over television across the country. Rockefeller's prestige then would have been hurt far worse than it was.

The Governor's basic problem concerned that old bugaboo of state government: taxation. Throughout his 1962 election campaign, he had pledged time and time again that he would propose neither new tax increases nor deficit spending, but would finance higher levels of state spending with revenues increased by accelerated economic activity.[5] That was his pledge in November, 1962. But by January, 1963, it was clear that state revenues would fall short of expectations, and Rockefeller would indeed need higher taxes to avoid deficit spending. His answer was to ask for $105 million of increases in state charges—he called them "fees"—on auto licenses and liquor.

The semantical distinction between "fees" and "taxes" was lost upon millions of New York taxpayers and a good many Republican politicians as well. To Rockefeller, the auto and liquor charges might be "fees." But to most New Yorkers, they were "taxes"—particularly when they were going to be raised. The result was a major tax revolt. The *Buffalo Evening News* and other staunchly Republican upstate newspapers accused Rockefeller of a breach of faith. The Legislature's Republican leadership rebelled. Faced with the alternatives of humiliating defeat and compromise, Rockefeller chose compromise. The increased auto license charges were dropped, but the Legislature agreed to some increases—less than Rockefeller wanted—in liquor charges (in deference to the Governor's political problem, the legislators called their increase "a brand label use fee"). To balance the budget, the Legislature then cut some $67 million out of Rockefeller's spending program. It was Rockefeller's worst annual legis-

---

[5] Morgenthau, the hapless Democratic candidate, correctly warned that Rockefeller was smoking fiscal opium, and that either a tax increase, deficit spending, or a cut in spending would be needed. But Morgenthau's powers of communication were such that nobody paid much attention to him.

lative showing by far. The *New York Times,* which had endorsed Rockefeller's bid for reelection a few months earlier, was mightily displeased. In an April 6 editorial entitled "A Poor Session at Albany," the *Times* scolded:

> The 1963 record of the New York Legislature was disappointingly poor. A few beneficial actions were taken but there was a stunning failure to live up to opportunities and responsibilities. The fault lay in considerable part with Governor Rockefeller, but the Legislature eagerly made things worse by rebellion against his faltering leadership.
>
> The session started with two strikes against it. The first was Mr. Rockefeller's major political and fiscal blunder, committed last summer in his re-election campaign, in promising that there would be no tax increases for four years. This not only laid him wide open to charges of bad faith when he proposed $105 million in tax increases (called "fee" increases); it also imposed a budget ceiling that made it impossible to meet adequately the needs of this state. The second impediment was the Rockefeller interest in 1964; it was obvious from the start of the session that he would, if possible, shun issues not helpful to him politically.

Some of the men around Rockefeller feared that the Governor's retreat before the wrath of the Republican-controlled Legislature might damage his national reputation with party leaders. But this was but a nagging little irritation compared to a scandal in the New York State Government, long regarded as a model for efficient Republican administration. Here again, Rockefeller was protected by the newspaper strike, which blacked out the worst of the revelations.

These revelations were coming out of an investigation of corruption in the Republican-controlled State Liquor Authority conducted by Democrat Frank Hogan, District Attorney of Manhattan. The first victim was Martin C. Epstein, who was named Liquor Authority chairman by Rockefeller as one of the Governor's first appointments in 1959. Asked to waive immunity from prosecution for any testimony he might give Hogan's grand jury, Epstein pleaded ill health. Rockefeller immediately fired him.

Then came the most stunning development: the fall of L. Judson Morhouse, state party chairman and a close political adviser to the Governor since the 1958 campaign. Morhouse resigned as state chairman two weeks before appearing before the grand jury, then refused to waive immunity when he did appear. On the day of his appearance, he quit as chairman of the New York State Thruway Authority.

Nor were Rockefeller's problems confined to the home front. While assiduously and successfully courting conservatives, Rockefeller was alienating some of his hard-core supporters from the party's progressive wing.

Rockefeller was committing the cardinal political sin of taking support for granted. While Hinman burned the midnight oil in wooing conservatives, he simply couldn't find time for such liberals as Senator Clifford Case of New Jersey. One day in April, Hinman dropped into Case's Washington office to talk things over with the Senator. Unfortunately, Case wasn't in town that day. That was the last that either Case or his office staff saw of Hinman or anybody else from the Rockefeller camp until later in the year when Rockefeller's Presidential fortunes had reached their nadir.[6] Case was not happy over this neglect. Neither were Jacob Javits and Kenneth B. Keating, New York's two Republican Senators, pleased by one Rockefeller snub—quite likely an unintentional snub—in April. During a quick Rockefeller trip to Washington, Javits and Keating waited for nearly an hour on the Senate floor in expectation of a visit from the Governor. But Rockefeller never showed up. One liberal Republican Senator, considered a steadfast Rockefeller man, became so

[6] Perhaps Hinman was falsely reassured by a *New York Times* account in April that Case had endorsed Rockefeller. Case insisted privately he had been misquoted, but declined to get in a public brawl with the *Times* over the matter.

exercised about this sort of thing that in April he asked an aide to work up a memorandum about George Romney's potential as a Presidential candidate.

But the irritation of Republican progressives with Rockefeller was not merely a matter of snubs and slights, real and imagined. Many felt that Rockefeller had overcompensated to the right in his effort to secure a broad base of party support. Their reaction provides additional proof of the inherent difficulty any Republican finds in getting simultaneous support from both wings of the party.

Irritation by the liberals reached its peak after an April 9 news conference in Washington. When Rockefeller was asked to comment on the Kennedy Administration's efforts to restrain hit-and-run raids against Cuba by Cuban exiles, this exchange followed.

> Rockefeller: I hope it is not as a means or as an endeavor to placate or to appease the Soviets.
> Q. Do you think it is?
> Rockefeller: I hope it is not, I said.
> Q. Governor, does this mean that you think there is a possibility of some secret arrangement between the President and Mr. Khrushchev on the matter of holding back the freedom fighters in Cuba?
> Rockefeller: Well, I have no idea. But maybe Mr. Khrushchev will release some more of the correspondence and we will find out.

This exchange raised some understandable doubts about whether or not Rockefeller was accusing Kennedy of appeasement. So a reporter brought up the Cuba question again later in the same press conference.

> Q. Governor, on Cuba again, you said that you hope that our restrictions on the exiles is not an attempt to appease or placate the Russians. Do you have any indication or any feeling that it is an attempt to appease or placate the Russians?

Rockefeller: Well, I only said that because it is hard to see what other reason there would be, in view of our past policy, and it seems to me this is a very sharp change of policy concerning which the public has not been advised as to what the reason, what our objective is, what our plans are as to how ultimately to rid the hemisphere of this cancerous growth.

Q. Governor, does that mean you are saying that the Kennedy Administration is following an appeasement policy on Cuba?

Rockefeller: No. . . . I said I hoped it wasn't.

Progressive Republicans were appalled by the Governor's performance. So were some influential Republican newspapers. The *Washington Evening Star*'s attack on Rockefeller was brutal.

Governor Rockefeller, in a press conference yesterday, made it clear enough that he wants to be President. But, in our eyes, he offered no evidence that he deserves to be.

His performance with respect to Cuba was a shabby bit of politicking. And if anyone were to take it seriously, it could be harmful to the national interest. . . .

Plainly, the Governor is trying to smear the President by expressing a "hope" that he is not an appeaser. There is no charge and no proof—only the insinuation. This is unworthy of a presidential aspirant and quite revealing of the Governor's qualifications, or, rather, the lack thereof.

An attack closer to home came from the *New York Herald Tribune*, symbol of the eastern seaboard Republican Establishment whose approval was absolutely essential for Rockefeller. In an editorial entitled "Relax, Governor!" the *Herald Tribune* was far more sympathetic than the *Evening Star* but more to the point. After acknowledging that Rockefeller had been under a strain during the difficult session of the Legislature, the *Herald Tribune* called his statements on Cuba an "extraordinary mishmash," and then fired off this broadside.

We suggest that Gov. Rockefeller calm down. If he engages
in a contest with Sen. Goldwater to see who can throw the
most matches into the most inflammable material, someone is
going to set up an opposition line, peddling asbestos garments
and fire extinguishers. And such a polarization of American
opinion into "war" and "anti-war" groups could be disastrous.

There was more criticism—public criticism from the press
and private criticism from Republican politicians—about
Rockefeller's insinuations of appeasement. And the very intensity of the reaction suggested trouble deeper than just
anger by the party's progressive wing because Rockefeller
had traveled too far to the right this time in his courtship of
the conservatives. After all, when Senator John F. Kennedy
had taken a strikingly similar stand in regard to President
Eisenhower's Cuba policy in 1960, liberal Democrats were a
bit embarrassed, but did not lash out at Kennedy either privately or publicly. But Kennedy was the acknowledged
leader of his party then. Rockefeller was not. In fact, the
reaction to the April 9 press conference was a warning sign
that Rockefeller was not wearing too well with his fellow
Republicans.

Indeed, the real weakness of the Rockefeller bandwagon
in April, 1963, was its lack of jubilation or happiness. Rockefeller was far in front of the pack, but not many Republicans
were terribly happy about it—even if they weren't particularly unhappy about it. The truth is that Rockefeller was
failing to excite real enthusiasm on his speaking engagements around the country. He was failing to pick up new
converts on such expeditions as his April 30 journey to the
heart of the Taft country. Rockefeller was invited as honor
guest and principal speaker at a hundred-dollar-a-plate fund-
raising dinner in Cincinnati honoring Representative Robert
Taft, Jr., and Ray Bliss, the Ohio state chairman. Young
Taft, a figure of rising importance in the Ohio Republican
Party, had been leaning toward Rockefeller. Fearing that

Goldwater's stands on labor issues and other questions might hurt the entire ticket in Ohio, Taft was looking for a moderate Presidential candidate who could unite rather than split the party. He thought Rockefeller might be the man. There was nothing objectionable in what Rockefeller said at Cincinnati April 30, but Taft was unimpressed by the Governor's general performance there. Taft had not found his candidate.

None of this was enough to stop or even slow down the Rockefeller bandwagon. It did mean there were ·enough structural weaknesses in the bandwagon that one truly serious jolt would be enough to stop it—perhaps for good. Rockefeller was front runner by process of elimination rather than because of his inherent political strength. If he should run into one critical setback of more transcendent importance than a State Liquor Authority scandal or inept remarks to the press about "appeasement," there would be precious few Republican leaders willing to defend him to the end, and a whole army of them eager and willing to defect. In short, for all of the careful years of missionary work by George Hinman, Rockefeller's campaign was a house of cards. And though hardly anyone outside Rockefeller's inner circle realized it at the time, the Governor himself was winding up for the blow that would topple the entire precarious edifice.

There was one cryptic clue that the blow was coming. Republican leaders had been puzzled for some months in the winter of 1963 that Hinman had flatly refused to accept commitments of support from Republicans who wanted to climb on the bandwagon as early as possible. When a member of Congress and party official offered to announce his support for Rockefeller, Hinman would say "no"—politely but firmly. When anybody would write offering to announce his support or set up a Rockefeller-for-President club, he would receive a form letter from the Governor's office which said in part:

> The Governor's strong feeling is that the party should avoid the mistake of becoming rigidly committed far in advance of the convention. No one can now foresee the situation that will prevail in 1964. In the meantime, he feels the party should remain flexible, giving all of its many attractive leaders full exposure, and above all developing, on the broadest possible base, a positive program on which it can go to the country in 1964. He sees his present role entirely in terms of working with others in the development of such a program.
>
> Since he feels the party should not be committed at this time, he is not seeking any commitments himself and he personally intends to remain wholly uncommitted.

This wasn't just talk. In April, Goodwin Knight, the irrepressible, mercurial former Governor of California, opened up a Rockefeller-for-President club in Los Angeles without any authorization from Albany. Rockefeller immediately asked Knight to close up shop, pull down the posters, and hold off future action until approval from Rockefeller. Regretfully, Knight complied. The incident, widely reported across the country, showed Rockefeller meant business in accepting no commitments.

But why? It seemed inexplicable on any rational basis. Some politicians ascribed it to arrogance or overconfidence or a combination of both. They guessed that Rockefeller believed himself to be out so far in front for the nomination that there was no particular hurry in gathering up commitments and setting up an organization.

Nobody outside the Rockefeller inner circle guessed the real truth. The refusal to pick up commitments was an act of political good faith. Rockefeller had made his momentous decision. He would marry Happy Murphy that spring shortly after her own divorce proceedings were final. Neither the Governor nor any of his aides could predict with any degree of accuracy the extent and depth of the political reaction to the remarriage. But to his great credit, Rockefeller didn't want to trap any Republican politicians with commitments for his candidacy before the remarriage. He felt that would have been an act of bad faith. This was the real reason for the strange reticence by Rockefeller, Hinman, and company.

IX

★ ★ ★ ★ ★ ★ ★ ★ ★ ★ ★ ★ ★ ★ ★ ★ ★ ★ ★ ★

Draft Goldwater

Late in the summer of 1962, a select group of conservatives scattered about the country received a typewritten two-page letter from New York City dated August 24 and marked CONFIDENTIAL MEMO. The subject of the memo was not listed. Nor was its author, who happened to be F. Clifton White, a public relations consultant from Rye, New York, and a Republican party worker since his twenties. The memo began:

> There are four months left in 1962. Many important and significant things will happen in these four months. We have several encouraging signs which have already developed.

White quickly began to tick off some of these "encouraging signs" as follows:

> In Illinois, Hayes Robertson has become Chairman of Cook County and is doing a tremendous job to insure that county and state being with us in 1964. I had an excellent meeting with Hayes and Charlie Barr earlier this month.[1]
>
> Tad Smith had a regional meeting for his area in Phoenix, Arizona, on August 18 and 19, which I attended. This was a highly successful meeting, all states in the region being represented by key people and commitments made to fulfill the 1962 objectives.[2]

[1] This was a reference to Charles Barr of Chicago, an executive with the Standard Oil Company of Indiana.

[2] Tad Smith was then Texas state Republican chairman.

We have just had the election of a conservative County Chairman in Allegheny County (Pittsburgh), Pennsylvania. I am meeting with him right after Labor Day to discuss his work and association with us.

Nowhere in the course of this newsy memorandum was there a single mention of Barry Goldwater. Yet these scattered events in Chicago and Phoenix and Pittsburgh were small steps forward toward one objective: the nomination of Goldwater for President in 1964. The August 24, 1962, "confidential memo" from Clif White was a reflection of the work by an underground Goldwater-for-President organization that really started functioning the day after Nixon's defeat in 1960.

Although secrets have a notoriously short life span in the gossipy world of partisan politics, the underground organization for Goldwater managed to keep out the sunlight for a surprisingly long time. Republican politicians from state after state honestly reported in 1962 and early 1963 that they could see no organized activity for Goldwater in their home areas, and that Rockefeller seemed to be headed for the nomination in a walkaway. Behind their backs, however, Clif White and his associates were carrying on one of the most remarkable clandestine operations in American political history, slowly and carefully building a national organization without the help of a candidate.

White's memo of August 24 reveals the scope and care of the Goldwater effort. This was a time when almost all the party was fixing its sights on the 1962 elections, just a little more than two months away. Rockefeller, Nixon, Romney, and Scranton—along with their supporters—were preoccupied by gubernatorial contests. As chairman of the Senate Campaign Committee, Goldwater was interested in capturing some new Senate seats in 1962. But the White group was looking beyond the 1962 preliminaries to the main event in 1964.

White's reference to "the election of a conservative County Chairman in Allegheny County (Pittsburgh)" is particularly revealing. He was talking about the election as Republican chairman there of Paul Hugus, not only an old Taft Republican and a conservative but also an ardent admirer of Barry Goldwater. It's doubtful that Rockefeller, Nixon, Romney, or, for that matter, Goldwater, had ever heard of Paul Hugus. Representative William W. Scranton, his hands full running for Governor of Pennsylvania, was aware of Hugus's election but scarcely connected it with Presidential politics. Clif White did. He realized that the strongest drive against Goldwater within the party would come from the highly industrialized, heavily populated states east of the Mississippi and north of the Ohio. Consequently, White was delighted to see an ardent Goldwater man elected to the top party post in the second largest county in Pennsylvania (a doubly gratifying victory if it turned out that Scranton was elected Governor and became a Presidential contender himself). Similarly, White was happy that so fanatically devoted a Goldwaterite as Hayes Robertson had been elected to lead Chicago's Republican organization at a time when it seemed that Senator Everett Dirksen and Illinois State Chairman Victor Smith were leaning toward Rockefeller.

This concern with the need for friendly faces at key places on the county level would be standard operating procedure for a run-of-the-mill Presidential campaign with a willing candidate. What makes it so remarkable in this case is the fact that White and his associates had virtually no personal contact with Goldwater. To the contrary, August, 1962, was a particularly bleak moment for millions of Goldwater admirers all over the country. Goldwater had been telling friends that Rockefeller would do nicely as a candidate for President, and that he was going to curtail drastically his 1963 speaking engagements so that he could mend some fences both in the Senate and back home in Arizona. But

White and his associates—what was to become the National Draft Goldwater Committee—wouldn't take "no" for an answer.

The real germination date for the Draft Goldwater movement may have been October 17, 1960. F. Clifton White, director of organization for the National Nixon-Lodge Volunteers, had boarded Richard M. Nixon's campaign plane that day on a routine assignment. At a rally in Polish Union Hall at Buffalo, New York, that night, Nixon was scheduled to present Walter J. Lohr, president of the Polish Union of America, with an album of postage stamps honoring Paderewski as a "champion of liberty." The album had been autographed in Washington by Postmaster General Arthur Summerfield, and was to be autographed now by Vice-President Nixon. White's mission was to carry the album aboard the plane, give it to Nixon, explain to Nixon the background of the presentation, and suggest some appropriate remarks that might accompany the presentation. White accomplished half his mission. He delivered the stamps but was unable to get time with Nixon for even one word. It was the closest he came to Nixon during the entire campaign.

This isolation from his own candidate, very much like the isolation experienced by other top staff men in the Nixon campaign, was not enough in itself to turn Clif White against Nixon. But it might have been the last straw. By the time of the Buffalo stamp presentation, White had just about reached the conclusion that Nixon was not the right kind of candidate for the Republican Party from the standpoint of either tactics or policies. It was significant in itself that White, heretofore a political tactician or technician, now was thinking about issues.

If casual acquaintances had been asked in October, 1960, to guess White's ideological leanings, they quite likely would have tagged him as a mildly liberal Republican because of his close association with Thomas E. Dewey's Republican organization in New York State. After distinguished World War II service as an Air Corps captain, White became an instructor of social sciences at Cornell University—and immediately began dabbling in Young Republican politics. Within a year or two, he was a key figure in New York State Young Republican politics and one of Governor Dewey's rising young political lieutenants. As chairman of "Youth for Dewey" in 1948, White helped subvert some of Robert Taft's own Young Republicans over to Dewey. As national chairman of the Young Republicans in 1951 and kingmaker behind the throne for half a decade following, White was Dewey's muscle in the YR organization.

Through all this exciting and remarkably successful career as a party politician, White never gave much thought to the great ideological issues that had so long divided his party. When White helped lead the charge for Dewey against Taft, it was a matter of loyalty to the Dewey organization rather than any devotion to the party's progressive wing. But as White gradually dropped out of Young Republican politics and began to mull over issues for the first time, he began to feel that conservatism was the wave of the future—not just for the sake of Republican Party victories but for the sake of his children and his country. White had come to believe that the heavy hand of big government was stifling individual freedom and opportunity throughout the land.

The first signs of this began to show through in 1958 when White was campaign manager for Walter J. Mahoney, Republican leader of the New York State Senate and a conservative, in his unsuccessful campaign for the gubernatorial nomination against Rockefeller. Most of the old Dewey men still active were backing Rockefeller. Some of them, particularly State Chairman Jud Morhouse, complained bitterly that White used unnecessarily tough tactics in promoting

Mahoney's losing effort. In fighting Rockefeller in 1958, White had broken his early political ties.

But the great watershed in White's political career came in 1960 at age forty-two. Disillusioned and disappointed by Nixon's showing, White was absolutely convinced that only a conservative would have a chance against Kennedy in 1964.

There were other rising figures in the party who completely agreed with White in 1960.

One was John Grenier, a bright young Birmingham lawyer who was soon to become Alabama state Republican chairman. Although he had voted for Eisenhower against Adlai Stevenson in both 1952 and 1956, Grenier did not really make his commitment as a Republican activist until the age of thirty. In August, 1960, he became alarmed at the liberal platform adopted by the Democrats at their National Convention in Los Angeles, and enrolled himself as a worker for Nixon. But he soon came to regard Nixon as a me-too candidate who was trying, without much success, to carry water on both shoulders. By the time of Nixon's defeat, Grenier was looking for a conservative.

Another was William Rusher, a White protégé who had become national chairman of the Young Republicans under his tutelage. Rusher really was not a party man at all, but a conservative ideologue who happened to gravitate to the Republican Party because it at least could potentially become a conservative instrument. Rusher, publisher of the militantly conservative *National Review,* never entertained the slightest illusions about Nixon. He was looking for a conservative champion long before the 1960 campaign even started.

Still another was Charles Barr, a public affairs officer for Standard Oil Company (Indiana). Barr was not one of the fuddy-duddy, old-line executives who believed that the captains of industry should play it safe in the background, making a campaign contribution here and there but staying away from the political crossfire. Barr was a political activist —a conservative political activist.

These four—White, Grenier, Rusher, Barr—are picked at random from scores of vigorous and competent men mostly in their thirties and forties who formed the nucleus of the Draft Goldwater organization. They are typical of the four types who composed that nucleus: White the party professional, Grenier the urban Southerner, Rusher the doctrinaire conservative, Barr the business executive. This was a far cry from the Old Guard of party hacks who fought so loyally but so ineptly for Robert A. Taft in 1952.

And behind the Goldwater nucleus were millions of rank-and-file Goldwater enthusiasts. True enough, they were not a solid majority of the Republican Party in 1961 and 1962. They were but a minority of a minority party. But they did constitute the closest thing to a genuine mass movement on the American political scene in the early 1960's.

Clif White and his associates met frequently and informally after the 1960 election to discuss the future. By the end of 1961, they had decided to set up a secret organization to promote the nomination of "a conservative"—obviously, the only man they were thinking of was Goldwater—at the 1964 convention. White was named chairman of the organization. Three well-heeled Republican campaign givers— Jerry Milbank of New York, William Mittendorf of Connecticut, and J. Stetson Coleman of Florida—were named as "trustees" of the organization.

Although he was operating on a financial shoestring, White began to pop up from time to time at party gatherings to look after Goldwater's Presidential interests (without Goldwater's approval or probably even Goldwater's knowledge). White was on hand, for instance, at Republican National Committee meetings at Oklahoma City and Seattle in 1962. Moreover, he started sending out those "confidential" memos to the nucleus of the Draft Goldwater organization. The first of these, on May 29, 1962, began:

> There are seven months left in 1962. We all agreed that it was essential to build our basic organizational forces this year. It is recognized that in some states it may be necessary to await the conclusion of the '62 elections before we make an official determination concerning those states. However, I do not think we should use this as an excuse to do nothing in those states. There is nothing that is easier or more fun for politicians than to sit down with one another and win elections by talk. However, as you well know, this is not the way elections are truly won.

White next proceeded to dole out routine but vital organization assignments (such as checking on "what the opposition may be doing"). White's first memo closed with this admonition:

> 1964 is just around the corner. 1963 is practically here. We never have time to do all of the preparation necessary to achieve a maximum effective political organization. Let's not kid ourselves into thinking that we have lots of time. We must stick to our agreed-upon schedule and get accomplished these things in an orderly fashion. If we do this, I have no serious concern as to our ability to be successful. But for want of a nail—a delegate—a convention—was lost.

This was the urgency of the underdog compared with the easygoing confidence of the front-running Rockefeller camp. But the fact that only the Goldwater camp was really putting its muscles to grass roots organization in 1962 was to pay off in due time.

However, by August 24, White complained in another memo that fund raising was running behind expectations and that organizational progress was disappointing.

> Since January, I have been in 28 states, at least once. We have contacts of varying degrees of effectiveness in 41 of the 50 states but we have not yet developed the depth and the

solid organization we listed as our objectives in the spring of
this year and which are repeated in the May 29 memo. We
must be prepared to move into high gear in January of 1963.
I know you recognize this. However, there are some of you
from whom I have not heard since April. I am anxiously awaiting word as to your state of health.

These were dark days for the Draft Goldwater movement.
White and a handful of other inner circle members talked it
over frankly in October in a room at the Avenue Motel in
Chicago's Loop—a meeting so secret that White didn't even
mention it in his confidential memos. All participants at the
October meeting expressed concern about Goldwater's attitude. The Senator was definitely unresponsive. When a member of the Draft Goldwater movement would approach him
with bids to run for the nomination, Goldwater would say:
"That's all right for you, but what about me? It's my neck
that would go on the chopping block—not yours." This
attitude and Goldwater's repeated praise of Rockefeller were
discouraging the Senator's rank-and-file supporters. Contributions were getting scarce. The Draft Goldwater organization was having trouble meeting its modest overhead.
Because of lack of funds, for example, White was unable to
attend the September convention in Phoenix, Arizona, of the
National Federation of Republican Women (where pro-
Goldwater women scored a coup by defeating candidates
slated by the nominating committee).[3]

The October gathering finally decided to press ahead
despite all the difficulties, and scheduled a meeting of the
entire organization in Chicago on December 1 and 2. White
announced it in a confidential memo of October 18.

This meeting will determine where we go—whether we are
serious or dilettantes. I would appreciate any information you
think you should submit between now and then. If the sheriff

[3] However, White was represented at Phoenix by Miss Rita Bree, White's
secretary and a competent party tactician in her own right.

has not attached everything we own by that date, Rita and I will look forward to seeing you on December 1.

The December meeting, held in downtown Chicago at the Essex Motor Inn, was the first full-scale meeting by all the recipients of White's confidential memos. With nearly one hundred persons present, it was inevitable that word of the Draft Goldwater organization finally would leak out. But nobody was prepared for the wave of publicity in newspapers across the country. Moreover, a new magazine published by young, progressive (and anti-Goldwater) Republicans and named *Advance* printed a long and detailed account of the December meeting—an account remarkably accurate in all but a few minor details according to those who actually attended.[4]

At the Essex Inn, there was a good deal of planning about the future, but also a good deal of trying to boost one another's morale. According to *Advance,* participants in the December meeting gave this breakdown of their prospects:

"Solid Goldwater States," yielding a total of 435 votes—Alabama, Arkansas, Colorado, Florida, Indiana, Louisiana, Maine, Mississippi, Missouri, Montana, Nebraska, New Mexico, North Carolina, Oklahoma, South Carolina, Texas, Utah, Virginia, and Washington.

"Almost-as-Solid States," yielding 81 votes—Georgia, Kentucky, South Dakota, and Tennessee.

"States That can be Won with Extra-Hard Work," yielding 142 votes—Illinois, Iowa, Ohio.

Total: 658 votes.

Adding pick-ups from split delegations: Connecticut—8; California—25; Michigan—10.

Grand total: 701.[5]

[4] It was so accurate, in fact, that White was certain a tape recorder had been smuggled into the motel room. The suspected "spy" was promptly dropped from all Draft Goldwater activity, and no future leaks occurred.

[5] This entire breakdown was based on the state-by-state delegate allocation for the 1960 National Convention. The 1964 allocation was approved six months later at the Republican National Committee meeting in Denver.

This was more than enough delegates for the nomination, but in December, 1962, this was clearly a case of whistling past the graveyard. The Goldwater camp had nothing close to this kind of strength, actual or potential. In fact, *Advance* reported, there was "some disagreement about these figures" at the Chicago meeting. Although the breakdown listed Indiana as a "solid" Goldwater state, the magazine continued, "Rep. Donald Bruce of Indianapolis, Indiana, told the group in Chicago that his state party organization at this point is 'lurching' toward Rockefeller."

But the Draft Goldwater organization was not really trying to calculate delegation strength accurately at this point. It was trying to revive its own spirits and, more important, encourage Goldwater to run. According to *Advance,* White told the Chicago meeting: "Barry Goldwater will not become a candidate until and unless he sees adequate financing and the energy of a full-scale professional operation."

Goldwater's reaction to the December meeting was discouraging. He told reporters he hoped the Chicago group would do nothing for all of 1963 and give him until January, 1964, to make up his mind. "I'd rather stay in a fluid position for the rest of the year [1963]," Goldwater said. "I hope they [the group meeting in Chicago] won't go ahead on this timetable." It was, in short, a request from Goldwater for White to close up shop. White didn't. But he did postpone January plans to establish openly a National Draft Goldwater Committee with Washington headquarters. Instead, a secret meeting of the Draft Goldwater inner circle was called for Chicago in late January.

This meeting was held at O'Hare Inn at Chicago's O'Hare International Airport. This time the invitation list was so select that there was not the slightest threat of a news leak. No more than a dozen men attended. Included were White and Charley Barr; Tad Smith, who had just resigned as

Republican state chairman of Texas; Peter O'Donnell, a Dallas millionaire who had moved up from his job as Dallas County Republican chairman to replace Smith as state chairman; Representative John Ashbrook of Ohio; William McFadzean of Minneapolis, who was to become Minnesota state chairman for the Draft Goldwater organization; and Tyrone Gillespie, assistant to the president of Dow Chemical Company in Midland, Michigan.

It was decided to keep going whether Goldwater liked it or not. They noted the tightening Rockefeller hammerlock on the nomination. It was no longer enough for the Draft Goldwater organization to operate underground. It had to surface and compete openly with Rockefeller. White, who had been elected chairman of the original organization by its entire membership, declared that somebody with a regular party position should be chairman of the new National Draft Goldwater Committee to show that the drive was headed by substantial party figures, not just backroom technicians. The consensus was that Peter O'Donnell, the new Texas state Republican chairman, should get the job. Before O'Donnell could accept or reject the offer, a waiter stepped into the motel room with a plateload of sandwiches. Everybody laughingly agreed that meant O'Donnell's answer would have to be "yes."

The actual unveiling came months later, on April 9 in Washington. Without prior warning, a morning press conference was called at the Mayflower Hotel for the purpose of announcing the formation of the National Draft Goldwater Committee. For a half hour before the press conference time, Clif White stalked around nervously, making last-minute arrangements. Then he ducked out. This was not to be a show for the professionals but for elected regular party officials. Along with O'Donnell at the speaker's lectern was another elected party official: Mrs. Ione Harrington, national Republican committeewoman from Indiana and now vice-chairman of the Draft Goldwater Committee.[6]

"We want to make clear," O'Donnell told the press conference, "that we have not consulted Senator Goldwater about forming this committee. We take him at his word when he says his present intention is to run for reelection to the Senate next year." The twenty to twenty-five Washington correspondents attending the press conference were a little patronizing about the whole affair. With Rockefeller seemingly assured of the nomination, what could be said for this fly-by-night band who weren't even in direct contact with Goldwater?[7]

But White and O'Donnell weren't worried about reporters' opinions. Their real crisis would come after the press conference when Goldwater's reaction would become known. They were well aware that a harsh comment by Goldwater would be enough to force the National Draft Goldwater Committee out of business before it really even opened its doors. If Goldwater were to make an angry plea for the White-O'Donnell group to leave him alone and desist from further activity until his own decision time in January, 1964,

[6] There was considerable private debate within party circles whether Mrs. Harrington's name on the masthead was an asset or a liability for the Draft Goldwater Committee. A charming and amiable matron personally, Mrs. Harrington is so fiercely conservative that she once tried to purge none other than Representative Charles Halleck of Indiana as a cryptoliberal. Moreover, she was a controversial figure with many enemies in Indiana, a state whose Republicans were then evenly divided between Rockefeller and Goldwater. Nevertheless, the Draft Goldwater organization needed a Northern female party official as vice-chairman to pair with O'Donnell, and Mrs. Harrington was the only committed Goldwater supporter in April, 1963, who met those specifications.

[7] There was much confusion among the press as to just when the O'Donnell-Harrington group started getting itself organized. Many reporters believed this was a completely separate enterprise from the December meeting in Chicago that had been repudiated by Goldwater. The *New York Times, in* reporting the O'Donnell-Harrington press conference in its April 9 edition, declared: "Another 'draft Goldwater' movement was mounted from Chicago late last winter, but apparently never got far." O'Donnell's cryptic answers at the April 8 press conference contributed to the confusion.

that would be enough to kill off the committee. The stillborn committee would then die for lack of money and supporters.

The suspense on April 8 wore on through the day. Goldwater earlier had been informed indirectly that formation of the committee was to be announced that spring, but he hadn't been informed of the exact day. When asked by the press to comment on the new committee on April 8, Goldwater's office announced firmly that there absolutely would be no comment. But seasoned Washington correspondents were aware that Goldwater usually forgot any self-imposed stricture of "no comment" if he could be contacted personally. A band of reporters did track him down during the afternoon at a reception given by the District of Columbia Republican Committee.

Goldwater's words were music to White and O'Donnell's ears. "I am not taking any position on this draft movement," Goldwater said. "It's their time and their money. But they are going to have to get along without any help from me." This was the kind of neutrality for which the Draft Goldwater movement had been praying. Goldwater had declined to try to force them out of operation. The National Draft Goldwater Committee had survived those critical postnatal hours.

Was Goldwater really aware of the importance of his attitude? Did he realize that he could have all but removed himself from Presidential consideration by firing a blast against the newly formed and still fragile committee?

He probably did. Only a few days earlier, he had discussed casually with Tony Smith, his press secretary, the action taken by Rockefeller in forcing Goodie Knight to close down a Rockefeller-for-President headquarters just set up in Los Angeles. Goldwater had remarked to Smith that Rockefeller could have permitted Knight's California operation to continue merely by remaining silent or disavowing himself from it. It required overt, positive action by Rockefeller to force Knight to desist.[8] It is clear then that Goldwater was aware he could have killed the National Draft Goldwater Committee within hours of its birth. The fact is that he didn't want to kill it.

This didn't mean that Goldwater was about to enter the lists as an avowed candidate. It didn't mean he had become so disenchanted with Rockefeller that he was about to wage all-out war to keep him from the nomination. Nor did it mean he had at last contracted White House fever. His failure to throttle the Draft Goldwater movement meant only that he wasn't going to run away from the nomination even if he wasn't going to run for it. This attitude was colorfully and characteristically explained by Goldwater himself in an interview with Cabell Phillips in the April 15 edition of the *New York Times*.

> I don't want the nomination. I'm not looking for it. I haven't authorized anybody to look for it for me. But who can tell what will happen a year from now? A man would be a damn fool to predict with finality what he would do in this unpredictable world.

Now that the Draft Goldwater movement had survived the ascent from underground to the open world, it had its work cut out for it. Rockefeller was far in front. He had made significant progress in winning over party workers during recent visits to Wisconsin, Kansas, and Nebraska in the conservative Republican heartland.[9] At their first press conference on April 8, O'Donnell and Mrs. Harrington announced a monster Draft Goldwater rally to be held in Washington

[8] Of course, Goldwater was not aware of Rockefeller's impending remarriage, the real reason for his harsh treatment of Knight.

[9] Rockefeller's successful trip to Omaha may have been the reason why O'Donnell picked Nebraska as an illustration that only a conservative Republican can be sure of winning in the Republican heartland. At the April 8 press conference, O'Donnell distributed material showing how all conservative Republican candidates had won in Nebraska in 1962 while the state Republican ticket's only progressive—Fred Seaton, who had been Eisenhower's Secretary of the Interior—was badly beaten in his race for Governor.

on the Fourth of July in order to demonstrate grass roots fervor for the Senator. This would keep up the morale of the Goldwater workers and perhaps recruit a few new ones. But those party leaders who were ready to commit themselves to Rockefeller whenever Albany gave the word would be singularly unimpressed with monster rallies.

Accordingly, White and O'Donnell plotted a three-part strategy to narrow the gap between Goldwater and Rockefeller. The first move concerned practical political maneuvering, the other two dealt with political propaganda.

1. The Favorite Sons

The greatest danger facing the Goldwater forces was the possibility that Rockefeller would have tied up an absolute majority of National Convention delegates long before Goldwater made up his mind whether to run. It seemed doubtful in April, 1963, that noncandidate Goldwater could really corral any great number of delegates before convention time. How to keep delegates away from Rockefeller—how to keep them neutral—so that Goldwater might be able to pick them up in a big drive at the convention itself? The answer: neutralize them with favorite son candidacies.

In the early spring of 1963, the best way to keep Rockefeller from a first-ballot nomination semed to be the encouragement of favorite son candidates who would lock up dozens of state delegations. The Draft Goldwater forces were privately trying their best to flush out more favorite sons. White was particularly eager to see favorite son candidates in states where key primary elections were scheduled. It then seemed unlikely that Goldwater could be prodded into a primary election, and uncertain that he could run very well against Rockefeller even if he did enter. But Rockefeller, running unopposed in the key primary states, would be able to pick up great batches of delegates and perhaps gain enough prestige to get his bandwagon rolling at breakneck speed.

Accordingly, the Draft Goldwater tacticians were delighted when Representative Melvin Laird and other Wisconsin Republican leaders decided to put up Representative John Byrnes, the highly respected chairman of the House Republican Policy Committee and one of the party's leading authorities on fiscal policy, as a favorite son candidate in Wisconsin's famed April Presidential primary. Wisconsin party leaders, trying to avoid a repetition of the 1944 and 1948 primary struggles that split the Wisconsin party and denuded its financial resources, asked that all national candidates honor Byrnes as a legitimate favorite son, and keep out of Wisconsin. Since Rockefeller seemed at that time the only Republican likely to enter the primaries, the Laird-Byrnes plan looked like Rockefeller's loss and Goldwater's potential gain.

The same trouble for Rockefeller was looming in California. While only thirty delegates were at stake in Wisconsin, California offered a rich harvest of eighty-six votes on a winner-take-all basis in the June primary. It was thought then that nobody would have a chance against Rockefeller there (even though his support from California party leaders was meager). But now there were rumbles about running a "harmony" slate of delegates headed by a favorite son— perhaps former Senator William F. Knowland, a strong supporter of Goldwater. Once again, Rockefeller would be asked to stay out in deference to a favorite son. Not only would Rockefeller lose the entire eighty-six-vote package from California on the first convention ballot, but at least thirty members of the "harmony" delegation—perhaps more— would be Goldwater men. This would give Goldwater his first breakthrough into the delegation of one of the Big Six states.

Obviously getting more and more interested in Presidential

politics, Goldwater commented publicly that the proliferation of favorite sons was a good thing for the party. Senator Thomas Kuchel, California's outspoken liberal Republican, angrily told friends that the Goldwater camp was trying to use the favorite son device to prevent internal democracy within the party and to stop Rockefeller short of the nomination.

2. Goldwater Can Win

As an old Dewey man, White had a sense of recent history. He remembered how Taft had been deprived of the nomination time after time with the use of the old battle cry: "Taft Can't Win!" The argument was the one that put over Willkie in 1940, Dewey in 1944 and 1948, and Eisenhower in 1952. As a minority party, the Republicans must woo away Democratic votes. The only Democratic votes that can be wooed away are in the industrial Northeast and Great Lakes regions. These are essentially liberal Democratic votes. Therefore, the Presidential candidate must come from the Republican Party's progressive wing. A conservative simply *can't* win.

It was indeed important that the Draft Goldwater forces should stamp out a "Goldwater Can't Win" slogan, and instead promote the battle cry that "Goldwater Can Win." What's more, the Goldwater forces had a cogent argument— much simpler and less sophisticated than the battle plan mentioned in Chapter V but strikingly similar to its general outlines.

The account by *Advance* of the December, 1963, meeting of the Draft Goldwater forces in Chicago revealed the basic formula behind the "Goldwater Can Win" battle cry. According to *Advance:*

> . . . the Goldwater strategists point out that the Democrats carried states worth 121 electoral votes by less than 51 per cent,

while Republicans carried only 43 electoral votes by less than
51 per cent. Thus, predict the right-wingers, with a conservative ticket the South and border states will go Republican, as
well as the states Nixon carried (except California), and Barry
Goldwater will be President.

This victory formula was explained fully in the first piece
of campaign literature distributed by the National Draft
Goldwater Committee. The pamphlet showed a map of the
United States with fourteen states conceded to Kennedy
against Goldwater—New York, Massachusetts, Connecticut,
Rhode Island, New Jersey, Delaware, West Virginia, Michigan, Minnesota, Missouri, Nevada, Oregon, Alaska, and
Hawaii—colored white. California, rated as "doubtful," was
colored gray. All the rest of the states, colored dark, were
claimed by Goldwater.

A table alongside the chart told what this meant in electoral votes.

	JFK	Goldwater	Doubtful
NORTH & EAST	118	11	
BORDER STATES	32	17	
THE SOUTH	NONE	128	
MIDWEST	31	106	
MOUNTAIN STATES	3	30	
PACIFIC STATES	13	9	40
	197	301	
NEEDED TO WIN	270		

In its text, the pamphlet then proceeded to embellish and
analyze these statistics:

> Barry Goldwater will take all 128 electoral votes of the eleven
> Southern States! In 1964 Goldwater will give "the solid South"
> dramatic new meaning! *This is the key to Republican success!*
>   In addition to sweeping the South, Goldwater will lead our
> party to a tremendous victory by carrying the dependable Re-

publican states of the Midwest, Rocky Mountains, and Northern New England.[10]

The secret to Republican victory lies in the fact that Senator Goldwater can convert a past weakness of the Republican Party into great strength. He alone can tap this new reservoir of votes, not only for President, but also for control of Congress!

Finally, the pamphlet put all this into historical perspective, showing how the Goldwater victory formula could at long last turn the Republican Party into the majority party.

For generations the South has given the Democrats their base of power with 22 Senators, 106 Congressmen, and 128 Electoral Votes. To control the country, the National Democratic Party only needed to win about ⅓ of the Electoral Votes and Congressional races outside the South.

Dewey would have been elected President in 1948 if he had carried the South. Nixon would now be President, if he had won the Southern electoral votes that went to Kennedy.

Recent elections show that the South is an area of tremendous future growth for the Republican Party. Goldwater's nomination will not only break the long-standing Democratic monopoly in the Southern states, but will also head off divisive third-party movements which might well spread into other areas.

This was revolutionary doctrine. The Draft Goldwater forces were as much as saying that the party should concede some of the traditional battlegrounds of Presidential politics —New York, Pennsylvania, Michigan, California—on the assumption that Goldwater would do what no other Republican in history had ever come close to doing: sweep the South.

---

[10] This is an exact paraphrase of the conservative battle plan described in Chapter V.

3. *Rockefeller Can't Win*

Rockefeller was still the front runner. It wasn't enough to
say that Goldwater could win. It would be necessary—later
in the fight—to claim that Rockefeller couldn't. That meant
proving that Rockefeller, admittedly weak in the South, was
no match for Kennedy in the industrial North. And what
better way to do that than to supply evidence depicting
Rockefeller as a loser in his home state of New York?

The Draft Goldwater tacticians weren't relying merely on
undocumented arguments that Rockefeller had lost in popularity because of his latest tax squabble with the Legislature
or because of the Liquor Authority scandals. They had some
evidence. The Draft Goldwater Committee had hired
Opinion Research Corporation, a large and highly regarded
polling firm from Princeton, New Jersey, to see how Rockefeller would fare against Kennedy in New York State (using
a sample of voters interviewed twice as large as usual).
The results were startling. Kennedy was the winner in a
landslide.

The Draft Goldwater Committee was ready to leak these
results to the press at the proper moment. It was because of
a remarkable personal decision by Rockefeller that the
proper moment never arrived.

Nobody will ever be able to know if this three-part
strategy would have stopped Rockefeller and nominated
Goldwater. Rockefeller's unprecedented act of political self-
destruction made any Goldwater strategy unnecessary.

Yet, the odds are that the Draft Goldwater Committee
would have failed. The favorite son ploy is an old one that
always tends to crumble when the front runner's bandwagon
really gets going. It's doubtful that the Southern strategy of
Goldwater would have proved so attractive had Rockefeller's

candidacy remained strong. As for the Kennedy-Rockefeller poll in New York, the ability of polls to move the minds of very many politicians is not great.

Instead, it was an event completely outside its own power that made the summer and early autumn of 1963 so delightful for the National Draft Goldwater Committee.

X

★ ★

Remarriage

The Goldwaters were spending the sunny, unseasonably warm Saturday of May 4, 1963, at their Washington home in the Westchester Apartments. Barry Goldwater, the inveterate gadgeteer, was on the roof trying to fix his television aerial when the telephone rang. His wife Peggy answered it.

"Hello," said a man's voice on the other end of the line. "This is Nelson Rockefeller."

"Well, hello yourself," Peggy Goldwater replied. "This is Mamie Eisenhower."

When the caller finally convinced Mrs. Goldwater that he really was the Governor of New York and not just one of the Senator's sidekicks hamming it up, she summoned her husband down from the roof. This was no casual call. Rockefeller informed Goldwater that he had been married that afternoon to Mrs. Margaretta Fitler (Happy) Murphy, and wanted to give the Senator the news before it was released to radio-television and the newspapers. Despite the friendship that had developed between the two party leaders, Goldwater felt uncomfortable, at a loss for words. He congratulated Rockefeller and wished him luck. After a few more words, the telephone conversation was over.

Goldwater was one of the very few party leaders who received a call from the Governor himself that afternoon.[1] But the telephone lines were kept busy by Rockefeller's closest associates.

Consider the way Senator Jacob Javits of New York was informed. Less than twenty-four hours earlier, Javits and Rockefeller had carried on a wide-ranging discussion of political topics over Friday morning breakfast in New York City, but Rockefeller gave no hint of the wedding to take place the next afternoon. In fact, the two men purposely skirted Rockefeller's personal life during their chat. Javits heard nothing of the marriage until Saturday afternoon. David Rockefeller, the Governor's brother and chairman of the Chase Manhattan Bank, telephoned Javits at his New York City home to inform the Senator before the word was passed to the news media.

Busiest of all that afternoon was George Hinman. The Governor's chief political missionary called Washington and points west to give a select assortment of presumed Rockefeller boosters—Congressmen such as Bradford Morse of Massachusetts, Abner Sibal of Connecticut, Charles Mathias of Maryland—advance word of the marriage. Unlike Nelson and David Rockefeller, Hinman did not confine his telephone call to straight reporting of the marital facts. He tried to get some idea of just how much each listener was disturbed by the news, and then tried to reassure him that any fuss over the remarriage would settle down quickly enough.

Only after all this frenetic telephoning ended were the news media informed—some three hours after the actual marriage. Reporters were told that the fifty-four-year-old Governor and his thirty-six-year-old bride were married on the Rockefellers' baronial estate at Pocantico Hills, New York, in the home of Laurence S. Rockefeller, one of the

---

[1] This tended to substantiate what by then had become a major complaint of Republican liberals. These liberals criticized Rockefeller for being over-attentive to Goldwater and other conservatives while ignoring the party's liberals.

Governor's brothers. The newlyweds left New York the next morning for a South American vacation at Monte Sacro, the Governor's ranch near Chirgua, Venezuela.

When Nelson Rockefeller returned to New York seventeen days later, he found that his plans for winning the Republican nomination—so carefully laid over the years—were in ruins.

Speculation that Rockefeller would marry Happy Murphy had been dormant for the better part of a year, but resumed on April 1 when she finally won her divorce from Dr. James Murphy of Philadelphia. By May 2 (just two days before the wedding), rumors that remarriage for Rockefeller was imminent were spreading through political circles. Outside Rockefeller's innermost circle, however, nobody—not even Senator Javits—had been told that the date was set for May 4. Indeed, outside that innermost circle, nobody—not even Senator Javits—was sure the wedding would take place any time before the 1964 Presidential election. Rather, there was a widespread belief among Republican politicians that Rockefeller would not himself endanger what would almost certainly be his last opportunity for the Presidency. By November, 1964, he would be either President or a political also-ran. That would be time enough for him to marry Happy Murphy.

Unlikely though it now may seem in light of the political upheaval that followed his remarriage, Rockefeller in May, 1963, did not see himself facing a hard choice between immediate marriage to the woman he loved and the glimmering goal of the Presidency that he had been pursuing for five years. He made it clear to his closest aides that he felt he could have both. Edward VIII may have given up the throne of England for Wallis Simpson. Princess Margaret may have given up Peter Townsend for the sake of the monarchy. But neither of these courses was for Nelson Rockefeller. He would sacrifice neither his happiness nor his political career.

Rockefeller's political instincts were never particularly acute, but this fatal miscalculation in his political career was not so gross at the time as it seems in hindsight. Rockefeller was not alone in believing that his remarriage would not prevent his nomination. Only a few Republican leaders—principally avowed Goldwater-for-President enthusiasts such as Peter O'Donnell of Texas, chairman of the fledgling National Draft Goldwater Committee—predicted (with the prediction reflecting the wish) that the second marriage would be Rockefeller's downfall.

Most party leaders were sanguine about the impact of the remarriage. Here's a fair sample:

Arthur Elliott, Michigan state chairman: "I don't think this marriage changes his political picture at all."

Robert Pierce, national committeeman from Wisconsin: "Just because no divorced man has ever been elected President doesn't mean we won't have one sometime."

W. Y. Walter, Washington state chairman: "If there was any impact at all, it would be from the original divorce and not the second marriage."

Webster B. Todd, New Jersey state chairman: "If this gal is all they say she is, she may help him."

Mrs. Ella Koeze, national committeewoman from Michigan: "I don't think it's going to make any more impact on the women of America . . . the whole thing depends on whether the man is qualified, a good candidate, and what he would do for the country as a whole."

J. E. Broyhill, national committeeman from North Carolina: "I don't think it would hurt him any more to get married than it did to get a divorce in the first place."

Jean Tool, Colorado state chairman: "People who might object to the marriage now will get used to the idea in a few months. I have heard many people say it would help Rockefeller's political future to remarry."

In view of the cloudy crystal ball employed by the party's leaders, the violent hysteria with which Rockefeller's remarriage was greeted came as a shock to most practicing politicians.

Representative Charles (Mac) Mathias, Jr., the Congressman representing the Washington, D.C., suburbs across the state line in Maryland, got a taste of the hysterical reaction early. His constituents were not thousands of miles away but right next door to Capitol Hill. A liberal Republican with a promising future in Maryland politics, Mathias was considered almost certain to wind up supporting Rockefeller for President (though, like other potential Rockefeller men, no commitment was asked of him in advance of the marriage). After the remarriage, however, Mathias began to have second thoughts about Rockefeller. The din of anti-Rockefeller sentiment from his own Congressional district was incessant. Just a few days after the wedding, twenty-eight Republican women dropped by Mathias's office at the Capitol ostensibly to discuss a subject not remotely related to Presidential politics. Yet, these women talked of little else except the "scandal" of Rockefeller's conduct. It's not surprising that within a week after the wedding, Mathias was telling friends that Rockefeller was dead—definitely in Maryland and probably in the rest of the country.

Other progressive Republican members of Congress were getting the same story in their mailbags. Senator Hugh Scott of Pennsylvania, who had been trying (without much success) to talk Governor Scranton into becoming Pennsylvania's favorite son for President but was expected to end up with Rockefeller, was amazed at the virulent tone of his anti-Rockefeller mail—particularly the letters from clergymen. One self-righteous Presbyterian minister from Philadelphia wrote Scott, "This may all go over with the jet set, but it will not go over with many decent-thinking persons like myself."

In fact, the loudest screams of outrage immediately following the wedding came from the clergy. The Reverend Charles H. Graf, rector of the Village Protestant Episcopal Church in New York City's Greenwich Village, got the ball rolling the Sunday morning after the wedding. In a sermon prepared when the Rockefeller remarriage was still in the rumor stage, he pointed to references in the Scriptures defining remarriage as adultery. The Reverend Graf was not alone for long. The many churches of Jesus Christ reunited briefly in an impromptu ecumenical movement for the purpose of denouncing Nelson Rockefeller and his bride.[2] Even the distinguished and liberal Dr. Reinhold Niebuhr, one of the nation's most eminent Protestant theologians, couldn't resist joining the chorus. He told how his cleaning woman, a pious Baptist, brought up the subject of the Rockefeller marriage. "She said she didn't like the quickness of the remarriage and the fact that a three-year-old child was involved," said Dr. Niebuhr. He paused, then added: "I share the view."

For the most part, Republican politicians—even Rockefeller's most bitter enemies—left the moralizing up to the clergy.[3] But less than a week after the wedding, there was clear proof of the reaction by some politicians. The occasion was a thousand-dollar-a-plate testimonial dinner for Goldwater at the Sheraton-Park Hotel in Washington on May 9. Rockefeller, who had been scheduled as one of the speakers, cabled regrets "from Mrs. Rockefeller and me" in Venezuela. When Senator Thruston Morton of Kentucky, toastmaster

[2] An exception was Dr. Eugene Carson Blake, stated clerk of the Presbyterian General Assembly. He said: "I think it is unfortunate that clergymen express excitement about the divorce and remarriage, however prominent, when it is quite clear that the moral and social question is widespread both inside and outside the churches which they head."

[3] One well-known Republican who did attack Rockefeller publicly from a moral standpoint was former Senator Prescott Bush of Connecticut. Coming as it did from a fellow Eastern Republican, Bush's attack was regarded as highly significant by some journalists and politicians. Actually, Bush never had much use for Rockefeller. As a member of the Platform Committee at the 1960 National Convention, Bush had battled furiously against Rockefeller's platform proposals.

for the dinner, read the cablegram from the honeymooners, the reaction was horselaughs and giggling. True, the Republicans who had paid a thousand dollars a plate in May, 1963, constituted just about the same group who had paid a hundred dollars a plate in February, 1963, to boo Rockefeller. But horselaughs and giggles were in their way more ominous than booing.

Still, some of the most astute political observers—men such as Representative William Miller of New York and Senator Everett McKinley Dirksen of Illinois—were not overly impressed. They cautioned more impulsive politicians to wait a bit before abandoning Rockefeller. They were certain the uproar would blow over in a few weeks. It was impossible for them to believe that the wedding could make political history.

They were wrong. The hysteria, instead of dying, grew ever more intense. The Governor and his bride seemed to help it along by the gaiety of their honeymoon. Good Republican matrons who were outraged by the very idea of this marriage were livid after seeing wire service photographs showing the girlish Happy Rockefeller, clad in blue jeans and a white shirt, cavorting with the Governor on his Venezuelan ranch. There was more righteous indignation when the Rockefellers, each clad in sport shirt and shorts, were photographed during a stopover at Caneel Bay, Virgin Islands, on the way back to New York. By the time the Governor returned on May 23 after a seventeen-day honeymoon, not even the Millers and Dirksens were at all sure that the reaction was only temporary. Rockefeller had been wounded critically, perhaps mortally.

The Rockefellers had been home only one day when criticism from the clergy hit its peak. The Hudson River Presbytery admonished the Reverend Marshall L. Smith of Protestant Union Church in Pocantico Hills for being "a disturber of the peace and unity of the church" when he married Governor Rockefeller and Mrs. Murphy at the home of Laurence Rockefeller. Smith, appearing before the Presbytery at White Plains, New York, confessed his "deep regret" for having violated the Presbyterian Church's requirement of a one-year waiting period before divorced persons may be married.

Moreover, letter writers were unremitting in their outrage. In a dispatch from Washington by Warren Weaver, Jr., the *New York Times* of May 26 reported the public reaction as seen by Republican Congressmen from New York. Weaver wrote:

> If Congressional mail accurately mirrors public sentiment, Governor Rockefeller's remarriage appears to have been a political disaster.
>
> Letters on the subject to New York Republicans are not particularly impressive by their numbers. A sampling of members of Congress and political leaders indicates the total received in Washington in the last three weeks can be few more than 1,000.
>
> What is impressive is the virtual unanimity of opinion expressed by the writers. With exceptions averaging less than 1 per cent, the letters are critical. . . .
>
> A random selection of several hundred letters received by one Republican—a strong political supporter of Mr. Rockefeller—indicates that few of them are coming from cranks. They are carefully written, clearly expressed and sincere.
>
> Almost all of them were written by women. . . .

Weaver quoted one choice letter from New York City as follows: "I am a staunch Republican and a Protestant, but I'd even sink to voting for Kennedy if Rockefeller runs, and I don't know a single female who doesn't say the same thing." Moreover, this stream of letters to Washington was puny when compared with the torrent of written complaint mailed into Rockefeller's own offices in New York City and Albany. Because the letter writer is habitually a complainer, the mailbag is not always a good barometer of public opinion. It was in this case, however.

Republican politicians spent the month of May asking both party workers and rank-and-file voters their reaction to the marriage. What they found shocked them. Typical of the politicians' own findings is this private letter by a member of the Republican National Committee who happened to be one of Rockefeller's closest friends and most enthusiastic supporters outside New York:

> Since his marriage . . . I have had hundreds of conversations with different people in different sections of the country. A very small percentage of the people have indicated that they felt his marriage made no difference. An overwhelming percentage of the people have been very definite in their statements that they could not support him for the nomination, and if he were the nominee, would not vote for him. What percentage of these people were Rockefeller supporters a year ago, I cannot answer. Many of them were. The female of the species seems to be a little more definite in this feeling than the male. However, there is not too much difference. . . . Does time change these reactions, or will this continue to be the feeling of the people? This, I cannot answer.

This last note of doubt was the vestige of hope, however frail it might be, still clung to by ardent Rockefeller supporters. But most Republican politicians, including a good many erstwhile Rockefeller men, believed the Governor was dead. This analysis was bolstered when the first post-marriage Gallup Poll showed that for the first time Rockefeller had slipped behind Goldwater as top Presidential choice of Republican voters. The last premarriage poll, showing 43 percent for Rockefeller and 26 percent for Goldwater, was very nearly reversed by the postmarriage results giving Goldwater 40 percent and Rockefeller 29 percent. In an age when politicians depend more upon public opinion polls than their own instincts, this was conclusive evidence indeed of Rockefeller's fall.

Why did the politicians so badly underestimate the probable effect of the remarriage? More to the point, why was the reaction so violent?

It's safe to say that Republican leaders, including Rockefeller himself, were badly misled by the relatively mild reaction to the Governor's divorce some fifteen months earlier. Divorce has become part of the American way of life, not some exotic practice of the gay and the rich. Public opinion surveys in New York State by both parties during the 1962 gubernatorial campaign showed a bare minimum of resentment against Rockefeller because of the divorce. Divorce touches almost every family sooner or later—and, quite likely, the divorced person remarries sooner or later. Why then, reasoned the politicians, wouldn't the public be as tolerant about the remarriage as it was about the divorce? The flaw in this logic was a matter of time—to be specific, a matter of one month elapsing between Mrs. Murphy's divorce decree and her marriage to the Governor. There was an involuntary sense of revulsion that swept across the country, a feeling that here was something tawdry and shameful. The quick remarriage by Mrs. Murphy confirmed the suspicions and rumors about "the other woman."

A further clue about why the reaction was so intense is the fact women reacted much more strongly than men. Many of these women insisted that they were not really concerned at all with divorce and remarriage but rather with the fate of Happy Rockefeller's four young children. The question of custody of the Murphy children, a boy and three girls ranging in age from three to twelve, was not settled before the Murphy divorce. This was the unforgivable aspect of the entire business, many women asserted. Taking this at face value, some Rockefeller supporters provided an after-the-fact judgment that the Governor could have cut his political losses considerably if he had only delayed the wedding until the custody question was settled.

Perhaps. But all this professed concern about the Murphy

children probably wasn't the real source of outrage for so
many millions of women. This was the familiar case of the
man marrying young, raising a family, watching his children
grow up and become parents in their own right, and then
noticing that his wife has aged much more rapidly than he
and isn't quite able to keep up with him. Enter the other
woman. It is a common enough chain of events in modern
life, but usually is seen only on a private, personal basis. The
great statesmen of the world seldom pamper their own desires for personal happiness. Rockefeller was the exception.
And it is not exaggeration to say that millions of American
wives saw the publicity given Rockefeller's divorce and remarriage as tantamount to public approval of this sort of
thing—a direct threat to their own personal happiness. What
if their own husband should get the same idea in a few years?
This is not mere speculation. Politicians of both parties, inclined to take a tolerant view of Rockefeller's conduct, were
amazed to find their own wives—even the most sophisticated
of them—as outraged as the good ladies in Bible Belt church
sewing circles.

Not even this fully explains the intensity of the public
reaction and the totality of Rockefeller's collapse. Given the
many unfortunate aspects of the remarriage, a really strong
political leader might well have weathered the storm. The
fact is that the Rockefeller campaign crumpled instantly
under the wave of public indignation. Front runner though
he was, Rockefeller was a politician with vulnerable weak
spots. The fiscal crisis and Liquor Authority scandal in his
own state hadn't helped his standing among party leaders
elsewhere. His recent campaigning efforts had been drab.
Because of his refusal to accept firm commitments of support
from politicians before his remarriage, Rockefeller had no
established organization (outside New York, that is) who
would loyally rally to his side in this moment of crisis. For

all of these reasons, Rockefeller was wobbly enough to be felled by one deadly missile.

However, the dramatic fall of Rockefeller cannot be attributed solely to the Governor's personal and political problems. It had a deeper meaning from the standpoint of the Republican Party. Rockefeller had failed completely during more than two years of trying to unite the party's progressive and conservative wings under his leadership.

If there had been neither remarriage nor some political catastrophe of similar magnitude, a good many conservatives would have backed Rockefeller at the National Convention and—under urging from Goldwater—all but the most doctrinaire and fanatic of party workers would have licked stamps and knocked on doors in Rockefeller's behalf during the fall campaign. But this amount of success by Rockefeller in winning the confidence of the Republican right did not constitute reconciliation of the party's two wings. Rather, the especially violent reaction to the remarriage by rank-and-file conservatives in the party shows they were just tolerating Rockefeller—willing to accept him as nominee perhaps, but hoping and praying for some miracle that would keep him from the nomination. It is not exactly a coincidence that the moral indignation about the remarriage seemed strongest among conservatives, who were delighted at Rockefeller's political discomfiture. The fact is that all those many months of "I am a Republican" talk and attempts to blur liberal-conservative distinctions in the party had gained Rockefeller very little. The reaction to the remarriage proved that he still remained a liberal Easterner much to be feared and suspected in the minds of thousands of party workers west of the Hudson River.

What Rockefeller's missionary work with the conservative wing did accomplish, however, was to erode his standing with the party's progressives. Perhaps the most remarkable aspect of the public reaction was the lack of spirited defense of the Governor outside his personal organization in New York. To be sure, no politician ever likes to risk his neck for another politician on a touchy issue, particularly a touchy moral issue. Yet if Rockefeller really had been the unchallenged and vigorous leader of Republican progressivism, he might have been blessed with enthusiastic stands in his defense by such militant Republican liberals as Senator Clifford Case of New Jersey and Senator John Sherman Cooper of Kentucky. Instead, when Rockefeller fell, his fellow liberals in the party didn't try to pick him up. They looked elsewhere —some with secret gratification—to find a new leader. Many looked to George Romney, a few to Richard Nixon, a very few to William Scranton. But hardly anybody expressed a desire to die on the barricades for Nelson Rockefeller.

This was indeed a sad harvest for all those months of politicking within the party. Rockefeller had detached himself from the Republican left without attaching himself to the Republican right. Instead of coalescing divergent elements in the party, he found himself suffering the worst of two political worlds when the great personal crisis in his life came.

XI

★ ★

Goldwater Takes the Lead

Before dinner actually was served at the thousand-dollar-a-plate testimonial for Barry Goldwater in Washington on the night of May 9, 1963, Senator Gordon Allott of Colorado beckoned a reporter over to his table. Flanking him were Governor John Love and Senator Peter Dominick, two up-and-coming Colorado Republicans who had been elected to statewide office for the first time in 1962.

"You might be interested to know," Allott told the reporter, "that we've just about decided I'm going to run."

"Run for what?" asked the reporter.

"Why, run for President, of course," replied the beaming Allott. "Isn't everybody?"

It seemed like it. Allott was not the first favorite son candidate for President. Nor did he figure to be the last. Partly as a result of the Draft Goldwater forces' attempt to stop Rockefeller, favorite son possibilities had been popping up all spring. Now, with Rockefeller fallen, there seemed to be a danger they would emerge in epidemic proportions.

Ray Bliss, Ohio's shrewd Republican state chairman, was passing the word that either Governor James Rhodes or Representative Robert Taft, Jr., would be a favorite son candidate from Ohio. There was serious talk about Senators Clifford Case of New Jersey and Leverett Saltonstall of Massachusetts going into the convention as favorite sons.

Senator Margaret Chase Smith made gestures as Maine's "favorite daughter" candidate. If they weren't bona fide Presidential aspirants by convention time, Scranton and Romney figured to be at least favorite son candidates from Pennsylvania and Michigan (though each protested in early May of 1963 that he didn't want his name to go before the National Convention even on a favorite son basis).

Furthermore, the epidemic of favorite sons was infecting some states whose Presidential primary elections had been traditional battlegrounds for White House hopefuls of both parties—a development that had the tacit approval of top party leaders, including Representative William Miller, the national chairman. Just a year earlier, Miller was rejoicing about an expected surplus of Presidential candidates competing in primaries to give the Republicans the same kind of newspaper publicity that the Democrats enjoyed in 1960 when John F. Kennedy was winning the nomination by fighting it out in seven primary elections. (With the nomination a foregone conclusion for Nixon, the Republicans had no such publicity opportunity that year.) But Miller was having second thoughts in May, 1963, because of Rockefeller's remarriage. Miller felt the remarriage threatened to rekindle such heated factional passions in the party between progressives and conservatives that it might be just as well if Rockefeller and all other Presidential possibilities stayed out of the primaries. The best way to prevent primary struggles? Put a favorite son in each of the habitual battleground states. Even before the remarriage, Wisconsin Republican leaders posted an "outsiders not wanted" sign by promoting the favorite son candidacy of Representative John Byrnes. Some influential Republicans in New Hampshire were urging Senator Norris Cotton to enter the first-in-the-nation primary there on March 10, 1964, keeping away serious Presidential hopefuls. Almost all the leaders of California's faction-riddled Republican Party wanted a favorite son candidate to keep outsiders out of their climactic primary on June 7, just before convention time, though the Californians characteristically had at least a half dozen Republicans who wanted to be the favorite son.

From a superficial viewpoint, it seemed in May, 1963, that favorite sons might well be the only names placed formally in nomination at the 1964 convention. Nixon was then a forgotten man. Whenever anybody bothered to ask either of them, Romney and Scranton would again deny any desire to run for President in 1964. As the full impact of Rockefeller's remarriage became clear, politicians began to doubt whether the Governor would become an active candidate. Their reasoning: if Rockefeller wouldn't try in 1960 when he was a bright new figure in the party with an outside chance to topple Nixon, why try now when plagued with an apparently insurmountable political handicap? That left Goldwater, who had passed Rockefeller in the Gallup Poll but could not quite be classed as a legitimate front runner in early May. The Senator still had no desire for either the torture of a Presidential campaign or the misery of filling that great office. Less than a week after the Rockefeller wedding, a friend told Goldwater that now, for the first time, he really had a chance to become the party nominee. The Senator's face clouded immediately. "Don't say that," he asked. "Please don't say that."

This complete vacuum at the top of the Republican Party for the first time since 1940 bemused some fairly experienced party leaders into believing that the 1964 convention might be a unique experience—no active candidates but a dozen, perhaps two dozen, favorite sons to choose from. An honest-to-goodness favorite son might be chosen for the first time since the nomination of James Garfield in 1880.

But the older heads in the party tended more to agree with the private analysis of Pennsylvania's canny Senator Hugh Scott, national chairman during Dewey's 1948 campaign and a member of Nixon's five-man strategy board in the 1960 campaign. Scott believed the confusion would disappear early that summer, certainly no later than August 1. He assumed that party leaders and party contributors from major industrial states east of the Mississippi—New York, Pennsylvania, Michigan, Ohio, and perhaps Illinois—would get together that summer to select the nominee. It might be Rockefeller if the furor over the remarriage seemed to be dissipating. If not, it probably would go to Romney or Scranton. Scott still ruled out the possibility of Goldwater's nomination. A good many of the party's old pros agreed with the Scott thesis.

The Scott thesis was wrong in detail and timing, mainly because he grossly underestimated Goldwater's potential strength. Yet, the cagey Pennsylvania politician was absolutely correct in predicting that the depth of confusion prevailing in early May, 1963, would not last for long. Political nature abhors a vacuum. Somebody was certain to try to move into it. That first try came quickly, from George Wilcken Romney of Michigan.

Actually, Romney's Presidential boomlet began the latter part of April, when nobody was certain whether Rockefeller would marry Mrs. Murphy, and few believed that the remarriage would hurt him badly. Never constructed of very sturdy stuff, the Romney boomlet was fueled chiefly by rumors—warmed-over rumors, in fact. In late April, a large number of top-level Republican politicians were peddling the story that General Eisenhower had privately designated Romney as his choice for President (a report that had been circulated from time to time ever since the 1960 election). This story went on to add that Nixon and Leonard Hall, the old pro from Long Island, also were moving into Romney's corner.[1]

[1] The Eisenhower-for-Romney reports triggered a long succession of rumors and newspaper stories speculating on the General's choice for the nomination. An equally long succession of reports about where Hall would land also was launched at this time.

Inevitably, the rumor found its way into print—in no less a showcase than the front page of the *New York Times*. In the May 2 edition, a Washington dispatch by Tom Wicker quoted "informed Republican sources" as revealing that Romney "was cooperating with the plans of some close associates of former President Eisenhower and Richard M. Nixon." Especially, the *Times* dispatch mentioned Hall and J. Clifford Folger, a Washington, D.C., financier and Nixon's chief fund raiser. Wicker added:

> Republican sources report that the Governor is hopeful of winning the nomination. But he is described as unwilling to appear at this time to be seeking it, and wary of drawing the fire of other candidates and hostile elements in the party. Mr. Folger and Mr. Hall appear to be emulating President Eisenhower, who has privately expressed great interest in Gov. Romney's candidacy in 1964. . . .
>
> . . . sources said Mr. Hall, Mr. Folger and other important backers of Gen. Eisenhower and Mr. Nixon had settled on Gov. Romney as the best possibility for 1964. Romney sentiment is reported to be particularly strong among the National Citizens Committee, an affluent and influential Republican group that was organized last year.[2]

Though exaggerated and premature, both the rumors and the *Times* dispatch contained a rather large germ of truth.

Eisenhower, who was acutely sensitive to criticism during his long career of public service, had never forgiven Rockefeller or Goldwater for public attacks on his administration. In his fight for a tough defense plank in the 1960 national platform, Rockefeller had suggested that Eisenhower's cost-consciousness on defense threatened to turn the United States into a second-class military power. Goldwater had called the Eisenhower Administration the "dime store New Deal" because it proposed watered-down versions of liberal

---

[2] It will be remembered that back in July, 1962, both Rockefeller and Goldwater were concerned that the Citizens Committee could become a launching pad for Romney. See page 104.

Democratic welfare legislation. Neither man maintained a
warm relationship with the General (even though Rockefeller
had served twice in his administration, first as Under Secretary of Health, Education and Welfare, and later as a special
assistant for cold war strategy). There's not much doubt that
some of the biting personal criticism of Eisenhower frequently unleashed by both Rockefeller and Goldwater found
its way back to Gettysburg.

Given the fact that Eisenhower wasn't rapturous about
either Rockefeller or Goldwater, who then would his choice
be in the spring of 1963? Perhaps Scranton. As a Pennsylvania voter and taxpayer, Eisenhower had built up an avun-
cular relationship with Scranton, admonishing him in 1962
that "duty" impelled him to run for Governor. But the General accepted at face value Scranton's plea that he wanted to
serve out his full four-year term as Governor ending in 1967
and had no interest whatever in the Presidency.[3]

So, it was natural that Eisenhower should turn to Romney,
the other bright new face emerging from the 1962 elections.
In many ways, Romney was peculiarly suited to Eisenhower.
The General could nod his head approvingly at Romney's
denunciation of big labor, big business, and big government. Moreover, Romney's nebulous goal of turning the Republican Party into a "citizens' party" wasn't too far from
what Eisenhower had been saying for years.

But none of this meant that Eisenhower had singled out
Romney as his final choice for the Presidency or was promoting his candidacy around the country. Never too realistic or
explicit in his political concepts, the General envisioned a
good-natured free-for-all at the National Convention with

[3] Returning to Gettysburg on May 1, 1963, after a four-month vacation
in Palm Springs, California, Eisenhower told the Associated Press: "I see by
the papers that Governor Scranton has absolutely removed himself as a
candidate next year." The statement revealed the General's absolute ingenu-
ousness in matters political.

Romney just one of many clean-cut and dynamic Republicans grappling for the big prize. Eisenhower had no intention of making any endorsement. Nor were the more sophisticated politicians—Nixon, Hall, and Folger—ready to make their move in May, 1963. They could be friendly to Romney, but it was much too early for them to endorse anyone.

However, gossamer rumors were not the sole ingredient of the Romney boomlet. Romney was helping it along himself. For all his protestations that he desired only to stay in Lansing and run the state of Michigan, Romney began to poke into the national political wars once April Fools' Day was passed. April 1 was the date of the statewide referendum on the new Michigan Constitution, Romney's pet project since his days as founder of Citizens for Michigan before he ventured into partisan politics. Despite open opposition from the Michigan Democratic Party and its allies in organized labor and despite clandestine (but more dangerous) opposition from Old Guard Republican leaders in rural counties, the Romney Constitution was approved by an 810,180 to 799,420 vote. This expression of confidence from Michigan voters, in itself a help to Romney's national prestige, freed the Governor for out-of-state speaking chores.[4]

Just three days after the vote on the State Constitution, Romney traveled down to Chicago to address the National Association of Broadcasters. Aiming to please, Romney gave the radio and television station owners exactly what they wanted to hear: a blistering denunciation of Newton Minow, Kennedy-appointed chairman of the Federal Communica-

---

[4] As an avowed noncandidate, Romney naturally enough professed disinterest in the impact of the Constitutional referendum on his own political career. He told a new conference in Lansing on April 2: "I'm not concerned about the impact of the vote on any one individual. I am deeply concerned about its impact on the state. My concern is Michigan. I got into this to do what I could to solve Michigan's problems. My position on that is unchanged. The talk of national office comes from others, not me." However, some key members on Romney's staff were deeply concerned about the referendum's national impact.

tions Commission and archcritic of the broadcasting industry. But the Governor also tossed in a generous helping of
Economic Romneyism. "There appears to be absent from
the thinking of those who are responsible for direction of
governmental power in this country the principle of competition," Romney declared. The broadcasters loved it.

A month later, Romney was ready for the speech to the
National Press Club in Washington that is a must for any
Presidential candidate, announced or unannounced. Motel
owner J. Willard Marriott and his wife, longtime friends of
Romney and generous contributors to the Republican cause,
took advantage of the Governor's visit to throw a party for
him in their Washington home on May 2. Some three hundred
Republican businessmen from the Washington metropolitan
area were invited. Even more interesting, Len Hall and Cliff
Folger helped the Marriotts plan the affair.

The Washington visit was an unmarred triumph for Romney. The *New York Times*'s implication that the Marriotts'
party was a launching device for his candidacy gave Romney
the opportunity to hold a Washington press conference to
deny it ("I want to keep a purely private affair from turning
into something it isn't intended to be," he said. "I am not a
candidate for President, and I am not going to become one").
The epitome of the dynamic American businessman-states-
man, Romney was a hit at his impromptu press conference,
at the Marriotts' party, and at the Press Club speech. Economic Romneyism and Political Romneyism sounded particularly exciting to listeners exposed to the Governor for
the first time.

It was natural that the Romney boomlet picked up in intensity after the Rockefeller wedding. And Romney was right
back flying to Washington before the memory of his first
visit was dim, this time for the thousand-dollar-a-plate Goldwater testimonial on May 9. His speech there was short,
punchy, and—unusual for Romney—partisan. There was

some thought that he had stolen the show from Goldwater.

Apart from rumors of support from Eisenhower and Romney's Lansing-to-Washington commuting, there was some solid political logic behind the Romney boomlet. In early May, most of the party's leaders still could not stomach the idea of anyone as far over to the right as Goldwater as Republican nominee even if the polls showed him now to be the choice of rank-and-file Republicans. The party leaders still adhered to the strategy followed by the party since 1940: pick somebody liberal enough to collect independent and errant Democratic votes. With Rockefeller in a state of political disrepair, the only nationally known Republican who met these qualifications was Romney. The Gallup Poll showed him slowly rising as a Presidential choice of Republican voters—from 13 percent in April to 16 percent in early May to 18 percent in mid-May. It was indeed a remarkable amount of public support for a brand-new figure in national politics.

True enough, Romney had some liabilities. The fact that he was born in Mexico of United States parents might raise the question whether he was a "natural-born" citizen, a Constitutional requirement for the Presidency. His Mormon religion was certainly no asset, and might even lose votes among Negroes because of the Negrophobic tendencies of official Mormon policy. A good many regular Republicans still distrusted Political Romneyism—his preachments about citizens' participation in politics and his condemnation of the existing party structure.

But Romney was one Governor who did not seem to be experiencing the postelection fiscal crisis that had so troubled Rockefeller in both 1959 and 1963 and now was afflicting Scranton. Besides winning adoption of the new Constitution in the referendum, Romney had escaped the deadlock that had been predicted to develop between the Governor and the rural conservative Republicans who run the Michigan Legislature. Romney, living up to his image of a man of action and a leader, had got most of what he wanted from the Legislature. This record unquestionably played some part in generating the Romney boomlet. What the national political leaders failed to notice was the ominous prospect of a showdown in the fall, when Romney's still unwritten tax program would go before the Legislature.

If the politicians in Washington weren't overly concerned with Romney's unfinished tax problems, some of his most important supporters back in Michigan certainly were. The *Detroit News* spelled this out in a blistering editorial on May 3 entitled "George—Come Home." It began:

> For what it's worth, our advice to Gov. Romney after that Washington coming-out party on the Republican Presidential circuit is:
> "Come home, George, and let's get on with the chores."
> . . . This White House talk is heady stuff for a governor in office only five months. It's all right for him to listen. To believe it could be fatal. It may even be intended that way.

After a few more paragraphs, the *News* editorial got down to brass tacks:

> Ahead of Gov. Romney lies a grinding tax reform session of the Legislature, the reorganization of a government made lopsided by one party rule, the implementation of a new Constitution. Here is challenge in plenty to test a man for any political future.[5]

> His way to solid accomplishment wouldn't be smoothed by demonstrations of national partisanship while pleading for political cooperation at home. His present posture is that of a governor elected by Republicans, Democrats and independents weary of excessive partisanship in a muddled state.
> Gov. Romney has said forcefully that he will not be a seeker of the 1964 Republican Presidential nomination. That isn't

---

[5] "One party rule" refers to fourteen unbroken years of Democratic control over the Governor's office. Republicans controlled both houses of the Legislature during this entire period, however.

enough. He should avoid even the possibility of being confused with one. . . .

We are proud as always to have a native son talked about for the Presidency. But there can't be a future for Gov. Romney without a present. For the present we think he'd be better off avoiding political jamborees in the big time and stick to his homework.

Almost every politician in the state of Michigan believed this editorial was either written or inspired by Martin Hayden, editor of the *News*. The relationship of Romney to Hayden and the *News* was by no means a casual one. They had been among Romney's earliest and most devoted supporters for Governor. What's more, the editorial of May 3 reflected a substantial body of Republican thinking back in Michigan. Apart from the unfinished tax business ahead, Michigan Republicans desperately wanted Romney to seek another two-year term as Governor in 1964. No other Republican was likely to beat the Democratic candidate, and the party was not willing to relinquish the Governor's office again after only two years of possession.

The attitude of Martin Hayden and other Romney supporters back in Michigan was not lost on the Governor. It was obvious that he could pursue his Presidential ambitions only at the risk of losing his home front support. The fact is that little was heard of Romney outside of Michigan after his May 9 appearance in Washington. And with that, the Romney boomlet promptly collapsed. It was a vaporous thing, more a state of mind than a grass roots movement or a grand design by professional politicians. To have kept it rolling, Romney would have had to keep himself in the public eye with personal tours throughout the summer and fall of 1963. This he did not do.

If he had, the complexion of the fight for the 1964 nomination might well have taken a far different course. But there is no certainty that Romney would have moved into the

Rockefeller vacuum if he had tried. Even more than Rockefeller, Romney was best at first glance. He didn't wear well.
He would have had a severe handicap in lack of enthusiastic
support from his home state party. And he would have faced
a determined and formidable antagonist named Barry Goldwater.

A good part of Goldwater's hostility toward Romney was
visceral rather than intellectual. Goldwater did give friends
reasons for it—for instance, Romney's preference for volunteer citizens over the regular party organization. But Goldwater generally was not given to personal feuding just
because of a difference over policy. Rather, something deep
within Romney's nature seemed to repel Goldwater. Nor did
he keep it a secret. Publicly and privately, he referred to
Romney as "just another Wendell Willkie" and quipped that
"the Republican Party can't afford more than one Eisenhower
in a generation."[6]

The fact that Barry Goldwater was not enamored of
George Romney is not just a matter of backstairs political
gossip. In those days, Goldwater used to say privately that
he probably wasn't strong enough to get the nomination himself, but did have enough power to veto an undesirable.
This was correct. Moreover, Goldwater left little doubt he
would do all in his power to veto Romney even if it forced
him to run for the nomination himself.

Republicans in Michigan reported that Romney recipro-
cated Goldwater's disregard. But during that brief Romney
boomlet, the Governor did make one fleeting effort to ingratiate himself with Goldwater. The result was a failure of
almost comical proportions.

Before flying to Washington for his May 2 visit, Romney

[6] Whatever the true depth of their attachment to Romney, Eisenhower
and his associates did not look kindly upon this gratuitous anti-Eisenhower
slur from Goldwater. The first definite sign that Goldwater was getting
serious about the Presidency came during the summer of 1963 when he began
resisting the impulse to insult the General.

had telephoned ahead to ask for an appointment with Goldwater. It was granted. Assuming that Romney wanted a private chat, neither Goldwater nor his staff mentioned the meeting to news media. Consequently, Goldwater's office staff was amazed to find a cluster of newspaper reporters waiting for Romney at the Goldwater office on the fourth floor of the Old Senate Office Building. Goldwater assumed that Romney had notified the reporters in an effort to imply to the public that he and the Senator had reached some meeting of minds. Goldwater, who began his private chat with Romney upset over the summoning of the newspaper reporters, wasn't mollified by Romney's words. Implausibly, the Governor said exactly what would be certain to irritate Goldwater. He began lecturing the Senator on a chief component of Political Romneyism: the need for citizens' participation in politics. Goldwater later confided he hadn't the slightest idea what Romney was talking about. Their meeting was a case of two ships passing in the night.

The cleavage between the two leaders was still further widened a week later when Romney returned to Washington for Goldwater's thousand-dollar-a-plate testimonial. When Romney entered the grand ballroom of the Sheraton-Park about fifteen minutes before the dinner began, press photographers immediately swarmed about him asking him to pose for photographs with Goldwater. Romney gruffly brushed them off. The word spread about the ballroom, and eventually reached Goldwater that Romney didn't want to be photographed with him. When the photographers tried again later in the evening, Romney did consent. But the damage had been done.

One further incident in connection with that dinner reinforced Goldwater's suspicions that what he called the "Eastern Establishment"—an amorphous power grouping of politicians and financiers—was plotting to give the nomination to Romney. Goldwater and his staff believed they had a commitment from H. Clifford Folger, Nixon's chief money-man, to take care of a large number of thousand-dollar tickets for the testimonial. But Folger never followed through with any help. Nor did he show up for the dinner itself. The fact that rumors and published reports had been linking Folger with Romney (exaggerated and premature though that alleged link was) raised suspicions by Goldwater of a general "Eastern" plot against him.

Indeed, now that Rockefeller had damaged himself so badly because of his remarriage, Goldwater believed that the "Eastern Establishment" would make an all-out assault to keep the nomination from going to either Rockefeller or himself. Goldwater never believed that this power group favored Rockefeller.[7] The Senator saw the party splitting off into two camps: Rockefeller-Goldwater and Eisenhower-Nixon-Romney.

This was not so wild a concept as it seems in retrospect. One party leader actually predicted privately that if Rockefeller was stopped short of the nomination, as now seemed likely, he would try to throw the New York delegation and any other support he had retained to Goldwater rather than permit Romney to get the nomination.

Goldwater and this party leader committed two basic errors. They believed the personal friendship that had been building between Rockefeller and Goldwater was really strong enough to bridge the immense doctrinal gap between them. They also assumed that Rockefeller would still be interested in trying to bridge that gap now that he no longer was front runner for the nomination.

Other political developments, which then seemed to be less important than the short-lived but noisy Romney boomlet,

[7] Accepting Rockefeller's advocacy of a balanced budget at face value at this time, Goldwater suspected that the big Eastern money interests would try to stop Rockefeller because they feared he would cut down on foreign aid. Goldwater was correct in perceiving this hostility from the money interests, but it had nothing to do with foreign aid.

accompanied the Rockefeller remarriage in the spring of 1963.

May 2, the date for Romney's Washington debut in Presidential politics, also marked Richard M. Nixon's announcement that he was forsaking his native California to become a Wall Street lawyer. Almost exactly six months after the conclusion of his unsuccessful campaign to become Governor of California, he was moving his wife and two daughters to an apartment at 810 Fifth Avenue in Manhattan (right next door to Governor Rockefeller's apartment at 812 Fifth Avenue). It was scarcely a surprise. After Nixon's loss to Kennedy in 1960, there had been much speculation among Republicans that Nixon would follow Thomas E. Dewey's example by entering a lucrative law practice in New York. The speculation was just two years premature. Nixon, who had been building up a bankroll through his writing ever since the 1960 election, was now going to make big money as a lawyer.

But it was not entirely the enticement of Wall Street money and the utter boredom he found in Los Angeles life that impelled Nixon eastward. Though realistic enough to recognize that the chances did not seem to be favorable, Nixon had not totally abandoned his White House dreams. In the spring of 1963, he probably was thinking more in terms of 1968 than of 1964 for a second Presidential bid. Whenever that bid might come, however, Nixon had decided that it would better be launched from New York City than from Los Angeles.

He said as much to close California friends before his move east. He told them that because news travels east-to-west across the continent and not west-to-east, a private citizen couldn't exercise anywhere near the influence and impact in Los Angeles that he might in New York. He recognized that he would be abandoning a political base by becoming an immigrant in New York. But by 1963, California hadn't become much of a political base for Nixon. The aftermath of his defeat for Governor was absolute chaos in the never-orderly ranks of California Republicans. With his own authority there understandably diminished by his defeat, Nixon was in no position to cope with the insistent thrust of militant right-wingers.[8]

Events that seemed even less pertinent to the fight for the 1964 nomination than Nixon's cross-country move were taking place during May at Harrisburg, Pennsylvania.

National interest in Governor Scranton, which always had been markedly less than the interest in Romney, gradually subsided from the high point of his landslide election in November, 1962. One reason was the way Scranton managed to sound so much more convincing than Romney in his disavowals of Presidential ambitions. Another reason was the fact that Scranton, who needed national exposure even more than Romney, flatly refused to accept the choice invitations that might have dented his national anonymity. In April alone, he turned down to bid to address the Young Republicans' national convention in San Francisco and a particularly coveted invitation to be Republican representative at the annual Gridiron Club dinner in Washington. But the biggest reason for the flagging interest in Scranton may have been his troubles on the home front.

When political correspondents from Washington would make the quick trip up to Harrisburg for an interview with Scranton, the Governor inevitably would point to the overwhelming problems he was facing in Pennsylvania, and declare he wouldn't have run for this trouble spot if he really had Presidential ambitions. He had a point. While Romney seemed to be sailing along in Michigan during his first few months in office, Scranton was in real trouble. By winning the election, he had inherited a fiscal crisis. His solution was

---

[8] However, many California Republicans, including some staunch Nixon men, were angry that Nixon left the state without first trying to restore order to the party there.

a highly unpopular tax increase package including a boost
in the four-cent state sales tax to five cents. In an act of poli-
tics-as-usual, Democratic members of the Legislature declared they would not give the tax program a single vote. Because Republicans held wafer-thin control of both the House
and Senate, a defection of only two or three Republicans in
either chamber would kill Scranton's program. The odds
were against Scranton winning that kind of loyalty from Old
Guard Republicans (some of whom had been dragooned into
his nomination a year earlier).

But Scranton slowly and carefully built up support. On
May 14 came the breakthrough. The House passed the program with only one defection. The Senate was tougher. It
waited until May 17 to pass his package by a 27 to 23 tally.
It was perfect party-line voting with no defection from either
party.

Scranton's low-keyed conciliatory tactics in getting the tax
package passed reflect his entire approach to politics. When
asked at his May 15 press conference about the lone Republican defector in the House vote, Scranton resisted the temp-
tation to revile this renegade (a gentleman named Enos H.
Horst). Instead, the Governor said: "Representative Horst
told me that he had made a thoroughgoing survey of his own
particular district, and that the people there were opposed
to the 5 percent sales tax and therefore he would not vote for
it." There would be other votes where he would need Mr.
Horst's vote. Moreover, Scranton went more than halfway
when incipient trouble between the Governor's office and
Republican Senators threatened to derail the tax program in
the Senate. As soon as the House approved the tax hike, an
aide in the Governor's office was quoted as saying: "Once we
get 106 votes for the sales tax bill in the House, no Republican Senator would dare oppose the bill." Enraged, a number
of Republican Senators threatened to bottle the bill in the
Finance Committee. Scranton did not stand on ceremony but

instead paid an unusual visit to the Finance Committee while it was considering the tax program. He told the Senators that he had never made the objectionable statement, and that he was certain none of his aides had made it. In any case, the Governor continued, the statement is without foundation. That was enough to repair the bruised Senatorial feelings.

Passage of the Scranton tax program, though not widely noted outside the borders of Pennsylvania, unlocked the possibility of a Scranton campaign for the Presidency. For one thing, it averted a prestige-killing defeat in the Legislature that would have aborted any Presidential possibilities for him. For another, it lifted from Scranton the specter of fiscal crisis and the responsibility for major unfinished business ahead. Bill Scranton's worst legislative ordeal lay behind him. George Romney's lay ahead.

Though his great tax fight was behind him, Scranton's presence was felt only dimly across the country. Nixon, a displaced Californian in Gotham, seemed to be out of the running. Romney, his brief boomlet now but a memory, had retired to Lansing. Rockefeller was now a political cripple. But political nature still abhors a vacuum. And by the end of May, the startling fact was that Barry Goldwater, genuinely reluctant and amazed at the process himself, was filling the vacuum.

This was the phenomenon that such battle-seasoned veterans of the Republican wars as Senator Hugh Scott and Representative William Miller had been telling friends simply couldn't happen. Goldwater, the embodiment of the party's downtrodden conservative masses without even any of the liberal veneer that the sainted Robert A. Taft had acquired, was front runner for the nomination. On the surface, it might seem that Goldwater had forged in front by a process of elimination. The four Republican figures who in one degree or another were representative of Republican progressivism—Rockefeller, Romney, Nixon, and Scranton—were disqualified or impeded for one reason or another. But there was more to it than this. Transcendent, even historic, events were at work in pushing Mr. Conservative to the front of the Republican pack in the spring of 1963. Nor was this a totally involuntary, passive process. Though great political trends were on Goldwater's side at this time, human forces were helping accelerate those trends.

The work of the newly constituted National Draft Goldwater Committee was significant. When its existence had been formally revealed at the Mayflower Hotel press conference on April 8, Washington's political reporters were faintly condescending. But the committee was no head-in-the-cloud gaggle of conservative zealots. Indeed, with Rockefeller and his personal organization immobilized following his remarriage, the Draft Goldwater Committee was the only team in the field playing Presidential politics that spring. By the middle of May, National Chairman Miller and other top Republicans began to note this. Two instances of the Draft Goldwater Committee at work particularly made their mark on Miller.

One instance came during the eleventh annual National Republican Women's Conference in Washington on April 27. Miller observed that on the chair of each lady participant was a copy of a recent article in *U.S. News & World Report*, an exposition of the theoretical manner in which Barry Goldwater could defeat John F. Kennedy in November, 1964, by capturing the Solid South. That was the only Presidential literature distributed at the conference.[9]

The other instance came a short while later when Miller paid a routine political visit to Maine. He found that Cyril Joss, Mayor of Waterville, Maine, and an experienced politi-

[9] This was an interesting illustration of the Goldwater propaganda machine at work, but the good ladies at that April 27 meeting hardly needed convincing. Their war whoops when Goldwater appeared to address the conference were testimony to that.

cian who once worked on the staff of the Republican Congressional Campaign Committee, was quietly building up a Goldwater-for-President campaign organization in Maine. It was the first sign of honest-to-goodness political groundwork in behalf of any Presidential possibility that Miller had seen.

Propaganda and organization. These were the two chief activities of the National Draft Goldwater Committee under the day-to-day supervision of Clif White from ground-floor office space rented at 1025 Connecticut Avenue in high-rent midtown Washington. Besides Miller, other Republican leaders began to view the Draft Goldwater organization with new respect.

Moreover, Goldwater's hands-off attitude toward the Draft Goldwater Committee was not nearly so rigid and harsh as it seemed on the surface. He did live up to the letter of his promise not to cooperate with any Goldwater-for-President organization until he made up his mind about running for President in January, 1964. But this didn't preclude informal, indirect contacts between the Senator and 1025 Connecticut. Texan Peter O'Donnell, chairman of the Draft Goldwater Committee, was in frequent and intimate contact with Senator John Tower, his state's first Republican Senator since Reconstruction days. In turn, Tower was regarded as Goldwater's chief disciple in the Senate and consequently in constant contact with his mentor. Information from the Draft Goldwater Committee often flowed from O'Donnell to Tower to Goldwater. However, a more direct route was often used. Tony Smith, the Senator's press secretary and an increasingly close personal aide, gradually became acquainted with the top staff of the Draft Goldwater Committee. Vic Johnston, the Senator's informal political adviser, provided another link. To be sure, these makeshift arrangements were clumsy and just a little ridiculous. It's doubtful whether anyone would have minded very much if Goldwater maintained

direct contact with Peter O'Donnell and Clif White. In fact,
considering the grievous problems that were to arise some
nine months later, it would have been in the Senator's own
interests if he had become better acquainted with O'Donnell
and White and developed some confidence in their political
skills. At the time, however, leaders in the Draft Goldwater
Committee were quite content that Goldwater was fairly well
acquainted with their efforts and doing nothing to discourage
them.

The fact is that Goldwater's attitude toward seeking the
Presidency was changing significantly. He long ago had
discarded—and probably forgotten—his resolve to curtail
drastically his speaking engagements outside Arizona during
1963.[10] This signified no conscious decision on his part to
generate more national political support. It was simply a case
of his being constitutionally unable to turn down plaintive
requests for him to appear at the convention of the beauti-
cians or the hardwood lumber dealers. Just because he was
doing more cross-country stump speaking than any other
politician in America by itself signaled no Goldwater desire
for higher office. Goldwater did not start turning his personal
political corner until after Rockefeller dropped from the lead
after the wedding.

Goldwater was sincerely shocked at how badly Rockefeller
had been hurt by the marriage. But he was even more surprised when he saw himself, not Romney, taking over that
lead from Rockefeller. For the first time, he began to see his
own nomination as a real possibility. He talked to friends of
the latent power in the grass roots conservative movement
and wondered whether it might not be strong enough to
nominate—perhaps elect—its champion. Tony Smith and
other aides close to Goldwater began to perceive a subtle
softening taking place in his attitude. Perhaps the drum-
beating activities of the Draft Goldwater Committee served

[10] See page 76.

one of their intended purposes by encouraging Goldwater's own Presidential interest. More likely, however, it worked the other way around. Goldwater's less adamant stand generated greater efforts from his volunteer forces.

But the front position for so uncompromising a conservative as Barry Goldwater cannot really be explained in terms of the Draft Goldwater Committee's energies or the Senator's personal attitude toward making the race.

A clue to what really was happening may be found in an April postcard poll of delegates to the 1960 Republican National Convention conducted by *Congressional Quarterly,* the political news and research agency. Conducted well before speculation about Rockefeller's remarriage began, the poll revealed that 64.4 percent of the delegates responding to the inquiry believed Rockefeller would be the nominee, while only 26.4 percent predicted Goldwater would be selected.[11] That was their expectation but not their preference. This same poll showed that the 1960 delegates personally favored Goldwater over Rockefeller for the nomination, 46 percent to 34.5 percent.[12]

These figures are deeply significant. More than any convention since the 1920's, the 1960 National Convention's delegates reflected perennial party workers rather than volunteers loyal to one Presidential possibility or another. Because Nixon so obviously had the 1960 nomination sewed up,

---

[11] Ironically, the *Congressional Quarterly* poll was published under the headline "Poll of '60 Delegates Gives Rockefeller Nomination Edge" in the Washington *Post* of May 5—the same edition that revealed the news of the Governor's politically disastrous remarriage.

[12] Here are the full results of the postcard poll with replies from 1,045 out of 2,662 convention delegates.

Who do you think is likeliest to receive the 1964 Republican Presidential nomination? Rockefeller, 673; Goldwater, 276; Romney, 31; Scranton, 20; Nixon, 8; Senator Thruston Morton of Kentucky, 5; Governor Mark Hatfield of Oregon, 2; scattered or blank, 30.

If the 1964 Republican Convention were being held now and you were a delegate, whom would you personally favor for the Presidential nomination? Goldwater, 481; Rockefeller, 361; Romney, 45; Nixon, 22; Scranton, 18; Morton, 11; Hatfield, 8; scattered or blank, 99.

there were few fights over delegates in 1960. This meant that the perennial party workers tended to fill these largely ceremonial slots. The *Congressional Quarterly* poll reveals that these party workers were quite ready in April, 1963, to acquiesce in Rockefeller's nomination though they themselves preferred Goldwater. Harboring some of the defeatist complex in the wake of quadrennial National Convention victories by the less numerous progressive wing since 1940, these conservatives assumed that once again liberal-leaning party leaders would dictate the choice of a me-too candidate.

For these party workers then, Rockefeller's remarriage was an act of emancipation. Now there was a perfectly valid reason for repudiating Rockefeller. Now they could turn to Goldwater, whom they had wanted in the first place.

So Goldwater was in first place. But for him to stay there, it was essential that his supporters be able to demonstrate more convincingly that Goldwater really might be able to beat Kennedy in 1964 and certainly would run a better race against him than any other candidate. Otherwise, a liberal-leaning successor to Rockefeller (or possibly even Rockefeller himself) would be back to reclaim the lead from Goldwater.

The Southern victory formula enunciated by National Draft Goldwater Committee propaganda was a step in this direction. But some validation was needed to make it really believable. This validation came not from the imagination of the Draft Goldwater Committee strategists but from one of the great postwar social movements in the nation: the Negro revolution of 1963. This social revolt and the white reaction to it not only kept Goldwater in front through the summer and autumn but very nearly triggered another revolution—a political revolution within the Republican Party.

XII

★ ★

The White Man's Party

George Hinman of Binghamton, New York, attorney-at-law and member of the Republican National Committee, was as usual the picture of calm and urbanity on Saturday morning, June 22, 1963, as he entertained reporters in his suite at the Brown Palace Hotel in Denver, Colorado. Hinman had called a press conference to reassure newsmen covering the summer meeting of the Republican National Committee that the Rockefeller camp, bloody though it was, certainly was unbowed.[1] While acknowledging that Goldwater had gained an unspecified amount of ground and Rockefeller had lost an unspecified amount of ground since the Governor's wedding, Hinman declared: "Our conclusion is that the race is wide open." Then, noting that no candidate actually had announced for the Presidency, he smiled and murmured that "it's hard to tell which horse is ahead when there's nobody on the track."

In truth, however, Hinman was deeply disturbed about what he had seen in Denver that week. So were other members of the enormous New York entourage attending the National Committee meeting. So were some of the other Eastern Republicans at Denver. "There's an insanity in the air around

---

[1] The major piece of official business by this National Committee meeting was the selection of San Francisco as site for the 1964 National Convention. The only major opposition came from Chicago.

here," Hinman confided to a reporter the night before his
cheery press conference.

Hinman probably would have classed under the heading of
"insanity" the fact that Goldwater now seemed far in front
for the nomination and the fact that support for Rockefeller
had dwindled to the point of invisibility. Some of the New
York entourage—perhaps Hinman among them—did not
really recognize the extent of Goldwater's rise and Rockefeller's decline until they reached Denver. But what really
troubled Hinman was a development within the party much
deeper than the rise of Goldwater or the decline of Rockefeller. What was bothering Hinman and a good many others
at Denver was unmistakable signs that party leaders from
outside the industrialized states of the eastern seaboard were
seriously contemplating transforming the Republican Party
into the White Man's Party.

Telltale signs were abundant at Denver.

Item: During one closed-door luncheon session of Republican state chairmen at the Denver Hilton Hotel, two Southern
state chairmen carried on a boisterous conversation about
"niggers" and "nigger-lovers" while Negro waiters were serving lunch. "The amazing part of it was," an Eastern state
chairman recalled later, "that nobody criticized them for
doing it and only a few of us were uncomfortable."

Item: Some of the biggest headlines produced by the Denver meeting came from a press conference held by Wirt
Yerger, the fire-eating young segregationist who was Mississippi's Republican state chairman and head of the Republican Party's Association of Southern State Chairmen. Yerger
blandly accused Kennedy of fomenting that spring's racial
violence in the South in order to win the election.

Item: The "omnibus resolution" adopted by the National
Committee as a matter of routine came close to implicit support for Yerger's outrageous claim. The resolution's only pro-
vision dealing with civil rights condemned the Kennedy

Administration for "its failure to deal effectively with the problems of civil rights and to foster an atmosphere of understanding and good will in which racial conflict can be resolved." Though the nation then was embroiled in the worst racial crisis since the Civil War, the Republican National Committee officially had no word of support—not even a lukewarm word of support—for the Negro movement.

Item: A major address to the National Committee by Senator Gordon Allott of Colorado slurred over the question of civil rights, disposing of it with a cryptic reference to the need for preserving "a Federal Union in which the rights of the Federal Government, the states, and municipalities are backed and where they can respond to the conscience for the lawful desires of every group and race for equal-handed opportunity and justice." This was all the more remarkable in view of Allott's strong position for Negro rights over the years.

Even more revealing than these specific clues was the overriding mood of the Denver meeting. It was a mood of rebellion. Republican politicians from the low-population states of the West and South in effect were declaring their independence. They were tired of the Easterners' long hegemony. They were determined to seize party control, nominate Barry Goldwater for President, and draft the most conservative party platform since the 1920's. Moreover, these Southern and Western conservatives were determined to break from forceful support of civil rights, as spelled out in party platforms of recent years, and move to a neutralist stand no more favorable to the Negro position than the civil rights statement contained in the National Committee's "omnibus resolution" adopted in Denver.

Craig Truax, the vigorous, thirty-four-year-old Pennsylvania state chairman, perceived the mood at Denver soon after he arrived a day late because of an engagement in Pennsylvania. "This is absurd," Truax complained in private. "These people are talking about picking the nominee without regard to what we think. They talk about writing off Republican states like Pennsylvania and New York." Indeed, state chairmen and National Committee members from the South had suddenly pushed themselves into new prominence. For the first time, the Republican Party had its own Southern problem.

One nasty little incident at the Denver meeting reflected the tension. Fred A. Young, a battle-hardened little Italian-American politician who had stepped down as a state judge to replace Jud Morhouse as New York state chairman, was shocked by all the pro-Goldwater and anti-civil-rights talk at Denver. Outspoken, frank, and prone to mix obscenities with his political declarations, Young could not contain himself. When introduced to National Committeeman Tom Stagg of Louisiana at a cocktail party thrown by the Colorado State Republican Committee, Young blurted out to him: "Why don't you get some sense and quit _____ _____ off with Goldwater." Stagg, twice Young's size and a good twenty years younger, bristled with indignation. It was a tense moment, but Stagg did no more than express his resentment to Young in sharp tones.[2]

All this pointed to an unmistakable conclusion: A good many, perhaps a majority of the party's leaders, envisioned substantial political gold to be mined in the racial crisis by becoming in fact, though not in name, the White Man's Party. "Remember," one astute party worker said quietly over the breakfast table at Denver one morning, "this isn't South Africa. The white man outnumbers the Negro 9 to 1 in this country."

The sound of quasi-segregationist sentiments coming from the mouth of a "Black" Republican—a "Black" Republican

[2] This and similar indiscretions at Denver by Young helped ruin the weekend for Hinman, who was still trying to ingratiate Rockefeller among conservatives. Young's ingenuous conduct also turned his debut in politics into his farewell appearance. No more was seen of Young outside New York State until the next National Committee meeting the next January in Washington, where he obviously was under wraps.

from the North, at that—is not so strange as may seem. From the moment of its birth, the Republican Party has harbored an ambivalence on the question of the Negro.

True enough, opposition to slavery was not only a precept of the party but a key reason for its founding. But an anti-slavery man in the late 1850's was by no means pro-Negro. Apart from the New England abolitionists, most of the party's founders displayed a distinct streak of Negrophobia. Moreover, it was the Negrophobic Midwesterners, not abolitionist New Englanders, that made up the Republican Party's basic strength. Then as now, the true measure of rank-and-file party sentiment was to be found in the Midlands.

In the late 1850's, that sentiment was firmly antislavery—but antislavery for economic rather than humanitarian interests. The great national fight over the export of slavery into the Western territories was no academic question for the Midwestern farmer and artisan.

In the first place, Midwesterners from East of the Mississippi wanted to migrate beyond the great river to the Kansas and Nebraska territories. If this area were to be developed by slave-owning Southerners with the plantation system, there would be no place there for free white yeomen and mechanics from Illinois and Indiana.

In the second place, even those Illinois and Indiana yeomen and mechanics who had no intention of westward migration were genuinely afraid that their own states might be next. If slaves could be brought to Kansas and Nebraska, why not Illinois and Indiana? These fears were fanned by the rantings of Southern zealots, who became so exercised in extolling slavery as a positive good that they actually suggested the extension of their peculiar institution into every state of the Republic as a replacement for capitalistic "wage slavery."[3]

[3] In his infamous *Sociology for the South*, published in 1854, George Fitzhugh of Virginia declared that imposing slavery on the white laborer would

Thus, the prevailing racial sentiment in the Midwestern heartland of the Republican Party was fear of the Negro as a competition—not sympathy for him as a fellow mortal. The Midwest wanted no Negroes at all, not as slaves and not as free men (who would accept a lower wage than whites) either. Most of the Midwestern states flatly prohibited Negroes, slave or free, from entering their boundaries (the prohibition being written into state constitutions in many states). When "Bloody Kansas" finally came under Republican control, the State Legislature immediately prohibited immigration of all Negroes, free or slave.

Though his views were quite liberal and advanced for a Midwestern Republican of the late 1850's, Lincoln in many ways typified the party position.

In his famed June 26, 1857, political speech at Springfield, Illinois, Lincoln made it clear that he was all for segregation of the races—even to the point of shipping all Negroes off to Liberia.

> . . . separation of the races is the only perfect preventive of amalgamation. I have no right to say all the members of the Republican Party are in favor of this, nor to say that as a party they are in favor of it. There is nothing in their platform directly on the subject. But I can say a very large proportion of its members are for it, and that the chief plank in their platform—opposition to the spread of slavery—is most favorable to that separation.
>
> Such separation, if ever effected at all, must be effected by colonization. . . . Let us be brought to believe it is morally right, and at the same time favorable to, or at least not against, our interest to transfer the African to his native clime, and we shall find a way to do it, however great the task may be. The children of Israel, to such numbers as to include four hundred

---

relieve him "of many of the cares of household affairs, and protect and support him in sickness and old age, besides preventing the too great reduction of wages by redundancy of labor and free competition."

thousand fighting men, went out of Egyptian bondage in a body.[4]

This segregationist strain in Lincoln, thoroughly in tune with contemporary Illinois Republicanism, came up time and again during his 1858 campaign for the Senate against Stephen Douglas, the Democratic incumbent. Referring to a speech the night before in which Judge Douglas warned of race mixing, Lincoln told a Chicago audience on July 10:

> The Judge regales us with the terrible enormities that take place by the mixture of races; that the inferior race bears the superior down. Why, Judge, if we do not let them get together in the Territories, they won't mix there. I should say at least that is a self-evident truth.

If this left any room for doubt, Lincoln resolved it a week later. In a July 17 speech at Springfield, he declared: "What I would most desire would be the separation of the white and black races."

The Civil War and Lincoln's martyrdom radically changed the facade of Republicanism. Ironically, the claim today of liberal Republicans that theirs is the true civil rights party (or, as usually proclaimed in partisan oratory, the "Party of Lincoln") stems not from Lincoln but from the vindictive Reconstruction program of the postwar Radical Republicans who detested Lincoln. Only in these Reconstruction years was the Republican Party truly a civil rights party. But Wilfred E. Binkley, a historian generally sympathetic to the Republicans, pointed out that even these years of pro-Negro sentiment among the Republicans were tainted with hypocrisy. In *American Political Parties: Their Natural History*, Binkley

---

[4] The Great Emancipator never quite discarded his notion that foreign colonization could provide the best solution to the Negro question. In the midst of the Civil War, he intermittently tried to sell Negro leaders on colonization but never was successful. One plan to place a Negro colony in the Latin-American republic of New Granada (now Colombia) reached a rather advanced state but eventually fell through.

tells of the way an idealized Lincoln influenced postwar Republicans:

> The prestige attaching to the Emancipator for two genera-
> tions bound whites and blacks together in the compelling
> conviction of a common purpose and enthusiasm. Indeed many
> a Republican veteran who, upon receipt of the news of the
> Emancipation Proclamation, had flung down his musket and
> resolved never to fight to free "niggers," lived to sit among his
> comrades each autumn upon the platform, beaming with pride
> as the campaign orator pointed to those "battle-scarred heroes"
> who had "struck the shackles from four million slaves." There
> was just enough historical basis to make it difficult to argue
> the point.[5]

Moreover, it required no sacrifice for a Radical Republican from the Midwest such as Benjamin Wade of Michigan or Schuyler Colfax of Indiana to impose harsh and uncompromising racial equality upon the South. The nation's Negro problem was then limited almost entirely to the South. Not until nearly a century later following World War II would the Negro migration to the North begin in earnest. The civil rights acts passed by the Reconstruction sessions of Congress really affected only the South. Rank-and-file Republicans of the Midwest could impose a biracial society upon the prostrate South while still maintaining a lily-white—in fact, a Negrophobic—Midwest.

But civil rights legislation was more than just a vindictive trophy of the war. The legislation also had its practical purpose. It ensured that Negro Republican voters of the old Confederacy would send Republicans—often Negro Republicans—to Washington to ensure the party top-heavy majorities in both Houses of Congress and would give Republican Presidential candidates the South's electoral votes to ensure them of victory.

[5] Wilfred E. Binkley, *American Political Parties: Their Natural History,* New York: Alfred A. Knopf, Inc., 1958.

But by 1876, enthusiasm over Negro rights had subsided enough for Republican politicians to end Reconstruction without shedding many tears. The outcome of that year's election between Republican Rutherford B. Hayes, Governor of Ohio, and Democrat Samuel J. Tilden, Governor of New York, was disputed. To get agreement by Democratic leaders to Hayes as the winner, Republican leaders agreed to pull Federal troops out of the South—signaling the effective conclusion of postwar civil rights activity. The Republican rank and file was tired of postwar vengeance and the civil rights issue anyway. Although Hayes probably would have won an undisputed victory over Tilden had not renascent white supremacy governments of some Southern states illegally deprived Negroes of their votes, there was no grass roots hue and cry in the North to resume the Civil War. Even more significant was the bare minimum of protest when President Hayes, living up to the bargain that put him in office, handed the Southern Negro over to the tender mercies of his erstwhile master by removing Federal bayonets from the South.

The inevitable result was the disenfranchisement of the Southern Negro and the emergence of the Democratic Party's Solid South supported by a lily-white electorate. It was the death of the dream of Thaddeus Stevens and his Radical Republicans for a Negro Republican South that would always ensure their party of a President in the White House and majorities in Congress.

Why did Republicans accept this with so little protest? To a great extent because the Civil War had broken the impasse over admission of new states. These new Western states were invariably Republican, more than compensating for the surrender of the South. The new members of Congress and Presidential electoral votes from the West were enough to maintain Republican hegemony until 1912.

Even after 1876, the Negro was to remain steadfastly Republican for better than a half century more. But there was little to sustain him except memories, tradition, and the portrait of Abraham Lincoln on the wall. Largely ignored now by the Republicans, the Negro was not wooed at all by the Democrats. Actually, the great majority of Negroes—still living in the South—were voteless. The enfranchised Negroes of the North were not numerous enough for Democratic political leaders to worry about.

In the years immediately following Reconstruction, Negroes were active in politics chiefly as leaders of the all-black Republican parties in the South. Their sole function was the dispensation of Federal patronage. These Southern Negro politicians became pitiable pawns as delegates to the party's national conventions, putting their votes up for auction to the highest bidder. This scandal dropped to its depths at the 1912 convention during the furious struggle between Roosevelt and Taft that led to the party's great schism. Estranged from the mainstream of both their party and their country, the Southern Negro leaders did not share the fervor of either the Roosevelt progressives or the Taft conservatives. Like most Republican leaders of their day, Taft and Roosevelt were patronizing and condescending to the Negro. Consequently, the Negro delegates at the Chicago convention found no trouble at all in switching back and forth between the Taft and Roosevelt camps. Charges and rumors of money changing hands were common. No wonder then that the latent Negrophobia of Republican politicians was enhanced by the conduct of the Negro delegates at the Chicago convention.

It may seem strange that the Roosevelt of 1912, so far to the left on most social issues, was unsympathetic to the Negro cause. The truth is, however, that there had been a minimum of civil rights sympathy within the Republican Party's progressive movement since 1900.[6] In fact, when Colonel Roosevelt and his followers bolted the Republican Party to form

[6] However, progressives within the Democratic Party were even less sympathetic to the Negro's plight. For all his liberalism in foreign policy and economic policy, Woodrow Wilson was a standpatter on the race issue.

the Progressive Party, they contemplated forming an all-white Southern branch to break the Solid South. How to accomplish this and still attract Negro voters in the North naturally posed a dilemma. A description of it by George E. Mowry in *Theodore Roosevelt and the Progressive Movement* affords a revealing glimpse of Bull Moose enlightenment on the Negro question.

> Hoping to retain the support of the colored voters of the North, Roosevelt argued that North and South had quite different race problems. In the North many Negroes were educated and deserving men. They had, he said, a long history of political action singularly free from corruption and venality. Therefore he had encouraged his party leaders north of the Ohio River to take the Negro in on the same terms with the white man. In the South, however, despite forty-five years of experimentation with racial equality within the party structure, Republicans had succeeded only in making themselves a minority party, in forcing every white man of character into the Democratic party, and in corrupting instead of helping the Negro. "I earnestly believe," Roosevelt said, "that by appealing to the best white men of the South . . . and by frankly putting the movement into their hands from the outset we shall create a situation by which the colored man of the South will ultimately get justice as it is not possible for them to get justice if we are to continue and perpetuate the present conditions."[7]

Clearly, the mutual affection between the Republican Party and the Negro masses had worn thin as early as 1912. The Negro vote was ripe for the taking by Democrats twenty years later when relief checks and special attention by the New Deal moved Negroes across the country to turn Abraham Lincoln's portrait to the wall and replace it with Franklin D. Roosevelt's. The informal Congressional alliance, beginning in 1937 between Republicans and Southern Democrats

[7] George E. Mowry, *Theodore Roosevelt and the Progressive Movement*, Madison, Wis.: The University of Wisconsin Press, 1946.

to stop Roosevelt's court-packing scheme, was a natural enough development. In return for Dixiecrat help against New Deal economic measures, it was no ordeal for Republicans to oppose civil rights measures proposed by Northern Democrats newly attentive to the Negro's interests. After all, it had been sixty years since Republicans had crusaded for Negro rights.

There is no single explanation why the Republican Party— or at least the Eisenhower Administration—took up the party's long discarded mantle as champions of civil rights in 1957 and pushed through Congress the first civil rights act in a century.

Mostly it was a matter of historical necessity. The Supreme Court's 1954 decision against segregated public schools had unleashed generations of Negro frustration. By 1957, there seemed to be a national consensus for some kind of legislation, even if limited to protecting the Negro's right to vote.

Moreover, there had been a gradual shift in attitudes toward the Negro. Theodore Roosevelt's concept of Negro progress via paternalism was repulsive to the liberal mind of the mid-twentieth century. An educated liberal oblivious to the problems of the Negro was a rarity—actually nonexistent —in the 1950's. Unlike Colonel Roosevelt, the Republican progressives of the post-World War II generation were deeply committed to what they called their Lincolnian heritage.

There was also a matter of politics. The immense migration of Negroes to the North after World War II had ballooned their political significance. Republicans began to speculate that the rising Negro middle class was more interested in civil rights than bread-and-butter issues. More than a few Republican politicians asked themselves this question: Why wouldn't a Republican Party solidly committed to civil rights be more appealing to the Negro who has struggled above the subsistence level than a Democratic Party whose Congres-

sional wing was controlled in large part by Southern segregationists? After passage of civil rights legislation in 1957 and
1960 under the auspices of the first Republican Administration since Herbert Hoover's, Republicans expected dramatic
gains among Negroes in 1960.

The overwhelming Negro support for Kennedy in 1960
proved mainly that the Negro vote was still essentially an
economic vote.[8] But many Republicans felt like a lover
spurned and betrayed. In 1961, increasing numbers of Republicans were saying that the Negro vote was unattainable.
The experience of the elections of 1962 confirmed this view—
particularly for Senator Everett McKinley Dirksen of Illinois.
As Republican floor leader of the Senate, Dirksen had helped
push through the 1960 civil rights act. He had been co-
manager in an unsuccessful attempt in 1962 to pass Federal
legislation emasculating the literacy tests still widely used in
the South to prevent Negroes from voting. As a result of these
activities, Dirksen and his political aides expected impressive
gains among Chicago's vast Negro population. Dirksen was
appalled and angered to find his comfortable reelection
marred by a drop in Negro support for him compared with
1956. Even Senator Jacob Javits, one of the most militant civil
rights advocates in the Senate, won less than a majority of
the Negro vote while winning a landslide reelection against
a nondescript Democrat suspected of crypto-segregationist
views. The fate of Dirksen and Javits coupled with the remarkable success by a few segregationist Republicans set the
Republicans to wondering after the 1962 elections. They
were still wondering when the Negro revolution erupted
without warning in the spring of 1963.

For all Wirt Yerger's charges that it was a Kennedy plot,
the Negro revolution came as a most unpleasant surprise for

---

[8] Political mythology records Kennedy capturing the Negro vote with a
single act in 1960: a telephone call to the wife of Martin Luther King, the
militant Negro leader who had been jailed. This is nonsense. Kennedy had
the Negro vote in his hip pocket long before the famous telephone call.

the Kennedy brothers. Attorney General Robert Kennedy had hoped that the Reverend Martin Luther King would not trigger the Negro demonstrations in Birmingham, Alabama, in May, 1963. But the Birmingham demonstrations coupled with the violent reaction against them by the city's lame-duck segregationist administration set off a chain reaction of Negro militancy not seen before in the nation's history. It spread to all parts of the country, North and South. The Negro, placid and patient, was making angry noises after a century of indignity under freedom.

What's more, a good many whites—South *and* North— were making angry noises right back. For the first time since the Civil War, the Negro question had become a truly national issue of immediate concern to tens of millions of voters. Until the Birmingham riots, the only civil rights mail received by Northern Congressmen was a thin volume of letters from cranks (anti-Negro) and clergymen (pro-Negro). Now civil rights was becoming the most frequently mentioned subject in Congressional mailbags. And, to their great amazement, many Northern Congressmen of both parties were finding a good bit of it hostile and antagonistic to the Negro movement.

The impact on Republican Presidential politics of the Negro revolution and the white counterrevolution in May, 1963, was all the more pronounced because it coincided perfectly with Rockefeller's disastrous marriage. Rockefeller, the Republican Party's foremost champion of civil rights, was in decline. Goldwater, the party's national figure most beloved by segregationists, was in ascent.

Actually, Goldwater's views on the race question were murky. Though personally opposed to racial segregation, Goldwater insisted that the states should have the right to deal with this problem. In other words, if the Negroes of Mississippi were to come out from under the burden of racial discrimination, it would have to be at the volition of Mississippi whites. Obviously, this was a perfectly acceptable stand to Mississippi whites.

While declaring his support for racial integration, Goldwater's public statements seemed to put the greatest emphasis on the Southern-oriented doctrine of States' Rights. An example is his civil rights stance in "A Conservative Creed," a brief summary of views specially prepared for *Mr. Conservative: Barry Goldwater* in 1961.

While the rights of union members are consciously denied, the Kennedy administration makes much ado about civil rights of racial minorities. I continue to believe that it is both wise and just for Negro children to attend the same schools as whites. But I believe the matter of school integration is left to the states under the Tenth Amendment.[9]

Those who have become obsessed with the subject of civil rights seem determined to destroy the right of association guaranteed us under the Constitution. This may prove to be a double-edged sword. It will affect those Negro organizations that rightfully prevent whites from joining, and white organizations that rightfully prevent Negroes from joining. The right of association is one of our most sacred rights and it need not be disturbed in solving the problem of what we call civil rights, which, in my mind, is a problem of civil liberties.

There is a different aspect, however, to the problems raised by Negro sit-ins and the riders of public transportation. As a merchant, I feel that a man in business who advertises for customers to come to his store or place of business and to make purchases from him cannot deny that customer, regardless of race, creed or color, the opportunity to purchase in any department of that store or business.

I also feel in relation to the "freedom riders," that while the organization back of them made a bad mistake in continuing this activity, under the commerce clause of the Constitution, bus companies, airlines, railroads, etc., engaged in interstate commerce, cannot deny any citizen the right to their facilities.

[9] However, Goldwater modified this stand late in 1963. Denison Kitchel, a Phoenix, Arizona, lawyer who became Goldwater's Presidential campaign manager, convinced the Senator that school integration was the law of the land under the Supreme Court's 1954 ruling, no matter what the Tenth Amendment said.

When I consider the over-all issue of civil rights, I come back
to the concept that the states have all of the rights not specifically reserved to the federal government in the Constitution.

This civil rights stance, despite its opposition to segregation
as such, was by far the most sympathetic statement to the
Southern position by a national politician since the Supreme
Court's school segregation decision in 1954. If any Republican
were going to carry the whole South and not merely nibble
at it as Eisenhower and Nixon did, it would be Goldwater.

Still, prior to the Birmingham riots, Republicans were
showing plenty of sales resistance to the Southern strategy
peddled by the National Draft Goldwater Committee. The
skeptics conceded Goldwater's popularity in the South. They
conceded he could easily pick up the Southern states carried
by Nixon in 1960 (Tennessee, Virginia, and Florida) and perhaps South Carolina and Texas as well. But no more. When
it came to the showdown on election day, the voter of the
deep South would revert to the ways of his pappy, hold his
nose if necessary, and vote Democratic. Besides, these skeptics argued, the Southern victory formula contained one basic
flaw. Even if Goldwater did perform a miracle and carry most
or all of the South, his position would have to be so blatantly
sympathetic to segregation that he would lose the rest of the
country. The price of victory in the South would be defeat
everywhere else.

After Birmingham, these skeptics started turning into true
believers.

Infuriated at the spectacle of Negroes rearing up and
demonstrating in the streets, the white Southerner turned his
wrath on two easily available scapegoats: the brothers Kennedy. By June, Southern Democratic politicians were nearing
a state of panic. They conceded that Goldwater could sweep
Dixie against Kennedy. Even Georgia, the only state always
to give its electoral votes to the Democratic candidate for
President, might defect. A Goldwater sweep of the South, the

keystone ingredient in the Southern victory formula, was hardening into reality.

But the rise of Kennedyphobia among the white Southerners was neither the most important nor most dramatic political by-product produced by the Negro revolution of 1963. What really breathed new vigor into the Goldwater-for-President drive was the Negro revolution's impact on the North.

The Birmingham demonstrations fathered a new wave of demonstrations not only in the South but everywhere, North and South, where Negroes lived in great numbers. No longer could the Northerner look upon the racial problems of the South in a patronizing and condescending fashion. The racial struggle had reached to his very doorstep—or more properly to his very pocketbook. The demands of the Southern Negro —voting rights, desegregated education, access to public accommodations—were essentially noneconomic. They touched on theoretical questions of racial relations rather than dollars-and-cents questions of financial security. Not so in the North. The wave of demonstrations by Northern Negroes after Birmingham were aimed at elimination of the color bar in housing and employment. These were matters of economic interest important enough to draw out the latent vein of anti-Negro sentiment in Northerners who had been mouthing pious anti-segregationist sentiments for years.

It was most obvious in the lily-white suburbs of the North —particularly the middle-income and lower-middle-income suburbs. The middle-class suburbanite's biggest investment usually is his home. If its property value precipitously depreciates, his personal financial loss is severe. And once a Negro —just one Negro—moved into a lily-white suburb of Detroit or Chicago or Philadelphia, a combination of unscrupulous real estate speculators trying for a quick buck and panicky suburbanites ready to accept the first offer would combine to drive down property values throughout the neighborhood. No wonder then that the suburbanite, who in earlier years would tell anybody who cared to listen of his utter lack of racial prejudice, blanched in the spring of 1963 when he heard Negro demonstrators chanting for an end to segregation in the suburbs.

The mail from the suburbs started pouring in to Democratic Congressmen. Worried middle-class homeowners did not bother to sugarcoat this threat: If you back up the Negro demands, we'll vote against you. Michigan Democrats, at least, knew this was no idle threat. They regarded Governor John B. Swainson's advocacy of open occupancy housing as a key factor—perhaps even the deciding factor—in his narrow loss to George Romney in 1962.[10]

What was infinitely more troubling to Democratic strategists than trouble in the suburbs (most of which were traditionally Republican anyway) was the danger that rising anti-Negro sentiment in the heart of the cities might produce Republican gains in these traditionally Democratic strongholds. Many city dwellers echoed the fear of the suburbanites that integrated neighborhoods would depress property values. An even more critical breadbasket apprehension involved the fearful (though not very likely) prospect of white workingmen being squeezed off their jobs if Negroes were admitted to the lily-white building trades union.[11]

By the end of June, Democratic politicians were faced with unsettling political developments, tied to the Negro revolution, in big cities of the North from one end of the country to another. What follows is just a sample:

CHICAGO: The city's big Polish-American community, whose loyalty to the Democratic Party is an absolute essential in any statewide Democratic victories, was furious over the support from Democratic leaders in Chicago and across the nation for racially integrated housing. The Polish-Ameri-

[10] See page 92.
[11] This illogical, unreasoning terror was reminiscent of the worries by Midwestern white laborers in the 1850's that Negro labor, free or slave, would take their jobs.

can workman on Chicago's South Side, who had turned his meager bankroll into a two-by-four white frame house, was near hysteria over the possibility that a Negro might move in next door, sending the value of his home tumbling. The notorious Negrophobia of the American Pole for the Negro now had an economic justification.

PHILADELPHIA: The Philadelphia Irish, masters of the city's building trades unions, certainly weren't about to open the union hall's doors to the Negroes. Consequently, the rank-and-file Irish weren't a bit pleased when not only President Kennedy but Mayor James Tate seemed to be sticking up for the Negro in the struggle over Jim Crow unionism.

LOS ANGELES: This city's immense Mexican-American community, assiduously wooed by Kennedy in an effort to pull California (carried by Nixon in 1960) into his column in 1964, was restive over all the attention paid to the Negroes—particularly the appointment of a Negro as Los Angeles postmaster while no comparably lofty Federal patronage was channeled to Los Angeles's Mexican community. Responsible Democratic leaders in California were talking among themselves about the possibility of massive defections by the Mexican vote.

DETROIT: The white population of one of the world's great blue-collar cities was aligning itself against the Negro demands for equal employment opportunity and open occupancy in housing. The latent Negrophobia found in Detroit's Polish community, which had burst into violence before, was on display once more. Democratic politicians feared the political consequences.

Similar paragraphs could be written about New York, Boston, Cleveland, Baltimore, St. Louis, Buffalo, and the other great polyglot cities. The Democratic Party's great union of minority groups seemed at the point of dissolution. This clearly was more than just a case of the Northern white losing enough sympathy for the Negro's plight so that a Goldwater-led Republican Party could woo the South without fear of losing the North. Rather, there was every bit of evidence that this Southern-oriented racial policy actually would *appeal* to the North enough to deprive Kennedy of needed strength in the big cities.

It was strikingly reminiscent of the 1961 Goldwater battle plan, which then had seemed so dangerous and so totally removed from reality.[12] Now, in the spring of 1963, cool-headed Republican professionals saw a chance for success in November if Goldwater were the candidate leading a White Man's Party.

Of course, no responsible Republican politician was screaming from the rooftops about the strategy of the White Man's Party—either at the Denver meeting or after it. That kind of strategy is never proclaimed publicly. This scarcely made it less real. But a good many Republican politicians, particularly the party's small minority strongly in support of Negro rights, protested shrilly after the Denver meeting that Democrats and muckraking columnists were impugning the motives of the Republican Party and trying to give it a Southern-fried aroma.[13] Moreover, some nonpartisan observers expressed doubt that the Grand Old Party was seriously contemplating turning its back on the Negro revolution.

What really brought home the great revolution within the party was the tumultuous national convention of the Young Republicans, which convened in San Francisco just one week after the National Committee session in Denver. Paradoxically, the Young Republicans' meeting in San Francisco was an event of no inherent importance. Its only significance lay in the way it dramatized the rightward movement of the party itself.

[12] See Chapter V.

[13] Senator Jacob Javits of New York protested on the Senate floor about a column, written from the Denver meeting by Rowland Evans, Jr., and the author, entitled "The White Man's Party?" At that early date, Javits simply could not believe that responsible Republicans were considering such a course.

The fact that 75 percent of the delegates to the YR convention favored Goldwater for President was not surprising. At that time, Goldwater would have picked up the same percentage of support in any representative national gathering of Republicans. The uniquely disturbing quality of the YR convention was the senseless race among its delegates to outdo each other in embracing a radical and raucous brand of conservatism.

Moderate delegates were appalled. Their own words best tell the story.

In an official report on the convention, Dale M. Hiller, chairman of the Delaware delegation, declared:

> The public press has reported that our convention was rather turbulent. Actually, the reports were quite restrained . . . this convention had a new element, a group of people who came with the deliberate and openly admitted purpose of obstructing and disrupting the proceedings, so that the convention could be prolonged to the point where many delegates would be forced to return home, leaving the convention in the hands of the few who remained behind. When asked about the time wasted by their disruptive tactics, their typical reply was, "That's all right. I can stay another week!" The disruption was so effective, during the early part of the convention, that one twenty-four-hour period elapsed in which no business was accomplished at all. . . . We had to give up the convention hall in the Sheraton-Palace by 6:00 A.M. on Saturday, at the latest. So, at 5:15 A.M., having accomplished no business except the adoption of the Statement of Principles and the election of officers, the convention was adjourned by consent of both major factions. . . .
>
> Who were the disrupters? They came mostly from California and Arizona, with a scattering of individuals from New England and the Northwest. Many were avowed members of the John Birch Society. They came more to manipulate the convention than to participate in it, and showed by their tactics their utter contempt for their fellow delegates and for the

parliamentary institutions which undergird the practice of freedom. They form a force with which the Young Republicans, and the whole Republican Party, will have to reckon. We have seen them in action; we know.

"Trunk Line," a mimeographed bulletin of the Maryland Young Republicans, reported:

> To a large extent, the disturbances were created by ultra-right wing elements in the party who seemed determined to take over the Republican Party and the YRs for their own selfish ends, hiding behind the mask of honest conservatism in the process. Actually, of course, they are not conservatives at all but extreme radicals of the right.

Stan Adelstein, YR national committeeman from the solidly conservative state of South Dakota, was genuinely concerned by the rightward drift at the convention. He reported:

> We thought we knew exactly what it meant to be conservatives until we saw these people. The only question seemed to be who was mere pro-Goldwater and suddenly we found ourselves—mostly pro-Goldwater—becoming "middle-of-the-roaders" in comparison with extremists.

None of these reports quite captures the true flavor of June 27 and 28 on the floor of the YR convention in a banquet hall of San Francisco's Sheraton-Palace Hotel. Even for the seasoned political reporter accustomed to the conflict of words, it was a new experience to watch these hard-faced, implacable young men with crew cuts and buttoned-down collars, shrieking into floor microphones and chanting and stamping their feet in union in a systematic effort to disrupt the convention. Silver-haired Robert Gaston, the mercurial leader of the Birch-infested California delegation, paced in and out of the convention hall as he directed the tactics of disruption. One time-consuming roll call after another was demanded on arcane parliamentary points. It was all too much for moderate Republican Leonard Nadasdy, a public relations executive for General Mills, Incorporated, in Minneapolis, who was finishing out a two-year term as president of the YR's. "This is incredible," Nadasdy muttered to himself at one point as he surveyed the scene of pandemonium. He was watching nothing less than the tactics of disruption long utilized by the Communists: come early, vote late.

Even worse than the antics on the convention floor were the endless, vapid political bull sessions between YR delegates over cocktails or in the hotel lobbies. Their conversation was primarily a game of conservativemanship. The winner was the YR who could show that he was really the furthest to the right of all. One litmus test of conservatism applied by the YR's was the lunatic "Liberty Amendment," which would amend the Constitution to prohibit a Federal income tax (with the loss in resulting Federal revenues to be compensated by selling unspecified Government-owned industries). A foe of the "Liberty Amendment" was a liberal.

To many of these fierce young men, support of Goldwater was a bare essential prerequisite of genuine Republicanism and a kind word for Rockefeller was the deepest heresy. The depth of their approach may be seen in the fact that many delegates declined to show up for a beer party thrown by the New York delegation out of fear that some of their colleagues might interpret their fraternization with Rockefeller supporters as a sign of apostasy in the direction of liberalism.

The sight of all these well-scrubbed young monsters would have been the worst of omens for the Republican Party if the Young Republicans had really served as an incubator for party officials over the years. In fact, it had been no such thing. With a few illustrious exceptions (most notably F. Clifton White; Charles McWhorter, the extremely capable aide to Richard Nixon during his Vice-Presidential days; Representative John Ashbrook, a fiercely conservative Congressman from Ohio) leaders in YR circles seldom have graduated into similar roles in the real political world. Such outstanding young leaders in the Republican Party as Representative John Lindsay of New York, Representative Bradford Morse of Massachusetts, and State Chairman Craig Truax of Pennsylvania preferred to step directly into party politics without dabbling in YR fun and games.

Moreover, the bad manners exhibited at the San Francisco convention were the unhappy product of years of neglect by adult Republicans. The handful of Republican professionals gazed with horror upon the antics of the YR delegates in San Francisco as would a father who had permitted his children to grow up like weeds for years only to discover that, surprisingly enough, they had turned into juvenile delinquents.

Ironically, the one important Republican politician who paid much attention to the YR's at all seriously was Nelson Rockefeller, who was reviled at San Francisco as a me-too Republican, no better (and perhaps a little worse) than John F. Kennedy, and certainly not fit for party leadership.

But apart from his own liberal-oriented New York State YR's, even Rockefeller did little to influence the impossibly muddled and complicated YR picture politically. Indeed, Bruce Chapman, a precocious young politician who had founded *Advance* as a provocative magazine of liberal Republicanism, got nowhere in his efforts to warn the Rockefeller camp of the coming right-wing *Putsch* within the YR's. Chapman, who had been an active YR member as a Harvard undergraduate, delivered this message in January, 1963, during a private luncheon with George Hinman at the Senate dining room in the United States Capitol. Chapman bluntly asked Hinman for Rockefeller money—at least $50,000—to forestall a Birchite takeover in the YR's. Hinman, who then was scoring one success after another in his efforts to blur right versus left distinctions in the party so that Rockefeller could be the nominee of *all* Republicans, politely thanked young Chapman but made it clear he wasn't at all interested.

There is no sign that Chapman's warning ever reached Rockefeller himself.[14]

The national publicity given the YR carnival in San Francisco coming on the heels of speculation about a real Republican push for the white segregationist's vote signaled that the movement to the right within the party was genuine. Actually, the extremism at the San Francisco convention was not really so much concerned with racism as with far-out economic concepts (the "Liberty Amendment" is the horrible example) and neo-McCarthyite fears that the Federal Government was infiltrated from top to bottom with pacifists and appeasers ready to turn the nation's war-making potential over to Moscow. But there was enough segregationist sentiment in evidence at the Sheraton-Palace to give the entire convention a distinct Southern accent.

A civil rights resolution adopted by the convention's resolutions committee (but never actually brought to the convention floor because of the uproar there) expressed the convention's "opposition to state laws prohibiting voluntary service of certain individuals in public facilities as well as federal laws compelling involuntary acceptance in privately-owned public facilities (a violation of freedom of association)." This was outdoing conservative Republicans in Congress. Not only were the YR's opposing the pending Congressional proposals barring racial discrimination in public accommodations but were putting themselves on record against the state statutes that had been adopted over the past century by a vast majority of states and almost every state outside the South with any sizable Negro population. Indeed, the civil rights resolution went on to imply its opposition to any kind of new Federal legislation at all by expressing "support of the *individual's good will* as the final solution of the 'social revolution' now besetting the nation."[15]

[14] During a July 19 press conference in New York City, Rockefeller categorically denied receiving any request for funds.
[15] Italics are added.

There is no doubt this unabashed hostility toward the Negro rights movement was fully shared by the overwhelming majority of convention delegates. In the cocktail lounges at the Sheraton-Palace, delegates from North and South talked with a single voice on the race question. Nor was there much fear their conversation would embarrass a Negro delegate. Only a handful of Negroes were there. This was very nearly a lily-white convention. For instance, Michigan sent an all-white delegation that in no way suggested that state's enormous Negro population.

For the Young Republicans at San Francisco, their party was now a White Man's Party. Whatever its intrinsic importance, this fact was emphasized as the notoriety of the San Francisco convention spread across the country.

XIII

★ ★

The Declaration of July 14

There is no question that Nelson Rockefeller was aware of exactly what happened at the Young Republicans' convention in San Francisco and was significantly impressed by those events. He had special sources of information quite apart from the public prints. Bobby Douglass, George Hinman's assistant, went west from the Denver meeting for a brief vacation in San Francisco that included a quick visit to the YR convention. In addition, members of the Rockefeller-dominated New York delegation to the YR convention supplied the Governor with full reports. And as the professional politicians inside Rockefeller's vast entourage frequently grumbled among themselves, he spent more time worrying about the Young Republicans than they deserved.

But it would be marking down Rockefeller as a simpleton to say that the antics of a few hundred postadolescents in San Francisco were the cause of the Governor's extraordinary political declaration of July 14, 1963. The YR convention two weeks earlier might have been the last shred of evidence that convinced Rockefeller that this declaration was needed. Or, it might just have been the pretext for issuing the declaration.

For this was more than the usual run of hastily thought-out and hastily issued political pronouncements. This was a document that obviously was intended to change the course of Republican politics. To a great degree, it did just that. The

202

point here is, however, that it was being talked about and argued about within the Rockefeller inner sanctum long before the Young Republican bedlam in late June.

Indeed, the debate about the Declaration of July 14 was really no more than an extension of a continuous debate within the Rockefeller camp that predated the 1962 elections, and that predated the 1960 election. This was the old conflict between the Hinman school and the Morhouse school—Hinman proposing that Rockefeller seek to blur ideological distinctions within the party and present himself as the great unifier of Republican left and right, Morhouse proposing that Rockefeller declare war on the Republican right and seek to remake the party in his own image.[1] On every political question until July 14, 1963 (with the exception of the platform fight at the National Convention in 1960), Rockefeller followed the Hinman line—with apparent success in 1963, judging from Rockefeller's front-running position and his *rapprochement* with Goldwater.

But Hinman himself began to run into a mild conflict of interest early in 1963. In Hinman's opinion, a strong position in California was vital in importance—second only to the paramount goal of establishing Rockefeller as the nonfactional leader of all Republicans. Hinman foresaw the June 2, 1964, Presidential primary election in California as a potentially crucial battleground, not only because of the state's rich harvest of delegates (second only to New York's) but for the psychological push just a month before the National Convention. Accordingly, shortly after the 1962 election, Hinman became a transcontinental commuter, hopping between New York City and Los Angeles via jet aircraft in order to line up support in California for Rockefeller. And Hinman's chief quarry in California was Senator Thomas H. Kuchel, California's senior Senator and Republican whip of the Senate.

Tommy Kuchel, inheritor of the Earl Warren tradition of

[1] See Chapter V.

progressive Republicanism in California, had become the state's most formidable Republican figure with the defeat of Richard Nixon in 1962. While Nixon was losing the Governor's race by some 300,000 votes, Kuchel was winning reelection to the Senate by 750,000. What's more, Kuchel's great victory followed two years of incendiary statements by him condemning the infiltration of the California Republican Party by the John Birch Society. Politician after politician, including Senator Barry Goldwater, warned Kuchel in 1961 and 1962 that he was unnecessarily risking his political career by provoking the Republican right. Speaking both as a friend and as a chairman of the Senate Republican Campaign Committee, Goldwater privately informed Kuchel that he might lose the general election, or perhaps even the primary, in 1962 if he didn't tone down statements offensive to conservative party workers and contributors of campaign funds. A jaunty bulldog of a politician with one of the most delightfully profane vocabularies in Washington, Kuchel ignored the warnings. Now in 1963, pointing to his impressive vindication at the polls, Kuchel told Hinman and other Rockefeller aides that the Governor ought to follow the same course—lashing out against the right—on a national level.

George Hinman, the most cautious of politicians, and very nearly the antithesis of tempestuous Tommy Kuchel, was not about to propel Rockefeller down Kuchel's hazardous road. A resounding broadside against Birchers would wash away years of Hinman labor in creating a mildly conservative image for Rockefeller and simultaneously destroy the hothouse friendship with Goldwater. Besides, why rock the Rockefeller campaign boat at a time when it was sailing so far in front? There wasn't even any certainty that the California primary would be contested. If it weren't, Kuchel's support would be a nonessential luxury.

Like so many other aspects of Republican politics, these factors disappeared overnight in May when Rockefeller remarried. Now that he was running far behind Goldwater, a

win in the California primary was absolutely necessary if the
Governor were to have any chance at all for the nomination.
And if the California primary did turn into a Goldwater versus Rockefeller contest (as was becoming increasingly probable in June, 1963), Rockefeller wouldn't stand even an outside chance without Tommy Kuchel's support. What's more,
some of Rockefeller's aides were convinced that a strong public stand by the Governor against the radical right was absolutely essential if they were to win support from Kuchel, who
was continually urging that just such a statement would be in
order.[2]

Quite apart from California considerations, some of Rockefeller's advisers were coming to feel there were national political gains to be found in an all-out onslaught on the
Republican right. Since the remarriage, the political beneficiary of harmony within the Republican Party was no longer
Nelson Rockefeller. It had become Barry Goldwater. If the
party plodded toward the 1964 convention at San Francisco
within the framework of Rockefeller-conceived armistice,
Goldwater seemed the sure nominee. Party discord now was
necessary for Rockefeller to stage a comeback. He needed to
stir up ancient animosities, to purposely reopen the schism he
had spent two and a half years trying to close. He needed to
become the champion of the party's "Eisenhower wing"
against the right. Without the internal bloodletting, Rockefeller was dead.

But there is yet another dimension to Rockefeller's motives
at this point. From the time of his entrance into elective politics in 1958, Rockefeller often confused personal and political
considerations. He looked on a political victory as a personal
compliment, a political defeat as a personal slight. So it was
that he was deeply and personally hurt in late 1959 when the
leaders and moneybags of the Republican Party informed
him that Richard Nixon was their choice for President in

[2] Actually, Kuchel almost certainly would have lined up for Rockefeller
in any contest with Goldwater in California even if no antirightist statement
had been issued.

1960. And so it was that his deep personal hurt over the reaction to his remarriage influenced his decision to attack the Republican right.

The violent reaction to his remarriage had come as a complete surprise to Rockefeller.[3] It was beyond his scope of comprehension that the remarriage spontaneously set off the wave of indignation across the nation. He confided to aides that the reaction *must* have been promoted by his foes in the party's conservative wing as a means of shooting down his Presidential campaign. Moreover, Rockefeller told these aides that Goldwater, while playing the role of friend and co-protector of party harmony, was tolerating—perhaps even encouraging—the torrent of anti-Rockefeller abuse.

As was the case so often in matters political, Rockefeller was completely wrong. He understood Goldwater not at all. In truth, Goldwater was personally appalled by the invective against Rockefeller and suspected (incorrectly) that it was instigated by Nixon supporters. But he was incapable of marshaling the party's conservative legions in Rockefeller's behalf. He probably didn't even contemplate such a move. Goldwater was one political leader who seldom tried to shape great events. His conduct usually was shaped by them.

But Rockefeller could see only betrayal. When he realized finally that the tide of sentiment against his second marriage was not receding, he seriously began considering the attack on Goldwater and the Republican right—partly as a matter of simple vengeance.

Thus, the furor over the rightist antics by the Young Republicans in San Francisco was the pretext, not the reason, for the Declaration of July 14. But even after the San Francisco convention, admonitions of caution came from within the Rockefeller camp. Hinman was characteristically chary about intraparty conflict. So was State Chairman Fred Young. The strongest objection of all came from Harry O'Donnell, gregarious, Coca-Cola-guzzling publicity man from the Re-

[3] See page 142.

publican State Committee who had been inherited by Rockefeller from the old Dewey political organization. A shrewd
political veteran, O'Donnell advised that Rockefeller might
possibly wound Goldwater but certainly would destroy himself by provoking a party rupture. The warning was ignored.

The irrevocable decision was made the week of July 8. The
battery of Rockefeller researchers and speech writers in New
York City hammered out draft after draft. By the end of the
week, the final draft was approved. Hugh Morrow, an ex-
Saturday Evening Post staffer who had been writing Rockefeller speeches since 1959, carried a copy on an airline shuttle
flight to show to Senator Kenneth B. Keating in Washington.
Jacob Javits, the state's other Senator, happened to be in New
York City, where he was shown his copy of the declaration.
Outside New York, only a few Republican leaders (including
Kuchel) were given an advance peek. For the rest of the
party, the Declaration of July 14 was another of those unexpected Rockefeller weekend bombshells.[4] Indeed, what they
heard over television and radio that weekend couldn't have
been more of a surprise.

Like most political papers issued in Nelson Rockefeller's
name, the Declaration of July 14 was marked by the characteristically hurky-jerky quality of a committee-written document. Its failure to flow told of too many collaborators, too
many revisions, too many editors.

Even with these handicaps, the declaration might have
come across with an air of conviction had its sole function
been to unite the Republican Party on a middle ground of
moderation against the radical John Birchers as Kuchel had
in California. But the Declaration of July 14 was too much
tied to reviving Rockefeller's personal political fortunes to
sound a stirring battle cry.

It began with an apologia explaining why Rockefeller had

[4] The December, 1959, announcement that he would not seek the 1960
nomination; his wedding in May, 1963; the Declaration of July 14, 1963—
all came on weekends.

not until now denounced the Republican right. In the first paragraph, Rockefeller explained that "many leaders of the Republican Party, myself included, have been working" to shape the party" as a strong and united fighting force" for the 1964 election. He continued:

> In making this effort toward unity for principle, it was my conviction that the activities of the radical right, while deeply disturbing in many ways, would represent an inconsequential influence on the Republican Party.
>
> It was my conviction that despite differences in emphasis among the party's responsible elements, there was an overwhelming consensus within the party on the fundamental articles of Republican faith.

He then ticked off these "articles of faith": preservation of freedom throughout the world, equal opportunity for all (civil rights, that is), the Federal system of government (with home rule for local government units), the free enterprise system, fiscal integrity, freedom of speech and information.[5] Next came a sudden warning "that many of us have been taking too lightly the growing danger to these principles through subversion from the radical right," followed by this startling announcement of the party's imminent subversion:

> I am now convinced that, unless the vast majority of Republicans who subscribe to these principles are aroused from present inaction—whether this inaction stems from complacency, from fear or from a fantastically short-sighted opportunism— the Republican Party is in real danger of subversion by a radical, well-financed and highly disciplined minority.
>
> For it has now become crystal clear that the vociferous and well-drilled extremist elements boring within the party utterly reject these fundamental principles of our heritage. They are,

[5] Anyone who had heard very many Rockefeller campaign speeches had heard the first five of these "articles" pronounced incessantly. The sixth "article"—pledging faith in freedom of speech and information—was apparently a part of Republican criticism of the Kennedy Administration's "news management" techniques.

in fact, embarked on a determined and ruthless effort to take over the party, its platform and its candidates on their own terms—terms that are wholly alien to the sound and honest conservatism that has firmly based the Republican Party in the best of a century's traditions, wholly alien to the sound and honest Republican liberalism that has kept the party abreast of human needs in a changing world, wholly alien to the broad middle course that accommodates the mainstream of Republican principle.

But as evidence that the party is in imminent danger of a rightist coup, Rockefeller mentioned only the Young Republicans' convention two weeks earlier in San Francisco. Nothing else.

. . . every objective observer at San Francisco has reported that the proceedings there were dominated by extremist groups, carefully organized, well-financed and operated through the tactics of ruthless, rough-shod intimidation. These are the tactics of totalitarianism.

Unfortunately, this cannot be brushed off as irresponsibility. For youth is responsible. The leaders of the Birchers and others of the radical right lunatic fringe—every bit as dangerous to American principles and American institutions as the radical left—who successfully engineered this disgraceful subversion of a great and responsible auxiliary of the Republican Party are the same people who are now moving to subvert the Republican Party itself. They claim initial success and predict ultimate victory for their efforts.

At this point, the declaration abruptly changed cadence, scene, and mood (with scarcely any attempt at smooth transition) to denounce the proposed transformation of Lincoln's Party into the White Man's Party in an effort to lure Southern states away from the Democrats.

Completely incredible as it is to me, it is now being seriously proposed to the Republican Party that as a strategy for victory in 1964, that it write off the Negro and other minority groups, that it deliberately write off the great industrial states of the

North (representing nearly 50 per cent of the country's population), that it write off the big cities, and that it direct its
appeal primarily to the electoral votes of the South, plus the
West and a scattering of other states.

The transparent purpose behind this plan is to erect political
power on the outlawed and immoral base of segregation and to
transform the Republican Party from a national party of all the
people to a sectional party for some of the people.

No such plan ever has, or ever will succeed. It cannot stand
the light of day. It will be rejected out of hand by the Republican Party. It will be rejected by the Nation. It will be rejected
by the South. . . .

A program based on racism or sectionalism would in and of
itself not only defeat the Republican Party in 1964 but would
destroy it altogether.

This was followed by a contention that "the invocation of
States' Rights" in the area of civil rights "can only be regarded
as pretext." The rest of the declaration moved downhill, con-
sisting of a conventionally partisan attack on the Kennedy
Administration. The climax was a claim that the Republican
Party's destiny "is to save the Nation by first saving itself."

Even when viewed from perspective friendly to Rockefeller, the Declaration of July 14 is a mishmash. Opening
with a warning that the party was in dire danger of subversion from the right, he cited only the lunatic antics of some
postadolescents two weeks earlier in San Francisco. While
contending that the rightist danger was imminent, he reassur-
ingly added that there was no possibility that Republicans
ever would want to do business as a lily-white party.

Much worse from Rockefeller's own standpoint was his
failure to define clearly the target of his attack. Although
Kuchel's bombardment of the far right in California was
carefully zeroed in on Birchers as an unruly but small splinter
group within the party, Rockefeller's attack on Southern
strategy made it seem as though he were listing all Republican conservatives—including in this indictment a vast majority of the party's workers—among the radical right. That was

the interpretation of the party's conservatives—including Barry Goldwater.

Now it was Goldwater who felt himself betrayed—betrayed and humiliated. Goldwater was visibly shaken when he arrived at his Washington office on Monday morning, July 15. He was declining any comment to the press. He had even given the cold shoulder to Jack Bell of the Associated Press, his neighbor and biographer, the night before. When Bell came pounding on the door of the Goldwater apartment in The Westchester, the Senator did not answer the door. The performance was repeated an hour or so later when the persistent Bell returned.

But in private conversation that Monday morning, Goldwater repeated over and over his shock at the Rockefeller declaration. He felt that he had not only been betrayed but humiliatingly played for a sucker. In those secret breakfast meetings at the Governor's Washington mansion on Foxhall Road, Rockefeller had talked incessantly about the need for party unity and harmony.[6] That was when Rockefeller was far in front for the nomination. Now that he was trailing, the talk of unity was shunted aside like an obsolete weapon.

Hurt and perplexed as he was over the Declaration of July 14, Goldwater did not quite yet perceive that Monday morning that Rockefeller intended a total rupture in their relationship. Goldwater noted that Rockefeller telegraphed him on July 13 (a Saturday when nobody was in Goldwater's office) advance word that a statement of "common interest" was to be issued the next day. Goldwater also noted that an airmailed copy of the declaration arrived in his office on Monday. Coupling this attention with the fact that he was not specifically mentioned by name in the Declaration of July 14, Goldwater supposed that Rockefeller might be inclined to try to warm up their old romance—perhaps over breakfast again on Foxhall Road. Goldwater would have none of

[6] See page 103.

it. "There'll be no more breakfasts," he told his staff that morning. "None at all."

In fact, Rockefeller had not the slightest intention now of asking Goldwater to breakfast or any other meal. The lower-level huddles between Hinman and Victor Johnston, Goldwater's unofficial political adviser, also ceased. After the Declaration of July 14, Hinman no longer phoned up Johnston for lunch during his frequent visits to Washington.[7]

Of course, Rockefeller regarded the break with Goldwater as complete and final. The alerting telegram of July 13 and the airmailed copy of the declaration received July 15, misinterpreted by Goldwater as a special attention from Rockefeller, actually were sent every Republican member of Congress and every Republican governor. As for the absence of Goldwater's name from the statement of charges in Rockefeller's declaration, this was soon to be remedied. The impersonal tone of July 14 was soon to escalate into a two-way name-calling contest that would persist into 1964.

Goldwater and his friend contributed to this escalation. Because sphinxlike silence from Goldwater's office just wouldn't do on July 15, a "spokesman" was enlisted. By mid-morning, press secretary Tony Smith was advising inquiring reporters that Goldwater would have nothing to say, but they might try Senator Carl Curtis of Nebraska. Curtis, one of the first Senators publicly to endorse Goldwater for President, was primed with a pungent anti-Rockefeller statement. But predictably, Goldwater himself couldn't keep quiet the entire day. He told the Associated Press in late afternoon he regarded Rockefeller's Declaration of July 14 as "just a formal declaration of candidacy."

But the real return fire against Rockefeller was not ready

[7] When this was reported in the *New York Herald Tribune* column written by Rowland Evans, Jr., and the author, however, Hinman telephoned Johnston to reassure him he bore no grudges and to invite him to lunch at the Senate dining room in the United States Capitol. The gesture was typical of Hinman's unfailing good manners as well as his conciliatory approach to politics but hardly signaled a revival of the Goldwater-Rockefeller alliance.

until Thursday afternoon. Once again Carl Curtis served as Goldwater's cannoneer. With a general mien appropriate to a baby with colic, Curtis was best known in the Senate for tenacity in monotonous questioning of Kennedy Administration officials for hours on end when they appeared before him in the Senate Finance Committee. His formal delivery on the Senate floor was high-pitched, monotonous, and unmemorable. Nevertheless, he was the chosen instrument to deliver the rebuttal with a speech carefully prepared in consultation with Goldwater and Vic Johnston.[8] The speech dispensed with the circumlocution usually found in Curtis's speeches. With the white-moustached, crimson-faced Johnston beaming down from the gallery, Curtis opened with a blunt statement of charges that set the tone for his entire attack:

> This last weekend an intemperate and, in my opinion, ill-judged, attack was made on the conservatives of the Republican Party. Since the conservatives constitute quite clearly the great majority of the party, it seems all the more strange, even suicidal, for a man sometimes thought to have been a Republican leader to turn on the great majority of his party such a destructive attack. The potential damage to the party is incalculable. The effects of the chasm which these attacks are opening in the party will be felt not only on the national level, but right down through the ticket to the local offices. It is no longer possible to remain silent in the face of such self-serving tactics by a man desperately trying to retrieve his declining political fortunes. This brazen attempt to cast a shadow over all conservatives by pinning an extremist label on them is the same tiresome and hypocritical game which for years has been the principal weapon of the northern Democrats. It is false in their hands, and it is equally false in the hands of a Republican.
>
> It is my considered judgment that a man who would take such desperate and destructive measures against his own party

---

[8] The *Congressional Record*'s transcript of the Curtis speech was reproduced by the thousands and dispatched to Goldwater clubs throughout the country. It became the approved text for rebutting Rockefeller.

in a gamble to gain some temporary, personal advantage has already forfeited any claim to loyalty from any part of the party organization.

The rest consisted of variations on this theme. In contrast to the meandering organization of the Declaration of July 14, Curtis's reply kept to a single point: to alienate Rockefeller from the mainstream of the Republican Party by calling him a party splitter playing into the hands of the Democrats.

Charging that liberal Democrats were trying "to create a broad public impression that the conservative movement is dominated by irrational and dangerous 'rightists' who are addicted to violent solutions of political problems," Curtis added:

> . . . it is a shocking fact that their greatest assist has now come from a member of our own party. It is a sad and bitter fact that this so-called Republican leader is helping them to accomplish their precise objective by his current attack on his own party. He is using exactly the tactic which the Democrats themselves have decided would be the most destructive of Republican chances in 1964, right down the line, right down to the local offices.
>
> I find it almost incredible that one who has received such favors from the party and who, it is rumored, looks to this party for even greater favors could fail to see that even his selfish interests would not, in the long run, be served by de-structive tactics.
>
> If such tactics should succeed and a hostile gap be opened inside the Republican Party, the nomination would not be worth anything to anyone, in any case. I say it is time to call a halt to reckless and destructive behavior of this kind on the part of anyone who holds a position of responsibility in the party.

It was a masterful exhibition in the art of political polemics. Curtis ignored Rockefeller's concern over the Young Republicans at San Francisco. He ignored Rockefeller's charges about selling the Lincolnian birthright for Dixie pottage. He confined himself to tarring Rockefeller as a renegade giving aid and comfort ot the enemy.[9]

Following the example set by the Declaration of July 14, Curtis never once mentioned Rockefeller by name. But political diatribes cannot long continue on an anonymous basis. Rockefeller broke the anonymity rule the next day during a New York City press conference, describing Goldwater as the dupe and puppet of sinister right-wing forces.[10] Once again, Rockefeller placed disproportionate importance on the Young Republicans' convention. But the real meat of the New York press conference was his challenge to Goldwater to disavow right-wing support.

> The great threat is whether the radical right wing, part of Senator Goldwater's following, will be able to capture its leader. Senator Goldwater is a conservative and not a member of the radical right wing. On many issues we have the same views. I can't believe that if Senator Goldwater realized the danger he would not extricate himself. He is a patriotic American and a devoted Republican.

It was faint praise. Painting him as a feckless moron in the clutches of the far right was not calculated to win back Goldwater's friendship. Indeed, Goldwater's reply to Rockefeller's challenge was less good-natured than his brief comments about the Declaration of July 14. Avowing that he was worried about the "radical left" inside the Kennedy Administration rather than "any rightist society members who are not in government," Goldwater said of Rockefeller: "I don't know what he's following—his own dictates, maybe."

[9] Inexplicably, Curtis's diatribe ended on this note of implicit forgiveness: "Surely this man has spoken inadvisedly. I cannot believe the wholesale and intemperate attack on the conservatives represents his mature reflection." These were the only faintly sympathetic words in the entire speech.

[10] This press conference had its ironic aspect. At a time when Rockefeller was demanding a pro-Negro rights stand within his party, Negro militants were conducting a "sit-in" at the converted brownstone containing his Manhattan office. Accordingly, the press conference was moved to a hotel.

I'm not going to answer this sort of thing from Rockefeller. He's using an old trick which the Democratic forces used against us for a long time, and I'm not going to fall for it.

By the first week of August, bare knuckles were exposed. On August 5, Rockefeller told an Albany press conference that he would not support Goldwater as nominee for President against Kennedy "if he were a captive of the radical right." Goldwater, who had been so reluctant July 15 to make on-the-record slurs against Rockefeller, fired right back in an August 6 interview with Cabell Phillips of the *New York Times:*

The primordial battle between Republican right and left was joined again. Conservative Republicans from one side of the country to the other, armed with Curtis's July 18 speech, were denouncing Rockefeller. Rockefeller expected all this. What he didn't expect was the reaction—or rather, the lack of reaction—from his own wing of the party.

Soon after Rockefeller's declaration was issued, Kuchel told the Associated Press that Rockefeller had "performed a splendid service to his country and to his party in his vigorous and courageous statement." A similar statement was made by Keating. Next came predictable support from Javits (who purposely delayed his commendation for one day in order to give the impression of a rising tide of support for the Declaration of July 14). Kuchel, Keating, and Javits—who were virtual collaborators with Rockefeller in drafting the declaration—were supposed to trigger a wave of support for Rockefeller that would isolate Goldwater on the far right wing of the party.

To the horror of the Rockefeller camp, however, the Kuchel-Keating-Javits endorsements were followed only by silence from other progressives within the party. Total silence. There was nothing to be heard from Eisenhower at his Gettysburg estate, from Nixon on Wall Street, from Romney in Lansing, from Scranton in Harrisburg. It was Rockefeller, not Goldwater, who was isolated.

Indeed, many progressives expected by Rockefeller's aides to line up solidly alongside the Governor privately assailed the Declaration of July 14 as a poorly contrived document that did the party far more harm than good. One of these was Governor William Scranton of Pennsylvania. While deeply sympathetic with Rockefeller's concern over right extremism and his dedication to Negro rights, Scranton told friends that the Declaration of July 14 implicitly included too great a section of the party in his indictment. By not pinpointing his attack on the Birchers, Rockefeller was declaring war against most of the party. A good many Republican progressives around the country agreed with Scranton.

Within forty-eight hours after its issuance, the havoc wrought upon Rockefeller's Presidential hopes by his Declaration of July 14 was clear.

The Hinman plan was now dead. Hinman's years of missionary work to depict Rockefeller as an orthodox party loyalist, to blur distinctions between liberal and conservative, and to nurture the friendship with Goldwater were erased in that one volley of biting words. The latent vein of anti-Rockefeller hostility among party conservatives was exposed. Now, they despised Rockefeller as the conservative-baiting party splitter they always had suspected him to be, and would do their best to keep the nomination from Rockefeller even if Goldwater fell short of the mark—a sentiment now fully shared by Goldwater himself. Worst of all from Rockefeller's standpoint, he had failed to enlist the forces that had nominated Willkie, Dewey, and Eisenhower into a holy war against Goldwater and his allies. The party's internal warfare had resumed under a frame of reference least favorable for Rockefeller.

And there was also the question of Rockefeller's sincerity. His protestations that he did not appreciate the full extent of rightist penetration in the party until the Young Republicans' convention just didn't wash. From vantage points both inside and outside the party, it was obvious that Rockefeller did not

manage to see the rightist danger until he was far behind
Goldwater in the race for the nomination. Politicians talked
among each other about the impossibility of discerning which
was the real Rockefeller.

To be sure, the Declaration of July 14 was not a completely
unrelieved disaster for Rockefeller. It did cement the valuable alliance with Kuchel in California. On a lower level, it
attracted some party workers who were deeply concerned
with the rise of Goldwater and the possible triumph of conservative Republicanism but until then were not personally
committed to Rockefeller.

One of these was Alexander (Sandy) Lankler, a young
Washington lawyer who had been asked to go on the Rockefeller payroll for the Presidential campaign. As the son of a
Presbyterian minister in Brooklyn, Lankler had become a
teen-age worker and orator for Thomas E. Dewey. From that
start, he had come to feel that it was in the country's best
interests for both parties to occupy the middle of the road
with no great ideological distinction between them. Accordingly, Lankler felt that an all-out fight should be waged to
keep the party out of the hands of Goldwater and his allies.
Not until Rockefeller's Declaration of July 14 showed that he
shared the same concern did Lankler commit himself to the
Governor's cause.[11]

Perhaps the most lasting effect of the Declaration of July
14, however, was its subterranean effect on Goldwater's
cause. On the surface, Goldwater was not scratched at all.
But he had suffered deep internal injuries. Now it would be
impossible for him to lead a united party. Now an anti-
Goldwater underground in the party would form, ready to
strike at the proper moment. The proper moment, however,
was most certainly not the summer and early autumn of 1963.
The Goldwater bandwagon was rolling then.

[11] Lankler later became coordinator of Rockefeller's New Hampshire campaign.

XIV

★ ★

Goldwater's Autumn

By mid-September, 1963, the contest for the nomination was very nearly a Goldwater runaway. On September 15, the Gallup Poll furnished proof in the form of answers to this question:

> Suppose the choice for President in the Republican Convention in 1964 narrows down to Barry Goldwater and Nelson Rockefeller. Which one would you prefer to have the Republican Convention select?

Republicans queried favored Goldwater by landslide proportions, 59 percent to 41 percent. Furthermore, Mr. Conservative had eaten deeply into Rockefeller's supposed backing among independent voters. Dr. Gallup's independents backed Goldwater nearly as heavily as the Republicans, 56 percent to 44 percent.[1]

But Goldwater's strength was not limited merely to his superior popularity over Rockefeller or any other Republican Presidential possibility. The Gallup Poll showed that Goldwater would crack the not-so-solid South against Kennedy with the greatest of ease, capturing 54 percent of the Dixie vote (to Kennedy's 34 percent and an undecided tally of 8 percent)—surpassing even Eisenhower's 51.4 percent

[1] Democrats questioned by Gallup favored Rockefeller over Goldwater, 58 percent to 42 percent. But this only confirmed suspicions of the Republican orthodox that Rockefeller was a Democrat at heart.

Southern total in 1956.[2] True, Kennedy outpolled Goldwater in every other section of the country. But this was more than a year before election day, and Goldwater had what no other Republican could match: a head start in the South that seemed invulnerable to any campaign gain by Kennedy.

Nelson Rockefeller, always a great believer in the reliability of polls, had his own private surveys to show him just how badly he had slipped. They also revealed the principal reason for his decline: his remarriage. Appearing on NBC's "Meet the Press" on September 14, he declared: "I have a very deep understanding of the reactions of individuals in this situation. I have no sense but one of feeling for people's concern. I think it's a situation which in political life is difficult."

But there really was no need for polls to convince Rockefeller of his political plight. Just one week before his "Meet the Press" appearance, he had seen with his own eyes the deterioration of his political standing. That week was, by chance, the tacit starting date for Presidential barnstorming by both Rockefeller and Goldwater. By chance, each picked Illinois among his targets. The contrast between the two trips to Illinois was vivid.

The debut of Nelson and Happy Rockefeller as a new campaigning team came on Saturday, September 7, 1963, at the second annual Sixteenth Illinois Congressional District Picnic at the Ogle County Fairgrounds in Oregon, Illinois

In brilliant sunshine and unseasonable heat that reached into the 90's, the Governor and his new bride arrived at high noon at Rockford Airport in Rockford, Illinois, largest city in the Sixteenth District (population: 130,000) and second largest in the state. As usual, Rockefeller arrived in style, airborne from New York in his own Convair. Besides the

[2] Surprisingly, this same Gallup report gave Romney a slim edge over Kennedy in the South, 47 percent to 40 percent. But Kennedy was favored over Rockefeller by Southern voters, 44 percent to 39 percent.

pilot and copilot, his entourage included press secretary, speech writer, advance man, stenotypist, and bodyguard.[3] Political reporters from Washington, New York, Albany, Chicago, and Milwaukee traveled to Rockford to record the event.

The airport welcoming delegation of some seventy local party dignitaries was courteous enough. In fact, had it not been for one unplanned little incident, there would have been no hint of Nelson Rockefeller's status in the Republican heartland of Northwestern Illinois. As Rockefeller inched along the rails at the airport, grinning his fixed campaigning grin and shaking hands, a gawky, middle-aged man dressed in an Uncle Sam suit elbowed his way to the front, grabbed Rockefeller's hand, and bellowed: "I'm Lar Daly, and I'm one candidate for Governor who's not afraid to be here."

Lar (America First) Daly, a Chicago furniture jobber whose hobby was politics, was in the habit of entering all manner of elections, from local contests to Presidential primaries, sometimes as a Republican, sometimes as a Democrat. Now he was trying to enter the Republican primary for Governor of Illinois. And he was indeed the *only* avowed candidate who cared so little about his chances in the April, 1964, primary to rub elbows with Rockefeller in September, 1963. Goldwaterism had become the established religion in rural Illinois, and any contact—even the most casual contact —with the Rockefeller heresy was dangerous business.

Although Rockefeller's appearance at the Ogle County Fairgrounds was expected to attract thousands of curious Illinoisans, none of the serious candidates for Governor was quite able to find enough time to attend. Not Secretary of State Charles Carpentier, the plumed knight of Illinois Old Guard Republicanism and front-runner for the gubernatorial nomination. Not Cook County (Chicago) Republican Chair-

[3] Soon after the Illinois trip, this entourage was expanded to include a press secretary for Mrs. Rockefeller and a radio-television adviser for the Governor.

man Hayes Robertson, a national leader in the Draft Goldwater movement. And not Charles M. Percy.[4]

It was Percy's absence that really bothered Rockefeller. Blond and boyish at age forty-two, Percy was the great white hope of progressive Republicanism on the prairies. As the *Wunderkind* of Chicago business who had fought his way up to the presidency of Bell & Howell camera makers when just twenty-nine, Percy was a director of the Rockefeller family's Chase Manhattan Bank.[5] He became intimately connected with Nelson Rockefeller during the platform fight of the 1960 Republican National Convention, when, as platform committee chairman, he sided with Rockefeller and Nixon against the committee's majority in the battle over civil rights. During the next three years, Rockefeller often talked privately of Percy as the Midwestern anchor of his Presidential campaign. It was a case of personal affection as well as expectation of political assistance.

That was before the Rockefeller remarriage and the Goldwater boom. Now, Chuck Percy was sliding away from his past strong stands for civil rights and was displaying a newborn affection for Barry Goldwater. While Rockefeller was shaking hands through a bigger than expected turnout of five thousand at the Ogle County Fairgrounds, Percy—along with his conservative rivals Carpentier and Robertson—was making do with no more than five hundred Republicans at a picnic in Joliet, just two hours' drive away. The turnout was smaller, but the situation was safer.

Representative John Anderson, the district's ambitious young Congressman, also had his misgivings about close association with the Governor of New York. Some two weeks

[4] Percy won the primary the next year. Carpentier suffered a heart attack in January and withdrew from the race. He died after a second attack a few weeks later.

[5] To erase all links with East Coast Republicanism generally and Rockefeller Republicanism specifically, he resigned as a Chase Manhattan director early in 1964.

before the picnic, he phoned Senator Everett McKinley Dirksen for advice. Was Dirksen going?

"Why, of course not, John," Dirksen boomed back. "I'll be busy."

Anderson took the hint. When Rockefeller came to the Sixteenth District, Anderson was back in Washington attending a "Congressional seminar." Dirksen, who had been ready to hop onto the Rockefeller bandwagon before the remarriage, also stayed in the Capital—to prepare for debate on the disarmament treaty, he said.

Add to this a threatened boycott of the picnic by the fiercely conservative local Young Republicans (a boycott that was forestalled at the last minute) and it is understandable that the Sixteenth District Republican leaders who had invited Rockefeller in the first place were a bit edgy as they waited for the Governor's plane to arrive. Stanley Guyer, former state chairman and now a state committeeman from the Sixteenth District, explained apologetically to newsmen that Rockefeller was by no means the first choice to speak at the picnic and was invited only after Goldwater and other party leaders had turned down invitations because of prior commitments.

For all the lack of warmth in his reception by the Illinois party leaders, Rockefeller put the best face on the day—choosing to be pleased by the huge crowd that swarmed over the fairgrounds in search of hot dogs, Northern Illinois' justly famous sweet corn, and a glance at—or even a handshake with—the fabulous New York millionaire and his new bride. Mrs. Rockefeller, no *femme fatale* but a warmly congenial matron, performed admirably. The Governor even managed to warm up his crowd, sullen at first, with a few stale jokes and an unmemorable give-Kennedy-hell speech. ("We are not on the New Frontier," he shouted. "We are lost in the woods.")

But the Goldwater buttons dominating his audience were

not removed. Nobody was converted, not the people and not the politicians. Typical of the people was Roy Larsen, who brought his wife and young children from Rockford to hear the Governor. "I'm glad I came," he said as he prepared to leave the fairgrounds. "It was a good speech, a conservative speech. But I expected him to make a conservative speech here." Typical of the politicians was Emmett Folgate, Winnebago County (Rockford) Republican chairman. Folgate confided that Rockefeller once looked to him a better bet against Kennedy than Goldwater. Before the remarriage, that is. Now it wasn't safe politically for the Winnebago County chairman to even hint of being anything other than a Goldwater man.

There was a smell of political death about the day in Ogle County. It was like observing a political corpse who did not realize that he was dead.

There was no such funereal mood four days later in Chicago. This was one of ten stops on a loosely connected "tour" by Goldwater, now a candidate for President in all but name. Goldwater traveled like any commercial salesman, with nothing approaching the splendor of Rockefeller. The "tour" consisted in Goldwater's catching a commercial plane out of Washington for a speaking engagement, making his speech, and then catching another commercial plane either to his next destination or, more likely, back to Washington.

His Chicago stop was a study in unorganization. After arriving at O'Hare Airport from Washington via commercial jet, his first stop was the WBKB (ABC) studios at State and Lake, in the Loop, for a taped television discussion program. Goldwater was relaxed and masterful under faintly hostile questioning. When the program was completed, a young reporter from the local CBS outlet approached Goldwater. The cameras were set up in the basement, and couldn't the Senator spare just a minute or two for an interview? Goldwater replied, with a smile, that he just couldn't give filmed interviews to CBS. "I haven't anything against you," he told the reporter, "but I just don't trust your people in New York. I know what they do with tapes."[6]

If a Presidential candidate's refusal of free television time was unprecedented, what followed was even more bizarre. Goldwater was past due for his major date at the twenty-fifth annual convention of the National Federation of Republican Women, held at a hotel some ten minutes' drive from the television studios. Incredibly enough, nobody had thought of transportation. There was Goldwater, accompanied by a couple of reporters, standing at the corner of State and Lake in the rain at the evening rush hour trying to hail a taxi. It was hopeless. Luckily, a young man driving home from work stopped his car. "I don't know where you're going, Senator," he said, "but I'm for you, and I'll take you there."

Not just the good ladies of the National Federation of Republican Women were waiting for Goldwater at the banquet. All the candidates for Governor who hadn't the time to meet Rockefeller the previous Saturday were there, falling all over themselves trying to shake Goldwater's hand—Carpentier, Robertson, and even Percy, the great white hope of progressive Republicanism on the prairies. As usual, Goldwater's flat, essentially undramatic style of oratory let down the exuberant ladies. But nobody really cared. Goldwater was the leader of the Republican Party, in fact if not in name.

Illinois in early September was no exception. Everywhere that autumn, it was the open-armed welcome for Goldwater and the cold shoulder for Rockefeller.

The most spectacular occasion of the autumn for Gold-

[6] Goldwater's major irritation was a CBS documentary about the rightist movement. He claimed that Fred Friendly, the show's producer, had ordered miles of film of Goldwater shot but had used only a few minutes' worth, squeezed in between sequences showing neo-Fascist groups. Goldwater's relationship with CBS did not improve markedly, hitting a low point at the Republican National Convention the following July.

water came on September 17, when he was awarded a hero's reception in Los Angeles. Some forty thousand admirers, a political audience of heroic proportions even in an election year, gathered in Dodger Stadium to cheer, whistle, and clap in unison. Cabel Phillips of the *New York Times* called it "a welcome such as is usually reserved for a Presidential candidate."

There were no hero's greetings for Rockefeller. On his 1959 travels to test his Presidential strength, he had been troubled by support from party mavericks, losers, and renegades. Now, he had no support at all. In fact, his 1963 appearances were studiously avoided by politicians. When Rockefeller addressed the Virginia Municipal League at Roanoke, Virginia, on September 23, Representative Richard Poff, the district's Republican Congressman, somehow couldn't manage to attend. And when the Governor addressed the Indiana State Bar Association in French Lick, Indiana, on October 12, there was hardly a partisan politician to be found, in a state that thrives on partisan politics. Among the absent was H. Dale Brown, boss of the Indianapolis Republican organization and recently deposed as state party chairman. In fact, it was precisely Brown's unannounced but obvious backing of Rockefeller that had caused his overthrow as state chairman—a post in Indiana as precarious as the French premiership before De Gaulle.[7] Now Brown wanted no part of Rockefeller. He pleaded the demands of a forthcoming municipal election in Indianapolis and stayed away from French Lick.

So, in the autumn of 1963, Goldwater versus Rockefeller was rapidly becoming no contest. But the real reason for Goldwater's widening lead was the utter failure of a third candidate to emerge.

Well into the autumn, strategists in the Draft Goldwater organization in Washington were worried most about Rom-

[7] See page 107.

ney as the man to watch. The fact that Romney was pulling from 20 to 25 percent in Gallup Poll listings of all Republican possibilities was some cause for concern. Aside from some spontaneously organized Romney-for-President clubs in Wisconsin and Texas, there was no activity for him outside Michigan. Romney, the imperious lone wolf, had no friends to speak of in the party structure. Since the admonition from the *Detroit News* back in May, Romney had made no overt attempts to promote himself through national barnstorming.[8] Yet, he managed to keep a Gallup rating that surpassed Rockefeller's and rivaled Goldwater's. This was indeed cause for concern by the Goldwater men, who still believed Eisenhower, Nixon, and the Eastern Establishment might wind up uniting behind Romney.

Moreover, there was no doubt now of Romney's hostility toward Goldwater. This became clear enough at the annual Michigan state party meeting on Mackinac Island in mid-September. Cliff White, director of the Draft Goldwater organization, and his Michigan lieutenants met privately with Romney at the Governor's official summer residence on the island. At that meeting, Romney sounded out a three-point indictment against Goldwater:

1. Goldwater is not strong enough on the issue of Negro rights.

2. Goldwater is biased in favor of business interests.

3. Goldwater has not made it clear that he repudiates the far right.

Added to this hostile attitude was the fact that some liberal Republicans in Michigan had changed their minds and were now urging Romney to get into the Presidential race. Their reasoning: Goldwater now was a cinch for the nomination unless challenged by Romney. With Goldwater at the top of the ticket, Romney probably would be beaten for reelection as Governor in 1964 anyway. So, why not go for broke?

[8] See page 162.

Romney might have done just that, save for an event of immediate concern only to the state of Michigan. The day before that Republican conference on Mackinac Island began, Romney submitted to the Michigan Legislature a tax reform program more progressive and more audacious than anything fourteen years of Democratic Governors had dared offer. Whatever Romney's tendencies to play the role of the sawdust political evangelist, there was no bunkum about this. Reform of Michigan's archaic tax statutes was overdue, and Romney—using the metaphor of fixing the roof when it's not raining—felt the reform should be made in 1963, when Michigan's auto-geared economy was booming, rather than when the state was suffering under the plague of an automotive recession and the state government's treasury was nearly dry. It was a courageous gamble, but he lost it. Old Guard conservative Republicans and pro-labor Democrats (who had consistently backed such tax reform programs under Democratic Governors) formed an unholy coalition in the Legislature to block Romney's program. A wrathful Romney denounced "legislative members of both parties—not just Republicans and not just Democrats—who are more interested in self-preservation or in playing narrow partisan politics than in supporting needed state programs."

Romney was on the side of the angels in this fight. But there is serious question about how skillfully he had waged his greatest fight as Governor. In *The New Republic*, Charles A. Ferry, a former (and obviously disenchanted) aide of Romney, put on paper a frequently voiced criticism of Romney's generalship in the tax fight. He wrote:

> As Romney began to push his tax program through the legislature, the mathematics of the situation dictated only one course of action: coalition. The legislature had 58 Republicans and 52 Democrats in the House, and 22 Republicans and 12 Democrats in the Senate. The Democrats had traditionally

supported tax reform. The Republicans had opposed it. There-fore, the Governor had first to win over the Democrats and then pick up the Republican votes necessary for passage— four in the House and six in the Senate.

But to nearly everyone's amazement, Romney followed an opposite course: he went after Republican votes and tended to freeze out the Democrats. "He stumbled over his Presidential ambitions," said one legislator. "He didn't want to lose the tax fight, but he didn't want to risk alienating his own party either."

Recognizing that Romney was headed for trouble, Senator Stanley G. Thayer, GOP Senate leader, apparently with the Governor's sanction, sought help from the Democrats. But when the news leaked out, Romney issued a stunning rebuke of Thayer, from which Thayer has yet to recover.

In desperation, Romney made an 11th-hour plea for Demo-cratic votes. It was too late. A series of Romney tactical errors had placed Democrats in a position where they could with some justification oppose the Romney program.[9]

This analysis seems overly harsh with Romney and cer-tainly is overly lenient with the Democrats. Nevertheless, this kind of criticism confirmed Republican leaders around the country in their own prejudices that Romney was more of a soapbox orator than an effective political leader. He had fumbled in his generalship of an issue on which he had staked his full prestige. Although his supporters in Michigan had felt that the tax fight would not affect his Presidential possibilities one way or another, they were wrong. On the day his tax bill died, his Presidential possibilities died along with it. Although Romney's flamboyant personality was to surface nationally from time to time over the next six months of confused contention for the Presidential nomination, he was never again mentioned as a serious threat.

[9] Charles A. Ferry, "George Romney Gone Bust," *The New Republic,* January 25, 1964. Although Ferry's criticism of Romney's legislative general-ship was echoed privately by many of the Governor's friends, this article has all the earmarks of a hatchet job.

One governor who did rule his legislature with an iron hand, William Warren Scranton of Pennsylvania, seemed to have vanished from the national scene. He had agreed to become a Presidential favorite son, but his motives were local rather than national. To prevent Pennsylvania Goldwater forces from taking over the delegation to the National Convention and the state party itself, Scranton was using his mighty patronage powers to ensure a state delegation pledged to him as the state's favorite son. But he would do nothing more. When his youthful, aggressive aides warned him that he might have to enter the Presidential race in order to head off Goldwater's sure nomination, Scranton would reply: "Oh, Barry's not so bad."

Would-be Wendell Willkies would suddenly appear and then disappear even more rapidly. Trial balloons for General Lucius Clay, an Eisenhower intimate in war and peace and now associated with the Wall Street brokerage firm of Lehman Bros., appeared on two occasions. They returned to earth without anybody's paying much attention to them. Boyish, handsome General Lauris Norstad, retired from the Air Force and from his longtime NATO command in Paris, made it clear that he was available in 1964, and he even went to the trouble of attending a Republican "citizens' " conference in Hershey, Pennsylvania, in May. Nobody paid much attention to him either. There were whispers about Henry Cabot Lodge for President, but they ended after Lodge volunteered to become John F. Kennedy's Ambassador to South Vietnam.

Then there was Nixon. Telltale Nixon footprints were appearing that autumn. Their message was unmistakable: Nixon was very much interested in the Republican Presidential nomination, despite his 1962 catastrophe in California. There was his remarkable statement of October 1 in which he publicly announced to the New York Press that he had refused an "implied" request from Rockefeller to support

him for President during a chat at the Governor's Fifth
Avenue apartment a month earlier. There were repeated
instances of Nixon's meeting old political acquaintances in
hotel lobbies and cautioning them not to climb on the Goldwater bandwagon just yet. And there were letters to close
political associates that bared his political thoughts at that
time. Like the hotel lobby conversations, the letters sought
to keep the loosely knit Nixon organization uncommitted in
the race for President. One of them read as follows:

> I still believe that it is best for our friends not to become
> committed because the real testing period . . . will come from
> now on out. Presidential candidates get much closer scrutiny
> than candidates for Senator or Governor. How Goldwater,
> Rockefeller, Romney and all the others are measured by
> columnists and political experts for potential Presidents will
> determine which one will merit our support.

As Nelson Rockefeller put it, Nixon was "standing in the
wings." But in the autumn of 1963, Nixon hadn't attracted
much more support than had Lucius Clay or Lauris Norstad.

Instead, the Eastern Republican Establishment was just
waiting. It was waiting for the same forces which had snatched
the nomination from Robert A. Taft and given it to Dwight
D. Eisenhower in 1952 to strike again. But there was no
Eisenhower this time. Moreover, the kingmakers of 1952—
Thomas E. Dewey, Herbert Brownell, Sidney Weinberg,
Lucius Clay, Henry Cabot Lodge—were now far removed
from the sources of Republican power. They were supplanted
by a whole new breed of thus far anonymous party leaders.

But the most amazing truth of the autumn of 1963 was
that Goldwater, leader of the party's right wing, stood a
chance of unifying the party from the right. It was a rare
moment for him, not fully appreciated by him and not to be
granted him again.

On his ten-state tour, Goldwater displayed a subtle change
in his approach. He was no longer the crusader for a return
to the tried-and-true Republican orthodoxy, but had become
the pleader for party unity. His speech in Chicago before the
National Federation of Republican Women on September
11 is a case in point. "We are a big political party, and there
is all kinds of room for a difference of opinion," Goldwater
declared. "But in differing, we need not beat the hides off
those we differ with." While Rockefeller was continuing to
flail away at Goldwater as the captive of the radical right
with increasingly less success, Goldwater was the calm and
even-tempered proponent of party unity.

The evolution was duly noted by Walter Lippmann. In
his syndicated column of September 19, Lippmann wrote:

> The peculiar genius of American politics, which is to draw
> candidates away from extreme positions, is now working on
> Senator Goldwater. Like every other man who has ever taken
> himself seriously as a Presidential candidate, the Senator is
> now engaged in remodeling his ideas, in moving away from the
> far Right and towards the more moderate Center. . . .
>
> This fudging process is characteristic of serious candidates
> for election. I say serious candidates. For the fringe candidates
> —Socialists, Prohibitionists, Vegetarians—are able to keep their
> views sharp and unfudged because they are not really running
> for office but are talking to influence opinion. But Senator
> Goldwater, who is now in big league politics, is well along
> on the road where he will sound less and less like Goldwater
> and more and more like Eisenhower. . . .[10]

In mid-September, Lippmann was essentially correct. Furthermore, a combination of Goldwater's apparent new moderation and the ever-increasing momentum of his bandwagon
was attracting ambitious Republicans who had dismissed

[10] Curiously, this column (called "The Evolution of Goldwater") troubled
Goldwater and some of his supporters more than Lippmann's frequent
frontal attacks on the Senator. This shows how deeply the Goldwater camp
felt about any significant sacrifice of principle.

him as nothing more than a factional leader six months earlier. In Illinois, Percy was being drawn ever closer into the Goldwater orbit. In Indiana, Lieutenant Governor Richard Ristine, a candidate for the gubernatorial nomination and a moderate conservative, all but endorsed Goldwater. Most remarkable of all was the news from Wisconsin. Wilbur Renk, wealthy dairy farmer from Sun Prairie, Wisconsin, and foremost of the state's liberal Republicans, had supported Rockefeller's abortive 1960 Presidential drive against Nixon. But in 1963, Renk was running for Governor. He endorsed Goldwater and ignored Rockefeller.

Simultaneously, the Draft Goldwater organization in Washington, under the direction of Peter O'Donnell and Clif White, was making every effort to screen John Birch Society members and other rightists out of their state organizations. The effort was only partially successful, but successful enough to give the movement a new respectability in the eyes of the party leaders across the country. In Michigan, for instance, the guiding light of the Draft Goldwater organization was no raving fanatic, but shrewd, highly respected Ty Gillespie, a top-echelon executive for the Dow Chemical Co. Gillespie ruthlessly barred from his organization all manner of right-wing extremists, including Richard Durant, a fanatically militant and highly influential Detroit Republican leader who had filed a multimillion-dollar libel suit against his opponents in the Republican Party (including George Romney). Gillespie even kept Arthur Summerfield, Eisenhower's postmaster general but a much disliked figure in Michigan Republican political circles, at arm's length.

As Goldwater extended his influence, his only avowed rival—Nelson A. Rockefeller—became more and more isolated. Even the eastern seaboard Republicans who still had misgivings about Goldwater hesitated to oppose Mr. Conservative at this stage of the game.

Rockefeller's pathetic attempts to find a campaign manager

for himself disclose the extent of his isolation. His first choice was Leonard Hall, the Oyster Bay, Long Island, Republican stalwart who had run the 1956 Eisenhower campaign as national party chairman. Hall turned down Rockefeller flatly. Next the offer went to Meade Alcorn of Connecticut, Hall's successor as national chairman in 1957 and close political associate. Alcorn took a few weeks to think it over but also turned it down. Then Rockefeller tried Hall again, inviting him to dinner in baronial splendor at the Rockefeller estate in Pocantico Hills. Never before had Hall been admitted this closely into the Rockefeller inner sanctum. But once again, he refused. Finally, Rockefeller picked John A. Wells, an experienced and highly competent political professional in New York State who had managed Javits' spectacular re-election campaign in 1962. But Wells was no national figure with the prestige of a Hall or an Alcorn. Even after Wells' appointment, the offer was made to Hall yet again. This time it came not from Rockefeller but from Wells, a friend and sometime fellow worker of Hall. He proposed that Hall be campaign chief, with Wells as staff director. Like Caesar, Hall refused the crown for the third time.

The extremity of Rockefeller's position was further hammered home to him in November. On a visit to Washington, the Governor invited several Senators to dinner at his Foxhall Road estate. Rockefeller spoke earnestly of his plans for the Republican Party. But a chilling response came from Senator Jack Miller of Iowa, a moderate conservative not then committed in the Presidential race.

"Governor," Miller said, "we're all happy you're in the race. We could support either you or Senator Goldwater. But there's one question that occurs to us. Would you support Goldwater if he's the nominee? He's said that he would support you."[11]

[11] Goldwater had said so many times. Asked in Atlanta on August 23 whether he would back Rockefeller as nominee, Goldwater said yes and added: "The country can't stand another four years of Kennedy." In truth,

Rockefeller replied he would "support the man nominated by the convention." Some Senators present thought this meant a pledge to back Goldwater. Others regarded it as a prediction by Rockefeller that someone other than Goldwater would be nominated. The point here is that Miller, representing a widespread Republican viewpoint, was viewing Rockefeller as the potential party splitter and Goldwater as the party regular.

Goldwater was very nearly unchallenged as leader of his party. This was the theme of Goldwater's autumn. It was a pinnacle he would not reach again, even on the day of his nomination.

---

however, Goldwater was so hurt by Rockefeller's continuing attacks on him as a captive of the radical right that he now confided to friends that choosing between Kennedy and Rockefeller would be a bitter choice indeed.

★ ★

XV

"Just Pooping Around"

In his breezy Sunday column in the *Washington Post* of September 8, 1963, Robert C. Albright led off with this item:

> Though his presidential balloon is soaring, Sen. Barry Goldwater still conducts a one-man, understaffed operation that is the despair of the pros and the joy of his loosely organized rooters.
>
> Requests for speeches and personal appearances pile up daily.
>
> He fills as many as he can, often taking only one hastily typed copy of his speech and not even a researcher for company. There's seldom any follow-up to the appearance. . . .
>
> Goldwater, the only candidate in history to pilot his own jet plane, runs his campaign like a broken-down jalopy. He doesn't even keep a written card index of the names behind the countless hands he's shaken.
>
> Not long ago, Victor Johnston, the GOP Senatorial Committee's top political pro, decided the time had come to give the informal campaigner a talking to.
>
> "I hate to suggest it, Senator," said Johnston, "but the least you can do is take somebody along to keep a record of the people you meet. It's a standard procedure."
>
> Goldwater dismissed him with a grin. He said: "You leave me alone, Vic. I'm doing all right just pooping around."

Hardworking staffers at Draft Goldwater headquarters on Connecticut Avenue in Washington read Albright's column that Sunday morning with mildly amused chuckles. While Goldwater was "just pooping around," they were working far into the night and on weekends at the monumental task of building a national Presidential organization. So were volunteer workers at the state and local levels.

Actually, Goldwater's help was not really needed at this stage. Nor was the Senator, no great shakes at the nuts and bolts of political organization, ever to take a hand directly in the great search for delegates. Nevertheless, Goldwater supporters were disturbed by Goldwater's tendency to "just poop around"—that is, to live the carefree life without the pangs and pains that go with seeking the Presidency. There was a paradox at work here. At precisely the time Goldwater seemed to consolidate himself as leader of the party, with an insurmountable lead over Rockefeller, he was alienating an ever-increasing number of Republicans by the most damaging aspect of his "pooping around": his damn-the-consequences tendency to shoot from the hip. It was a slow, corrosive process—one that Goldwater did not become fully aware of until January, 1964.

It really began in late August, 1963, when Stewart Alsop, Washington editor of *The Saturday Evening Post*, wrote a full-dress article about Goldwater.[1] It was, on balance, a sympathetic treatment of a unique political personality. But Goldwater aides bitterly denounced Alsop. What upset them were Alsop's verbatim quotes of Goldwater's off-the-cuff sallies, particularly in this brief account of an Alsop-Goldwater airborne conversation:

> REPORTER: "You have been quoted as saying that you oppose the progressive income tax, that everyone should pay the same rate as a man with five thousand?"
> GOLDWATER: "Yes. Yes, I still believe that."
> REPORTER: "But do you really think it's fair that a man with

[1] Stewart Alsop, "Can Goldwater Win in '64?" *The Saturday Evening Post*, August 24–31, 1963.

five million a year should pay the same rate as a man with
five thousand?"

GOLDWATER: "Yes, Yes, I do."

(Goldwater explains that the poor man would benefit from
the rich man's investments, while in his mind's ear the reporter
hears liberal orators make mincemeat of candidate Goldwater
as "the rich man's candidate" in 1964.)

GOLDWATER (*volunteering*): "You know, I think we ought to
sell TVA."

REPORTER (*scribbling busily*): "You really do?"

(Oops, thinks the reporter, there goes the whole Tennessee
Valley.)

REPORTER: "You were quoted some time ago as favoring the
'prompt and final termination of all farm subsidies.' Do you
still believe that?"

GOLDWATER: "Yes, I believe that. Might take three years,
might take five. But it's not right to force an inefficient farmer
to stay on the farm when he'd be much better off in industry."

(Oops again, there go the farm states.)

Alsop's article was liberally sprinkled with similar Gold-
waterisms (including the Senator's comment that "I haven't
got a really first-class brain"). Goldwater had been taking
nonconformist stands in blunt language for years along the
banquet circuit and in private bull sessions. But now there
was a new element introduced. He was running for President of the United States. His every utterance would be
minutely examined.

Of course, the remarks of every Presidential contender
undergo this scrutiny. But by the time they seek to enter the
White House, most politicians have learned to fuzz over their
views and deal exclusively in glittering generalities. But in
the strictest sense, Goldwater was not really a politician at
all, but a preacher. And as a preacher of the new conservative
doctrine, he had sought not to moderate and blunt his views,
but to sharpen them to the point where their impact would

be felt hardest. In his interview with Alsop, Goldwater was acting like a preacher and being treated like a politician.

Consider his volunteered remark to Alsop that "I think we ought to sell TVA." On the conservative banquet circuit, sale of the Tennessee Valley Authority was a no more revolutionary proposal than balancing the budget. As the symbol of socialism in free-enterprise America, why shouldn't it be sold? Nor had Goldwater ever hidden his distaste for the TVA. He told the Senate on August 9, 1957: "TVA was conceived in socialism, born during a period of economic chaos and has been nurtured and expanded in deceit." In another Senate speech, on September 23, 1961, he said: "I knew this socialistic octopus had a deathlike grip on the area it serves and that it dictated the economy of that area."

All perfectly consistent for a political preacher. But as a politician, Goldwater should have known that the TVA is the most sacred of sacred cows in the Southeastern states served by the big power-dispensing utility. It is defended by conservative and liberal, by Republican and Democrat, by segregationist white and integrationist Negro. In fact, it is a common political ploy in Tennessee and other TVA states for a candidate to put his opponent on the defensive by calling him a foe of the TVA.

Consequently, an enterprising Democratic Congressman from Tennessee named Richard Fulton took a long shot in October, 1963, and wrote Goldwater a letter asking whether he really and truly still wanted to sell the TVA. To Representative Fulton's surprise, Goldwater answered the letter. To his utter amazement, the answer was yes. Without consulting any of his political advisers, Goldwater had dictated a letter to Fulton advising that the TVA should be sold because "it would be better operated and would be of more benefit for more people if it were part of private industry."

What followed was a fairly substantial political explosion in the Tennessee Valley, right in the heart of the Goldwater country absolutely necessary to his Southern strategy. Representative Howard Baker of Tennessee, dean of Southern Republican Congressmen, called Goldwater's stand "a serious mistake, not only politically, but also from the standpoint of the best interests of the nation." Ultraconservative Republican Rubel Phillips, candidate for Governor of Mississippi and a staunch Goldwater man, disavowed the Senator's position on the TVA.[2] On a less public level, a friendly Tennessee newspaper publisher wired Goldwater that the reaction to his letter to Fulton was far worse than he had dreamed possible.

And then there were the letters to Goldwater from rank-and-file residents of the TVA area, many of them from erstwhile Goldwater supporters. Here is a sample:

From Chattanooga, Tennessee: "I have contributed to your campaign and helped to organize the Goldwater club here . . . but since you have . . . come out . . . for sale of the TVA, I am taking off my Goldwater stickers."

From Florence, Alabama: "As a Democrat who had hoped to have the privilege of supporting you . . . I am disappointed to learn of your advocating that TVA be sold to private power trusts. I am confident that the almost 7 million who reside in the TVA power district are likewise disappointed."

From Atlanta, Georgia: "For some time now, I have thought I would vote for you if you are nominated. But why in hell did you say that about the TVA? . . . The Southeast will never vote for anyone who advocates turning over TVA to the . . . monopolists."

From Waverly, Tennessee: "Being against TVA has given the damn Kennedys and their followers more votes in this TVA area than you can ever gain for the GOP."

Goldwater was unmoved. When a delegation of Southern

[2] While losing, Phillips ran the best race of any Republican in Mississippi since Reconstruction days. But Mississippi supporters of both Goldwater and Phillips agreed that Phillips' vote in the Northern Mississippi counties served by TVA power had been hurt by Goldwater's position.

Republicans came to remonstrate with him, he brushed them off with this remark: "You either take Goldwater or you leave him."

He did, however, on November 14 release a memorandum clarifying—and, in some respects, softening—his letter to Fulton. It began:

> I meant that the Federal Government should sell or otherwise dispose of TVA in its present form. I meant it then. I mean it now. But this hardly means that I propose to abolish all TVA services or stick up a sign outside the TVA offices and wait for a rich buyer to stroll along and snap it up.

He went on to explain that he would not sell all of the TVA but only enough to turn "a Federal white elephant into a more productive and useful part of the economy." Specifically, this would include the TVA's steam-generating plants and fertilizer-production program. He continued:

> There are sound ways to return them to the non-Federal control of the state involved, private industry, or to a special corporation such as that formed for Telstar and other communications satellites.

Softer though it was, the memorandum did not come close to satisfying Goldwater's partisans in the TVA area. As matters turned out, Goldwater himself ended the crisis he had fomented—by simply remaining mute on the matter of the TVA for the next six months. But the TVA rhubarb was not forgotten by strategists in the Goldwater camp. To them, it was the dangerous result of "just pooping around." With no other Republican really grappling with Goldwater for the National Convention delegations of the Southeast, the TVA was not a burning issue in the months to come. But Goldwater was to be troubled deeply by similar off-the-cuff remarks on national issues of far wider application.

A preview of this came on October 24 in a press conference at Hartford, Connecticut, when newspaper reports quoted Goldwater as urging that NATO field commanders be given discretion to use tactical nuclear weapons. Goldwater argued that he had been misunderstood and misquoted. He had referred to *the* NATO commander, not to the several local NATO commanders.[3] Even in this form, however, the position was to haunt him down to the floor of the San Francisco convention.

The growing confusion over the volume of words pouring out of Barry Goldwater was badly needed fuel for the stalled Rockefeller campaign. Rockefeller tried to capitalize on it. But his onslaught really didn't worry the Draft Goldwater organization's strategists. With a great deal of justification, they felt that Rockefeller himself was no danger. What worried them was attacks from the Democrats. At the least, these attacks would make the fall campaign against Kennedy more difficult. At the worst, they could erode Goldwater's position within his own party as front-runner for the nomination.

And the Democrats, now convinced that Goldwater really was about to push the Republican Party to the right, were zeroed in on Mr. Conservative.

The opening barrage was fired on September 18 by Senator Frank Church of Idaho, keynote speaker at the 1960 Democratic National Convention. Keynoting the Western States Democratic Conference in Salt Lake City on September 18, Church declared that Goldwater "is committed to a policy of initiating the use of force in the struggle with communism," adding:

> Beware of a leadership which has nothing to offer but reaction at home and jingoism abroad.

[3] Goldwater said exactly what he meant on this point in an article ("My Proposals for a 'Can-Win' Foreign Policy") under his own by-line appearing in *Life* of January 17, 1964. He wrote: "I have suggested that the supreme commander in Europe be given authority over the tactical nuclear weapons appropriate to NATO's defenses. The best authorization ultimately must be worked out with NATO itself."

One man, in this day and age, clothed with the power of the Presidency, can deliver us into fiery oblivion—foolishly, needlessly, and finally, by just one error of judgment.

An American President who mistrusts the winds of freedom and tampers cavalierly with the delicate balance of terror upon which the peace presently depends might well be the last American President.

This is a chance I don't want to take. That's why I am here.

Church was painting Goldwater as the trigger-happy gambler with nuclear holocaust. The supplementary Goldwater image painted by Democrats was the amiable, eccentric bumbler. This latter type of attack appealed to Kennedy himself. Planning to use it against his old Senate colleague right through to November 3, 1964, he began early. Asked at his October 31 news conference to reply to some criticism of him by Goldwater, the President unleashed his satirical wit in this reply:

> Well, as I have said before, I think it would be unwise at this time to answer or to reply to Sen. Goldwater. I am confident he will be making many charges even more serious than this one in the coming months, and in addition, he himself has had a busy week selling TVA and giving permission or suggesting that military commanders overseas be permitted to use nuclear weapons, and attacking the President of Bolivia while he was here in the United States, and involving himself in the Greek election. So, I thought it really would not be fair for me this week to reply to him.[4]

[4] In the case of the Greek election, Goldwater was an innocent victim. A Greek newspaper, the *Athens Post*, had interviewed Goldwater weeks earlier—posing questions that had no apparent relationship to internal Greek politics. When they appeared in print, just before the Greek national elections, however, Goldwater's answers were presented in a way that seemed to put him on record, ironically enough, against the right-of-center incumbent premier and for the left-of-center opposition leader. The remarkable part of this incident is the fact that the *Athens Post* interview, given virtually no notice in the U.S. press, was noted by Kennedy. It indicates how closely the White House then was observing Goldwater as the probable Republican nominee.

Goldwater was not totally oblivious to his problem. Before the end of the year, he imported to Washington two items of assistance designed to ensure that his "pooping around" wouldn't get him in trouble. One was a computer to sort out all the many pronouncements he had made in his career as a political preacher, to make sure that he wouldn't get them mixed up. As an incorrigible gadgeteer and devotee of *Popular Mechanics*, Goldwater was delighted with the computer. But it is doubtful whether it served a useful purpose. Of infinitely more value was the other imported aid: a taciturn fifty-five-year-old lawyer from Phoenix, Arizona, named Denison Kitchel.

Kitchel, deceptively boyish looking because of his grayish-blond crop of crew-cut hair, was one of Barry Goldwater's closest confidants. He had been scheduled months before to manage Goldwater's campaign for reelection to the Senate in 1964. Now, as he quietly arrived in September of 1964 to assume a position without portfolio in the amorphous Goldwater "organization," it was clear that he was going to manage something far more ambitious than a sure-thing reelection campaign in a remote Western state. Goldwater had named his national campaign chief of staff and had thereby tipped his hand to those who still had to be convinced that he was running for President.

Within days after arriving in Washington, Denny Kitchel made it clear that he was no politician. He had had no experience in Arizona politics, much less in Presidential politics, except on a tangential basis. Abrupt and often tactless, Kitchel quickly found that he didn't like a way of life that puts inordinate stress on patience and tact. Slightly hard of hearing, he found for the first time in his life that he couldn't even understand everything that was being said. "When I went to the doctor for a hearing aid," he recalled later, "I told him I had entered a line of work where everybody whispers." He detested the small talk, circumlocution, and wasted time that are part of the day-to-day business of politics. Lawyer Kitchel couldn't understand why the politicians couldn't just come directly to the point.

Apart from his lack of political experience, Kitchel scarcely had the personality of a great political manager. A wellborn son of Bronxville, New York, and graduate of St. Paul's School, Yale, and Harvard Law School, Kitchel had migrated to the West after college. The years in the desert had not put much of a dent in the austere reserve of this erstwhile member of the East Coast gentry.

Kitchel's early problems in communicating with politicians produced at least one unfortunate result. Leonard Hall, having three times turned down pleas to become Rockefeller's campaign manager, was ready to cross his Rubicon from the eastern seaboard Republicanism that was his heritage to the new conservative Republicanism of Barry Goldwater. Goldwater men were anxious to have Hall on their team, partly because of his prestige and know-how, but also partly because they thought that he would serve as a bridge between them and the East. At that time, the Goldwater men thought of Goldwater as leading a unified party—not as leading a factional take-over of the party through sheer strength of numbers. Representing Goldwater on an informal basis, Senator John Tower of Texas was in private contact with Hall several times that summer in an effort to get him to climb aboard. Hall was interested, but insisted on talking to Goldwater himself. Goldwater was interested, but was still religiously maintaining the position of noncandidate—and, as a noncandidate, couldn't possibly offer campaign jobs to anybody. A compromise was arranged. Hall would lunch in a Washington hotel with Kitchel, who was the next best thing to Goldwater himself. During the course of the lunch, Kitchel presumably would offer the post of campaign staff director to Hall. Presumably, that is.

The luncheon was a disaster. Hall got the impression that

Kitchel expected him to volunteer his services. Kitchel got the impression that Hall was beating around the bush and really didn't want to go to work for Goldwater at all. It was a case of two ships passing in the night. The two men parted amiably after the lunch with nothing whatever decided. There was no second lunch.

If Kitchel was not a professional politician, neither was he a conservative theoretician (as his early notices around Washington described him). He had written a thin book embroidering the conservative dogma that repeal of the Connally Amendment restricting U.S. participation in the World Court would be "too grave a risk" for the U.S. in its cold-war death struggle with the Communist world.[5] That seems to have been the extent of Kitchel's career as a conservative philosopher. He was not known to conservative intellectuals, and they were not known to him.

One incident points this up. Interviewed that fall by Chalmers M. Roberts of the *Washington Post*, Kitchel told him that Robert Strausz-Hupé, director of the Foreign Policy Research Institute at the University of Pennsylvania, had volunteered his services to Goldwater. Strausz-Hupé, one of the most highly respected conservative intellectuals in the field of foreign policy, had indeed written Goldwater a letter offering his services several weeks earlier. But all he received in return from Goldwater was a form letter of acknowledgment. The blunder was quickly reported to Kitchel. But his first reaction was: "Who is Strausz-Hupé?"

If not a politician and not a theoretician, why then was Kitchel so important? Because he was precisely what Barry Goldwater needed most: a close friend he could confide in and whose advice he could rely on. It quickly became evident that Kitchel alone, among all the Senator's political associates, was his peer. He alone could dare talk back to

[5] Denison Kitchel, *Too Grave a Risk: The Connally Amendment Issue,* New York: William Morrow and Company, Inc., 1963. The book's foreword is by Barry Goldwater.

Goldwater, to advise him in the strongest of language, without fear of a snappy retort at the time or of being ignored by the Senator in the future. Whatever Kitchel's shortcomings as a politician, the politicians themselves began to treat him with the utmost respect when they perceived how close he really was to Goldwater.

Kitchel set up a nameless quasi-advisory unit for Goldwater, renting a suite in the Carroll Arms Hotel on Capitol Hill, just down the street from Goldwater's office in the Old Senate Office Building. Edward A. McCabe, Washington lawyer and middle-level White House official under Eisenhower, was brought in by Kitchel as director of research. A few weeks later, a thirty-six-year-old Tucson, Arizona, lawyer named Dean Burch unobtrusively slipped into Washington as Kitchel's assistant. Like Kitchel, Burch was a Goldwater intimate. But he was a protégé, not a peer; a faithful admirer, not a constructive critic. Crossing east of the Mississippi River for the first time at the age of twenty-eight, Burch had come to Washington in 1955 as Goldwater's administrative assistant and had returned to Tucson in 1959 to practice law (specializing in clients with problems before the Arizona State Legislature). Burch and McCabe slowly began to build a set of position papers for Goldwater. They also served as liaison men with the Draft Goldwater headquarters miles away in midtown Washington, improving communications between the O'Donnell-White group and the Senator.

But Kitchel's greatest service to the Senator was highly personal. His cool-headed calm was an effective antidote to Goldwater's mercurial impulsiveness. His supreme mission was to impress upon the Senator the gravity of running for the Presidency, the necessity to weigh his words most carefully and to bite his tongue once or twice before he spoke.

Would Kitchel have been successful? Even if he weren't, was Goldwater's "pooping around" damaging him enough to significantly reduce his vast lead over Rockefeller and every-body else? The answer to both questions is "probably not." But nobody will ever know. One of the great tragedies of our generation was to transform the political situation in such a way that a peaceful Republican Party united under Barry Goldwater would be impossible.

XVI

★ ★

Dallas

On Friday, November 22, 1963, Denison Kitchel was having a long, talkative lunch with Tony Smith, Senator Goldwater's press secretary, and two political reporters at the Sheraton-Carlton Hotel's dining room.

Both Kitchel and Smith expressed annoyance and concern over what they considered misreporting in the press of Goldwater's remarks about selling the TVA and giving authority over nuclear-weapons use to the NATO commander. Aside from that, however, they scarcely seemed to have a problem in the world. They frankly admitted that they could see no possible impediment in Goldwater's path to the nomination.

Their confidence was justified. On November 2, a poll of the Republican Party's state and county leaders conducted by the Associated Press showed that an overwhelming majority favored Goldwater for the nomination. Out of 1,404 grass roots party officials responding to the survey, 1,194, or 85.1 percent, chose Goldwater as the "strongest candidate" against Kennedy. Nelson Rockefeller was an out-of-sight second with 56 votes, or 3.9 percent. As an afterthought, Richard M. Nixon was selected by 44, or 3.1 percent, of the party leaders replying.[1]

[1] However, only 901 of the party leaders responding to the AP poll, or 64.2 percent, thought that Goldwater actually would be nominated. This reflected the lingering fear of many conservatives that the "Wall Street internationalists" would at the last moment do to Goldwater what they had done to Taft in 1952.

Nor was this immense edge limited strictly to party wheelhorses. On the same day, a Gallup survey showed that Goldwater was expanding his lead over Rockefeller, Romney, and Scranton among the party's rank and file. This was Gallup's November survey as compared with the October rating:

	Percent, November	Percent, October
Goldwater	45	42
Rockefeller	23	26
Romney	16	15
Scranton	5	6
Others, no preference	11	13

So, on that late-autumn afternoon, campaign manager Kitchel was not much worried about capturing the nomination. That was taken for granted. What really concerned him was the forthcoming struggle against John F. Kennedy for the Presidency itself. Even now, he was talking of plans for the general-election campaign. Just that afternoon, for instance, a well-wisher had stopped by Kitchel's office in the Carroll Arms to offer a campaign gimmick: a contest to predict what crisis the Kennedy brothers would uncork just in time for the election. Half-seriously, Kitchel said that the idea was worth considering. Fully serious, Kitchel told of the beginnings of an informal brain trust to help Goldwater right through to November 3, 1964. He disclosed that he and the Senator were meeting in the evenings every so often at friends' homes in the Washington area with groups of three or four conservative academicians brought in from all parts of the country.

Kitchel acknowledged that Goldwater faced an uphill fight against Kennedy. But, lingering over coffee after lunch, Kitchel told in loving detail an incident intended to indicate Goldwater's abilty to win over hostile listeners. The Senator was addressing a junior high school in Tucson, Arizona. To hear Kitchel tell it, the entire student body had been indoctrinated with liberal Democratic dogma by the pervasive influence in Tucson of the Udall brothers (Secretary of the Interior Stewart Udall and Congressman Morris Udall). The students were sullen, even discourteous, when Goldwater first entered the auditorium. But in less than thirty minutes, they were eating out of his hand, cheering his conservative axioms. The implied moral of Kitchel's story: the same thing could happen with the American people.

As the four left the Sheraton-Carlton to enter a taxi, they heard the unbelievable news blaring over the taxi's radio. President Kennedy and Governor John B. Connally had been shot and seriously wounded in the sun-drenched streets of Dallas. As the taxi drove off, the four listened in stunned silence. Tony Smith was the first to speak. "My God," he said, "I'll bet one of those Birchers did it."

Smith's concern probably was shared by thousands of dedicated Goldwater supporters in those first confused hours after John F. Kennedy's assassination. If a member of the John Birch Society or any other extremist group had fired the shots, the reaction against respectable conservatism generally and Barry Goldwater specifically would have instantly removed any possibility of his winning the Republican nomination.

Assassin Lee Harvey Oswald turned out to be no Bircher, but instead an avowed Marxist. That meant that the tragedy of Dallas had not completely destroyed Goldwater's candidacy. However, even Goldwater's staunchest supporters knew that it had been badly damaged.

On November 22, Charles Barr, the Chicago oil-company executive who had been one of the founders of the Draft Goldwater movement, was in St. Louis attending a Midwestern regional party conference. Even before he had learned of the assassination, he had heard an analysis of the tragedy's political impact that was to be repeated incessantly in the coming weeks. As Barr walked through a hotel lobby, a fellow Republican politician grabbed him by the arm and said: "I'm sorry for you, Charlie. I'm afraid your man's all through."

It was a commonly stated opinion. It became the great cliché of Washington to say that the bullet that killed Jack Kennedy also struck Barry Goldwater. Once Congress reconvened after the Kennedy state funeral, the Speaker's Lobby just outside the House of Representatives was filled with Republican Congressmen whispering to one another and to newsmen that Goldwater no longer had the slightest chance for the nomination.

There were two basic reasons behind these arguments:

First, Goldwater's Southern-based victory plan seemed to be an immediate victim of the transformed political climate. Goldwater had had a better chance to beat Kennedy than any other Republican precisely because of his undeniable strength in the South. Now, with the first citizen of a Confederate state to occupy the White House since Andrew Johnson, that strength had all but disappeared. In December of 1963, it seemed most unlikely that Barry Goldwater would win many electoral votes in the South against Lyndon Johnson.

Second, the vote-rich industrialized states of the eastern seaboard, which had been John F. Kennedy's private political property, now seemed open to challenge by a Republican candidate—by the *proper* Republican candidate, that is. Goldwater certainly didn't seem to fit the specifications. The proper strategy for challenging Texan Johnson seemed to dictate opposing him with a "Republican Kennedy"— that is, a moderately liberal, handsome sophisticate. The suburban and urban Democrats who might not be entirely impressed with Johnson's Southern homilies would be attracted by such a Republican.

But these two entirely justifiable political arguments

do not in themselves account for the instant writing off of Goldwater's chances for the nomination by so many Republican politicians who only the day before had been perfectly willing to acquiesce in Mr. Conservative's nomination. Outside of the hard core of Goldwater zealots, Republicans who had been leaning toward him suddenly were leaning the other way. Indeed, there was a sense of emancipation within the party over the apparent end of Goldwater's Presidential bid, much like the sense of emancipation that followed the virtual elimination of Rockefeller following his remarriage back in May.

The truth is that Goldwater's unified support within the party before November 22 was only skin deep. His conservatism had not really been accepted by key party leaders. They were not about to fight his nomination, partly because he seemed to have a better chance than any other Republican of beating Kennedy, but mainly they saw no valid excuse for depriving Goldwater of the nomination. The growing party consensus saw 1964 as the year when the party's conservative wing might as well have its own candidate. If they didn't, there might be an open party schism. But now, with the assassination, there were excuses for stopping Goldwater. Thus, the feeling of emancipation.

This meant that Goldwater no longer had the slightest chance of leading a truly united party into the general-election campaign even if he managed to win the nomination. The party no longer would stand aside for him to walk through unanimously on the first ballot as it had for Alf Landon in 1936 and Thomas E. Dewey in 1944. Now it was certain that the party's liberal, or progressive, wing—or, as it now had taken to calling itself, the "moderate" wing— was sure to oppose Goldwater right up to the balloting at San Francisco.[2]

[2] By the end of 1963, the Goldwater influence was such that "liberal" had become a dirty word. "Progressive" was an outmoded label of a bygone era, connoting nothing very definite. So gradually through 1963, the anti-

But this opposition was to be fragmented, split among a half-dozen ambitious men. When Rockefeller had fallen after his remarriage in May, Goldwater moved into the vacuum after only a brief delay. When Goldwater fell (or, at least, seemed to fall) after the Kennedy assassination, there was nobody to move into the vacuum. If one moderate had had the backing of the rest of the Republican moderates, Goldwater might have been finished before ever really beginning his campaign. As matters turned out, however, the fragmentation of the moderates was to prove one of Goldwater's greatest strengths—perhaps his greatest strength.

During the month-long political moratorium following the assassination, here was how Goldwater's rivals stood:

Rockefeller: Despite Goldwater's obvious slip, Rockefeller showed no perceptible gain. His closest advisers were bitterly disappointed that the party's fence-straddlers, who now regarded Goldwater as a political corpse, did not immediately switch back to Rockefeller. Instead, most of the party felt that the Governor had not recovered from the political trauma of his remarriage.

This didn't bother Rockefeller. He was the only announced Republican candidate for President, having made political history of a sort on November 6 by announcing his candidacy at eight o'clock in the morning in order to appear on NBC's widely watched "Today" show over nationwide television.[3] He wasn't quitting yet. Rather, he was building a massive campaign staff that made the Draft

---

Goldwater forces appropriated for themselves the label of "moderates." Goldwater men complained, with some little justification, that "moderate" was a euphemism for "liberal." Nevertheless, for the sake of convenience, the label "moderate" to describe the anti-Goldwater forces will be used for the rest of this book.

[3] Rockefeller did not go whole hog and become a full-fledged television-age candidate by making his announcement from the NBC studios. Instead, his televised announcement originated from the Governor's ceremonial office in the State Capitol in Albany.

Goldwater headquarters staff and the meager handful re-
cruited by Denny Kitchel look like a bush-league operation.

Besides campaign manager John A. Wells, the most important addition to the Rockefeller staff was Charles Moore,
one of the nation's most brilliant public-relations men. A
onetime newspaper reporter who had become vice-president
for public relations of Ford Motor Co., Moore had been an
intimate of George Romney and had helped mastermind his
rise to the Governor's chair. He had left Ford and had come
to the East for an early retirement in 1963, but Rockefeller
talked him into running his campaign's public-relations
operation. Moore quickly became a part of the Rockefeller
inner circle.

On a lower level, Rockefeller was hiring top professional
politicians around the country who would serve under the
general command of George Hinman. Lawrence Lindemer,
former Michigan state party chairman, was named Midwestern coordinator. Mort Frayne, former Washington
state chairman, was named Pacific Coast coordinator.

But Rockefeller realized that not even professionals of
the Lindemer-Frayne caliber would enable him to win a
delegate-hunting competition with Goldwater. He told
friends in December that the party's leaders were still blinded
by his remarriage and would not accept him under any conditions—unless they were forced to. How to force them?
Through the primaries. The entire high-paid Rockefeller
campaign apparatus was geared to beating Barry Goldwater
in the primaries—all the primaries that they could entice
Goldwater into entering—and thus to force Rockefeller's
nomination on the party. That he was still regarded as an
underdog in the primaries, even against the politically
weakened Goldwater, bothered Rockefeller not at all.

Romney: Despite his tax-program debacle, Romney was
showing definite signs of new interest in national politics—
even before the assassination. Shortly after the defeat of

his tax program, Romney invited all his old supporters in the Citizens for Michigan and in his race for Governor to a private, informal party in Detroit. When all were assembled, he informed them that, though he certainly was not becoming a candidate for President, he was to embark on a speechmaking tour around the country early in 1964.

"Why, George," replied one of his oldest friends, "everybody will say you're running for President. What will you do then?"

"I'll just tell them I'm not," Romney replied blandly.

Everybody did interpret Romney's renewed speechmaking as a hat, if not exactly in the ring, then on the edge of the ring. But no skyrockets were launched, because the defeat of the tax program had set Romney off on one of those political escalator rides that are impossible to stop. It was just as difficult to explain why party workers and rank-and-file Republicans alike suddenly lost their interest in Romney as it was to explain why there had been so much interest in him during the summer and early autumn. His speaking engagements in January generated no Presidential enthusiasm. A speech before the National Press Club was a pale imitation of his triumphant appearance before the same body in May. His volunteered declaration that "I'd have a duty to accept" a draft "if it should come" aroused only the murmur from the newsmen that it almost certainly wouldn't come. Next came another rebuke from the *Detroit News*, again urging Romney to stick to his knitting as Governor of Michigan.[4] Romney once again retired to obscurity in Lansing.

Scranton: The politically sophisticated, in both parties and in the press, immediately thought of Scranton as the "Republican Kennedy" to oppose Lyndon Johnson. That started a steady flow of politicians and political writers on that two-hour auto ride from Washington to Harrisburg. During the thirty-day political moratorium, the political traffic to Bill

[4] See page 162.

Scranton's office was of rush-hour proportions. So was the volume of telephone calls into his office.

Scranton was still the reluctant dragon in chats with his visitors. True, he expressed the opinion that Johnson was by no means the surefire winner that Kennedy would have been and was particularly vulnerable in the Northeast. But Scranton quickly took pains to point out that *he* certainly wouldn't be the man to do the job. Conceding that he had first declined to run for Congress in 1960 and for Governor in 1962 and then had consented both times, Scranton told visitors that he had agreed to run on those occasions only because the party was on the brink of factional warfare and party leaders felt that he alone could unite them. Neither of those conditions existed today, he added.

But the visitors got quite another story from his aggressive young aides and particularly from his administrative assistant, William Keisling, a twenty-seven-year-old ex-newspaper reporter from Scranton, Pennsylvania, who first entered politics as Scranton's aide in the Congressional race of 1960. He idolized the Governor. Plump, extroverted Bill Keisling pulled out all the stops in singing the praises of his boss in the harsh, guttural accents of Pennsylvania's hard-coal country. He would point out to politicians either visiting in Harrisburg or telephoning long distance that Scranton had first turned a deaf ear to pleas that he run in 1960 and 1962, only to change his mind. The implication was that he would change his mind again. Nor were representatives of the communications media discouraged from coming to Harrisburg and writing about Scranton. It was not entirely accidental that most of the big magazines prepared full-dress articles on Scranton soon after the assassination. Scranton's mass appeal as measured by his ratings in the polls was still miniscule. But the top level of politicians was definitely interested.[5]

[5] There was much more than this to the post-assassination Scranton build-up. The story is told in greater detail in Chapter XVII.

Nixon: The assassination caught Nixon in mid-sentence—
or, to put it more accurately, in mid-contract. On November
22, he had been set to sign a lucrative contract with a large
publishing house to write a long book about the campaign
of 1964 (with a publishing date sometime in 1965).[6] That
commitment, while further fattening the expanding bank
account of Wall Street lawyer Nixon, would have eliminated
Nixon from dark horse consideration for the nomination.
When news of the assassination came, the appointment with
the publisher was canceled. It never was rescheduled. Nixon
now was a serious, significant contender for the nomination,
though not an avowed candidate.

If Goldwater was indeed eliminated, Nixon was definitely
a possible replacement. Although national party leaders of
all ideological persuasions had tended to sour on Nixon in
his 1960 campaign and his 1962 disaster in California, he was
remembered by millions of rank-and-file Republican voters
and party workers as the man who came within a hair of
beating John F. Kennedy for the Presidency, not the man
who was trounced by Pat Brown for the Governorship of
California. This was his one great asset in the new, fluid
situation: if Scranton was still a town somewhere in Pennsylvania to most Americans, Nixon was a household word.[7]

Lodge:The most surprising development of the post-assas-

[6] Actually, Nixon wasn't going to "write" the book in the old-fashioned
sense. Political reporters were to have been hired as stringers for Nixon
around the country. Their reports would flow into a central desk, where a
Nixon aide would write a straightforward account of the 1964 campaign.
Nixon would then put on the finishing touches by inserting commentary and
analysis.

[7] Nixon's residual name identification was demonstrated shortly before the
assassination, when he narrowly beat Goldwater among rank-and-file Republicans, 52 percent to 48 percent, in a two-man Gallup Poll. In the preassassination political climate, this was not regarded as a sign of strength
for Nixon or of weakness for Goldwater, but rather proof that newcomer
Goldwater was beginning to match Nixon in name identification. Similarly,
Adlai Stevenson, the 1952 and 1956 Democratic nominee, led Kennedy in
Gallup Poll ratings until the primary election campaigns identified Kennedy
to the public early in 1960.

sination moratorium was the sudden emergence of the other half of the 1960 Nixon-Lodge ticket, Henry Cabot Lodge, the archetypical liberal Eastern Republican, as a nonavowed candidate. And he did it while staying on the other side of the world, in Indochina, continuing to serve Johnson as he had Kennedy as Ambassador to South Vietnam.

A few unsuccessful trial balloons had been shot up for Lodge before the assassination. In the first few days after November 22, there was renewed talk by his friends about Lodge being the prototype candidate who ought to take on Johnson, but there was still not much of a reaction. If Nixon was less than popular with the national-level Republican politicians, Lodge was considered a public enemy. They were still incensed over his leisurely Vice-Presidential campaign of 1960 and particularly his pajama-clad midafternoon nap (though most of them did not go so far as Goldwater in claiming that Lodge's languid style had cost Nixon the Presidency).

But the politicians' eyes opened wide on the Sunday morning of December 1 at the sight of this headline in the right-hand corner of the *New York Times*:

EISENHOWER URGES

LODGE TO PURSUE

GOP NOMINATION

It was followed by a Washington dispatch by Felix Belair, Jr., the *Times* White House correspondent during the Eisenhower days and one of the few Washington reporters who had a working relationship with the General. Belair began:

> Former President Dwight D. Eisenhower has asked Ambassador Henry Cabot Lodge to make himself available for the Republican Presidential nomination.
>
> Without going into such details as preferential primary elections or pre-convention campaign tactics, General Eisenhower

urged Mr. Lodge to return to the United States soon from
Saigon to take part actively in the Republican party effort to
develop a consensus in a candidate before the national convention in July.

The move was part of General Eisenhower's personal re-
appraisal of Republican prospects in next year's Presidential
elections. He has been telling friends recently that the political
upheaval resulting from the assassination of President Kennedy
and the emergence of President Johnson as the Democratic
standard-bearer in 1964 calls for a re-evaluation of the Republican position.

As General Eisenhower sees that position, the Republicans'
best chance of winning the Presidential election in November
is with a moderate, common-sense candidate with an impressive background in international affairs. He regards Mr.
Lodge as one of the very few Republicans who could compete
on equal terms with President Johnson on the paramount issue
of war and peace.

Belair went on to say that Eisenhower felt that Rockefeller had not "recovered sufficiently" from his remarriage,
that Nixon "may have a limited appeal to Republican voters"
because of his 1960 and 1962 defeats, that Scranton is "not
available" because of his desire to finish his four-year term
as Governor, ending in 1966. The dispatch continued:

It was against this background that General Eisenhower
urged Mr. Lodge in their only conversation recently to consider coming back and indicating his availability by making
some speeches on the big political issues of the day.

Lodge was Topic A in the Capital the next day. The general bewilderment over the *Times* dispatch was illustrated
by Senator Thruston Morton, the wry and witty Kentuckian
who himself had been mentioned by Eisenhower in private
discussions as a dark horse possibility for President. "Until
yesterday," drawled Morton, "I would have thought Lodge
would have some trouble getting a seat at the convention,

much less be nominated for President. But now, I just don't know."

Other Republican members of Congress were harsher than Morton. They were enraged. Three years of grumbling that Lodge had dogged it on the 1960 campaign trail now were reinforced by what they considered his act of apostasy in serving first Kennedy and then Johnson in a critical overseas crisis that could be made into a 1964 campaign liability for the Democrats.[8]

Some of these Republicans quickly contacted Bryce Harlow, White House chief of Congressional liaison under Eisenhower and now Washington representative for Procter & Gamble. Still the intimate of the General, and writer of most of his speeches, Harlow called Gettysburg and reported back to the Congressmen with this account of what really had happened: Eisenhower had not fingered Lodge as *the* candidate for the nomination. On the contrary, the General would continue to remain scrupulously neutral. But he did hope that as many outstanding Republicans as possible would seek the nomination, and he hoped that his old friend Cabot Lodge would be among them. He had told Lodge only that if he did intend to make a race for the nomination, he ought to hurry back home. That was all there was to it, Harlow reported to the Congressmen. It was not to be the last apparent commitment, followed by a rapid withdrawal, by Eisenhower in the Presidential race.

Whatever consternation the *Times* story caused among party officials and workers, it created no discernible support for Lodge. Talking to friends, Nixon declared: "If Cabot comes home, it will have to be with either a blast or victory." Immediate "victory" against the Communist guer-

---

[8] According to Belair's *Times* dispatch, Eisenhower did not criticize Lodge for taking the Vietnamese assignment, but felt that he should return now that Kennedy was dead. Belair wrote: "As General Eisenhower viewed the matter, any obligation that the Ambassador felt he owed the Administration had ended with the death of President Kennedy."

rillas in Vietnam was out of the question. And Nixon expressed the view that Lodge could hardly "blast" a situation in which he himself was intimately involved. Most Republican leaders agreed that Lodge was a prisoner in Saigon.

But some of Lodge's old friends were at work building a Draft Lodge movement. The first of these was Colonel Irving Saloman, a retired Chicago industrialist and Republican campaign-fund contributor, now living in San Diego, California, who had been named by President Eisenhower to serve on the U.S. delegation to the United Nations under Ambassador Lodge. Weeks after the assassination, Saloman talked about getting something going for Lodge to another intimate: Washington public-relations man Robert Mullen. Mullen was skeptical at first. But in the changed and confused post-assassination political climate, Mullen came to agree with Saloman.

Mullen had first come in contact with Lodge back in 1936. As a fledgling Boston political reporter, Mullen was spellbound by young Henry Cabot Lodge's satirical speech in Boston's Orchestra Hall mimicking James Curley, Lodge's Democratic opponent for the Senate. The Lodge-Mullen friendship was formed that night. They were together again just after World War II, when Senator Lodge was helping push through the Senate the Marshall Plan for rehabilitating Europe and Mullen was in charge of publicity at the Marshall Plan's Washington office. And in 1952, Mullen was one of Lodge's aides in the Draft Eisenhower movement that succeeded first in getting the General to come back from his command in Europe and then in getting nominated. Now in 1964, Mullen wanted to do for Lodge what Lodge had done for Eisenhower.

He started by enlisting the informal cooperation of George Lodge, the Ambassador's son. Young Lodge in turn reassembled the youthful, energetic campaign organization that had worked for him in his unsuccessful but spirited 1962 campaign for the Senate against Edward M. (Teddy) Kennedy. It was a start, but it was a good deal short of being a professional nationwide organization.

However, the public was interested. To the rank-and-file Republican voters, Lodge was not the querulous, aging Brahmin who napped too frequently in the 1960 campaign, but the handsome, full-voiced Ambassador to the United Nations who had never hesitated to tell the Russians off during their nationally televised confrontations. Indeed, Lodge was the only surprise of the new Gallup Poll ratings after the assassination. Nixon, with his enormous name identification, was running well. Goldwater had slipped. Rockefeller and Romney showed no signs of recovery. Scranton was still an unknown. The one surprise was Lodge. Here are the first two Gallup Polls taken after the assassination:

	Percent, December	*Percent, January*
Nixon	29	29
Goldwater	27	23
Lodge	16	19
Rockefeller	13	12
Romney	7	8
Scranton	2	4
Others, no preference	6	5

By the time that second Gallup Poll appeared, the Lodge phenomenon was in full swing.

As a political amateur, Kitchel's immediate political reaction to the assassination was the feeling that Goldwater's prospects to win the Presidency had been improved. Now that Kennedy the political champ was dead, he told fellow members of the Goldwater staff, wouldn't it be easier for Goldwater?

But Goldwater's more politically sophisticated supporters had no such illusions. Particularly Clif White at the Draft Goldwater headquarters. As a political professional, White

knew well the importance of momentum in politics. Goldwater had lost his—perhaps temporarily, perhaps perma-
nently. The changed political climate had made no difference
to the hard core of Goldwater supporters who were the
essence of the national political organization that White and
Peter O'Donnell were building. But the Goldwater zealots
by themselves were not enough for the nomination. What
also was needed was the shrewd fence-sitting politicians who
had leaned first to Rockefeller, then to Goldwater, and now
were eyeing Nixon and Scranton. Momentum was needed to
get them back aboard the Goldwater bandwagon.

How to get momentum? White recognized fully that most
Republican leaders now doubted that even Goldwater could
make much of a dent in the South. Thus, it was necessary
to convince them that Goldwater could run well against
Johnson in the *North*. And the only way to do this effectively
was by a long, unbroken chain of primary-election victories.
Thus, the primaries now took on more importance than
ever before in White's view. Believing, as most Goldwater
men then did, that the Senator was by far the party's best
vote-getter and would easily win any primary, White wanted
him to enter as many primaries as humanly possible and win
them all—just as Kennedy did in 1960. A long, unbroken
chain of primary victories, coupled with the grass roots support from party workers, would be bound to lead to an easy
first-ballot victory—perhaps by acclamation.

But unlike the Rockefeller forces, White was not relying
exclusively on the primaries. Even after the assassination,
when the political moratorium was in effect, the Draft Goldwater organization was slowly building and perfecting its
delegate-hunting machinery. Take the case of New Mexico.
In December, 1963, Goldwater men were pouring into and
dominating precinct mass meetings throughout New Mexico.
These mass meetings elected pro-Goldwater delegates to
county conventions, which in turn elected pro-Goldwater

delegates to the state convention. Predictably, the state convention, which met on June 6, 1964, elected an all-Goldwater fourteen-member delegation to the National Convention. But it all began six months earlier with those precinct meetings—meetings neglected by all the other candidates. It was a procedure repeated in more than one state.

Actually, Barry Goldwater personally was oblivious to all these plans and any talk of lost or regained momentum in December of 1963. The more immediate question bothering him was the basic one of whether he should run for President.

Goldwater tipped his hand in an Associated Press interview on December 5. While going through the motions of the conventional political statement that "I don't think my support has changed from what it was," he also revealed some more candid sentiments about the status of his unannounced candidacy: "I feel you can't say for sure. The whole country is in a position of flux. There's no way to assess it." In the same interview, Goldwater talked of "a new ball game with a new pitcher," and he hinted broadly that he had less philosophical reason to oppose Johnson than would have been the case with Kennedy. Speaking of the new President, Goldwater said: "I like him. I think he has a chance to be a good President, a great President." He added that Johnson has the ability for "seeing problems quickly, cutting through the red tape and junk and coming to a solution."

Among his friends, Goldwater praised Johnson in even stronger terms. He was particularly impressed by the new President's address to a joint session of Congress on November 27. Johnson had promised to cut back on wasteful Government spending and to pay greater respect to the independence of Congress. Goldwater even authorized Tony Smith, who was doubling as press secretary and frequent ghost writer of the Senator's nationally syndicated column, to write a column praising Johnson's speech. Moreover, he told friends that if Johnson lived up to his promises of budget balancing and respect for Congress, no Republican—implicitly, not even Barry Goldwater—would have a chance in the South. As long as three weeks after the assassination, when Goldwater conferred with Senator John Tower of Texas, his close political associate, about the Johnson record to date, the two conservatives agreed that they could not find any major issue on which to attack Johnson.

As word of these private comments by Goldwater began to seep out, Republican politicians interpreted them as a sure sign that Goldwater was getting ready to bow out of the Presidential race. Their expectation was supported by his doleful air in the first days after the assassination.

Goldwater was genuinely bereaved by Kennedy's death. The two men had entered the Senate together in January, 1953, had fought many battles with each other on the Senate Labor Committee, and had become casual, though certainly not close, friends. Moreover, Goldwater's spirits were not raised in the days immediately following the assassination by the torrent of angry, semihysterical letters and telephone calls blaming him and the conservative movement for Kennedy's death.[9] Finally, it should be added that Goldwater's dolefulness immediately following the assassination was aggravated by severe physical pain. A painful calcium deposit, or spur, had developed in his right heel, forcing him to walk with a pronounced limp. He spent much of his time riding back and forth between the Capitol and Georgetown University Hospital for cortisone injections. It was not a time to anticipate eagerly the rigors of a Presidental campaign.

By mid-December, Republican Congressmen in the House Speaker's Lobby were willing to give odds that Goldwater would not run. The fact is that Goldwater did toy with the

[9] The same kind of frenzied phone calls poured in to other conservative leaders, Senator John Tower was so alarmed by it that he moved his family out of their Washington home on November 22 as a precautionary measure and spent the night with friends.

idea of dropping out. He was deeply concerned with the fate of the conservative movement if he should run and lose— not so much if he should lose the race for the nomination, but if he should be nominated and then snowed under by a Johnson landslide. This could postpone the nomination of another conservative candidate for a full generation.

Furthermore, there were personal reasons. Just as he had expected, Goldwater found that he didn't at all enjoy the life of a Presidential contender. What bothered him most was the invasion of privacy. An essentially private person, Goldwater liked to ride an airliner without having the aisle filled with well-wishers wanting to shake his hand. He liked to walk into a cocktail lounge with friends for a drink or two without provoking a riot. These simple pleasures had become unobtainable during the last few months, and Goldwater liked it not at all.

Yet, the Goldwater-for-President drive had gained such momentum that it could not be stopped. The movement was bigger than the man. Goldwater had not really started it all himself, and now he couldn't turn it off. His millions of hard-core followers began deluging his Washington office with impassioned pleas urging him to run. Typical is this telegram from the Young Republicans Club of La Puente, California:

> We . . . want to extend our support to you both financially and with determined precinct activity for your nomination and election as President of the United States. If we are to continue as a free people, this nation must have a type of leadership you have consistently displayed.

Among these true believers, there were no doubts about the political wisdom of running Goldwater against Johnson. These were the zealots who cared naught for talk of momentum and bandwagons and Republican Kennedys. But Goldwater began to see that they would not remain true believers for long if he should bow out of the Presidental race. The conservative movement might be hurt if he were humiliated by Lyndon Johnson in November, but it might well be totally destroyed if he did not run at all.

Goldwater was scheduled to leave Washington on December 21 to spend Christmas at home in Phoenix. But his doctors decided that the cortisone injections had been ineffective and that the spur in his heel must be removed. They operated that afternoon, and he finally left for Arizona on Christmas Eve with his right foot in a walking cast. But by then, his decision had been made and transmitted to the key staff personnel at the Draft Goldwater headquarters. He would run.

Goldwater showed his hand on December 26. He telephoned his Washington office from Phoenix and dictated an angry two-paragraph blast against Johnson for keeping Congress in session over the Christmas holidays to pass the foreign-aid bill. The Senator said:

> I recall that President Johnson in his speech to us on November 27 spoke of the Congress as his home and indicated his respect for an independent Legislative branch. His actions on the foreign aid bill contradicted that by trying to treat Congressmen as his personal errand boys.

The honeymoon obviously was over. The statement of December 26 removed all doubts about Goldwater's intentions.

The actual announcement came January 3 in Phoenix on the patio of his $150,000 hillside home. Carrying crutches and with his foot in a walking cast, he was anything but the happy warrior. Nor was he the great advocate of party unity. He made it clear that he was going to run as a militantly conservative candidate "because I have not heard from any announced Republican candidate a declaration of conscience or of political position that could possibly offer to the American people a clear choice in the next Presidential election."

After asserting that a majority of Republicans believe "in the essential emphasis on individual liberty," he continued:

> I have been spelling out my position now for 10 years in the Senate, for years before that here in my own state. I will spell it out even further in the months to come. I was once asked what kind of Republican I was. I replied that I was not a "me-too" Republican. That still holds. I will not change my beliefs to win votes. I will offer a choice, not an echo.

A choice, not an echo. Goldwater had a campaign slogan. But he also had set for himself a course of ideological inflexibility that would have profound implications for his party.

XVII

★ ★ ★ ★ ★ ★ ★ ★ ★ ★ ★ ★ ★ ★ ★ ★ ★ ★ ★ ★

The Scranton Boomlet

On the bleak, chill evening of January 9, 1964, in Washington, William Warren Scranton made his debut as a national politician. It was a busy week for Republican politics in Washington. George Romney and Nelson Rockefeller each were making addresses to the National Press Club. Barry Goldwater, now an avowed candidate, was opening his national campaign headquarters in the Duryea Building on Connecticut Avenue (just up the street from the old Draft Goldwater offices). The Republican National Committee was holding its winter meeting at the Mayflower Hotel. And the Governor of Pennsylvania, heretofore a shrinking violet when it came to national political festivities, arrived on January 9 to join the fun.

There was the smell of a Presidential campaign about Scranton's one-day visit. A hearing room in the Old Senate Office Building was jammed with reporters for a press conference at the inconvenient hour of 6:30 P.M. While not saying much of great interest about anything, Scranton performed with assurance, grace, and a Kennedy-like style at the press conference (even managing to call the Washington political writers by their first names when answering questions, a feat that has eluded far more experienced politicians). Later in the evening, Scranton was the object of pawing, curious Republican politicians of both sexes when

270

he showed up at a Republican National Committee reception in the Mayflower Hotel. Scranton never had a moment to himself at the reception, as his aides expertly herded politicians toward the Governor whenever it appeared that he was running out of hands to shake.[1] Emphasizing the Presidential campaign aroma about Scranton's visit was the fact that one of his traveling companions happened to be writer Theodore White, author of the best-selling *The Making of a President: 1960,* friend of John F. Kennedy, and now commissioned to do a Scranton article for *Life.*

Of course, Scranton insisted that he was not in any way a candidate for President. The fact that his visit to Washington (purportedly for a dinner in his honor given by Republican members of Congress from Pennsylvania) coincided with the National Committee meeting was dismissed by Scranton as strictly accidental. His press conference was given over largely to verbal sparring with reporters over whether he was or wasn't coming closer to becoming a candidate for President. He opened a new frontier in political hairsplitting by announcing that he was not a "favorite son *candidate*" from Pennsylvania, but would be a "favorite son" (provided, that is, "there is not a runaway situation" at the beginning of the Republican National Convention and that the Pennsylvania delegation to the convention "wants me to do this").

At the beginning of that January 9 press conference, Scranton again disavowed any knowledge of the efforts made in his behalf. When asked about a statement issued by Senator Hugh Scott and Pennsylvania's Republican Congressmen that called on him to run for President, the Governor expressed his ignorance of the move, adding that he would have to talk it over with Scott. The Senator, puffing contentedly on his pipe by Scranton's side, looked like the boy who

[1] With no such adroit crowd-herders helping him and without Scranton's fresh appeal to the curious, Nelson Rockefeller was left to himself much of the time when he attended a National Committee reception the next night.

had been caught in the cookie jar. Next, another reporter asked Scranton what two of his top aides—William Keisling and James Reichley—were doing entertaining National Committee members and newsmen in a suite in the Mayflower the night before.

"Why, I didn't know anything about that," said Scranton. Then, turning to Keisling, he asked: "Is that right, Bill?"

"Yes, sir, Governor," Keisling replied, looking even more sheepish than Scott.

The sophisticated political correspondents of Washington looked upon all this as an elaborate charade. In fact, it was not. In January, 1964, Scranton was determined not to run for President—buttressed in that determination by his highly intelligent, highly aggressive, and politically perceptive wife, Mary. The push came from political allies, from friends, and —most of all—from his personal staff.

Actually, the push—in a very subtle form—began even before the assassination, under the auspices of septuagenarian Philadelphian Thomas McCabe, head of the Scott Paper Co. Though for decades a generous contributor to the party, McCabe's political role never before had been more than tangential. Now he was toying with the idea of playing kingmaker for Bill Scranton. The beginning was discreet enough. Working in cooperation with Keisling in Harrisburg, McCabe would invite prominent Republican leaders and businessmen to meet Scranton at private lunches in the boardroom of Scott Paper in Philadelphia. Scranton then would explain his legislative and administrative program intended to restore the economic health of Pennsylvania. There was never a word said about the Presidency, but nobody had any difficulty in understanding the purpose of these meetings. Another highly respected Philadelphian behind Scranton was Thomas Gates, former Secretary of Defense and now chairman of the Morgan Guaranty Trust Co. in New York. Particularly after November 22, Gates became active in preaching the virtues of Scranton in Wall Street.[2]

But the surest sign that the Eastern Establishment was lining up for Scranton came with support—qualified support, but support nevertheless—from John Hay Whitney and Walter Thayer, publisher and president, respectively, of the *New York Herald Tribune*. Never really delighted with the prospect of Nelson Rockefeller as Republican candidate for President, the *Tribune* had been looking around for an alternative to Goldwater for some time. On December 23, much to the displeasure of the Rockefeller camp, this semi-official organ of Eastern Republicanism signaled that the alternative had been found. In a full-page editorial entitled "Calling Governor Scranton," the *Tribune* stopped just short of an outright endorsement. The editorial began:

> Pennsylvania's Governor William Scranton is a man with a weakness for one temptation: the call to duty.
>
> He answered that call when, after first refusing, he finally agreed to run for Congress in 1960. He answered it again two years later, when—again reluctantly—he bowed to repeated entreaties that he run for governor.
>
> It seems clear to us that duty again calls William Scranton. This time the highest political duty of all: to place himself open in the running for the Republican Presidential nomination.

The editorial went on to write off Rockefeller, primarily "for personal reasons, which unfortunately cannot remain private in such a political situation" and to declare Goldwater's Southern strategy null and void with Johnson in the White House. That, according to the *Tribune*, put the spotlight on Scranton.

[2] Actually, Gates might well have become a Presidential possibility himself if he had gone along with the original plans of Pennsylvania kingmakers in 1962. They wanted to run Gates for Governor and Scranton for Senator. If both had won, the Presidential opportunity probably would have been Gates's, not Scranton's.

. . . he [Scranton] appears to have just the combination of qualities, both personal and political, that the Republican party needs to oppose Lyndon Johnson.

To his campaigns, Governor Scranton has brought many of the same qualities that made John F. Kennedy so exciting a candidate—youth, poise, style, articulateness, combined with a genuine zest and talent for person-to-person politicking.

Simultaneously, Scranton was actively cooperating with —in fact, leading—a well-executed, often ruthless campaign against the Goldwater forces in Pennsylvania. Fearful in May, 1963, that Goldwater insurgents might control Pennsylvania's delegation to the National Convention, Scranton had whittled the threat down to manageable proportions by the end of the year.

What was visible of the anti-Goldwater operation in Pennsylvania seemed naïve and ineffective. With a great fanfare of publicity, Scranton asked for private, separate meetings with both Goldwater and Rockefeller to impress upon them the importance for party unity in Pennsylvania and how Presidential candidates in search of Pennsylvania delegates might prove fatal to that unity. With Rockefeller a potential ally who was not about to cause Scranton any trouble in his home state, Scranton's proposal for a meeting with the New York Governor was sheer facade—necessary only to show that he wasn't discriminating between Goldwater and Rockefeller. What Scranton really wanted was the meeting with Goldwater.

Scranton and Rockefeller went through the formality of an eighty-minute meeting in New York on November 20, with Rockefeller "agreeing" not to contend for Pennsylvania delegates. That put the onus on Goldwater to make a similar commitment. Scranton and Goldwater had been scheduled to meet in Washington on November 19, but it was canceled when Goldwater left for Muncie, Indiana, to attend funeral services for his mother-in-law. In the confusion following the assassination, the meeting could not be rescheduled until mid-January. To avoid publicity, Scranton suggested that they meet secretly in Goldwater's apartment rather than in his office on Capitol Hill. Inevitably, word of the meeting leaked out. Scranton refused to talk about it; his aides hinted that Goldwater had agreed to keep hands off Pennsylvania; Goldwater proclaimed that he had said no such thing.

Whatever commitment Scranton might have thought he got from Goldwater, the Goldwater forces in Pennsylvania never showed any sign of letting up in their drive to split off delegates from the Governor. Actually, Scranton did not at all depend upon any nebulous commitment from Goldwater to keep order in his own house. Rather, he used his own version of the velvet glove and mailed fist—the velvet glove for Pennsylvania Goldwater backers willing to lay down their arms voluntarily and come over to Scranton, the mailed fist against those who insisted on fighting for Goldwater until the bitter end.

Once Scranton showed that he meant to use the mighty patronage powers of the state of Pennsylvania to keep the delegation loyal to him, most of the defections to Goldwater ceased—particularly after the assassination had apparently lessened the likelihood of a Goldwater nomination. By January, many of the Goldwater men of the previous summer were Scranton converts. The most important of them was James F. Malone, president of the Pennsylvania Manufacturers Association and an original member of the Western Pennsylvania Goldwater Committee. In a January 24 interview with the *New York Times*, Malone confirmed what politicians in Pennsylvania knew: "I would say he's [Scranton] in a pretty good position to get the nomination. . . . Goldwater has a lot of ground to make up since President Kennedy's assassination." Malone's defection was a severe blow from which the Pennsylvania Goldwater forces never quite recovered.

For one Pennsylvania Goldwaterite who did not capitulate

to Harrisburg, the reward was grim retaliation. The victim
was Paul Hugus, Allegheny County (Pittsburgh) Republican
chairman and one of Goldwater's earliest and most steadfast
supporters in the state.[3] The long story of the negotiations
between Scranton's office and Hugus is too convoluted to be
retraced here. Suffice it to say that two Scranton agents—
William Murphy, the Governor's secretary, and Craig Truax,
the state party chairman—applied the screws to Hugus with
such unflinching tenacity that he became an object lesson
of what befalls the Republican politician who defies Harrisburg. State patronage was stripped from Allegheny County.
Hugus' salary as county chairman was terminated. Ultimately, after a long and bitter fight, Hugus was kept off
Pennsylvania's delegation to the National Convention.[4]

More than discreet meetings with Scranton in the inner
sanctum of the Scott Paper Co. and more than qualified
endorsements from the *New York Herald Tribune,* this raw-
meat exhibition of power politics impressed party leaders. It
was one reason why a Scranton boomlet was running strong
by the time that the Republican National Committee convened during the week of January 6 at the Mayflower Hotel
for its winter meeting. Considering Scranton's continued
anonymity among rank-and-file voters (as witnessed by his
still-microscopic Gallup Poll ratings), it was just a boomlet
and not a genuine boom. But the boomlet was running
strong among the politicians gathered at the National Committee meetings—most of them from the eastern seaboard
states, but including some left-of-Goldwater party leaders
from the Midwest and West, such as State Chairmen Jean

[3] Hugus' election as county chairman was celebrated by Clif White as a
step forward for Goldwater in one of his early confidential memorandums
to the nucleus of the Draft Goldwater forces. See p. 118.
[4] At one point, Hugus thought he had won a seat to the convention. This
was when the Allegheny County organization slated him as an endorsed
candidate for delegate in the primary election over the objections of the
Scranton forces. But in an unprecedented move, Scranton fielded his own
candidate against Hugus in the primary. Hugus lost.

Tool of Colorado and Robert Forsythe of Minnesota. Forsythe was so anxious to get his first glimpse of Scranton in action that he traveled crosstown from the Mayflower to Capitol Hill for the Governor's January 9 press conference.

Moreover, some of the kindest words uttered about Bill Scranton during that National Committee meeting came from the "three musketeers" of eastern seaboard Republican politics—Leonard Hall of New York, Meade Alcorn of Connecticut, and Fred Scribner of Maine. They controlled no delegates, but the residual prestige of the Eastern Establishment was theirs. True, none of them was coming out for Scranton at this time. But they made it clear in private conversation where their sympathies lay.

The weeks of winter and early spring also saw a quiet pilgrimage of the Eastern Republican eggheads to Harrisburg. Dr. Arthur Burns, professor of economics at Columbia and chairman of the President's Council of Economic Advisers under Eisenhower, came to talk economics. Dr. Malcom Moos, a White House speech writer in the Eisenhower days and now a Johns Hopkins University professor, came to volunteer as a speech writer. Dr. Milton Eisenhower, president of Johns Hopkins and the former President's younger brother, came to talk about Latin-American problems.

There was no question that the obscurity of preassassination days had been pulled from Scranton (though not with his energetic cooperation). What worried his aides was how soon more dramatic advances could be made. Walter Alessandroni, a tough, pint-size Philadelphia lawyer who had been named attorney general of Pennsylvania by Scranton after managing the 1962 gubernatorial campaign, thought that the time to strike was now. Early in January, he mapped out a plan of drumming up a write-in campaign for Scranton in the New Hampshire primary on March 10 to show the Governor's vote-getting prowess. Scranton flatly forbade Alessandroni to start off on any such venture.

Though generally more bullish than Alessandroni, Scranton's younger aides believed nothing could be gained by getting mixed up in the New Hampshire maelstrom. Bill Keisling, the Governor's assistant, toyed with the idea of running a clandestine campaign for Scranton in the May 15 Oregon primary (where Scranton's name would be on the ballot anyway because of the state's strange primary-election law). But State Chairman Craig Truax, at thirty-four an instinctively shrewd political strategist, wanted Scranton to lie low until after the Oregon primary. By then, it would be too late to enter the California primary, and Scranton could become an avowed candidate without having to contend with Rockefeller and Goldwater in the California showdown on June 2.[5] The strategy was ideal for Scranton. As a new political face, he could not hope to contend with Goldwater and Rockefeller in the primaries. By staying out of the primaries, he would avoid a ruinous defeat and—more important—avoid bruising his relationships with any of the other contenders.

This was the heart of the Truax plan. Avoid insulting anybody. Truax was particularly industrious in maintaining the warmest of relations with not only the conservative party leaders leaning toward Goldwater, but also the Goldwater staff itself. At every party gathering, Truax was to be seen drinking, joking, and earnestly talking with Clif White and with John Grenier, the Alabama state party chairman who had been named Goldwater's Southern regional director.[6] In the spirit of political banter, Truax assured White and Grenier that there would be a place for them high in the Scranton organization once he had won the nomination. It

[5] The tactic of announcing a candidacy only after it is too late to enter any primaries often is used by a candidate without great popular support but with important backing among the party leaders. This tactic was followed by Senator Stuart Symington of Missouri in the 1960 Democratic competition, but, of course, it failed in the face of Kennedy's all-victorious record in the primaries.

[6] Truax' courtship of White and Grenier was so obvious that some Republican politicians assumed that he was angling to get Scranton the second spot on a Goldwater ticket. He was not.

was a good bit more than banter, and both White and Grenier knew it.

The Truax strategy was sound. Rockefeller, whose political stock had slipped so badly that he could not possibly be nominated no matter how he fared in the primaries, seemed sure eventually to give what delegate strength he had to Scranton as a fellow moderate. Nixon, Lodge, and Romney did not seem to be likely to control large blocks of delegates. That left Goldwater as kingmaker. If Goldwater-Scranton amity could be maintained, Scranton could become not only the nominee, but a unity nominee with Goldwater's blessing.

Of course, one element was essential: Goldwater had to stay down after his post-assassination dip. But in January, 1964, there seemed no danger of his resurrection. Goldwater's big slip after November 22 was no fault of his own. However, the fact that he kept dropping through the month of January was nobody's fault but his own.

On the Sunday afternoon of January 5, 1964, Barry Goldwater decided to walk the mile from his apartment in The Westchester to the National Broadcasting Company studios, where he was to be the guest on "Meet the Press"—his first public appearance as an avowed candidate. Goldwater, an outdoorsman at heart, had been chafing over the inactivity forced by the minor surgery on his ankle and had decided that this sunny winter day was perfect for some exercise.

It was a mistake of serious proportions. The walking cast encasing his foot was intended for the briefest of strolls, not cross-country hikes. By the time Goldwater reached the studios, he was in agony, but he tried his best not to show it.

David Broder, political writer for the *Washington Evening Star* and a member of the "Meet the Press" panel that day, greeted Goldwater and asked him, by way of casual conversation, whether he had been briefed in preparation for the show.

"Oh, no," the Senator replied. "The last time I was on this

show, I spent hours getting briefed, and then nobody asked the questions I was briefed on."

That, along with the ill-timed hike, was a grievous mistake for Goldwater. His "Meet the Press" performance (the last time he would appear on the program prior to the National Convention) was an absolute disaster. Never before had a politician's appearance on a televised question-and-answer show hurt him so badly.

Distracted by pain, Goldwater seemed not the dynamic apostle of conservatism, but querulous and unsure, hoping that the endless half hour would end. Moreover, Goldwater committed one factual blunder after another as the situation worsened.

Lawrence Spivak, permanent member of the "Meet the Press" panel, opened the show by asking whether Goldwater still adhered to his past proposals to break off diplomatic relations with the Soviet Union. When Goldwater replied that he as President would use a threat to break off diplomatic relations "as a bargaining effort with the Soviet Union to try to get some things accomplished," the colloquy took this turn:

> SPIVAK: What do you think would be the consequences if we broke off relations with the Soviet Union for any reason at this time?
>
> GOLDWATER: I think the Soviet Union would do a lot of things to keep from having us do that. We have to keep in mind, though, this would take an action of the Senate of the United States. . . .

As a constitutionalist, Goldwater shouldn't have forgotten that the Senate has no role whatever in granting or withdrawing diplomatic recognition to any country. This is completely the prerogative of the President. But Goldwater tripped again two questions later when Spivak asked whether, if elected President, he would renounce the test-ban treaty. Goldwater replied:

I would have to cross that bridge when I got to it. I still think it is of no advantage to the United States, and just the other day, Dr. Hans Morgenthau, one of the greatest physicists in the world, backed my position up on that by stating what I said on the floor, that the treaty had more accrual of good to the Soviets than it did to the United States. . . .

Only complete distraction can explain this lapse. No nuclear physicist and certainly no foe of the test-ban treaty, Hans Morgenthau was amazed when told of Goldwater's remarks. A professor of political science at the University of Chicago, author of many books about world affairs, and ranking member of the liberal elite, Morgenthau had served as a member of the Democratic National Committee's advisory council during the Eisenhower Administration. Moreover, Goldwater had engaged in friendly debate with Morgenthau on a televised panel discussion in Chicago just three months earlier.

The third big blooper came during a colloquy with Broder over civil rights. Referring to the use of Federal troops by President Kennedy, Goldwater said:

He didn't use Federal troops, as I recall. He sent Federal marshals in. If an edict had been issued by a Federal court, then I believe that he has the right to use Federal marshals.

Actually, President Kennedy *had* employed Federal troops in his two major civil rights crises, at the University of Mississippi in 1962 and at the University of Alabama in 1963.

Writing about these and two less serious errors (concerning details of the Tennessee Valley Authority's operation), Broder wrote in the *Washington Evening Star* two nights later:

These whiffs were, as anyone who knows Senator Goldwater would testify, anything but deliberate efforts to mislead. But they represent, to some of the Senator's friends, an inattention to detail and an impreciseness of utterance that could be troublesome to his presidential campaign.

Troublesome, to say the least. Actually, there were to be no more outright bloopers—a sign that physical pain played a part in the performance of January 5. But the same vagueness, the lack of preparation, and the general distraction were to prove troublesome indeed throughout the winter and particularly in the dreary New Hampshire campaign. The "Meet the Press" debacle also had its more immediate impact. Party leaders, many of them gathered in Washington for the National Committee meeting beginning the next day, watched Goldwater's performance over television with unbelieving eyes. Quite apart from any ideological disagreements, they wondered whether this was the man whom they wanted to lead the party.

Nor were the party leaders arriving in Washington for the National Committee meeting reassured by the obvious turmoil within the Goldwater organization. It was clear that the Draft Goldwater organization, a fairly efficient operation by political standards, had been replaced by sheer chaos once Goldwater became an avowed candidate.

Most Republican politicians had assumed that the Senator, inheriting a campaign staff-in-being in the Draft Goldwater organization, would keep it pretty much as is—Peter O'Donnell as chairman and Clif White as operating director, with Goldwater confidant Denison Kitchel superimposed, with or without the title of campaign manager. O'Donnell and White shared this view. But such speculation showed an imperfect understanding of the nature of Barry Goldwater.

Curiously enough, no decision had been made about a campaign organization until just before Goldwater's formal announcement of his candidacy. The decision was hammered at the Senator's home in Phoenix by Goldwater, Kitchel, and a few other close associates without consulting O'Donnell and White in Washington. The hierarchy of the new Goldwater for President Committee, announced in Phoenix shortly after the announcement of his candidacy, was a shocker to party leaders.

Kitchel was general director of the Goldwater for President Committee. Dean Burch, who had been helping Kitchel in the temporary office at the Carroll Arms Hotel in Washington, was assistant general director. Richard G. Kleindienst, a Phoenix lawyer, was named director of field operations. Still a fourth Arizonan, ex-National Committeewoman Ann-Eve Johnson, was named director of women's activities. Not a word was said about O'Donnell and White and their fate under the new regime. The Arizona Mafia was in complete command.[7]

The omission of O'Donnell and White was one surprise. Another was the last-minute introduction of Kleindienst to the Goldwater team. A partial reason why Kleindienst was suddenly rushed from Phoenix to Washington to play a key role in a Presidential campaign was to be found embedded in the secretive, inbred Republican politics of Arizona. It was clear by early January that Kleindienst was getting ready to run for Governor, an event that Goldwater at that moment most certainly did not desire. It was simple enough to exile him to Washington.

Although appointment of the all-Arizona high command was announced publicly on January 3, the Draft Goldwater headquarters in Washington didn't receive a word of explanation (or a hint about the fate of O'Donnell and White) until Sunday, January 5. That night, in a suite at the Mayflower, Clif White met with Kitchel, Burch, and Kleindienst. Kitchel declared that he wanted White on board for the campaign—as Kleindienst's lieutenant. Kitchel then offered White the title of executive assistant to Kleindienst. Understandably, White—who was far more responsible than anybody else for building the Draft Goldwater organization—turned the proposal down flat.

[7] Goldwater quickly followed these appointments up with the announcement that a non-Arizonan—Ed McCabe, the ex-Eisenhower staffer who had been helping Kitchel at the Carroll Arms office—would be director of research for the campaign. But McCabe was well below the Kitchel-Burch-Kleindienst triumvirate in the Goldwater hierarchy.

"Well, we're sorry to hear that," replied Kitchel icily. "If you can stick around for another week, we'll figure out a way to announce that you're leaving."

That probably would have been the end of Clif White in the Goldwater campaign had it not been for Kleindienst. Though anonymous nationally, Kleindienst, forty, had far more practical political experience than either Kitchel or Burch, serving as state party chairman in Arizona from 1956 to 1962. He recognized how difficult it would be for the Arizona Mafia to take over the Draft Goldwater national network without guidance from White, the man who had constructed it. Accordingly, Kleindienst suggested that everybody calm down and try to work out a place in the organization for White. The suggestion was agreeable to Kitchel. A few days later, the solution was found. White would work as Kleindienst's subordinate, but with the face-saving title of coordinator of field operations.

If the Arizona Mafia's treatment of White was abrupt, it was absolutely brutal in the case of Peter O'Donnell. After the meeting with White was over, the Arizonans convened another session in another Mayflower suite, attended by a half-dozen Goldwater supporters—including O'Donnell. His name was not mentioned as Kitchel gave a routine briefing on the campaign ahead. Nobody said so, but everybody knew that the young Dallas millionaire was being given his pink slip without so much as a "thank you."

O'Donnell was outraged. During the National Committee meetings that week, he complained bitterly to his colleagues on the Committee how the amateurish Arizonans were endangering the Goldwater campaign by their take-over. Partly in response to these complaints, Kleindienst cornered O'Donnell to ask him whether there was any job in the Goldwater organization that he would like to fill.

"There sure is," replied O'Donnell with a grin. "I'd like Kitchel's."

O'Donnell returned to Dallas and his job as Republican state chairman of Texas without further comment.[8]

Party leaders were not enraptured by their first glimpse of the Arizona Mafia. There seemed to be more of New England asceticism than outgoing Westernism in Kitchel and Burch, who were viewed by the politicians as correct, icy, and distant. Kleindienst was another matter. As a former state chairman, he was better known to party leaders around the country, but not always in the most favorable light. Though a Harvard man and a Phi Beta Kappa, husky, good-looking Dick Kleindienst played the part of the Western cowboy roughneck: tactless, boisterous, and professionally profane in two languages (English and Navajo). Kleindienst's was not necessarily the most suitable personality for wooing political support.

But the impact of the three Arizonans on neutral party leaders across the country was adverse, not so much because of their personalities, as because of their lack of experience. Even Kleindienst, the one member of the trio with any prior background in party work, had never before functioned outside Arizona. At this particular point in the campaign, when Goldwater's status within the party was dropping so precipitously and his own performance seemed so inadequate, his campaign badly needed the appointment of a prestigious general staff to give it a boost. Naming an old pro like Len Hall as campaign manager (even if only as a figurehead campaign manager) would have been therapeutic. The appointment of Peter O'Donnell or Clif White, fairly well known around the country, would have helped some. The naming of the Arizona Mafia was a minus, not a plus.[9]

[8] Subsequently, O'Donnell was named to a post in Goldwater's national fund-raising operation. Furthermore, strictly acting on his own, he worked in both the New Hampshire and the California primaries. But he never rejoined the Goldwater high command.

[9] It must be conceded that John F. Kennedy's Irish Mafia was composed of political newcomers when Kennedy formally announced for the Presidency in January, 1960. But the Irish Mafia had worked together as a close unit

But Goldwater was not really thinking about the problem of giving his campaign a shot in the arm when he named his campaign staff. Nor was he, at this particular point, in tune with the desires of White and the rest of the original Draft Goldwater group to assume control of the Republican Party with a band of hard-boiled young conservative politicians. Rather, Goldwater's motives in naming the all-Arizona high command were intensely personal.

At one point during that winter, when Goldwater's prospects seemed to be reaching a new low, a friend asked the Senator just what advantage he saw in Dick Kleindienst as chief of the delegate-hunting operation.

"Sure, I know Dick's clumsy and bad-mannered sometimes, and I know he hurts me," Goldwater replied. "But he's a hell of a stump speaker." Goldwater paused for a moment, perhaps reflecting that stump-speaking talents were not really a prerequisite for a political manager. "I guess what I really like in Dick is that he's always been loyal to me."

This was the key. In purging O'Donnell and in downgrading White without so much as an apology or an explanation, Goldwater was certainly guilty of bad manners, but he was not really being ruthless. He was merely searching—rather desperately searching—for men he knew well and could trust completely to help carry him through the greatest endeavor of his life. And for all the hundreds of politicians, businessmen, and academicians Goldwater had come in contact with over the past decade, the circle of friends he truly trusted and could rely upon in times of crisis was pitifully small, limited almost entirely to those from his native Arizona. Seemingly gregarious and extroverted, Goldwater was in truth suspicious and introverted, a man who made friends slower than most and came to trust them only after

---

in Kennedy's 1958 Senate campaign and by January, 1960, had become all too familiar to party leaders around the country as agents of the early-starting Kennedy campaign. In contrast, the Arizona Mafia was not in being before January, 1964.

a long testing period. He also was a man who demanded absolute loyalty. So long as Kitchel, Burch, and Kleindienst met these requirements, their shortcomings as politicians bothered him not at all.

The jarring, wrenching replacement of the Draft Goldwater team by the Arizona Mafia was damaging for more than reasons of prestige. The winter weeks at the Duryea Building were sheer confusion.

Clif White came close to quitting more than once—mainly because he now had no authority, partly because of the confusion and uncertainty. Early in January, Kleindienst told a reporter that he and White would evenly divide up the delegate-hunting chores. Kleindienst would handle the states that selected delegates through primary elections; White would be in charge of the states that picked them through state conventions. But nearly a week later, White had not been told about this division of labor.

To make matters worse, Goldwater's fund raisers were having trouble financing the Senator's lagging campaign and were demanding that they be given authority to pump some life into it. Head of the fund-raising effort was Daniel C. Gainey, sixty-six, a wealthy Minnesota businessman who spent his winters at an Arizona ranch. A political veteran who was national party treasurer during the second half of the Eisenhower Administration, Gainey regarded the Arizona Mafia as a bunch of political amateurs who needed expert advice. He was not deterred when his advice was repeatedly refused.

An illustration of the early fumbling at Goldwater headquarters was the "decision" not to enter the West Virginia primary against Rockefeller on May 12. Confident Goldwater forces in West Virginia urged the Senator to enter, promising to give him an impressive win that would propel him to victory just as John F. Kennedy's West Virginia triumph over Hubert Humphrey had all but clinched the Democratic nomination for him in 1960. But the Arizonans were bearish. Remembering the part that Kennedy money had played in West Virginia four years earlier, the Arizonans feared that Rockefeller (already entered in West Virginia) would spend his way to victory in this impoverished state. But no decision ever really was made. The Goldwater headquarters was so disorganized that the February 1 filing date passed without anybody realizing it. The decision to stay out of West Virginia was made by the calendar.

Even if the Arizonans had been fully aware of the February 1 deadline, it is likely that they would not have entered Goldwater in West Virginia. This represented a vast transformation in the spirit at Goldwater headquarters. In the days of the Draft Goldwater organization, O'Donnell, White, *et al.*, had been imbued with an extravagant self-confidence about Goldwater's vote-getting capabilities. Just as Kennedy's all-victorious string of seven primaries had forced him on the Democratic Party's Old Guard in 1960, so would Goldwater travel the primary route to victory. White's first reaction to the Goldwater slump after the assassination was a plan to regain momentum by entering—and, presumably, winning—every primary election possible.[10]

But this *élan* disappeared in the grim, drab weeks of January. The audacity was gone. Caution was the watchword. It was a case of the candidate and the staff reacting unfavorably to each other's shortcomings, each tending to lose faith in the other. As Goldwater's ratings in the polls continued to tumble and his New Hampshire primary campaign began to assume disaster proportions, his campaign staff—the Arizonans and Clif White alike—began to lose faith, perhaps subconsciously, in his vote-getting power.[11] And it can be fairly argued that the inefficiency and confusion within his

[10] See page 264.
[11] The New Hampshire campaign is discussed fully in the next chapter.

staff were partially responsible for Goldwater's dismal campaigning.

Besides West Virginia, two other illustrations of the new Goldwater caution worthy of note were the Goldwater pullbacks from all-out war in Ohio and Wisconsin. Along with West Virginia, these were the two states that daring and audacity had transformed into stepping-stones toward the nomination in the Kennedy campaign, which O'Donnell and White once had hoped to emulate.

Ohio had been Kennedy's first major breakthrough to make him more than just a New England regional candidate. Warning hostile Ohio Democratic leaders that he would file his own slate against theirs in the primary election unless they pledged themselves to him, Kennedy grabbed Ohio's big delegation—and an incalculable hunk of prestige—early in the game. The situation there was similar in 1964. Governor James Rhodes and State Chairman Ray Bliss had turned openly cool toward Goldwater since the assassination and had talked privately of turning over the state's fifty-eight member delegation, pledged to Rhodes as a favorite son, to Richard M. Nixon at the proper time in San Francisco. Clif White and Representative John Ashbrook, an aggressive young conservative Congressman from Ohio and an original in the Draft Goldwater movement, wanted to fight this head on just as the Kennedys had in 1960: threaten Rhodes and Bliss with running a Goldwater slate of delegates against the Rhodes slate unless the Rhodes slate were pledged to Goldwater. Because it seemed certain that Bliss would not capitulate, the stage was set for a showdown in the Ohio primary on May 5. In fact, a Goldwater slate was named and ready to go.

That is, the stage was set until Kleindienst moved in shortly after being named director of Goldwater's field operations. At the winter National Committee meeting in Washington, Bliss and Kleindienst—friends from the days when

Kleindienst was Arizona state chairman—got together for a heart-to-heart talk. Bliss, claiming that he had nothing against Goldwater, declared that a contested primary would destroy the party in Ohio. He added that about one-third of the Rhodes slate of delegates consisted of dedicated Goldwater advocates anyway and that the other two-thirds might join the Goldwater bandwagon in time. That convinced Kleindienst.

From him, the foxy Bliss got an assurance that Goldwater would stay out of the Ohio primary. From Bliss, Kleindienst got a warm handshake and a smile. John Ashbrook and the other Goldwater leaders in Ohio were not consulted. Acting on Kleindienst's advice, Goldwater on January 9 ordered his forces in Ohio not to oppose the Rhodes slate. What was lost was not just two-thirds of the Ohio delegation. The real loss was the regained sense of momentum that a decision to challenge the mighty Ray Bliss in his home ball park would have imparted throughout the party.

In Wisconsin, the original decision to run Representative John Byrnes as a favorite son was originally a pro-Goldwater move (made before Rockefeller's remarriage, when the Governor of New York was far in front for the nomination) to load the Wisconsin delegation with pro-Goldwater conservatives and keep Rockefeller out of the state's primary. But since the political demise of Rockefeller, the Goldwater leader in Wisconsin—Wayne Hood, a La Crosse, Wisconsin, industrialist and veteran party worker who was staff director of the Republican National Committee during the 1952 campaign—was urging Goldwater to enter. If he did, Byrnes would quickly drop out as a favorite son candidate and Rockefeller would immediately enter. Hood was certain that Goldwater would run far ahead of Rockefeller in Wisconsin on April 7, a victory that would be needed to counteract the bad effects of the increasingly likely defeat in New Hampshire on March 10.

This time the word of caution came from White. He feared the uniquely "open" nature of the Wisconsin primary, which does not restrict voters to registered party members. White believed that Democrats would stream over into the Republican primary to vote for Rockefeller in sufficient numbers to threaten Goldwater. White's advice was followed, and Goldwater stayed out—much to Hood's chagrin.

In addition to the loss of verve and audacity, the Goldwater forces were putting their money on the wrong horse in some states. Such a blunder endangered Goldwater's hold in conservative Florida, which should have been his for the asking.

Alabamian John Grenier, chief Goldwater agent in the South, made the mistake of interfering in a Florida family quarrel. As part of an old factional feud, Representative William Cramer was trying to seize control of the party from State Chairman Tom Fairfield Brown and had entered his own slate of convention delegates against the regular slate in the Florida primary on May 26. The Cramer insurgent slate was pledged firmly to Goldwater. The Brown regular slate was dominated by pro-Goldwater Republicans (including Brown himself), but was uncommitted.

Against the better judgment of some Goldwater strategists, Grenier endorsed the Cramer slate in the primary. Even Goldwater himself was disturbed by Grenier's move. In a telephone call from Washington to Birmingham, the Senator pointed out to Grenier that Goldwater's old friend and a generous contributor to the party—Miami Beach millionaire William D. Pawley—was on the Brown slate. Since Goldwater was opposing the Brown slate, it was all very embarrassing. Grenier replied that the Senator should have made known his feelings sooner. It was too late to switch. On March 5, Goldwater formally endorsed the Cramer slate.

As a result, Brown was no longer on speaking terms with Grenier, Goldwater's designated Southern lieutenant. More important, Brown was playing footsie with Pennsylvania State Chairman Craig Truax, who was quietly scouring the South for possible Scranton support. Because the Brown slate figured to win on May 26, there was danger of a big hole being blasted in Goldwater's Solid South. When Goldwater suffered a humiliating defeat in New Hampshire on March 10, Brown no longer disguised his feelings. Asked by United Press International for his reaction, Brown replied: "From the way it's going, it looks like the Goldwater staff people didn't know any more about the situation in New Hampshire than they did in Florida."

The flavor of the dreary and disorganized month of January for Goldwater was clearly seen in capsule form on January 18, when his schedulers interrupted his crucial New Hampshire campaign and dispatched him for a quick speech in Kingston, North Carolina, a state that Goldwater had wrapped up anyway. Incredibly, even at this stage of the game, the Goldwater speech-writing operation was still catch-as-catch-can. On the plane trip to North Carolina, Goldwater excused himself from a conversation with the explanation that he had better get to work on his speech. He then moved to another seat on the plane, pulled out a note pad, and started writing his speech in longhand.

In truth, Barry Goldwater, though a candidate for eighteen days, was still "just pooping around." Luckily for him, however, so was Bill Scranton.

The Scranton boomlet was not turning into a boom. Even with Goldwater slipping further, Rockefeller failing to recover, and Nixon standing still, Scranton's stock was not rising.

The fault lay with Scranton himself. He was playing his noncandidacy too closely, too cutely. One of the shrewdest members of John F. Kennedy's Irish Mafia always referred to Scranton as "the *cute* bastard." There was much justification in this. Throughout his brief political career, Scranton had shown a penchant for avoiding risks and playing sure things. Not until he had pinned down complete party support did he run for Congress or Governor. Moreover, his brief tenure at Harrisburg showed some of the same traits.

On August 16, 1963, the *Pennsylvania Guardian,* a liberal Democratic publication in Philadelphia, assessed Scranton, after his first legislative session, in an article entitled "Scranton: The Image Unimpaired." With due weight given to the publication's liberal bias, the article nevertheless points to some of Scranton's weaknesses. It concludes:

> Because he supported good government legislation, Scranton has a good image. As the *Guardian* predicted in January (1963), Scranton tried to get . . . governmental reforms enacted. . . .

So this is the picture of Scranton eight months later:

> A nice decent guy, ahead of his party—but not prepared to fight—only to negotiate with his Assembly leaders—unable or unwilling to act as the political boss of his party, yet wishing he could change its image. His greatest chance to do this came when a choice was made for the Philadelphia Mayoralty candidate—but he didn't do what he could and so the party boasts an unknown and relatively untried candidate. . . .
>
> Scranton's political future now hangs in the balance. Without doubt he has Presidential ambitions. His time table calls for 1968, not 1964, but he will have to demonstrate more leadership than he has so far to be sold even with the help of his relatives on *Time* and *Life.*[12]

Without question, Scranton had played it close to the belt in the 1963 mayoralty situation in Philadelphia. An outstanding liberal Republican candidate could have picked up considerable support from dissident Democrats fed up with the corrupt regular Democratic machine. But no such Repub-

[12] This was a reference to James Linen, Scranton's brother-in-law and president of Time, Inc., publishers of *Time* and *Life.*

lican would make the race without clear assurances of all-
out support from the Governor. Grossly overestimating the
power of the machine, Scranton decided not to squander his
prestige on a futile gesture and kept to the sidelines while
the Republican nomination went to a nonentity named James
McDermott. Too late, Scranton discovered the real weakness
in the Democratic machine and incumbent Mayor James
Tate. In one secret meeting, he asked McDermott to drop
out of the race. McDermott refused. In November, Tate won,
but by less than a comfortable margin. A topflight Republican candidate could have beaten him. In that same
1963 election, Pennsylvania's voters narrowly turned down
a Scranton-backed call for a state constitutional convention
when the Governor refused to commit his prestige in support
of it.

If he had decided to fight, Scranton probably could have
had his constitutional convention and been the first Republican mayor of Philadelphia since 1951. Those victories would
have enhanced his national prestige. But it also can be
argued that Scranton was avoiding the fate of George
Romney, who faded from national consideration after risking
all on a controversial state issue.

At any rate, what really bothered Bill Keisling and Scranton's other ambitious aides was a new image of Scranton that
was being formed as a result of his reluctance to enter the
Presidential race. *Newsweek* called him the "Hamlet of
Harrisburg." The popular political wisecrack of the day became: "If Bill Scranton were only half the man his mother
was"—a reference to the late Margery Scranton, the indomitable "Duchess" of Pennsylvania's Republican politics.[13]
What bothered Scranton's aides most of all was the tendency
now to call Scranton not the Republican Jack Kennedy, but
the Republican Adlai Stevenson.

[13] When Mary Scranton's aggressive and vigorous campaigning abilities became better known, the crack became: "If Bill Scranton were only half the
man his wife is."

From this, it was but a short step to emphasizing Scranton's more unfortunate characteristics—his languor, his super-civilized Eastern airs, his tendency to flash quick, embarrassed grins that made him appear to be simpering. Out of all the massively favorable publicity early in 1964, two passages hit a raw nerve in the Scranton camp, irritating both the Governor and his entourage.

One was a single sentence in a *Newsweek* cover story of January 27. Describing life at Marworth (the Scranton estate) under Margery Scranton, the magazine said "liveried footmen served swan for dinner." Here was the image of an effete Eastern society foreign to the rest of the nation.

The other passage was contained in a *Wall Street Journal* analysis of Scranton by Alan L. Otten appearing on February 10. Writing about Scranton's internal paradoxes, Otten said:

> His heavy-lidded, mobile face, with its wide mouth, can alternately appear charming or simpering. His lean, loose-jointed body makes him appear trimly athletic one moment, limp the next. He displays deep emotion with such expressions as "golly gee" or "jeepers cat" and yet can ruthlessly put the political squeeze on Pennsylvanians backing Senator Barry Goldwater of Arizona.

It was the "jeepers cat" phrase, with its suggestion that Scranton never really had outgrown the nursery school, that struck the raw nerve. The Governor heatedly denied he had ever used the phrase. Similarly, he denied that swan ever was served at Marworth.

For all the concern at Harrisburg over this slight deterioration in the Scranton image, more experienced party leaders across the country who wanted to cast their lot with Scranton were concerned about more substantial matters—namely, Scranton's continued anonymity outside the eastern seaboard states. The only antidote was a heavy barnstorming tour by the Governor, to put him on display to the workers for the first time.

Scranton supporters were encouraged by his travel plans for the winter months, featuring "nonpolitical" visits to Detroit, Cincinnati, Kansas City, and New York. Some of these "nonpolitical" trips tended to become a bit "political." In Kansas City to address a soil-conservation convention, he spent better than an hour shaking hands at a political reception. In his "nonpolitical" appearance before the New York Economic Club, he declared: "It's time the Republican Party became once again the majority in America."[14]

But what Scranton really needed was overt, frankly political trips during which he could make contact with the party faithful—trips such as his January 29 appearance in Indianapolis. That was the night for one of those national fund-raising extravaganzas at which Republicans dine for $100 a plate in cities from coast to coast, hear one of the party's leading lights in person, and listen to four minutes apiece from the others over closed-circuit television. On the closed-circuit screen were National Chairman Miller, Eisenhower, Nixon, Goldwater, Rockefeller, Romney—and, for the first time, Scranton.

Indiana was clearly Goldwater country. With Goldwater unlikely to face opposition in the Indiana primary, the state's thirty-three-member delegation would be pledged to him for at least one ballot. After that, most of the thirty-three would be inclined to continue to vote for Goldwater on future ballots. Yet, Indiana was by no means a closed proposition when Scranton made his late-January excursion there.

Goldwater was immeasurably weaker in Indiana than he had been three months earlier. Some of the moderate conservatives who had jumped on the Goldwater bandwagon during Goldwater's glorious autumn—such as Lieutenant Governor Richard Ristine, now running for Governor—were having second thoughts about Mr. Conservative's prowess as

[14] This speech was highly publicized as the work of Malcolm Moos, the ex-Eisenhower speech writer. Actually, Moos submitted only a first draft, which was completely revised by Keisling.

a vote-getter. Former Senator Homer Capehart, eyeing a political comeback in Indiana, was looking toward Scranton. So was Indianapolis party leader H. Dale Brown, who had lost his state chairmanship because of his support for Rockefeller but was still firmly anti-Goldwater. Indeed, Scranton had cheer leaders in Indiana he didn't even know about. At one reception preceding the January 29 dinner, Representative William Bray, a moderate, pro-labor Congressman from Southern Indiana, herded party workers toward Scranton with these words: "You ought to meet this fellow. He's good people, real good people."

Enough Hoosiers were curious to see firsthand the newest thing in Republican politics to fill the ballroom of the Indiana Roof to its fifteen-hundred-seat capacity. They liked what they saw. Putting aside his usual low-keyed, let-us-reason-together style of oratory, Scranton gave the Democrats hell, establishing his own credentials as a bona fide Republican. It was the kind of conservative speech that Indiana Republicans like. What they liked even more was the way Bill and Mary Scranton table-hopped at the Indiana Roof in order to shake as many hands as possible before the formal speech and then stood beaming and gracious in an endless reception line at a postdinner reception in the mansion of an Indianapolis millionaire.

At that reception, Indiana moderate leaders agreed over highballs and cigars that Scranton easily outshone the party's established stars—Nixon, Goldwater, Rockefeller, et al.—in his four-minute closed circut television stint. "Scranton was the only one with something fresh to say," said Homer Capehart. "The others had the same tired old stuff we've been hearing for years."[15]

[15] However, those who saw Scranton over closed-circuit television were not impressed. A thick coat of makeup made him look pasty, and that tendency to flash an embarrassed, simpering grin whenever the crowd applauded was particularly disconcerting over television. The makeup problem was solved quickly, but try as he would, Scranton was unable in the months ahead to overcome his tendency to grin out of embarrassment.

But beneath the surface of Scranton's Indiana triumph were ominous rumblings. As they started the auto ride back to town from the reception that night, for instance, Mary Scranton called out to Bill Keisling: "Now be sure to close the door, Bill. We wouldn't want to lose you. Or *would* we?"

As the junior member of the Scranton inner circle, Keisling was the constant target of gibes. But there was a special cutting edge to Mary Scranton's voice this time. She hadn't enjoyed this visit to Indianapolis at all. Downtown Indianapolis in midwinter never is known for its gaiety, and the threadbare suite given to the Scrantons at the Columbia Club (then undergoing a noisy but overdue renovation) added to the depression. This mood aggravated Mary Scranton's irritation over the trip. She felt that it was only a thinly disguised Presidential campaign trip, and she most certainly did not want her husband to run for President.

Keisling, who had arranged the trip, was the natural target of her irritation. She was unhappy when Keisling arranged an early breakfast meeting at the Columbia Club between the Scrantons and a nationally syndicated columnist. She flatly vetoed a Keisling effort to open his speech at the Indiana Roof with a little joke about feeling a Presidential draft. She didn't like the give-'em-hell tone of the Keisling-written speech. Most important, she made it clear that she was opposed to any overtly political excursions in the future.

There was none.

In February, March, and April, Scranton turned down gilt-edged political invitations that would have had other politicians drooling. David Scull, the Maryland state party chairman, journeyed to Harrisburg to ask Scranton to address a $100-a-plate dinner in Baltimore (and, though Scull didn't mention it, to boost a burgeoning Scranton-for-President movement in Maryland). Scranton declined. New Jersey State Chairman Webster Todd, fighting hard to hold back a vigorous Goldwater grass roots movement in his normally liberal state, begged Scranton to help him by addressing a fund-raising dinner. Scranton declined.

Party leaders began to note other signs of languor in the Scranton camp. Early in January, for example, Keisling had been talking about formation of a "Friends of Bill Scranton" organization that would dispense propaganda and control volunteer efforts. Its nominal head was to be General Milton Baker, superintendent of Valley Forge (Pennsylvania) Military Academy and an intimate of General Eisenhower. Nothing came of it.

Then there was a January 17 luncheon called by Thomas McCabe (working in close cooperation with Keisling) in the Philadelphia boardroom of Scott Paper. This was of a different magnitude than the earlier McCabe luncheons. It was very nearly a summit meeting of the Eastern Republican Establishment, come to break bread with William Scranton. Old pros Len Hall and Meade Alcorn plus National Chairman Miller were there. So were ex-Eisenhower aides now high in corporate affairs: Neil McElroy (ex-Defense Secretary) of Procter & Gamble, David Kendall (ex-White House counsel) of Chrysler Corp., James C. Hagerty (ex-press secretary) of the American Broadcasting Company. The roster of corporate giants with less direct political ties included George Leness, president of the Merrill Lynch brokerage house; Keith Funston, president of the New York Stock Exchange; and many more.

But this was not the signal for action. It wasn't even a prelude to action. The Scranton candidacy was not even discussed over the luncheon table. Nor was there any follow-up to the meeting.

One more incident truly reflects the mood of the Scranton camp. On a January trip to Washington, Scranton met secretly with Representative Robert Ellsworth, a young moderate from Kansas, in Ellsworth's office on Capitol Hill. Also attending the meeting were Representative Charles (Mac)

Mathias of Maryland and Mathias' campaign manager, Jack Stark, a Washington lawyer and party leader in suburban Montgomery County, Maryland.

Ellsworth and Mathias told Scranton that they didn't expect him to announce formally his candidacy at this point. But they did feel that the time was ripe for them to start behind-the-scenes activity in his behalf. Their proposition to Scranton: would he guarantee that they could quietly begin to work for him without being publicly disavowed from Harrisburg?

Scranton replied that he could give no such assurance. Rather, he specifically urged them not to do anything just now. If conditions changed, he would phone them to give them a green light for quiet activities. In fact, he promised he would call them in any event. That telephone call was never placed.

The curtailed traveling by Scranton, the haphazard activity by his aides, the refusal to even condone *sub rosa* activity in his behalf—all this was having a profound impact on party leaders who were prepared during the first week in January to do battle for Scranton. One of a politician's greatest fears is having a limb sawed out from under him. Republican leaders who had backed Nelson Rockefeller for President in 1960, only to have him suddenly remove himself from contention, really never had recovered from the blow. Flirting with a Scranton candidacy now seemed equally dangerous. Gradually, these party leaders came to realize that Bill and Mary Scranton really didn't want to run.

By mid-February, the Scranton boomlet seemed over. Scranton had failed to fill the vacuum left by the fall of Goldwater after the assassination. The significance of this failure was not to be fully realized until July.

XVIII

★ ★

New Hampshire

The great year of the New Hampshire Presidential primary was 1952. Never before had it so directly or so significantly influenced national politics in both parties. Probably, it never will again. On the Republican side, General Dwight D. Eisenhower was challenging front-running Senator Robert A. Taft. On the Democratic side, Senator Estes Kefauver was challenging President Harry Truman. These were the results:

Republican		Democratic	
Eisenhower	46,661	Kefauver	19,800
Taft	35,838	Truman	15,927
Other	10,366	Other	525

Eisenhower's victory gave his bandwagon momentum and added validity to the "Taft Can't Win" slogan. Kefauver's victory made him a national figure for the first time and might well have helped make up Harry Truman's mind about not running again in 1952. But in the same state, these two victories were achieved by directly opposite routes. Eisenhower was the absentee candidate—keeping above the battle at his NATO headquarters outside Paris. In contrast, Kefauver's win opened up a new—and not entirely agreeable —vista for Presidential campaigning. The lanky, drawling Tennessean set off slogging through the New Hampshire snow with the indomitable purpose of shaking hands with every resident of New Hampshire, just as if he were running for county assessor back in Tennessee.

The Presidential primary in New Hampshire featured no contests in either party in 1956 and 1960. So, as the 1964 clash between Rockefeller and Goldwater seemed imminent, the last campaign to look back upon was 1952. And curiously, the supporters of Rockefeller and Goldwater both looked back to the example of Estes Kefauver, wandering through the snowbanks, and not to the example of Dwight Eisenhower, staying aloof in Europe.

Their New Hampshire managers tried to make both Rockefeller and Goldwater another Estes Kefauver. The fact that both ran so badly not only made for one of the strangest primary elections ever held, but also put a new complexion on the fight for the nomination. In this sense, New Hampshire was a watershed on the road to San Francisco.

Back in those glorious, preassassination days of autumn, 1963, when the Goldwater bandwagon was charging full speed, New Hampshire's first-in-the-nation primary on March 10 seemed an easy first step toward the nomination. The polls forecast a Goldwater landslide against Rockefeller—a landslide, that is, if Rockefeller were foolish enough to honor his promise to enter in New Hampshire. Rockefeller knew from his pollsters that the latter-day Puritans of Upper New England cared not at all for the Rocky-Happy romance.

And though Rockefeller was having trouble just reenlisting the team of amateurs he had lined up in his abortive New Hampshire campaign of 1960, Goldwater had no shortage of willing lieutenants in the state. Indeed, he had cornered the market on New Hampshire's Republican Establishment.

It went without saying that Goldwater had the loyalty of the leaders of the Republican right—Doloris Bridges, widow of the late Senator Styles Bridges and a prominent party leader in her own right, and William Loeb, publisher of the

influential *Manchester Union Leader,* the state's only morning newspaper and only paper with statewide circulation.
But the Senator also had won over most of the state's leading moderates. It was they, not the Bridges-Loeb right-
wingers, who would run his campaign. Heading the list was
Senator Norris Cotton, Senator Bridges' successor as the
state's Mr. Republican and chairman of the Goldwater campaign.[1] Close behind in stature were the two leaders of the
State Legislature: House Speaker Stewart Lamprey and
Senate President Philip Dunlap. And the bitterest blow to
Rockefeller was the enlistment in the Goldwater army of
former Governor Lane Dwinnell, a liberal by New Hampshire standards, who had been assiduously courted by Rockefeller. Just as General Eisenhower's supporters had in 1952,
the Goldwater forces swallowed up most of the state's reign-
ing party leaders.

But Goldwater should have sniffed trouble ahead when
he first tested the New Hampshire political climate with a
precampaign trip on October 29, 1963. As his state manager,
Senator Cotton arranged for Goldwater to make a New
Hampshire debut at a capital fund-raising banquet for little
New England College in Concord. But Doloris Bridges, trying
to make a political comeback after the losing 1962 bid for her
husband's Senate seat, realized that Cotton and the moderates were squeezing her out of the Goldwater show. She
counterattacked. As a member of the New England College
board of trustees, Mrs. Bridges persuaded her fellow trustees
to set October 29 as the time for establishing a Styles Bridges
Chair of Political Science at the college. In this way, Mrs.
Bridges—and the Bridges name—was at center stage for
Goldwater's first visit to the state.

---

[1] Actually, Cotton was just about as conservative as Goldwater on most
domestic matters and joined him in voting against the 1964 Civil Rights
Act. But Cotton's reputation as an internationalist who supported the Marshall Plan and the United Nations in the late 1940's made him the leader of
the moderate, anti-Bridges wing of the New Hampshire party.

The ploy moved Cotton to shed his usual New England reserve in a rare burst of emotion. At the ceremony, he cornered the widow Bridges and told her: "I want you to know, Doloris, that I disapprove and resent your resurrecting your husband to advance your own political future."

It was a portent that perhaps Goldwater had too many supporters in New Hampshire for his own good.

Nor did Goldwater and the New Hampshire Yankee take to each other in their meeting on October 29. Declaring that his first visit there "could not exactly be called a humdinger," Mary McGrory wrote in the *Washington Evening Star*:

> The Senator's murky generalities about freedom, liberty of opportunity and "the greatness of our Federal system and representative, balanced Government" were received with cordiality but not the ecstasy that the statement of his creed has evoked on other occasions.
>
> After it was over, the diners lined up quietly to shake the Senator's hand.
>
> One Peterboro Republican said he was going to go all out because of "the spiritual content" of the speech. But another from the same town said, "I could have written him a better speech myself. There was nothing I could get my teeth into."

It should be remembered that this less than satisfactory experience in New Hampshire came during Goldwater's autumn, when his mass popularity had reached a peak never to be attained again. It is natural then that Goldwater's post-assassination visits to the state, when his stock was dropping rapidly, were even less satisfactory.

Goldwater quickly came to understand why Republican factionalism in this rock-ribbed Republican state had led to the election of two unknown Democrats as Governor and junior U.S. Senator in 1962. Ultraconservative Doloris Bridges, the state party's biggest source of conflict, had been successfully shunted off to the side. But intense feuding had broken out among the pro-Goldwater moderates.

Though chairman of the Goldwater campaign, Cotton was tied down to his Senate duties in Washington and could not maintain day-to-day control. Cotton could have passed operating control to his administrative assistant, Chet Wiggin, a veteran New Hampshire politician assigned by Cotton to stay in the state for the duration of the campaign. But Cotton missed this chance, and actual operating authority was seized by House Speaker Lamprey, a rising new political star who had his eye on the Governor's chair. The Cotton-Lamprey dispute raged beneath the surface during the entire campaign. Because Goldwater had ceded complete authority over the primary campaign to his local leaders, without a disinterested proconsul representing the Senator, there was no Goldwater man on the scene to mediate the local disputes.[2]

Unwittingly, the Cotton-Lamprey problem was exacerbated by a quiet visit to New Hampshire from none other than Peter O'Donnell. Though Goldwater had written him out of his high command, O'Donnell simply couldn't rusticate down in Texas while Goldwater was facing his first challenge in New Hampshire. So without waiting for an invitation, O'Donnell came North, ready to preach and teach the doctrine of house-to-house canvassing, a technique he had perfected in wresting Dallas out of Democratic hands. In Lamprey, O'Donnell found a willing acolyte. Lamprey immediately set workers to the task of house-to-house canvassing—much to the displeasure of Cotton and his lieutenant, Wiggin. They argued that the New Englander didn't like political canvassers disturbing him in the sanctity of his home. More important, Cotton and Wiggin believed that Lamprey was wasting time and effort on this newfangled venture, neglecting the time-tested New Hampshire technique of lining up established county leaders. It was an argument that raged on weeks after election day.

[2] Goldwater's New Hampshire managers were extraordinarily jealous about interference from Goldwater headquarters in Washington. Midway through the campaign, Cotton flatly vetoed a troubleshooting visit from Clif White.

But all Goldwater's New Hampshire leaders agreed on how the candidate should campaign—an agreement that was to prove far more costly than all their disagreements. Both Cotton and Lamprey insisted that Barry Goldwater emulate Estes Kefauver by campaigning for the Presidency in New Hampshire as if he were trying to become county assessor. Their formula was simple: try to shake hands with as many of the expected one hundred thousand Republican voters as possible between January 7 and March 10. Against his better judgment, Goldwater acceded to the wishes of his New Hampshire managers.

It was perhaps his worst mistake of the year. Goldwater had pulled himself up from obscurity to national political status over the past decade as a preacher of conservatism before mass audiences of faithful supporters in banquet halls and auditoriums—audiences that were convinced in the first place and were given no opportunity to cross-examine the Senator in the second place. In New Hampshire, Goldwater was forced to operate under a completely new set of ground rules. Except for a nighttime rally or banquet, where the audience might number in the hundreds, Goldwater spent most of the time at the traditional forum for New Hampshire politicking: the intimate coffee hour, where the candidate briefly addresses an audience of forty to fifty and then accepts questions from the floor.[3] The balance of the time was filled by factory tours and other handshaking expeditions.

Goldwater hated this regimen. Essentially a private person who respected the privacy of others and expected them to respect his, the Senator rebelled at the Kefauver-style handshaking tours. On more than one factory tour arranged by Lamprey, Goldwater would plow through, eyes straight ahead, shaking no hands, and giving no greetings—while Lamprey looked on in impotent horror. After some six weeks

[3] Although the coffee hours proved to be a most unsatisfactory campaign vehicle for Goldwater, the Senator's later complaints that there were more news correspondents than voters attending many of the coffee hours were unjustified. It just seemed that way to the campaign-weary candidate.

of this schedule, Goldwater blurted out at a Hanover coffee hour on February 19: "I'm not one of these baby-kissing, handshaking, blintz-eating candidates. I don't like to insult the American intelligence by thinking that slapping people on the back is going to get you votes." It was, of course, an attack on Nelson Rockefeller's extroverted campaign style. But it was also a cry for help from a Barry Goldwater imprisoned by the Kefauver syndrome.

Moreover, Lamprey and the Senator's other managers in New Hampshire grossly overestimated Goldwater's stamina. Unlike Jack Kennedy or Bill Scranton or Nelson Rockefeller, he was not the iron-man campaigner who could maintain a frenetic dawn-to-dusk pace without tiring. Goldwater's limits of endurance were exceeded by the schedules imposed on him during those endless days of flitting across New Hampshire's snow-covered Currier and Ives landscape. What made matters worse was amateurish scheduling that on some days included far more traveling for Goldwater in his auto caravan—wasted time as far as the candidate is concerned—than actual campaigning.

The result was that Goldwater reached the end of every long day near the point of physical collapse. Facing his first fair-sized audience of the day during the evening rally, an exhausted Goldwater could do no better than mumble through a few conservative clichés loosely strung together— and often would then stalk out of the hall without holding the question-and-answer period so dear to the Yankee voters or waiting to shake hands. Such a performance by Goldwater at the town of Woodsville in the ultraconservative northern tip of the state left a hall of angry Goldwater supporters—or perhaps they were now *ex*-Goldwater supporters. At any rate, New Hampshire politicians seriously believe that Goldwater's refusal to shake hands in Woodsville accounts for his worse than expected showing there on March 10.

Indeed, Goldwater tended to run worst in the very areas

in which he had campaigned (with the major exception of
Manchester, the state's largest city). The truth was that
Barry Goldwater and New Hampshire did not take to each
other. Writing in the *Washington Evening Star* of March 5,
Mary McGrory concluded that Goldwater was no more comfortable there less than a week before election day than he
had been during that first visit back in October. She wrote:

> Senator Goldwater has yet to give a statistic about New
> Hampshire. He does not even trouble to mention the name of
> the town in which he finds himself. And it is weeks since he
> has heard that thunder of applause which greeted almost his
> every word in warmer climes.

Goldwater, invigorated by hearty applause (like most politicians) and accustomed to adulation, was hurt and surprised
by the icy reserve of Yankee audiences. But he made no
real effort to ingratiate himself with the Yankees by avoiding the ostentation that they deplore. On her first trip to
New Hampshire to campaign with her husband, Peggy Goldwater was garbed in a long and luxuriant black mink coat.
Goldwater sped across the ice-caked highways in a sleek
black Cadillac with the tasteless license plate designation of
CADDY. These trifles were not lost on the enigmatic and
inscrutable Yankee.

But the growing disaffection with Goldwater was not
based solely—or even principally—on trifles. The Senator's
big problem in New Hampshire was what he was saying, not
doing. Every time he opened his mouth, he seemed to lose
votes—for two basic reasons.

First, the question-and-answer format of New Hampshire
campaigning, totally new to Goldwater, was utterly unsuited
to his distinctive style. For the first time, Goldwater was
subject to cross-examination on his sweeping proclamations
of conservative dogma. Actually, he would have found no
great difficulty in fielding the normal run of questions at
coffee hours. But the Rockefeller forces took advantage of

the Q-and-A ritual, putting a pack of bright, young Harvard Law School students on his tail to spring loaded questions at each stop. A particularly effective technique called for the same question to be asked at every stop all day long. By day's end, Goldwater had lost not only his temper but also his coherence in trying to answer the question. Moreover, newspaper reporters following Goldwater—some openly hostile to the Senator, but most of them trying to be fair—added to his woes. At press conferences (sometimes running as frequently as four in a day), correspondents abandoned the normal line of political questioning in favor of dissecting the Senator's views in the most intimate detail.[4]

Second, Goldwater still had not settled down to the hard, deadly business of running for President. Although he had talked with friends some six months earlier about the possibility of colliding with Rockefeller in New Hampshire, he was totally unprepared for such a campaign. There was no briefing on the questions he might be asked. Nor did he have a formula speech—an absolute necessity for a candidate making several appearances daily—during those early weeks. In his remarks to those at the coffee hours before the questioning began, Goldwater seemed to say whatever popped into his mind at the moment. One of his favorites in the early weeks was a discussion of the superiority of a conservative-leaning statement of principles drafted by Republican members of Congress in 1962 over the liberal-leaning national party platform of 1960. A more arcane campaign topic would be difficult to imagine. This was Goldwater "just pooping around."

These two factors—the ritual of Q-and-A sessions plus Goldwater's shocking lack of planning—caused what never

[4] This phenomenon tended to feed upon itself. Goldwater's attempt to deal in terms of ideological concepts only inspired more questions from the press, which in turn produced more ideological pronouncements. In contrast, whenever reporters asked about Rockefeller's ideology, they were quickly discouraged by a stream of meaningless clichés. Rockefeller's was the safer and more traditional method of campaigning for the Presidency.

should happen in a campaign: the candidate lost control of the news. It was not Goldwater's prepared (poorly prepared, at this stage) remarks that usually were reported in the press and over television-radio, but his off-the-cuff answers to questions not of his choosing. The array of Goldwater headlines springing from his New Hampshire campaign were the products of snap answers, not carefully planned statements.

The first day was probably the worst day. After his disastrous appearance on "Meet the Press" in Washington on January 5, he flew to Grand Rapids, Michigan, for a fund-raising speech under the unfriendly eye of Governor George Romney. Leaving Grand Rapids as soon as the speech was finished, he arrived in Concord, New Hampshire, at the red-eyed hour of 2:51 A.M. After a few hours' sleep, he formally kicked off his New Hampshire campaign with a 10 A.M. press conference at his Main Street headquarters in Concord. It was a press conference whose ill effects he never was quite able to erase during more than two months of New Hampshire campaigning.

The banner headline in the January 7 edition of the *Concord Daily Monitor* was the cross Goldwater had to bear throughout the campaign:

GOLDWATER SETS GOALS: END
SOCIAL SECURITY, HIT CASTRO

With justification, the Goldwater camp complained that the headline contradicted not only what the Senator really had said, but also the *Monitor* reporter's account of what the Senator had said. But Goldwater's actual comments at that opening press conference were damaging enough. While not proposing that the U.S. invade Castro, he called for another exiles' invasion of Cuba with U.S. air support. While not demanding an end to Social Security, he proposed that the system be made voluntary (which, in the opinion of most experts on the subject, would have the effect of ending the program).[5]

The Cuba statement, though not really damaging in itself, did augment Goldwater's growing image as a trigger-happy warmonger. The Social Security statement was sheer disaster in a state with far more than its share of retired persons, many of them dependent on Social Security benefits. In short, the January 7 press conference was a classic example of Goldwater, fatigued by lack of sleep and distracted by the continuing pain in his foot, losing control of his own campaign. He certainly had not intended to include the end or even the revision of Social Security as a key campaign goal. But by failing to chart in advance an answer to a question about Social Security, Goldwater had put a heavy burden on his back for the entire campaign.

He simply was not thinking in terms of Presidential politics. On the conservative banquet circuit, it had been completely unexceptional to propose that Social Security be made voluntary, regardless of whatever havoc this might cause in the program. "Voluntary Social Security" was indeed a battle cry of the new conservative ideology as proclaimed by William Buckley, Jr., editor of the *National Review*. Goldwater simply had failed to consider what an adverse impact the idea of gutting a popular social-welfare program would have among an audience broader than the readers of the *National Review*.

For Goldwater, politically, nothing was ever as bad as that first week in New Hampshire. During the second week, Denison Kitchel dispatched himself to travel with Goldwater in New Hampshire and proved a steadying influence on his old friend. As a peer of the Senator, Kitchel was far more successful than press secretary Tony Smith and other aides had been in convincing Goldwater that running for Presi-

[5] Contradicting the banner headline, the first paragraph of the *Monitor* account read: "Sen. Goldwater said here today he favors turning federal Social Security into a voluntary program."

dent was a serious matter that required advance preparation, intense self-control, and the utmost caution. It was Kitchel who convinced Goldwater that, in response to questions, he should pause a moment and reflect before answering. It was also on Kitchel's advice that Goldwater, in the second week of the New Hampshire campaign, dropped his flat recommendation that Social Security be put on a voluntary basis and instead asserted that his staff was now preparing recommendations for constructive changes in the program.

Yet, throughout the New Hampshire campaign, Goldwater never really regained the initiative. The tone of the campaign was set by whatever questions happened to be thrown at him that day. Nor did Goldwater ever realize that the old-fashioned New England conservatism of New Hampshire was a world apart from the militant Western conservatism of Arizona. These Yankees liked to hear talk about balanced budgets, frugality in government, and low taxes, but they also wanted to retain the fruits of the New Deal—particularly the Social Security system. Even Goldwater's watered-down comments that he was merely studying some undefined change in the program hurt him. In New Hampshire, they liked Social Security as it was. Moreover, they preferred a cautious search for peace to militant anticommunism in foreign policy. Polls showed that Goldwater hurt himself with each hard-line foreign policy stand as the campaign rolled on—that the U.S. should quit the United Nations if Red China were admitted, that the U.S. should send the Marines into Cuba to restore the water for the Guantanamo Naval Base, that the U.S. should carry the Southeast Asian war into North Vietnam.

Wincing at these stands, Cotton and Lamprey urged Goldwater to moderate his statements to fit New Hampshire tastes—to no avail. Realizing that his campaign was failing,

Goldwater blamed Lamprey and Cotton. The chasm between managers and candidate widened.

The real point of no return between Goldwater and his managers came on January 28, more than a month before polling day. In Washington to visit his national headquarters, Goldwater told reporters that the March 10 results in New Hampshire would be of little importance. "I don't think the outcome can possibly be convincing," he said. To his New Hampshire managers, this was the final blow—and a further revelation of how little Goldwater understood New Hampshire. To a small, backwoods state (population: 606,921) sensitive about being a small, backwoods state, the fact that its Presidential primary attracted the attention of the nation was a point of great pride. To have a candidate dismiss it so lightly well before election day was not just incredible—it was suicidal.

Nelson Rockefeller, the multimillionaire who broke into elective politics in his 1958 race for Governor of New York by munching blintzes and pizzas on the sidewalks of New York, had none of Barry Goldwater's trouble in adjusting to the Kefauver-style handshaking ordeal in New Hampshire. He loved it. Indeed, the main reason why Rockefeller decided to challenge Goldwater in New Hampshire despite the adverse readings in his polls was a belief that he could do what Estes Kefauver did in a saturation campaign throughout the state. But on other points, Rockefeller's tactical disagreements with his local managers were even more severe than Goldwater's.

As early as the summer of 1963, Rockefeller had decided to hire professional campaign managers in New Hampshire rather than string along with the eager but inexperienced amateurs who had backed his abortive 1960 effort there. After the remarriage, there wasn't a wide choice of professionals willing to cast their lot with Rockefeller, who then seemed a sure loser against Goldwater. As Rockefeller's scout, George Hinman came up with a two-man team: former Governor Hugh Gregg and his close political associate Bert Teague.

When the Gregg-Teague political team signed on with Rockefeller in the autumn of 1963 as paid professionals to run his New Hampshire campaign, more than a few eyebrows were raised in the state. Certainly, nobody there regarded Gregg or Teague as liberal Republicans. They were established members of the state party's conservative wing (with Teague serving as a state director of the ultraconservative Young Americans for Freedom). Asked on September 22, 1963, by Station WBZ in Boston why he was supporting Rockefeller, Gregg's answer was less than satisfying:

> I'm a personal friend of George Hinman's. . . . George called me one day and said, "Hugh, would you be willing to give us a little lift in New Hampshire and sound out some sentiment among the people up there, as to where the Governor [Rockefeller] might stand in the event he might enter the race in New Hampshire?" Which I did, and was glad to do it. At that time I had no particular feeling for Gov. Rockefeller or any of the other potential candidates. But as I made these calls over a period of several weeks and talked to people I became quite interested. I did some more reading about the Governor's background and activities.

The way Gregg told it, it was all quite accidental and casual. When the WBZ interviewer asked whether Gregg would also have agreed to help if the phone call had come from a Goldwater aide, he replied: "Well, I suppose it would depend a little bit on who called me."[6]

It wasn't nearly so simple as Hughie Gregg told it. Gregg and Teague joined the Rockefeller team only after a long and difficult courtship. Prior to the Rockefeller remarriage, Hinman had cultivated Gregg as part of his nationwide cam-

---

[6] This unfortunate interview with WBZ was used incessantly against Gregg by the pro-Goldwater *Manchester Union Leader*.

paign of inducing prominent conservatives to climb on the
Rockefeller bandwagon. After the remarriage, Hinman
thought it all the more vital for a conservative to run Rockefeller's New Hampshire campaign.

The culmination of the courtship came in September of
1963, when both Gregg and Teague were brought to New
York City for a face-to-face confrontation with Rockefeller.
The two New Englanders were brutally frank. With Rockefeller's cause apparently hopeless both nationally and in New
Hampshire, they held all the high cards. If they did not go
to work for the Governor, no other experienced New Hampshire political hands were available. Their terms were stiff:
complete, absolute, and final control over all aspects of the
New Hampshire campaign. Rockefeller's aides, accustomed
to bowing and scraping around the Governor, gasped at the
audacity of these two hired hands from the backwoods. But
Rockefeller agreed to their terms.

Granting that Rockefeller met their conditions, however,
it still would seem difficult to understand why two conservatives would risk their prestige on a politically down-and-out
liberal. The answer is simple: they had no other place to go.

In one moment of candor in his remarkable September 22
interview with WBZ, Gregg just about let the cat out of
the bag. "Well," he said, "if somebody wants you to do them
a favor in politics, it makes you feel good, and I've been out
of touch for a while, so frankly, I was happy to do it." In
truth, the Gregg-Teague team was in the throes of a losing
streak. Gregg (with Teague as campaign manager) had lost
two bids to regain the Governor's chair. Teague (with Gregg
as campaign manager) had lost in the primary in a 1962 try
for a seat in Congress. With most of the state's top Republicans at his disposal, Goldwater was not about to summon
a losing team to his service. Rockefeller afforded Gregg and
Teague a long-shot opportunity for a comeback. If they could
somehow guide him through to an upset win, another chance
to regain the Governorship would open up for Gregg.

Gregg and Teague formed an ill-sorted combination. Crew-cut, lean Hughie Gregg, an Ivy League patrician, was intense, irascible, and too often abrasive. Gray-haired, hulking Bert Teague, from a New England working-class background, was phlegmatic, congenial, and immensely well liked in New Hampshire political circles. Yet, they worked well together, each utterly loyal to the other. And on the main campaign theme, they were in perfect agreement. Nelson Rockefeller must forget about his millions and wage a New Hampshire-style campaign: simple, frugal, folksy. The planning and organization were not to be handled any differently than they would be if Hughie Gregg were running for Governor or Bert Teague were running for Congress—or if Estes Kefauver were running for the Presidency back in 1952. The threadbare campaign that had been a necessity for Kefauver in 1952 because of empty pockets now was transmogrified into a virtue in 1964 for one of the richest men in the world.

The Gregg-Teague campaign plan was based upon a concept of the New Hampshire voter as a unique and special creature. Television commercials, brass bands, and lavish rallies might be just the thing for campaigns in New York— but not in New Hampshire. Here, the voter wanted only to look over the candidate, hear him say a few words, and shake his hand.[7] Anything more would be ostentatious.

Because Rockefeller's own staff categorically rejected the Gregg-Teague thesis, the seeds were sown for constant debate between the Rockefeller staffers and the Gregg-Teague team. Moreover, the debate was waged daily in Rockefeller state headquarters at the New Hampshire Highway Hotel in Concord. For Rockefeller, unlike Goldwater, was not willing to put his fate entirely in the hands of his New Hamp-

[7] Some New Hampshire politicians carried the idea of special tactics needed in their state to the point of the ridiculous by arguing that a candidate needed a special kind of handshake in New Hampshire—not exactly weak, but not overly robust.

shire managers. As his proconsul in Concord, he assigned Alexander (Sandy) Lankler, the young Washington lawyer who had joined the Rockefeller staff the previous summer.[8] Lankler, the debonair son of a Presbyterian minister from Brooklyn, scoffed at the concept of a distinctive New Hampshire voter. "I see nothing different about them," he would say. "Just like everybody else, they eat, they drink, they sleep. They also watch television and are impressed by what they see on it." Lankler's recommendation was a tasteful but well-financed campaign with heavy emphasis on television and not nearly so much reliance on handshaking.[9] He was proposing a Presidential campaign. Gregg and Teague were proposing a Congressional campaign.

True to his promise, Rockefeller gave Gregg and Teague the last word. The entourage of a dozen or so aides that usually followed him was kept home. On his first New Hampshire campaign trip on October 19, 1963, he bent over backward to follow Gregg's warnings—arriving without a single aide at the airport in Manchester. On later trips, he was accompanied by press secretary Robert McManus and perhaps one other aide (plus the State Police captain who served as Rockefeller's bodyguard and insisted on accompanying him after the Kennedy assassination). The simplicity fetish reached such a point that McManus was barred from bringing his personal secretary and had to hire a stenographer by the hour in New Hampshire. While Goldwater sped about in a Cadillac, Rockefeller rode with the press in a bus. While Peggy Goldwater was bundled in mink, Happy Rockefeller wore a tweedy cloth coat. As Gregg insisted, Rockefeller was on the sidewalks shaking hands with scores of voters rather

---

[8] See page 218.

[9] Such a campaign would collide with New Hampshire's puritanical state election code limiting total expeditures for a Presidential primary campaign to a paltry $100,000. But this could be and was circumvented by beaming television programs into New Hampshire from stations outside the state. Technically, the money wasn't being spent in New Hampshire and therefore need not be included in the $100,000 total.

than on the television screen asking for the votes of thousands.

The Gregg-Teague formula was deeply frustrating for the Rockefeller staffers. The Presidential campaign that they had awaited these past five years was finally at hand. The New Hampshire primary was critical. Unless he could win it, Rockefeller's chance at rehabilitating his candidacy was dim. Yet, a pair of backwoods politicians decreed that the richest man ever to run for President must operate on a Kefauver-size budget and without having his own staff accompany him for the critical test.

It was a stormy campaign at the New Hampshire Highway Hotel. When reports of Rockefeller dissatisfaction with Gregg were published, the taut-nerved Gregg offered to quit. But he stayed and was in full command until the closing days of the campaign. Not until then did Lankler disregard frantic Gregg-Teague objections and launch a program of saturation television and mass mailings of elaborate campaign literature.

Within the framework of the Gregg-Teague formula, Rockefeller's campaign was a fairly good one and infinitely superior to Goldwater's. He was, of course, a master of the Kefauver-style handshaking technique. He was no Daniel Webster on the campaign platform, but was certainly no worse than Goldwater. Rockefeller was best when flailing Goldwater's position on Social Security and the United Nations, worst when mouthing a dry-as-dust treatise churned up by his immense research staff back in New York City. The campaign usually had Rockefeller on the offensive and Goldwater on the defensive, with the Governor continually hounding his rival with demands (continually declined by the Senator) for face-to-face debates.[10]

[10] However, the fine cutting edge of this Rockefeller tactic was dulled considerably late in January, when Senator Cotton distributed to the press a six-year-old letter by Rockefeller declaring: "I cannot believe that series of debates between Republican candidates is the best way to strengthen the

Yet, even as Goldwater dropped precipitously in New Hampshire, Rockefeller was not picking up nearly enough erstwhile Goldwaterites. The reason was clear to all. Just as it had very nearly destroyed him nationally, the remarriage issue was crippling his New Hampshire campaign. Rockefeller's polls showed just how badly the remarriage issue was hurting him. But no professional pollster was needed to perceive the malevolent gaze in the eyes of grim young matrons as they shielded toddlers when the Governor of New York passed by them on the sidewalks of New Hampshire towns.

Happy Rockefeller, now expecting a baby in June, was displayed from one end of the state to the other so that the voters could see her as the fresh and wholesome girl next door. It did little good. There seemed little chance of the remarriage issue subsiding so long as William Loeb was exacerbating it in his *Manchester Union Leader*. Only occasionally did Loeb leap to heights of frenzy by denouncing Rockefeller as a "wife swapper." But almost every day, the state's most influential paper managed to dredge up some reminder of Rockefeller's great political problem. On January 22, for instance, the *Union Leader* carried an article by a Lewis E. Seale of Alexandria, Louisiana, under this headline:

THE ROCKEFELLER IMAGE
BLURRED BY DIVORCE, REMARRIAGE

The quality of the material about Rockefeller printed in the *Union Leader* is reflected in the concluding paragraph of Mr. Seale's article:

It looks like "Who Threw Rocky in Mrs. Murphy's Chowder?" is still an apt quip. The point here is that while

---

Republican Party." It was written by Rockefeller, then front-runner in the 1958 race for the gubernatorial nomination, to his closest contender, Leonard Hall, after Hall had challenged him to debate. Rockefeller men were indignant when they learned that Hall had volunteered the letter to Cotton.

history does repeat itself, not even the Queen of England dared to challenge public opinion, and Her Majesty does not have to appeal to the voter in order to succeed herself. Nearly 30 years have elapsed since the Duke [of Windsor] abdicated the throne "for the woman I love," and the royal pair still have no roots. Is America more gullible? We should soon know.

Indeed, Rockefeller and his aides came to feel in New Hampshire that their real foe was not Barry Goldwater but Bill Loeb.[11] Late in January, Rockefeller even went to the point of preparing a television tape that denounced Loeb (without mentioning his name) as a sick, pathetic man abusing freedom of the press. Fearing that it would only increase Loeb's attacks, however, Rockefeller never showed the tape.

Nor did he find any other means of neutralizing the re-marriage issue as the March 10 election day drew near and his last chance at the nomination trickled through his fingers.

One afternoon midway through the campaign, at Rocke-feller headquarters in the New Hampshire Highway Hotel, Bert Teague fell to musing about the differences between the 1952 and 1964 campaigns.

"You know," he said, "everything was simple back in 1952. Eisenhower against Taft. Two-man race. That's all there was to it. It was a good clean campaign—good for the state, good for the party. We thought it might be that way this time—Goldwater against Rockefeller. But it isn't. It's messy and confused, with so many candidates that nobody can understand anything."

The New Hampshire winter scene was indeed crowded with candidates, both avowed and unavowed. No fewer than

---

[11] Goldwater wasn't completely immune from Loeb's sharp pen. Curiously, ultraconservative Loeb was a close friend and business associate of Jimmy Hoffa, scandal-scarred president of the Teamsters Union. When Goldwater attacked Hoffa (a Rockefeller supporter) late in the campaign, Loeb publicly upbraided the Senator.

six men and one woman figured on the bed-sheet-size New Hampshire ballot. This was the lineup:

1. *Goldwater.*
2. *Rockefeller.*
3. *Senator Margaret Chase Smith* of Maine, trying to prove that a woman could run for President, was on the ballot as an avowed candidate.
4. So was that old perennial, *Harold Stassen.* The man who would have been the Republican nominee for President and quite possibly President of the United States had he not engaged in a disastrous radio debate with Thomas E. Dewey just before the 1948 Oregon primary, Stassen was making his pathetic last hurrah.
5. The last-listed candidate was somebody named *Norman LePage.*
6. A write-in campaign for *Richard M. Nixon* was directed by former Governor Wesley Powell, the stormy petrel of New Hampshire Republican politics who had supported a Democrat for Governor in 1962.
7. Another write-in, conducted by some unknown volunteers from New Hampshire and assisted by a cadre from Massachusetts, was being staged for *Henry Cabot Lodge*— still on the other side of the globe as Ambassador to South Vietnam.

Like Bert Teague, most politicians in New Hampshire believed that this plethora of candidates was confusing the primary and spoiling what otherwise would have been an exciting two-man race. They were confusing cause and effect. Actually, the plethora of candidates resulted from the mood of the voters.

The misinterpretation of what was really happening in New Hampshire—and, as was later seen, in the entire country—was typified by the way the Rockefeller camp reacted to the news that Margaret Chase Smith might enter the New

Hampshire primary. Although Rockefeller publicly was cheering this prospect ("She's a wonderful person and a very able woman, and I hope that she will come into the New Hampshire primary," he said on CBS's "Face the Nation" on November 16, 1963), he was privately—and unsuccessfully—begging her to stay out. His fear was that Mrs. Smith, a moderate liberal, would split the anti-Goldwater vote in New Hampshire and thereby ruin what slim chance Rockefeller had for victory.

In other words, Rockefeller—and Goldwater, too, for that matter—saw the New Hampshire electorate as a pie to be divided between the two avowed candidates, and any additional candidates would cut into the slice of either Rockefeller or Goldwater or both. This was totally unrealistic. In fact, Goldwater started losing votes badly in New Hampshire after the Kennedy assassination; but Rockefeller, unable to recover from the remarriage issue, was unable to pick up more than a small portion of them. This meant that Rockefeller was slowly catching up with Goldwater, but the number of voters who wanted neither of the two leading candidates was increasing even faster.

The results were that very nearly unbelievable totals in the "undecided" columns were showing up in the polls. Scientific surveys conducted for Rockefeller reflected an "undecided" total of more than 50 percent. In conducting his house-to-house canvasses for Goldwater, Speaker Lamprey was getting the same result. Canvassing voters in Pittsfield (supposedly a Goldwater stronghold), Lamprey found 130 for Goldwater, 51 against him, and 300 undecided.[12]

But a few conversations with New Hampshire voters on the street showed that the "undecided" label was a misnomer. Most of them had definitely *decided*—decided not to vote

---

[12] Amid much consternation within the Goldwater camp, Lamprey released the Pittsfield survey and others like it to the press. Although Lamprey apparently felt that these results revealed Goldwater strength, they actually confirmed suspicions of Goldwater weakness.

for either Rockefeller or Goldwater. This was the typical refrain: "I don't care much for either of them. Maybe another candidate will come along." The "undecideds" were voters in search of a candidate. More perceptive than the politicians, the *Concord Daily Monitor* came close to catching the mood of the state when it facetiously editorialized on January 24 that petitions ought to be distributed to put "the name of that great American, I. M. Undecided, onto the ballot." Even an imaginary candidate might appeal to the state's Republicans in their choice for an alternative to Goldwater and Rockefeller.

Margaret Chase Smith was not acceptable as that alternative. Though their neighbors in Maine might elect her to the Senate year after year, the New Hampshire voters were not accustomed to ladies in politics, at any level, much less the Presidency.

It seemed for a time that the Nixon write-in campaign might provide the alternative. But the write-in drive conducted by Powell was sporadic and haphazard. Powell was a bitterly controversial figure, so much so that he was losing Nixon votes. Finally, Nixon's reputation as a New Hampshire favorite was badly overblown, based entirely on a 22,000-vote "spontaneous" write-in for Vice-President in the 1956 primary at a time when liberal Republicans were plotting to dump him from the 1956 ticket. The write-in that year actually was the result of undercover work by Styles Bridges' well-oiled political machine. Now, in 1964, Bridges was dead, and Wes Powell was clearly a poor substitute.

But by mid-January, the alternative had arrived. It was Henry Cabot Lodge. What better alternative than this publicly popular, handsome, still-dashing statesman? Paul Grindle and David Goldberg, two vigorous young Bostonians who had helped run the George Lodge Senate campaign against Teddy Kennedy in 1962, were directing the Lodge write-in campaign with far more competence than Wes Powell's slapdash effort for Nixon. A massive mailing dispensed Lodge pledge cards throughout the state. An amazing amount of them were returned with promises of support.

By late January, the Rockefeller forces realized that Lodge, not Mrs. Smith, was their real problem. While Rockefeller was addressing a party banquet in Concord one Friday night, Sandy Lankler sat down at the same table with Grindle and Goldberg to try to pound some sense into their skulls. His argument was the standard Rockefeller line. As a write-in candidate on the other side of the globe, Lodge had no chance to win the primary himself, but might well drain enough anti-Goldwater votes away from Rockefeller to give first place to Goldwater.

"I wouldn't say this if you had a chance to *win*," Lankler told the Lodge men. "But as long as all you're doing is hurting us and helping Goldwater, why not pull out?"

Grindle and Goldberg agreed with Lankler that their man couldn't come in first. But they felt that even a second place finish to Goldwater or even a good third place would be a formidable accomplishment for a noncandidate.

On a higher level, Rockefeller was making the same overtures to Lodge—and meeting with no more success. On two occasions, Rockefeller asked the Ambassador to repudiate the write-in campaign—once relaying the message through the Ambassador's son George and once talking directly to Lodge in Saigon via transoceanic telephone. Static made U.S.-to-Vietnam communications difficult, but transmission was clear enough on both occasions for Rockefeller to see that Lodge was not going to call off his volunteers in New Hampshire.

Rockefeller was enraged. He felt that Lodge was double-crossing him and betraying the liberal wing of the Republican Party. During a private conversation the previous summer, Lodge had urged Rockefeller to run for President—

despite his remarriage—in order to prevent Goldwater from winning the nomination by default.

But Rockefeller and most politicians were guilty of two basic errors of judgment about New Hampshire:

First was their belief that Lodge could not place first. They were so permeated by the Kefauver syndrome that they simply could not believe that a noncampaigning candidate could win there. They had forgotten the Eisenhower performance of 1952.

Second was their belief that Lodge was taking votes that otherwise would have been Rockefeller's. The truth is that these were never Rockefeller's votes. They were denied him because of the remarriage. It's fair to say that if Lodge had not been available to pick up these non-Rockefeller, non-Goldwater votes, somebody would have—perhaps Nixon, perhaps even William Scranton if a Scranton write-in campaign had been organized.

At any rate, the "undecided" vote was rapidly transformed into a Lodge vote as election day neared. In the March 9 issue of *Newsweek*, pollster Louis Harris found that *if all contenders were listed* on the ballot, voters would prefer:

	Percent
Lodge	31
Nixon	24
Goldwater	18
Rockefeller	12
Mrs. Smith	4
Romney	2
Scranton	1
Stassen	1
Not sure	7

But Harris and all other pollsters were skeptical about the ability and will of the New Hampshire voter to write out L-o-d-g-e on March 10. While forecasting that "the combined write-in vote will be the greatest in state history," the *Newsweek* article accompanying the Harris poll asserted:

Many voters simply are reluctant to write in candidates not listed on the ballot—out of shyness, a fear of misspelling names, or other psychological reasons. Some feel, too, that only announced candidates deserve their vote. . . .

As a result, Harris found that *on a sample of the actual ballot,* voters preferred:

	Percent
Goldwater	29
Rockefeller	29
Lodge (write-in)	16
Nixon (write-in)	15
Mrs. Smith	7
Stassen	3
LePage	
Others (write-in)	1
(Blank ballots)	9

What Harris misjudged was not the mood of the voters but their dexterity at writing in Lodge's name. But Harris was not alone in forecasting a head-an-head Goldwater-Rockefeller race for first place. Nobody expected the Lodge landslide. The television networks' computers manned at CBS by Harris himself spotted the landslide within the first fifteen minutes after the polls closed.

These were the final results:

Lodge (write-in)	33,521
Goldwater	21,775
Rockefeller	19,496
Nixon (write-in)	15,752
Mrs. Smith	2,812
Stassen	1,285

This whopping 35 percent of the total (to 22 percent for Goldwater, 21 percent for Rockefeller, and 17 percent for Nixon) did not tell the full story. Besides the Lodge win in the popularity contest, the entire fourteen-member Lodge slate of delegates to the National Convention was elected.

This was the real stunner. While apprehenshive about

Goldwater's showing in the popularity contest, Goldwater forces were confident that most or all of their delegate slate would be sent to San Francisco. It was a matter of name identification. Such familiar New Hampshire names as Cotton, Bridges, and Dwinnell led the Goldwater slate. The Rockefeller slate contained some familiar names, but nothing to approach the star quality of the Goldwater slate.[13]

Serving as spokesman in Goldwater's Washington headquarters on election night, Clif White was exuding confidence about picking up delegates even after Lodge's win in the popularity contest was undisputed.

But the New Hampshire voters were having nothing to do with Goldwater on March 10. They passed over the familiar names pledged to Goldwater to mark the unfamiliar names pledged to Lodge.[14] At one point during the evening, it seemed that New Hampshire's Republicans would elect thirteen Lodge delegates plus the highly popular Norris Cotton, running first on the Goldwater slate. But soon after this, the fourteenth Lodge man passed Cotton in the counting and stayed ahead.[15]

Considering how badly the nature of the New Hampshire campaign was misunderstood even by the combatants, it was natural, then, that the results were badly misinterpreted. The vast majority of Republican politicians (as well as most of the press) dismissed Lodge as a "regional" candidate.

[13] At Nixon's specific request, no delegate slate was filed for him.

[14] This was facilitated by a "road map" of the king-size New Hampshire ballot contained in one of the mass mailings from Lodge headquarters in Concord. It gave explicit directions for casting a maximum Lodge vote. No such similar "road map" was mailed by either Goldwater or Rockefeller.

[15] Appearing on NBC's "Today" show on the morning of March 11, Cotton used his wry Yankee humor to find a silver lining in the election results. Because he now would not have to finance the cross-country trip to the San Francisco convention and back, he said that he could afford to remodel his bathroom back home and make Mrs. Cotton happy. This flip phrase, as well as his characterization of the New Hampshire results as "a disaster," did not endear him to the Goldwater staff.

As a native and resident of neighboring Massachusetts, he was supposed to have popularity in New Hampshire that would not show up elsewhere. Thus, the New Hampshire primary was dismissed as totally meaningless. The bogus concept that there is something distinctive and totally atypical about the Upper New England Yankee was now thought to be an established fact.

The fact is that Sandy Lankler had been quite correct in his analysis that the New Hampshire voter was not a great deal different from the voter anywhere else. As the nation-wide polls were soon to show, Lodge's popularity was by no means confined to New Hampshire. Nor were the problems of Rockefeller and Goldwater confined to New Hampshire. The truth is that, from the standpoint of reflecting national sentiment, the New Hampshire primary was to prove more meaningful than the many primaries to follow it. These were its major lessons.

1. Rockefeller and Goldwater, managing to collect less than 50 percent of the New Hampshire vote together, were in trouble—Rockefeller because of his remarriage, Gold-water because of his indifferent campaigning style and the ideological leanings that, it was now clear, caused trouble out of the immediate circle of Goldwaterites.

2. Rank-and-file Republicans were looking for an alternative to Rockefeller and Goldwater. Lodge was the best alternative on hand at the moment. But New Hampshire made it clear that Lodge's front-running position among rank-and-file Republicans was mainly a matter of being least unpopular rather than most popular.[16]

[16] The Harris poll in the March 9 issue of *Newsweek* pointed up this phenomenon. Asking Republican voters which candidate they would *not* support even if he were the party's nominee, Goldwater ran first and Lodge last. Specifically, the results were Goldwater, 25 percent; Mrs. Smith, 18 percent; Stassen, 18 percent; Rockefeller, 14 percent; Romney, 5 percent; Nixon, 5 percent; Scranton, 4 percent; Lodge, 2 percent; Not sure or none, 37 percent.

3. There was an unmistakable vacuum in the Republican Presidential race, unfilled since the post-assassination slump of Goldwater. But such vacuums do not stay unfilled for long.

On a candidate-by-candidate basis, this was the post-New Hampshire outlook:

Goldwater: His staff had been given a shocking—very nearly a disillusioning—look at his campaigning and vote-getting abilities. He was at his low point now. Most important, whatever chance Goldwater had in getting the nomination was to be found in painstaking collection of delegates, not in a Kennedy-style romp through the primary elections.

Rockefeller: The postmarriage strategy of forcing himself on a reluctant party by an all-victorious record in the primaries was now dead—because he had failed even to place second to Lodge and beat Goldwater, much less finish first in New Hampshire. His slim vestige of a chance for the nomination was gone.

Lodge: Neither his win in New Hampshire nor his soon-to-be announced boost in the national polls had diminished the intense dislike for him among party pros. Goldwater had no use for him. Rockefeller, still insisting that he would have won in New Hampshire had it not been for Lodge, was telling friends that he would never, never throw his delegates to Lodge at San Francisco. Even if Lodge were to enter and win all subsequent primaries, he would have only an outside chance.

There were then no winners out of New Hampshire and only two nonlosers—*Nixon* and *Scranton.* Nixon's fourth-place finish in New Hampshire was lackluster, but nothing much had been expected of his listless write-in campaign anyway. Scranton collected only 77 (repeat, 77) write-in votes, but he had no campaign at all.

The New Hampshire outcome emphasized Nixon's shopworn quality and Scranton's anonymity, but they seemed the most likely possibilities to fill the vacuum (with a big edge to Scranton because of his more impressive support within the Eastern Establishment). What nobody counted on was Barry Goldwater himself filling the vacuum he had created by his own slump.

XIX

Goldwater's Delegates

On April 9, 1964, an Evans-Novak daily column, entitled "Reassessing Goldwater," began:

> Sen. Barry Goldwater, whose chance for the Presidential nomination was pronounced dead by professional politicians weeks ago, may have been the victim of premature burial.
>
> In a hard-boiled reassessment of the fight for the nomination, a few Republican politicians have come to these conclusions:
>
> Goldwater never really has been stopped. To the contrary, he is still very much the man to beat. His chances for the top prize now are assessed at around fifty-fifty—perhaps even better. More important, Goldwater's foes today have no clear-cut plan for stopping him. This is his vital asset.
>
> Anti-Goldwater forces still are relying on the prospect of a convention deadlock between Goldwater and Gov. Nelson Rockefeller. But if Goldwater beats Rockefeller in the June 2 California Primary, as now seems likely, Rockefeller is finished. Goldwater could enter the convention with perhaps 550 votes (only 100 less than is necessary for nomination) and nobody else even a close second.

Cautious and carefully hedged though this reassessment was, it was revolutionary in the context of early April, 1964. It was less than a month since Goldwater's debacle in New Hampshire, and nothing discernible to the naked eye had happened since then to rejuvenate his candidacy. Rather, he was going from bad to worse in the national polls. Lodge had soared far into the lead in the Gallup Poll since the New Hampshire primary on March 10—indicating that his popularity was by no means merely a New England phenomenon. Nixon had slipped to second place. Rockefeller had rallied a bit in February, but fell to a new low after New Hampshire. Romney and Scranton managed no more than microscopic ratings. But Goldwater was going down, down, down.

Here is the month-by-month Gallup derby since the assassination (the figures are percentages):

	December	January	February	March	April
Lodge	16	19	12	16	42
Nixon	29	29	31	34	26
Goldwater	27	23	20	17	14
Rockefeller	13	12	16	13	6
Romney	7	8	7	6	4
Scranton	2	4		5	4

But nominations are won by convention delegates, not Gallup ratings. And Goldwater was slowly, inexorably picking up the delegates while everybody else was counting him dead.

Clif White, in charge of the delegate-counting charts at Goldwater headquarters in Washington, was quite aware of this process. Gradually, a few non-Goldwater Republican politicians also realized it. One of them was Charles McWhorter, who had been a protégé of Clif White in the Young Republicans. A former aide to Richard M. Nixon and now an executive with AT&T in New York City, Charley McWhorter maintained contacts with Republican leaders throughout the country dating back to his days as national chairman of the Young Republicans. Drawing on these sources, McWhorter found that Goldwater (with eighty-six more delegates and an incalculable boost in prestige that would come from whipping Rockefeller in the two-man California primary on June 2) would be unstoppable. Or, figuring out the arithmetical problem backward, McWhorter could find a hard core of non-Goldwater delegates no larger than four hundred, far less than needed to stop Goldwater.[1]

As they took up pencil and paper, other Republicans came to agree with McWhorter. By early May, anti-Goldwater elements in the party had finally come to realize that public-opinion polls and primary elections were not enough. In a May 7 editorial called "But Goldwater Got the Delegates," the *New York Herald Tribune* concluded:[2]

> Both polls and primaries have indicated that Goldwater is far from being first choice of the party's rank and file—i.e., the people who vote in November. But he's been steadily gathering in the delegates—i.e., the people who will vote in July in San Francisco. And of these, all he needs is 655.
>
> Those in the party who now are united only by their common aversion to a Goldwater nomination will have to be united on more that that if he's not going to walk away with the prize.

By mid-May, however, they at least were united in their common understanding that Goldwater was far from dead. Old pro Len Hall made it official at about that time with his own delegate count, which was the basis for a *Newsweek* prophecy in its May 18 issue that the fight was all but over. Said *Newsweek*:

> It was still nine weeks before the gavel's first crack in San Francisco, but the air was filled with premonitory thunder. By the simple arithmetic of power, the Republican Presidential nominee seemed all but chosen, and his name was Barry Goldwater.

What were the ingredients of Goldwater's resurrection, at once both spectacular and virtually unnoticed? How had he recovered from the New Hampshire debacle without any

[1] McWhorter's calculations were a principal source for the Evans-Novak column of April 9.

[2] Goldwater's showing in Indiana and the other primaries between New Hampshire and California is surveyed in the next chapter.

gain in the polls or any really meaningful primary-election victory? How had he seemingly defied the laws of pre-convention party politics?

One essential ingredient in Goldwater's resurrection was the rejuvenation of his campaign, from the standpoint both of the candidate and of his staff.

Facing his defeated and discouraged campaign workers in a ballroom at Washington's Madison Hotel on the night of the New Hampshire defeat, Goldwater said: "I did something wrong. I goofed up somewhere." Transmitted over nation-wide television, these remarks were Goldwater at his most refreshing and most candid. He meant it. Whatever hap-pened in the future, there would be no repeat of New Hamp-shire.

For one thing, Goldwater made up his mind that night never again to cede full authority for a campaign to outsiders as he had to his New Hampshire managers. More specifically, he determined never again to be hounded by local primary campaign managers into a Kefauver-style campaign or any other that didn't fit his temperament and nature. Finally, he never again would be pressed into a backbreaking sched-ule that exceeded the limits of his stamina.[3]

The New Hampshire defeat also showed Goldwater that he needed a speech writer, desperately and immediately. Though the most prolific speechmaker of his day, Gold-water never had found a speech writer who really satisfied him. In the past, his most eloquent speeches had come from the typewriter of Brent Bozell, a *National Review* editor and occasional ghost writer of Goldwater's syndicated news-paper column. But Goldwater never really felt perfectly com-fortable with high-flown conservative intellectuals such as Bozell. Tony Smith, a workmanlike political jack-of-all-trades, could bang out an acceptable Goldwater speech. But

---

[3] The implications of these resolutions were felt most strongly in the California primary campaign, which is discussed in Chapter XXI.

it usually lacked the ideological flourishes that the Senator liked. Though he often wrote his own speeches, Goldwater was the first to admit that he was no stylist. Moreover, the chilling experience of those New Hampshire coffee hours convinced him that impromptu speeches would not do. He must have prepared speeches—indeed, Goldwater needed two or three set speeches that could be used constantly through a campaign, embellished here and revised there to meet special occasions.

After New Hampshire, Goldwater finally found his speech writer (and the set speeches) in Karl Hess, forty-one, a moon-faced, slightly plump professional writer and militant anti-Communist. Though never before intimately involved in partisan politics, Hess's background was varied—journalist, researcher, ghost writer of books, speech writer. He had made contact with Goldwater through the American Enterprise Institute, a Washington-based research foundation run by William Joseph Baroody, one of Goldwater's closest friends and most influential advisers. Baroody had occasionally employed Hess as a researcher, and he recommended him to Goldwater. Hess did some part-time chores for Goldwater late in 1963 and early in 1964, and after New Hampshire, he was put on the full-time staff.

Goldwater and Hess hit it off from the start. Hess's hard-line anticommunism, his inclination for a strong military response to get the U.S. out of diplomatic problems, and his generally pro-military sentiments were right down Goldwater's alley. So was Hess's stressing of international over domestic affairs. Moreover, Hess could construct the phrases needed to help demolish the New Hampshire-built image of a trigger-happy warmonger ("Why, I'm the biggest peacemonger you ever saw," was a frequent line in Goldwater's Hess-written speeches).

But the Goldwater-Hess union was more than ideological. Goldwater, who had not finished his freshman year at the

University of Arizona and was sensitive about it, often felt uncomfortable under the haughty gaze of conservative academicians. This never happened with Hess, a self-trained intellectual who quit high school at the age of fifteen before graduating. Nor did Hess make the mistake (as did many of his predecessors) of annoying the Senator with scoldings and lectures. Most important, perhaps, Hess was a sincerely devoted admirer of Goldwater. In sharp contrast to other Goldwater aides, Hess didn't downgrade his chief in private. "I think the Senator's a political genius. I think he's just about perfect," Hess would say in private conversation—and mean it.[4]

Hess was no home-based speech writer. He became Goldwater's constant traveling companion after New Hampshire and, as such, was soon more than merely a speech writer. He became a key adviser without portfolio. Calm and placid, his advice began to carry great weight as he became one of the very few non-Arizonans to pierce the Goldwater inner circle. The fact that Hess was a conservative theorist rather than a practicing Republican politician helps to account for Goldwater's lack of an attempt to woo the party's moderates during these weeks.[5]

Simultaneously, one other non-Arizonan was upgraded at Goldwater headquarters in Washington during the post-New Hampshire shake-up. During the first months of the year,

[4] Hess even took to wearing a steer's-head Western-style silver belt buckle similar to Goldwater's. When an old friend kidded him about it, the usually bland and affable Hess flared up.

[5] One other, less important change on Goldwater's traveling staff was made after New Hampshire. Press secretary Tony Smith was sent to the hospital with recurrent ulcer trouble and was replaced by Edwin K. Nellor, a former colleague of Smith's on the old *Washington Times Herald,* a former speech writer for Senator Joseph McCarthy, and most recently public-relations man for the Washington office of the National Association of Manufacturers. Though a highly competent press officer when in good health, Smith was impeded in New Hampshire by his ulcer condition. Though distrusted by some liberal-minded reporters because of his background, Nellor proved extremely helpful to the press—too helpful in the opinion of some of the more secretive members of the Arizona Mafia.

Clif White had come close to quitting on more than one occasion. But he stayed on in hopes of lifting himself back up to a point of authority. After New Hampshire, the Arizona Mafia became convinced that they could not get Goldwater the nomination by themselves. White would have to be brought back into the high command.[6]

The idea of neophyte Dick Kleindienst serving as chief and the veteran White carrying out his orders was becoming manifestly absurd—especially to Kleindienst. One night in Washington, sipping brandy and talking into the wee hours of the morning, the two men reached a personal arrangement. Kleindienst asked why White hadn't stepped in more actively to direct the field operations or even to disagree with Kleindienst's own directives. As a subordinate, White replied, he was severely limited as to just how far he could go. Kleindienst then insisted that White feel free to contradict him and disagree with him whenever necessary.

This arrangement was formalized a few weeks later. In a full-scale staff meeting in the Duryea Building, Goldwater gave Kleindienst and White equal status, like the two consuls of Rome. Each would carry the title of codirector of field operations. Actually, however, White was being put in charge of the heart of the Goldwater campaign. He would be in charge not only of states picking their delegates via the convention system (which was the vast majority of the states), but also of floor tactics for the National Convention itself. While still maintaining his voice in strategy councils, Kleindienst was now to serve chiefly as overseer in the two primary elections—Oregon on May 15 and California on June 2—in which Goldwater would have major opposition.

The reformed high command was unveiled on April 5 in a national session of Goldwater regional and state chairmen from across the country. The scene of the closed-door ses-

---

[6] But not into their social circle. Kitchel and Burch kept to themselves after working hours, away from the non-Arizonan members of the staff.

sion was a suite in the O'Hare International Inn in Chicago—
the same airport hotel where, early in 1963, the nucleus
of the Draft Goldwater organization had decided under Clif
White's leadership to keep going despite discouragement
from Goldwater himself.[7] The ostensible purpose of the April
5 meeting was to plot strategy and tactics. But its underlying motive was to reassure the regional and state Goldwater leaders, many of them originals in the Draft Goldwater
movement and close friends of White. The local leaders had
been upset to read reports of the Arizona Mafia taking over
command and shoving White out of the picture. The April 5
meeting gave them a chance to meet the Arizonans for the
first time, and, more important, to note that White (newly
rehabilitated in the high command) was in on the ground
floor. It was White who ran the briefing sessions in Chicago.

The Goldwater leaders who attended the Chicago meeting
also came away with the clear impression that the chief
brunt of the Goldwater campaign henceforth was to be
the delegate-hunting operations at district and state conventions. The primaries, once seen as the avenue to the White
House, were now dismissed as a necessary nuisance.

This strategy was enhanced by the absence in the field of
any opposition in the hunt for delegates at local conventions.
Take a quick rundown of Goldwater's possible challengers:

Rockefeller's well-paid fieldmen continued to show up for
these conventions—but as observers, not contestants. As
Rockefeller himself was well aware, his only hope for support
came from rank-and-file Republicans and not from the party
workers who turned up as delegates to county conventions.
Crippled though he was, Rockefeller might give Goldwater a
run for his money in state primary elections but never in
county conventions.

After New Hampshire, the Draft *Lodge* movement tried to

[7] See page 128.

challenge Goldwater for delegates at county conventions, but with little success. Maxwell Rabb, administrative assistant to Lodge during his Senate days a dozen years earlier and a top staff assistant in the Draft Eisenhower movement of 1952, climbed aboard the Draft Lodge movement after his New Hampshire victory and took over the job of running down delegates. But Rabb had not participated in partisan Republican politics since the Draft Eisenhower movement. Most of the party leaders that Rabb had dealt with were dead, inactive, or powerless. Furthermore, the kind of rank-and-file Republican who took the trouble to write in Lodge's name in New Hampshire and other primary states was not the kind of Republican who took the trouble to show up for a precinct mass meeting. The Lodge following was passive rather than active and thus of no help whatever in controlling state conventions.[8]

Nixon had no interest at all in a state-by-state hunt for delegates. His only hope was a convention deadlock. He could not benefit from such a deadlock if he dirtied himself by digging for delegates.

That left *Scranton*. Despite his continued miniscule ratings in the Gallup Poll, he was the one candidate who could have become the focal point for non-Goldwater party leaders to gather about in a quest for delegates.[9] As it was, these non-Goldwater leaders fought for "uncommitted" delegations in their desperate efforts to head off the Goldwater hordes. But it was a case of running nobody against somebody, a concept against a man. If the anti-Taft forces had fought Taft with the concept of "uncommitted" delegations instead of the

[8] Rabb and other Lodge leaders made much of a temporary alliance with Rockefeller forces to stop Goldwater at the Iowa state convention on April 22. Clif White seemed justified in claiming six "certains" and six "probables" —half of Iowa's twenty-four-member delegation. At any rate, the Lodge-Rockefeller alliance was not repeated in any other state.

[9] Bill Keisling, the incorrigible optimist in Scranton's entourage, confided at this time that the anemic Gallup Poll ratings really did worry him. Actually, Scranton's own attitude should have been far more worrisome.

reality of Eisenhower in 1952, Taft, without question, would have been the nominee.

But Scranton's aides in Harrisburg, following the same line of reasoning as Nixon, wanted no down-and-dirty fight that would prevent Bill Scranton from becoming the unity candidate of the party at San Francisco. What's more important, Scranton would have no part of any activity in his behalf. Prodded by Mary Scranton, the Governor seemed to be getting increasingly firm in his statements against running for President.

At one point in mid-April, Scranton came close to ruling himself out of the race once and for all.

This was the background. On March 20, Scranton had scored his greatest legislative triumph by pushing a union-opposed reform of unemployment-compensation laws through the recalcitrant Legislature against heavy odds—marking the first time that a Governor of Pennsylvania had won major controversial legislation in his second year, after his patronage-dispensing powers had been depleted. It was a performance that showed the nerve, courage, and audacity that often seemed lacking in his public career. The holdout Pennsylvania conservatives who still regarded Scranton as a crypto-New Dealer were impressed by the way he took on organized labor in an election year. And Scranton's own Presidency-minded aides heaved a sigh of relief when his bill squeaked through the House without a vote to spare. They had feared that Scranton's national reputation might suffer the same fate as Romney's after the latter's tax program was scuttled by the Michigan Legislature.[10]

After his great legislative triumph, the Governor and his wife traveled to the Scranton family retreat in Hobe Sound,

[10] Scranton also realized this. At one point, when his unemployment compensation bill seemed to face certain defeat in the Legislature, he turned to Walter Alessandroni and said: "Once this bill is defeated, you and everybody else can forget this nonsense about running me for President."

Florida, for a brief spring vacation of tennis playing and sunbathing. When he returned, he seemed more determined than ever not to run for President. At this inopportune moment, Scranton learned that State Chairman Craig Truax had ordered one million Scranton-for-President write-in stickers printed for use in the Pennsylvania primary on April 28.[11] He was irritated that Truax and his other aides were forcing him to run against his will.

His decision: announce to the world that he not only was not a candidate, but also, in Sherman style, would not run if nominated—even if nominated by a draft. As his staff looked on in horror, Scranton ordered his press secretary, Jack Conmy, to summon political correspondents from Washington to Harrisburg for a press conference on Thursday, April 9. On Wednesday, the *Philadelphia Inquirer* correctly reported that Scranton planned to remove himself completely from Presidential consideration the next day.

Bill Keisling and Scranton's other aides pleaded with him on Wednesday night. They appealed to his sense of duty, claiming that he could not possibly play the part of a political ostrich if the Republican Party really did want to draft him as nominee. At the last minute, he relented. The press conference, attracting more than a score of reporters from Washington as well as the regular Harrisburg press corps, proved a dud. Scranton did little more than reaffirm his old position of noncandidacy in slightly stronger terms (including an appeal to friends to stop working for him).

Nevertheless, the incident did its damage. The headline on the front page of the *Washington Post* of April 10 was typical of the nationwide coverage:

SCRANTON

ALL BUT

QUITS RACE

[11] The background of this is described in the next chapter.

For many party leaders, it was the last straw.[12] Their ardor of early January had been cooling anyway. Scranton was too much the reluctant dragon. He was still turning down political speaking bids. Besides, his credentials as a practical politician were sullied a bit during March and April by his habit of predicting to visitors that the Presidential nomination probably would wind up going to Henry Cabot Lodge —the man that party leaders, liberal and conservative, wanted least.[13]

As a result, the Scranton boomlet was fast disintegrating. No longer confident that Scranton would run, the old pros— including the Len Hall–Meade Alcorn–Fred Scribner trio— were withdrawing their offers of support. Scranton's delegate strength in such Eastern redoubts as New Jersey, Connecticut, Delaware, and Maryland was vanishing.

Obviously, there was no basis now to challenge Goldwater for delegates in Scranton's name. Moreover, it was clear that Scranton now could be nominated only as the unity or compromise candidate following a deadlock—not as an active contender. The distinction was to be of immense importance.

But Goldwater's greatest asset in his post-New Hampshire recovery was not his reorganized campaign organization, Clif White's skill as a delegate hunter, or the absence of much organized competition in the delegate hunt. His greatest asset was a nationwide army of volunteers at the grass roots level.

Through his dozen years of preaching the conservative

---

[12] However, Truax tried to alleviate the damage by putting the best face on the press conference. "The forthrightness marking the Governor's statement is the very thing that is attracting growing numbers of supporters looking to him for leadership," declared Truax. It was a laudable, though not entirely successful, exercise in political gymnastics.

[13] Personal friendship may have colored Scranton's judgment here. The two men were warm friends. Lodge's only political speech during the 1962 campaign was in behalf of Scranton for Governor.

gospel, Barry Goldwater had won for himself what no other Presidential candidate ever had prior to nomination: a national mass movement. These were the Goldwaterites: a few wild-eyed extremists who huddled together in John Birch Society meetings in paranoiac fear of a "Communist" take-over from within; some Old Guard Republicans who thirsted for revenge after the defeat of Bob Taft by the Eastern Establishment in 1952; and, mostly, well-meaning Americans who wished for an America in which a man could make his living free from the pressure of the omnipotent Federal Government. What bound them together was a discontent with the liberal-dominated *status quo* and a nearly fanatical devotion to Barry Goldwater as the minister to end their discontent.

This was the Goldwater Movement. The apparent collapse of the Southern strategy after President Kennedy's assassination, Goldwater's steady decline in the Gallup Poll, and the debacle in New Hampshire (and other primary elections) did not and could not dim their ardor. There lay the real reason for the Goldwater recovery, breaking all the old political rules. The Goldwater Movement simply didn't follow the conventional rules. It would no sooner abandon Goldwater because of a few setbacks than the old Bolsheviks would have abandoned Lenin when he was outvoted in early Communist Party caucuses. Here was something new to contend with in American politics.

Its battle cry was Goldwater's slogan of "A Choice, Not an Echo." The Goldwater Movement's favorite pamphlet bore that motto. *A Choice Not an Echo,* a thin paperback by an attractive young housewife and party worker from Godfrey, Illinois (just across the Mississippi River from St. Louis, Missouri), named Phyllis Schlafly became a runaway best seller. Better than any other single volume, this pamphlet exposed the paranoia of the grass roots Goldwater worker.

The tone is defiantly conspiratorial. Mrs. Schlafly opens

by promising to tell how "a few secret kingmakers based in
New York have selected Republican presidential nominees
since 1936 and successfully forced their choice on a free
country where there are more than 34 million Republican
voters." She goes on to claim that Eastern-picked candidates for the party failed to campaign on the winning issues
—in 1940, "Roosevelt's policy of consenting to Stalin's in-
vasions of Poland, Finland, Latvia, Lithuania and Estonia—
while committing American boys to fight Hitler"; in 1944,
"how the Roosevelt Administration manipulated and invited
the disaster at Pearl Harbor"; in 1948, "Communist infiltration in Government"; in 1960, "Kennedy's sponsorship of
legislation helpful to the Communists." She then comments:

> How did it happen that in four major presidential campaigns,
> Republicans were maneuvered into nominating candidates who
> did not campaign on the major issues?
> It wasn't any accident. It was planned that way. In each of
> their losing presidential years, a small group of secret king-
> makers, using hidden persuaders and psychological warfare
> techniques, manipulated the Republican National Convention
> to nominate candidates who would sidestep or suppress the key
> issues.

Written in the winter of 1964, when the Goldwater tide
was at low ebb, and published in May, A Choice Not an
Echo is permeated with the haunting fear that these "secret
kingmakers" will once again prevail and substitute one of
their own, probably Scranton, in place of Barry Goldwater.
Mrs. Schlafly concludes:

> I speak for the thousands of little people who worked their
> hearts out for Willkie and Dewey and Nixon believing they
> had a just cause and the right leaders. These people were
> entitled to something better than the "me too" campaigns they
> got, and I want to help them get it in 1964. . . .
> A Republican victory in 1964 is dependent on our having
> candidates who campaign on the major issues of our time and

fight hard to win. All the Party unity and loyalty among the rank and file cannot give us victory if we lack this essential ingredient. Therefore, the most positive, constructive thing I can do for the Republican Party is to give our people the facts, in anticipation of the Convention, which will assist them to reject the efforts of the little clique of kingmakers who want to force upon us another "me too" candidate who will pull his punches and evade the vital issues.[14]

She was striking a responsive chord. In every part of the country, there emerged something not often seen in American politics: a political crusade with a real cause. This mass movement, channeled and guided by Clif White at Goldwater headquarters in Washington, revolutionized preconvention politics.

Until 1964, preconvention politics had been a matter of winning over county and state leaders in the hope that they would back your man—the sort of preconvention politics that George Hinman was playing so artfully for Nelson Rockefeller before the disaster of the Governor's remarriage. This old-style version of politics presumed that the county and state leaders were looking for a winner. Thus, it was important for the candidate to show victories in primaries and high ratings in polls. Otherwise, the leaders would swing their delegates to another candidate.

But the new Goldwater-style of preconvention politics did not waste time on winning over county and state organizations, but concentrated on actually taking over the county and state organizations by an inundation of the Goldwater volunteers. It was indeed a revolutionary doctrine. It meant that the Goldwater delegates sent to San Francisco would be not merely the run-of-the-mill party workers under the command and the bidding of regular party leaders. Here was a new breed of delegate, most of whom had never been to a

[14] Phyllis Schlafly, *A Choice Not an Echo*, Alton, Ill.: Pere Marquette Press, 1964.

national convention before. They were going not as a reward for faithful service, not to see the sights of San Francisco, and certainly not to ride the bandwagon of a winner. They were going there for one purpose: to vote for Barry Goldwater. To woo them away to another candidate would be as difficult as proselytizing a religious zealot. On April 14, Phyllis Schlafly was elected a delegate from Illinois. No matter what the primaries and the polls showed, she and hundreds of delegates like her would support "A Choice, Not an Echo" to the end.

One more point should be made about the effectiveness of the Goldwater Movement. It was, of course, not large in numbers—as witness Goldwater's anemic 14 percent national rating in the Gallup Poll at a time when so objective a source as *Newsweek* was conceding him the nomination. Yet, it is not generally understood how much preconvention politics is a game of hundreds or scores of votes—or sometimes even a single vote. The Goldwater Movement could not show its strength in the New Hampshire primary and was totally submerged in national polls, but the pyramidal nature of delegate selection (beginning with precinct mass meetings) was admirably suited to the Movement.

What happened in Fairfax County, Virginia, illustrates what was happening all over the country. Fairfax County, located across the Potomac River from Washington, D.C., is a burgeoning suburban area of more than three-hundred thousand population, evenly split in local elections between Republicans and Democrats. Fairfax County is a world removed from either the old Bourbon South and the fiercely militant new Republican South. As a middle-class Northern-type suburb, it did not figure to be solid Goldwater country. Moreover, the county's regular Republican organization was led by an anti-Goldwater moderate, Jack MacDonald, a former member of the Republican National Committee's staff.

Under old-style preconvention campaigning, the Goldwater

forces would have been trying their best to woo MacDonald so that Fairfax County's delegates to the tenth Congressional District convention might support the election of Goldwater delegates to the National Convention. They didn't. Instead, they tried to take the county organization away from Mac-Donald by flooding the precinct (in Virginia, the district) conventions with Goldwater men. MacDonald was well aware of the danger. He knew that the other Republican Presidential possibilities had taken no interest in Fairfax County. If Goldwater was to be stopped there, it would be up to MacDonald. He tried his best, through letters and personal contact, to get anti-Goldwater Republicans into the election-district conventions.

MacDonald failed. But the narrowness of his failure shows how much a game of inches preconvention Presidential politics really is. Because voters do not register by party in Virginia, any registered voter—even a hard-core Democrat—could walk into a district convention and cast his vote. Yet, no district convention attracted many more than one hundred persons. The Goldwater forces conceded several of these election districts to MacDonald and decided to wage a battle for just enough votes to win control over the county. The decisive battleground was the fashionable Lake Barcroft District, whose district convention was captured by the Goldwater forces by a *single* vote. This victory gave Goldwater control of the Fairfax County delegates to the tenth Congressional District, which in turn elected two Goldwater delegates to the National Convention.

This was the microcosm. Multiply it many hundredfold and the reason for Goldwater's recovery after New Hampshire becomes clear enough.

Through the spring, the Goldwater Movement was operating in high gear. On February 29, the North Carolina state convention concluded that state's delegation selection with twenty-five out of twenty-six delegates in Goldwater's corner.[15] On March 21, the South Carolina state convention concluded that state's delegate selection with a sixteen out of sixteen score for Goldwater. On April 18, the Arizona state convention pledged its sixteen-member convention to Goldwater. On April 25, the Nevada state convention picked an all-Goldwater slate of three men and three women.

But Arizona was the candidate's home state, and the Carolinas and Nevada were deep in the Goldwater heartland. These were the delegates certain to go to Goldwater, come what may. What was remarkable was the way he was winning most or all of the delegations from states that were not 100 percent Goldwater country. Four such states—Oklahoma, Georgia, Kansas, and Washington—provide a good cross section of how profoundly the Goldwater Movement affected the delegate-selection process.

Oklahoma: To the outsider, Oklahoma might seem solid Goldwater country. Certainly, a liberal Republican was a rare commodity there. But its conservatives were split into two distinct and warring camps—the moderates and the militants. Both were for Goldwater, but with varying degrees of emphasis.

The moderates were led by Governor Henry Bellmon, a former state party chairman who in 1962 was elected Oklahoma's first Republican Governor. As a conservative, Bellmon leaned toward Goldwater, but he was not at all hostile to Nixon and hadn't closed his mind to a new face such as Scranton. Above all, he wanted to lead an uncommitted Oklahoma delegation to San Francisco—probably to vote

---

[15] However, the overzealousness of North Carolina Goldwater forces tended to take the edge off their victory. Acting against the wishes of both White and regular Goldwater officials in the state, some Goldwater zealots attempted at the state convention to pledge irrevocably North Carolina's four at-large delegates to Goldwater. When the motion was voted down by an overwhelming margin, anti-Goldwater Republicans pointed to the North Carolina convention as a sign of the Goldwater slump in the South.

for Goldwater, but perhaps to go elsewhere if it was in Oklahoma's best interests.

This was what Phyllis Schlafly would call kingmaker politics. It was in complete violation of the precepts of the Goldwater Movement. Accordingly, the Oklahoma militants had no inclination to go along with Bellmon. Nor were these militants to be trifled with. They controlled the Oklahoma City Republican organization, a good portion of the party activists throughout the state, and a large percentage of the campaign money available to the Republican Party. What's more, they had made it clear in the autumn of 1963 that they would use roughhouse tactics to force Bellmon and the moderates into line, withholding support from the Governor in a coming statewide referendum over a state issue.

That autumn, a secret emergency session was called by Bellmon in a Tulsa hotel suite. Meeting with his close political associates, the Governor decided despite his desire for an uncommitted delegation, it wasn't worth splitting the Oklahoma Republican Party, still badly outnumbered by Democrats, with a spirited Senate race coming up in 1964.[16] Though some of Bellmon's advisers objected to knuckling under to a minority of a minority, Bellmon agreed to pledge irrevocably the Oklahoma delegation to Goldwater.

Oklahoma's 22 votes were the first toward the 655 for Barry Goldwater—thanks to the intransigence of his supporters there.

Georgia: While the postwar trend in the rest of the South had been toward a lily-white Republican Party that was more militantly segregationist than even the Bourbon Democrats, Georgia was the exception. Georgia Republicans were building a multiracial party, opening their doors wide to the

[16] The Oklahoma Republicans had a dream candidate for that Senate race in Bud Wilkinson, the former University of Oklahoma football coach. But many of the Oklahoma City militants, angered by Wilkinson's refusal to endorse Goldwater before the National Convention, opposed Wilkinson in the state primary.

Negro population so long rebuffed by the whites-only policy of the Democratic Party. Chief architect of this multiracial party was a courtly Atlanta businessman (and transplanted Yankee) named Robert Snodgrass, a senior member of the Republican National Committee and a moderate on most questions—including the racial question.

Bob Snodgrass, a personal friend and admirer of Nelson Rockefeller, was not about to back Goldwater for President. It would seem, then, that Georgia would be one Southern state not likely to wind up with Goldwater. But this assumption did not reckon with the new-style tactics of the Goldwater Movement. If Snodgrass would not surrender to the Movement, then the Movement would seize control of the party from him.

As early as the National Committee meeting at Denver in June, 1963, Snodgrass was telling friends that a Goldwater tide was running in Georgia and that his days as a party leader were numbered.[17] But he was powerless to stop that tide. The Goldwater militants overpowered the Snodgrass moderates in county mass meetings during February—even in Snodgrass' own stronghold of Fulton County (Atlanta). In March, the Goldwater forces captured nine out of ten Congressional district conventions in the state, committing eighteen out of twenty delegates to the National Convention.

The remaining four delegates from Georgia were to be picked by the state convention in Atlanta on May Day. It was an anticlimax. The Goldwater forces were in complete control. After hearing a keynote address from Barry Goldwater himself, the convention voted to pledge the state's four at-large delegates to him. That made it twenty-two out of twenty-four Georgia delegates pledged to Goldwater. Snodgrass was finished. So were the state's Negro Repub-

[17] The Young Republicans' national convention in San Francisco the next week added validity to Snodgrass' fears. For the first time in memory, Georgia was represented by an all-white delegation—which tended to be pro-Goldwater and anti-Snodgrass.

licans. Georgia's Republican Party had joined its sister parties in the South as a lily-white party.

Kansas: In 1964, Kansas was the most Republican state in the Union—the only state with a Republican Governor, two Republican U.S. Senators, an all-Republican delegation in Congress, and Republican control of both houses of the State Legislature. By any standard, Kansas was not a fertile ground for liberalism. But its conservatism was traditionally of the moderate rather than the militant variety. Its two senior Republicans—Senator Frank Carlson and National Committeeman Harry Darby—had been key figures in the early Draft Eisenhower movement against Taft in 1952.

By 1964, Carlson no longer dabbled in national politics, and Darby was about to end a long tenure on the National Committee. But others were carrying on the Carlson-Darby brand of Republicanism. A big majority of the state's Congressional delegation was opposed to Goldwater. Moreover, Governor John Anderson and State Chairman Richard D. Rogers were ready to fight for an "uncommitted"—that is, an anti-Goldwater—delegation to the National Convention. The militantly conservative Fourth Congressional District (Wichita) seemed sure to elect two Goldwater delegates, and the Goldwater forces might be able to round up a few more delegates. But in early April of 1964, Governor Anderson seemed sure to control at least sixteen of the twenty Kansas delegates.

Once again, the ability of the Goldwater Movement to flood precinct mass meetings and county conventions was underestimated. Actually Goldwater forces were in firm control of about half the delegates selected prior to the state convention in Topeka on April 18, when five at-large delegates were to be chosen. It was here that the Goldwater forces (directed by State Senator Tom Van Sickle, Clif White's top aide back in Washington) prepared a coup. They could not control the entire delegation. But they could deliver a rabbit punch to anti-Goldwater resistance in Kansas by keeping Governor Anderson off the delegation. The move to keep Kansas "uncommitted" would be blocked.

The choice to oppose Anderson was a masterstroke: Effie Semple, a seventy-five-year-old party worker who was stepping down as national committeewoman and wanted to conclude her political career with the trip to San Francisco (to cast her ballot there for Barry Goldwater). For sentimental as much as political reasons, the delegates in Topeka were inclined to choose Mrs. Semple over Anderson. When the vote stood at 626 to 282 in her favor (with Anderson even losing 20 out of 92 votes from his home county), the Governor stood on the floor of the convention to concede.

The twenty-member Kansas delegation then voted 11 to 9 for Goldwater partisans as the state's two new representatives on the National Committee. Those 11 votes represented Goldwater's minimum strength in a delegation in which he was not supposed to have more than four delegates. Moreover, without Anderson there to head off the Goldwater forces, the total could climb to as high as eighteen out of twenty.

Washington: The state of Washington was less of a conservative bastion than Kansas. In 1964, its Governor and two U.S. Senators were all liberal Democrats. Its last Republican Governor was a moderate of the Eisenhower type. It had voted 20 to 4 for Eisenhower against Taft at the 1952 convention.

But that was twelve long years ago. Now the Goldwater Movement was running hard in the Pacific Northwest. It was the same old story of Goldwaterites flooding party caucuses.

Consider the liberal stronghold of Seattle, containing 40 percent of the state's votes. Only the Goldwater activists bothered to show up for the party caucus. Goldwater was backed by 62 percent of the King County (Seattle) delegates, compared with 17 percent for Nixon, 10 percent for

Lodge, and 9 percent for Rockefeller. If Goldwater could swamp liberal Seattle, it naturally followed that he had no trouble at all in conservative Spokane—claiming sixteen hundred out of seventeen hundred delegates at the Spokane County caucus.

The state convention was scheduled for June 13, but it was obvious by mid-April that most or all of Washington's twenty-four delegates would be Goldwater men.

All this was repealing the rule of preconvention politics that required a candidate to appease the uncommitted rather than titillate his own committed followers. Goldwater was doing quite the opposite. Rather than appease the uncommitted, Goldwater was destroying them. And this required keeping his own committed followers in a state of high titillation. In other words, Goldwater was making no perceptible movement toward the left. He was now even less of a unity candidate than he was on January 1. He was conquering, not convincing, the Republican Party.

And he was paying the price for it: increasingly disappointing performances in primary elections. What titillated his committed followers often tended to repel the rank-and-file Republican voters.

This was not without significance. The Goldwater Movement was by no means all-conquering. It could not really penetrate deeply into Nelson Rockefeller's New York or William Scranton's Pennsylvania or George Romney's Michigan or such other havens of progressive Republicanism as Connecticut, Maryland, Massachusetts, Minnesota, and New Jersey. There was an upward limit to how many delegates Goldwater could collect by brute force—probably in the vicinity of four hundred.

To pick up the extra 255 delegates needed for nomination, Goldwater had to beat Rockefeller in that climactic California primary on June 2. Like the British, Goldwater could lose every battle (every primary-election battle, in this case) except the last. But he must win that last one. And as he continued to trip in primary after primary, even his devoted followers began to wonder whether that last, absolutely essential primary victory might elude his grasp.

XX

★ ★

The In-Between Primaries

James Burnham, one of the most highly respected intellectuals in the conservative movement, traveled cross-country early in the spring of 1964. No politician, Burnham was not looking for the Goldwater Movement's saturation of precinct conventions. Consequently, he saw scant sign of Goldwater strength and was instead troubled by what he correctly analyzed as a lack of mass support for the Senator. Writing from Sasabe, Arizona, for the *National Review* of April 21, Burnham delivered this candid and cogent analysis:

> Goldwater has not yet succeeded in establishing himself in the public mind as a *national leader*; therefore he has not, in strictly political language, yet made good a *claim* to the Presidency. He still figures, in the public mind, as a sectional leader and as an ideological leader of a tendency (the conservative leader). Here in the Southwest, and to some degree elsewhere in the South and West, everyone likes him and looks on him as a legitimate leader. Throughout the country, all conservatives like and admire him and recognize him as a legitimate leader. But he has not yet been able to project himself much beyond this geographical-ideological limit. In his campaign for the nomination he easily reaches those who are predisposed in his favor, and often rouses them to active, enthusiastic support; but he has not opened communications with the largely amorphous center that is not strongly committed one way or the

other. I have not talked to a single voter—West, North, South *or* East—who has said: "Since Barry Goldwater started campaigning, I've changed my mind and now I'm for him."

James Burnham had perceived and reported what most Goldwater supporters either could not perceive or were too loyal to report. Yet, neither the instinctively correct perceptions of Burnham nor the continued Goldwater slump in the polls were necessary to expose this problem. Any objective analysis of the primary elections between the first primary in New Hampshire on March 10 and the last primary in California on June 2 revealed Goldwater's continuing lack of mass appeal. Most shocking of all was what happened in the April 14 Illinois primary.

In many ways, Illinois was the national keystone of the Goldwater campaign. It was the only state out of what Nixon used to call the Big Six (New York, California, Pennsylvania, Ohio, Michigan, and Illinois) where Goldwater was solidly in command. He had an excellent shot at wrapping up all of the state's fifty-eight-member delegation (except for one or two Negro delegates). The wily Senator Everett McKinley Dirksen might once have flirted with Rockefeller and might now be flirting with Nixon, but he is not the kind of politician who swims upstream against a strong current. And the Goldwater current was running strong in Illinois. Goldwater had a stranglehold on precinct-level workers from Chicago in the north to Little Egypt in the south. Barring an absolute catastrophe in the Goldwater campaign, he could count on Illinois at San Francisco in 1964 just as Taft had counted on Illinois at Chicago in 1952, when Illinois was one delegation that never switched to Eisenhower, even after the General had enough votes to be nominated. Goldwater had reason to expect the same kind of Illinois loyalty.

For these reasons, the Goldwater strategists looked forward to the Illinois primary on April 14 with particularly keen anticipation. Here was the chance to prove that Barry Goldwater was a vote-getter after all. He might run badly in a vest-pocket, backwoods state like New Hampshire, but Illinois was where the electoral votes were (26 of them as compared with New Hampshire's 4). A smashing victory in the preferential primary in this big, industrialized state could well extend Goldwater's prestige beyond the devoted ranks of the Goldwater Movement.

Goldwater did seem to have a clear field ahead in Illinois. Rockefeller never even considered challenging him here in the conservative heartland. But Goldwater would have a foe on the ballot so that it could not be said that he won the Illinois primary only because he was unopposed. His opponent: Senator Margaret Chase Smith of Maine, who had yielded to requests by Illinois feminist groups to put her name on the ballot. If Mrs. Smith (best remembered nationally as a foe of Senator Joe McCarthy in the early 1950's) had run so badly in neighboring and moderate New Hampshire, how would she do in distant and conservative Illinois? Mrs. Smith was the ideal candidate for Goldwater in Illinois —respectable enough to make his victory look impressive, but not nearly strong enough to cause any concern over an upset.

Nor was there much chance of write-in votes causing another New Hampshire. In a March 29 background bulletin to political correspondents, Bob Mullen of the Draft Lodge operation summed up the Illinois situation in this fashion:

> We have had a good group in Chicago active since early January. After New Hampshire they were sought out by the news media . . . [were] half-persuaded to go for a write-in, and said as much. This boomed overnight, and when I heard about it in Portland, I called . . . to ask about it. By that time [the Illinois Lodge] group had time to sort things out and found that write-ins in Illinois are extremely difficult. The machines in Cook County [Chicago] require pressing a button,

lifting a flap, sliding out some jigger, finding a pencil, and in some places I understand even includes a requirement that the voter draw a box and mark his X in it!

The best write-in that they knew about was the one for Ike in 1952 when he got about 150,000 which represented about 12% of the vote. . . .

With the Illinois primary set for April 12 [sic], with all our energies and resources committed to Oregon, it just wasn't sensible to walk into it. So, they didn't.

Mullen's analysis omitted one important reason why a Presidential candidate never should rely heavily on an Illinois primary write-in. There is nothing in the Illinois state election code requiring county officials to tabulate write-in votes. With Goldwater men solidly in control of the vote-counting apparatus in most of the counties, it would be understandable—and perfectly within the law—if they just didn't bother adding up all those messy write-ins. Thus, there was no real write-in campaign conducted in Illinois in 1964. A few young party workers in Springfield tried to get one going for Nixon, but Nixon himself quickly squelched it.[1]

Besides his clear field in the preferential contest, Goldwater had an opportunity to demonstrate his vote-getting ability much more dramatically in the Governor's primary election on the same day.

The Governor's race is so central to an understanding of the mood of the Illinois Republican voter in April, 1964, that it deserves some explanation.[2] Going back to early January, there was a three-way race for the nomination between Secretary of State Charles Carpentier, aging leader of the Illinois Old Guard and close ally of Senator Dirksen; in-

---

[1] Considering the quiet assistance—in fact, guidance—Nixon gave to a later write-in campaign in his behalf in Nebraska, his decision in Illinois was based on the practical problems of a write-in campaign there rather than any desire to avoid a second Presidential nomination.

[2] See Chapter XIV.

dustrialist Charles M. Percy, the liberal Republican who had been edging toward the right and away from his old friendship with Nelson Rockefeller; and Cook County Republican Chairman Hayes Robertson, typical of the new breed of militant conservative and an original founder of the Draft Goldwater movement.

As 1964 began, Carpentier enjoyed an immense lead, Percy was running a poor second, and Robertson was running a still poorer third. This state of affairs was most unsettling to Charles Barr, the Standard Oil Co. (Indiana) executive who had (along with Hayes Robertson) been one of the Draft Goldwater originals and now was the real spark plug of the Illinois Goldwater forces.[3]

Barr was backing Robertson for Governor, but his real interest was in keeping the Illinois delegation safe for Goldwater. For this reason, the prospect of the wily old Carpentier leading the Illinois delegation gave Barr the cold shivers. Though he had remained blandly neutral when the national Goldwater boom was running high in the autumn of 1963, Carpentier ceased trying to conceal his hostility toward Goldwater after the assassination, chortling about the precipitous drop in Goldwater's fortunes in private conversations with fellow politicians. A close personal friend of Nixon, Carpentier was even more pronounced than Dirksen in his leaning toward the former Vice-President. Nor was this just a simple matter of one man's opinion. As nominee for Governor, Carpentier would handpick ten at-large National Convention delegates during the state convention at Springfield on May 1. As a savvy political pro who had built his own statewide machine during twelve years in the patronage-rich Secretary of State's office, he could command many of the state's other forty-eight delegates (elected directly by Congressional district in the April 14 primary). It was not

[3] See page 123.

inconceivable that Carpentier would swing most or all of the Illinois delegation from Goldwater to Nixon on the second or third ballot. And if Goldwater lost his Illinois keystone at the convention, he was finished.

As a ploy intended to force Carpentier and Percy into flat endorsements of Goldwater, the Robertson candidacy had failed. Florid, middle-aged Hayes Robertson just wasn't much of a candidate. Even by wrapping himself in Goldwater raiment, he failed to pick up much support.[4] What was needed was a younger, brighter, stronger pro-Goldwater candidate for Governor who would have a chance actually to win the nomination or, at least, to force Carpentier and Percy into endorsing Goldwater.

Such a man was more than a pipe dream. Perfectly fitting the specifications was State Treasurer William J. Scott, thought then to be the most promising young figure in Illinois Republican politics. Boyishly handsome at thirty-seven, Billy Scott was originally a Dirksen protégé but had drifted away from him to become a Goldwater stalwart. As early as October, 1963, Barr and other Goldwaterites tried to talk Scott into the Governor's race.[5] Scott refused—unless he was given a clear field, which meant that the other candidates would have to drop out. Of course, Robertson was willing to make way for Scott. It goes without saying that Carpentier and Percy were not.

There the matter stood until mid-January, when Carpentier suffered the first of two severe heart attacks—the first forcing him out of the race for Governor, the second ending his life. In a frantic forty-eight hours of political wheeling and dealing following the first heart attack, the Dirksen-led Old Guardsmen finally struck a political bargain with Percy. With

---

[4] This, of course, should have been a danger signal to the Goldwater forces in Illinois. But it was Robertson, not Goldwater, who was blamed.

[5] Though he wasn't formally a candidate at this point, Goldwater was kept informed of these developments.

Carpentier now off the scene and an open race possible, Bill
Scott agreed to enter (and Robertson naturally withdrew).
It was now a clear-cut race: Percy versus Scott, a non-
Goldwater Republican versus a Goldwater Republican.[6]

It was probably the roughest Illinois Republican primary
ever. Scott tried to link Percy with Republican hoodlum
elements in Chicago's notorious West Side Bloc. A scurrilous
pamphlet called "Mercy, Mr. Percy" labeled him as soft on
communism. Both charges were absurd calumnies. But the
major attack against him was built around the charge that
Percy might lead the Illinois delegation away from Goldwater at San Francisco. This had considerable basis in fact.
Though not to be compared with Charley Carpentier in
political power or political shrewdness, Chuck Percy was no
more reliable a Goldwater man. For his part, Scott wrapped
the Goldwater mantle about him just as tightly as Robertson
had.

At Goldwater headquarters in Washington, Clif White
(not generally given to unjustified euphoria) was telling
friends that an upset win for Scott in Illinois might be in the
wind—an upset that not only would put a hammerlock on
Illinois's 58 votes, but also would display the magically
wondrous impact of Barry Goldwater's coattails and dispel
once and for all those doubts about Goldwater's popularity
with rank-and-file Republicans that had been raised by the
New Hampshire debacle.

Why not? Why shouldn't a clean-cut young Republican
who had endorsed Barry Goldwater beat a clean-cut young
Republican who had not endorsed Barry Goldwater if they
were running in Barry Goldwater's heartland?

[6] Representative Edward Derwinski, a Chicago Congressman and chairman of the Illinois Goldwater-for-President Committee, announced that
the Goldwater forces were going to be scrupulously neutral in the Percy-
Scott race. This announcement produced a few amused chuckles from politicians who saw Barr and most of Goldwater's other top leaders in the state
working their hearts out for Scott.

Why not, indeed? The result was a shocking Percy landslide:

Percy	626,111
Scott	388,903
Other candidates	23,558

Nor had Goldwater run at all well in the Presidential
primary. His 500,000-vote total was some 125,000 votes less
than Percy's. With a great deal of justification, Goldwater
men claimed that this was a case of comparing apples with
oranges—particularly unfair in that a torrid race for Governor was bound to pull a heavier vote than a tepid Presidential primary. But the fact remains that Goldwater
collected little better than 60 percent of the Presidential vote
against 25 percent for Mrs. Smith (with the balance scattered
among write-in votes).

Campaigning in California that week, Goldwater scoffed
at the political commentators who were referring to his
Illinois "defeat" and *only* 60 percent of the vote. "I'll settle
for 60 percent any time," he told reporters during an airborne bull session between Los Angeles and San Francisco.
"Really, I expected Mrs. Smith would do better than she did.
I saw her on the Senate floor yesterday and told her I
thought she'd get close to 40 percent. Almost anybody can
get at least 33 percent of the vote. Anybody's got that many
enemies. I'll bet somebody could get 33 percent of the vote
against me in Arizona."[7]

But the full enormity of Goldwater's debacle in Illinois
did not become apparent until weeks later, when the official
vote canvass was released. Moreover, it never became apparent to most Republicans—a fact for which the Goldwater

[7] This is by no means always the case. It certainly wasn't the case in
the 1956 Illinois primary, when President Eisenhower and then Senator
William F. Knowland were both listed on the ballot. Eisenhower got 95 percent of the Presidential vote cast, Knowland got 4 percent, and other candidates picked up the remaining 1 percent. This is obviously an unfair
comparison but it serves to disprove the "anybody can get 33 percent of the
vote" thesis that was much bruited about that spring.

forces must be eternally thankful. This was the official canvass in the Presidential primary (with only Goldwater and Mrs. Smith on the ballot, the rest are write-ins):

Goldwater	512,840
Mrs. Smith	209,521
Lodge	68,122
Nixon	30,313
Rockefeller	2,048
Wallace[8]	2,203
Scranton	1,842
Romney	465
Miscellaneous	437

Considering the fact that champion vote-getter Dwight Eisenhower could manage no more than 150,000 Illinois write-ins in 1952 with a well-organized campaign, it is indeed remarkable that Lodge got at least 68,000 write-ins and Nixon at least 30,000 write-ins with no campaign. The words "at least" are used because of the probability that the county clerks did not tally nearly all the write-ins.

But the Lodge and Nixon write-in totals are not the most striking statistics of the Illinois primary as revealed by the official canvass. That distinction goes to Goldwater's own total. The widely quoted figure of 62 percent of the Presidential vote was misleading. Actually, the official canvass showed that his 512,000 votes represented *less than half*— about 49.1 percent—of the total Republican vote in the primary. In other words, more than two hundred thousand Illinois Republicans went to the polls on April 14 but were not recorded in the Presidential vote. Some of them probably cast write-in votes that were not counted. Many more probably just didn't vote for President. Opposed to Goldwater, they may have found Mrs. Smith an unacceptable alternative and had not given sufficient prior thought to the troublesome chore of writing in their own choice.

[8] This was Governor George Wallace of Alabama, the segregationist Democrat.

Still, the Illinois primary was not a complete disaster for Goldwater. Once more, the faceless horde of passive rank-and-file Republicans was throwing dirt in the Senator's face. But dedicated activist workers in the Goldwater Movement, not a faceless horde, were running for seats as National Convention delegates—unopposed in almost all cases. Here was the vital area in which the Goldwater Movement was in control. Out of forty-eight delegates elected that day, at least thirty-three (including such stalwarts as Phyllis Schlafly and Hayes Robertson) were firmly committed to Goldwater, and most of the other fifteen were leaning his way. This in a state where less than half of the Republican voters took the trouble to mark their ballots for him, despite the lack of any organized opposition.

Goldwater's other primary runs between New Hampshire and California were similarly dismal. Here is a rundown:

Massachusetts (April 28): Goldwater's showing in a write-in derby (no Presidential contenders were listed on the ballot) was expected to be poor. It was. Favorite son Henry Cabot Lodge ran far ahead with 64,000 votes. Trailing well behind were Goldwater, 8,000; Nixon, 5,000; Rockefeller, 2,000. Campaigning in California, Goldwater commented: "I expected to do the same in Massachusetts as he [Lodge] would do running against me in Arizona."

Pennsylvania (April 28): Like Massachusetts, this was strictly a matter of write-in votes, with nobody on the ballot.

Actually, State Chairman Craig Truax was spoiling for a head-on Scranton versus Goldwater clash on Scranton's home grounds. Scranton had given strict orders not to put his name on the ballot—unless some outside candidate invaded Pennsylvania to oppose him. Goldwater's Pennsylvania militants, carried away by their faith in the Senator's vote-getting prowess, wanted to put him on the ballot against Scranton. Hoping against hope that they would indeed make the challenge, Truax had collected petitions to put Scranton on the ballot. The petitions were ready in Harrisburg, like ammunition in a cocked pistol. It was Clif White in Washington who wisely prevented them from being fired. Well aware that challenging the regular party organization in a state where Goldwater had minimal appeal would be suicide, White ordered the Pennsylvania Goldwater legions to cease and desist.

Still, Truax was concerned about a Goldwater write-in vote in Pennsylvania that might challenge Scranton's control of the delegation in San Francisco. This is why Truax quietly organized Scranton's own write-in campaign, ordering one million Scranton-for-President stickers to paste on voting machines.[9]

Like many professional politicians, Truax was making two basic mistakes. First, he was mistaking the intense precinct-level activity in Goldwater's behalf for widespread voter strength. Second, he was mistaking the absence of any such precinct-level organization in Lodge's behalf for lack of strength among voters. In reality, it was Lodge, not Goldwater, who proved to be Scranton's real rival in Pennsylvania.

Scranton's write-in total of 220,000 votes was just so-so and well below the 300,000-vote target of his supporters.[10] But it was Lodge who was taking the votes from Scranton, finishing second with a remarkable 80,000 votes (25 percent of the total vote cast), despite little or no effort in his behalf. Following in order were Nixon, 37,000; Goldwater, 32,000; Rockefeller, 7,000.

However disappointing the Scranton write-in may have been, however overjoyed Truax was that Goldwaterites were limited to only three out of sixty-four National Convention delegates elected that day—a pittance, considering the fact

[9] See page 341.

[10] Truax had predicted a modest 100,000-vote write-in for Scranton, so that Truax would be certain to be "pleasantly surprised"—for public consumption at least—on April 28.

that they once had hoped to control a third of the delegation —most satisfying of all was the defeat of Goldwater leader Paul Hugus as a National Convention delegate.[11]

Texas (May 2): This was an added starter among primary elections, dreamed up by Peter O'Donnell after the New Hampshire debacle in an effort to restore Goldwater's sagging prestige.

As Texas state Republican chairman, O'Donnell ordered the Presidential preferential primary and prescribed some peculiar ground rules. Unavowed candidates *would not* be listed on the ballot. Avowed candidates for President *would* be listed, whether they wanted to be listed or not. That meant that Goldwater would be opposed by Rockefeller, whose Texas support was tiny to the point of invisibility. But Lodge and Nixon, boasting popular support in Texas as elsewhere, would not and could not be on the ballot. Considering the fact that Texas was solid Goldwater country, a substantial and badly needed Goldwater victory seemed assured. The New Hampshire defeat would be avenged and Rockefeller given the drubbing of his life.

Clever. A shade too clever, however. The decks were so transparently stacked in Goldwater's favor in this ersatz primary that anything short of 100 percent of the vote was bound to be analyzed as less than impressive.

That's exactly what happened. Goldwater totaled 100,000 votes, far ahead of the other three names on the ballot— Rockefeller, 6,000; Mrs. Smith, 5,000; Stassen, 5,000. But Lodge and Nixon spoiled it all with their write-in votes— 10,000 for Lodge, 5,000 for Nixon. O'Donnell and the other authors of the special primary grimaced in frustration when the press emphasized the Lodge write-in instead of the fact that this was the best Goldwater primary-election showing of the spring.[12]

[11] See page 276.
[12] The Goldwater Texans were particularly upset by the first paragraph of a May 3 Associated Press dispatch from Dallas: "Sen. Barry Goldwater's easy victory in the Texas Republican Presidential poll came as expected.

Indiana (May 5): It was Illinois all over again. Here in the Goldwater heartland, Goldwater faced only the token opposition of the pitiable Harold Stassen. Yet, he could win no more than two-thirds of the vote—260,000 votes to Stassen's 104,000. The Stassen vote could be interpreted only as an anti-Goldwater protest in an area of supposed strength.[13]

Nebraska (May 12): If Illinois and Indiana were Goldwater country, Nebraska was super-Goldwater country. Senator Carl T. Curtis was one of Goldwater's earliest and closest supporters, and most of the state's top Republicans followed Curtis' lead in backing Goldwater. What's more, there was not even a Margaret Chase Smith or a Harold Stassen to give Goldwater some opposition and serve as a vehicle for anti-Goldwater sentiment. Goldwater had the ballot all to himself.

But he didn't have the field all to himself. Ever since the Lodge landslide in New Hampshire, Nixon had been looking for a primary in which he could wage the same kind of write-in campaign to demonstrate his own vote-getting prowess. Nebraska was ideal. Nixon always had been strong here. Fred Seaton, Secretary of the Interior under Eisenhower and now back in Hastings, Nebraska, as a newspaper publisher, was one of Nixon's closest political advisers. Furthermore, he was ready and willing to direct a state write-in campaign. Finally, Nebraska Republicans had in the past shown themselves adept at the write-in.[14]

The whirlwind Nixon campaign showed long and careful

But Henry Cabot Lodge's surprise second-place showing with write-in votes indicated unexpected strength."

[13] Once again, the alibi here is that anybody—even Harold Stassen— could win one-third of the vote if his name were on the ballot. But in the 1960 Indiana primary, Nixon got 95 percent of the vote against an unknown candidate who was listed on the ballot.

[14] In 1960, with no Presidential candidate listed on the ballot, Nebraska gave Nixon nearly 75,000 write-ins. Even more impressive evidence was provided by the 1952 Nebraska primary, when Stassen was alone on the ballot but finished third. Write-in campaigns gave Taft 79,000 and Eisenhower 66,000 to Stassen's 53,000.

planning. Just five days before the primary, Nixon was in Omaha to deliver a long-scheduled "non-political" speech (accompanied by the usual political press conference) before a function of the National Conference of Christians and Jews. On the next morning, Seaton unleashed a blitz attack through the mails.[15] Closely modeled after the Lodge effort in New Hampshire, the letters urged a write-in vote for Nixon and explained how to execute it. It worked. The results were:

		Percent
Goldwater	67,369	49
Nixon (write-in)	42,811	35
Lodge (write-in)	22,113	16

Perhaps the most remarkable result in this Midwestern bastion of conservatism was the size of the Lodge write-in after only a haphazard campaign—proving again that the Lodge phenomenon was not regional in nature. Conveniently overlooking the Lodge vote, Seaton claimed that "Nebraskans have nominated the next Republican candidate for President with their write-in" for Nixon—a claim that was forgotten after the Nixon debacle in Oregon just three days later. Actually, Nebraska was important only in showing Goldwater's lack of popular strength even in his heartland. Alone on the ballot, he could not pull a majority of the vote in a state whose sixteen delegates were solidly committed to him.

Florida (May 26): This was Goldwater's only test of popular strength in the South, though admittedly an inconclusive one. He lost it. The Goldwater slate of insurgent delegates led by Representative William Cramer was snowed under by the unpledged slate of regular delegates led by State Chairman Tom Fairfield Brown.[16] With Brown casting

[15] Actually, the mail campaign would have started a bit earlier, but Goldwater forces threatened to try to cancel out Nixon's "non-political" speech if any organized campaign in his behalf began before his appearance in Omaha.

[16] See page 291.

moon eyes at Craig Truax and Bill Scranton, Goldwater was in danger of losing Florida's thirty-four delegates.

Oregon (May 15): Oregon was the most prestigious, the most confused, and probably the most important of the in-between primaries. Like the others, it was a dismal proceeding for Goldwater.

> I am not and do not intend becoming a candidate at the November election.

This is the cryptic pledge required by Oregon law if a Presidential contender wishes to remove himself from that state's strangest-of-all primary elections. The law requires the Oregon Secretary of State to comb newspaper clippings for news of prominant politicians mentioned for the Presidency. He then enters them on the ballot—there to stay unless they sign an affidavit containing the prescribed disavowal pledge.

Would a man signing such an affidavit actually be barred from running for President in November? Almost certainly not. The mind boggles at the thought of anybody going to court for an injunction to stop an affidavit signer from accepting his party's Presidential nomination.[17] Rather than legal, the questions posed by the Oregon pledge are essentially of a political nature. By refusing to make the pledge, does a candidate then compromise his position as a noncandidate? By taking the pledge, does he end whatever chance he might have of getting the nomination?

Of the Republican possibilities arbitrarily put on the 1964 ballot by the Oregon Secretary of State, only *Romney* removed himself by taking the pledge—while still insisting that he was open to a sincere draft at San Francisco.

Scranton chose to approach the pledge problem as a legal problem and asked for advice from State Attorney General

---

[17] For instance, Adlai Stevenson, though hoping to be drafted by the Democratic National Convention in 1960, did not hesitate to sign the disavowal pledge putting himself out of the Oregon primary.

Walter Alessandroni, his principal legal (as well as political) adviser. Alessandroni (perhaps with tongue firmly placed in cheek) solemnly advised the Governor that signing the Oregon affidavit would not be consistent with his position of being open to a fair and honest draft. After much soul-searching, Scranton accepted his attorney general's advice, whereupon Alessandroni and the rest of the Scranton staff sighed in relief. They felt that Scranton would frighten away every bit of potential support if he took the Oregon pledge.

But Scranton flatly forbade his staff to promote any kind of campaign in Oregon whatever. Disobeying him, Craig Truax purchased space in the official Oregon voter's guide (which is sent to all the state's registered voters) to tell Oregon of the virtues of Bill Scranton. When he found out about it, Scranton not only forced Truax to cancel the order for space, but also gave his state party chairman a thorough scolding.[18] There was no Scranton campaign in Oregon.

Originally, *Nixon* planned to sign the Oregon affidavit, believing that the pledge would not conflict with his willingness to accept a draft and assuming that everyone was aware of his availability anyhow. That was before March 10. The Lodge write-in in New Hampshire showed Nixon that he needed to reestablish his own vote-getting muscle, and the best two places for it seemed to be Nebraska and Oregon. Oregon had been Nixon country. He had built a strong personal organization there in the process of carrying the state against John F. Kennedy in 1960.

Nixon should have known that four years can make all the

---

[18] Lodge's name did not appear in the Oregon voter's guide either. The first that the young Draft Lodge staff had heard about the existence of any such guide were the newspaper reports that Scranton was pulling his name out of it. By then, it was too late for Lodge to purchase space. This oversight, plus the much more serious error of letting the filing deadline for the crucial California primary pass without trying to enter Lodge's name, lends credence to the suspicion that Lodge's write-in landslide in New Hampshire was more the product of a genuine ground swell than of terribly efficient staff work.

difference in politics. He soon found out the sad story from Leonard Nadasdy, a young Minneapolis public-relations man and Nixon protégé.[19] Dispatched by Nixon on a discreet mission to Oregon, Nadasdy returned with a grim report: that old Nixon gang had broken up. Some were working for Rockefeller, some for Goldwater. His advice: don't try a full-fledged campaign in Oregon.

Nixon was not to be put off, however. He quietly reassembled the old Nixon organization for a last hurrah in Oregon.

F. Clifford Folger, the Washington, D.C., financier and longtime Nixon fund raiser, was asked to raise a $50,000 bundle to finance the Oregon campaign. Even Len Hall agreed to lend a hand. While urging Nixon not to try for the White House in 1964 and insisting that he would not manage any such campaign on a national basis, Hall did consent to help in Oregon—and Oregon only. Robert Finch, Nixon's chief aide in the 1960 campaign and now a Los Angeles lawyer, and Hall tried to line up workers and supporters for Nixon. It wasn't like old times. Folger was facing amazing resistance from well-heeled businessmen who used to cough up sizable contributions for Nixon at the drop of a checkbook. Hall and Finch were finding that old Nixonites now were ignoring the call to battle. These were ominous beginnings. The fact is that the Nixon campaign never did get off the ground in Oregon—a massive blow to his national hopes.

Lodge's problem with the Oregon pledge was resolved by an elaborate charade. On active duty with the Foreign Service, he could scarcely *not* sign an affidavit. On February 27, Howell Appling, the Oregon Secretary of State, cabled to Lodge in Saigon the form of the pledge he must sign to get off the ballot. At the same time, Appling airmailed him an

---

[19] Backed by Nixon, Nadasdy had defeated a Goldwater supporter to become national chairman of the Young Republicans at their biennial convention at Minneapolis in 1961. He presided over the famed YR convention of 1963, when conservative forces gained revenge for 1961. See page 198.

unsigned affidavit making the disavowal of candidacy. The
deadline for disavowal was March 9.

From Lodge, there was silence until March 11—the day
after his stunning triumph in New Hampshire. Appling then
received this cablegram from Lodge:

> Have just now seen your letter. In reply wish to state I am
> not a candidate and I am precluded by foreign service from
> engaging in any political activity.

Appling chuckled. There was no mention of his cablegram
of February 27. Appling simply couldn't believe that it had
been misplaced in the embassy at Saigon. At any rate, the
unsigned affidavit was not returned. Nor did Lodge's cablegram use the explicit language of disavowal required by
Oregon law. Appling assumed that Lodge wanted his name
to stay on the ballot. It did.

The Lodge Oregon campaign was a carbon copy of the
Lodge New Hampshire campaign—except that the troublesome write-in was not a factor here. The young Massachusetts duo of Paul Grindle and David Goldberg were in charge
again. The emphasis was on mass mailings. The candidate
was silent and absent.

Of course, there never had been any question that *Rockefeller* would travel the Oregon trail—and travel it long and
hard, with lots of speeches and lots of handshaking. With no
New Hampshire Yankees gazing over his shoulder counting
the pennies, Rockefeller could run a typically lavish Rockefeller campaign—saturation television, big mass mailings, a
large professional staff. Mort Frayne, former Washington
state party chairman and Rockefeller's Pacific Coast coordinator, had lined up a topflight state organization heavily
peppered with former Nixonites. But Rockefeller was not
about to rely on strictly local talent in this one. A young New
Yorker named Robert Price, who had managed brilliant Congressional campaigns for Representative John V. Lindsay in

Manhattan's famed "silk stocking" district, was transported to Oregon to manage the campaign. Other Eastern talent (including entertainer Dave Garroway to narrate one television show) was shipped cross-country when needed.

Completing the field was *Goldwater*—who almost from the beginning wished that he wasn't on the Oregon ballot.

However, it did seem rosy—deceptively rosy—for a while. Governor Mark Hatfield, a liberal Republican and close friend of Rockefeller who was staying neutral in the Oregon primary, told friends through the autumn of 1963 and right past the assassination in 1964 that Goldwater was well ahead. In truth, he probably never was—at least, he wasn't after the assassination. Hatfield, like so many other Republican politicians, was blinded by the fervor of the Goldwater Movement, which had taken over the Multonomah County (Portland) Republican organization from pro-Hatfield liberals, under the Governor's amazed and disapproving eyes. Elsewhere in the state, the Goldwaterites were moving in.[20]

But Goldwater leaders were having trouble in controlling this energy and in routing it into useful avenues. While Rockefeller's organization was quickly and effectively constructed, the Goldwater troops remained in disorder. Dick Kleindienst came to Oregon to take personal command, but he couldn't straighten out the mess. Sig Unander, a highly respected Oregon Republican who was the party's nominee for U.S. Senator in 1962, was for Goldwater and had promised to lead his primary campaign. But wires were crossed somewhere, and Unander never played much of a role in the Oregon race. Instead, the state chairmanship for the Gold-

[20] The strength of the Movement in Oregon did give Goldwater a substantial chunk of the state's National Convention delegates, who were elected on May 15 separate from the Presidential preferential primary—another case of the Goldwater Movement's winning delegates but not the popular vote. In Oregon, however, the delegates are bound by law to vote for the winner of the preferential contest on the first ballot and on all ballots thereafter so long as the preferential primary winner has 35 percent of the total vote of the convention.

water campaign went to Dr. Edwin Durno, a dedicated conservative, but no great shakes at practical politics. Nor had Durno won many friends in 1962 when he gave up a sure seat in Congress (which was then captured by a Democrat) to run against (and lose to) Unander in the primary for the Senate seat.

At length, a troubleshooter was summoned: Arizonan Stephen Shadegg—prolific writer, tireless political organizer, militant conservative, imaginative tactician, and colorful political personality. Once, Shadegg had been in the innermost circle of the Arizona Mafia as national committeeman from Arizona, one of Goldwater's earliest speech writers and ghost writers, and one of his closest political advisers. It was generally assumed that if Goldwater ever ran for President, Shadegg would be his campaign manager. But in 1961, relations between Shadegg and Goldwater worsened when Shadegg publicized himself as the Senator's ghost writer. In 1962, their relations all but snapped when Shadegg defied Goldwater's wishes by running for Arizona's other Senate seat (and, for his pains, was defeated in the Republican primary). By the time the Goldwater Presidential campaign was running in full gear, Shadegg was nowhere to be seen.

But now (as the newly appointed Western states director for Goldwater) he was given a chance to square himself with the boss by performing the impossible in Oregon. The one Arizona politician respected nationally by the professionals, jut-jawed, crafty Steve Shadegg might just be the man to bring order out of chaos.

It was awfully late, though. Besides, Goldwater's problems in Oregon were not strictly a matter of a disorderly organization. Although Shadegg wouldn't have admitted it, Goldwater's major problem was really lack of political appeal among the passive rank and file. He just couldn't draw votes.

The early-April polls showed it. They also showed that Lodge's appeal was not limited to New England. Polls conducted by Louis Harris for the *Washington Post* and the research organization of Clark, Bardsley & Haslacher for the *Portland Oregonian* produced almost identical results (the figures are percentages):

	Harris	*Oregonian*
Lodge	46	40
Nixon	17	17
Goldwater	14	14
Rockefeller	13	18
Scranton	4	3
Mrs. Smith	1	1
Undecided	5	7

Lodge seemed set for his second straight absentee landslide victory, with a meaningless three-way fight for second place.

Nevertheless, Shadegg had hopes of making it close. Before election day, some six weeks remained during which Barry Goldwater would be traveling from one end of the state to the other. The beginning of the big push was set for Sunday, April 5. Goldwater was to arrive in Portland that day for a staff conference at the Hilton, to be followed by three intensive days of campaigning. But the visit started on a sour note, as described by Mervin Shoemaker in the *Portland Oregonian:*

> The 55-year-old Arizonan, looking tanned and fit, appeared more surprised than pleased at his reception by some 200 shouting, banner-carrying supporters who met him just inside the door to the airport. He did not stop and talk to them. He smiled, and paused briefly to shake hands here and there, but strode almost directly to his car through a small passageway opened in the crowd by airport security police.[21]
>
> It occasioned some grumbling in the crowd. The senator's

[21] Goldwater often displayed pique over unscheduled airport receptions, apparently regarding them as an invasion of privacy. Arriving in Atlanta to address the Georgia State Republican Convention on May 1, for instance, he was so angered by the unexpected crowd there that he refused to leave the plane until Denison Kitchel remonstrated with him.

plane had been delayed by mechanical trouble from its scheduled 11:21 A.M. arrival time, and many of the welcomers had
waited more than two hours. . . .

Goldwater went into seclusion in his hotel suite when he
arrived at the Hilton, and broke the news silence only with a
statement in tribute to Gen. Douglas MacArthur, who died
Sunday.

What went on behind closed doors in that hotel suite was
the announcement of one of the most daring and unusual
moves ever made by a Presidential contender. When Shadegg
and Goldwater's Oregon leaders were assembled, Goldwater
showed them his startling new plans. For openers, he was
cutting the proposed three-day swing through Oregon to a
day and a half, returning to Washington on Tuesday noon
instead of Wednesday night. That was by no means all. He
next informed them that this would conclude his campaigning there. *He would not return to Oregon for the balance
of the primary campaign.*

Shadegg and the Oregon leaders were flabbergasted. They
tried desperately to change Goldwater's mind, but the Senator was determined. Denison Kitchel had advised after New
Hampshire that Goldwater's schedule be trimmed down to
fit his style and stamina. What followed from that basic recommendation was a decision by Goldwater and Kitchel to
reduce radically the California schedule and eliminate completely the Oregon schedule.[22] It was one campaign decision
that had the full backing of all members of the Goldwater
high command—Dean Burch, Dick Kleindienst, and Clif
White.

It did make sense. The prospect of overtaking Lodge in
Oregon seemed remote even if Goldwater were to campaign
there every day for the next six weeks. Because he was definitely not going to campaign to the point of fatigue as he had

[22] This and other aspects of the California primary are discussed in the
next chapter.

in New Hampshire, Goldwater had only so many campaign hours a week. Because California was absolutely essential to getting the nomination, why divide his precious time between campaigning for the California primary and an Oregon election that he couldn't possibly win anyway? Why not forget Oregon and concentrate on California?

There were other factors. So long as he was going to lose in Oregon, he would minimize the impact of the loss by writing it off in advance rather than fighting it out to the last minute. And, as Goldwater sometimes told friends half-seriously, those voters in Oregon who seem to like absentee-candidate Lodge so well might also come to like absentee-candidate Goldwater.

But the withdrawal from Oregon did transform the probability of his loss there to a certainty. Of course, there was no actual announcement of any pullout from Oregon. The excuse for the canceled appearances was the need for Goldwater to attend Senate debate on the civil rights bill. The cancellation of his April 8 schedule was followed on April 21 by the announcement in Portland by Kleindienst that Goldwater's Oregon schedule of April 24–25 was canceled because "the Senator will not duck his duties as an elected representative of the people even though this may mean he has to curtail campaign appearances." But all pretense about Goldwater ever coming back to Oregon was ended by a United Press International dispatch of April 29 relating the comments of an obviously ruffled Dr. Durno:

> Asked if cancellations of scheduled Oregon appearances by Goldwater had hurt his cause, Durno said "to some degree."
> "I don't know if Goldwater will make any appearances in Oregon before the primary. I would hate to announce he was coming back and then have him cancel again," Durno said.

The withdrawal of Goldwater had the desired effect of generally downgrading the importance of the Oregon primary. It also had one undesired effect. This was no longer a Western carbon copy of New Hampshire with Rockefeller and Goldwater tearing at each other's innards while the serenely distant Lodge grabbed all the votes. Now the Oregon field was left to Rockefeller, describing himself as the *only* candidate who cared enough to come across the country to ask for Oregon's vote. "He Cared Enough to Come" became Rockefeller's new motto. In a postprimary letter published in the June 2 edition of the *National Review,* Steve Shadegg correctly analyzed what happened during the first two weeks of May:

> With Lodge in Saigon, Goldwater in Washington, Nixon diffident and aloof, Rockefeller had a political vacuum to huff and puff in. Rockefeller constantly repeated charges that Goldwater would eliminate social security, order the Marines into Cuba, and abandon missiles as part of our weapons system. Goldwater's enemies also said that he had ducked the Oregon primary because of the gloomy predictions of the pollsters. Voters, hearing the story, translated it to mean "he doesn't want my vote." Rockefeller hammered on the theme, "I'm the man who cares enough to come to Oregon to ask for your vote—the other candidates don't care."

Shadegg could have mentioned one other key point. Almost as small (in population) as New Hampshire and considerably more isolated from the mainstream of national events, Oregon was just about as proud of its Presidential primary as New Hampshire was of its contest. Rockefeller cared to come. In contrast, Ed Durno on April 29 declared that the Oregon primary "is not vital" to Goldwater's winning the nomination. It was a gaffe comparable to Goldwater's own statement three months earlier that the New Hampshire primary was meaningless.[23]

The pollsters were slow in perceiving the change, though Harris charted a Rockefeller upswing in the *Washington*

[23] See page 313.

Post. This was the Harris poll in Oregon (the figures are percentages):

	May 12	*May 3*	*April 12*
Lodge	35	40	46
Rockefeller	24	19	13
Nixon	21	22	17
Goldwater	16	14	14
Mrs. Smith	2	2	1
Scranton	2	3	4

Harris had caught a whiff of the Rockefeller trend, but insisted that Lodge seemed a sure winner. Samuel Lubell, pollster for the Scripps-Howard newspapers, was not so sure about the winner. Spotting the fact "that a dramatic shift is underway," Lubell wrote on May 12 that the heavy Rockefeller vote "is likely to produce something of a surprise and perhaps even an upset."

Lubell was probably the only unsurprised man in politics three nights later. The computers caught the big Rockefeller win within a half hour after the vote counting began, just as they had perceived the Lodge win in New Hampshire. The results:

		Percent
Rockefeller	85,000	33
Lodge	71,000	27
Goldwater	45,000	18
Nixon	43,000	17
Mrs. Smith	7,000	3
Scranton	4,000	2

The outcome had an impact on the Presidential possibilities of only *Lodge.* He alone of all the candidates on the Oregon ballot had no organization to speak of, no movement of zealous workers behind him, no money worth mentioning, no support from the old pros of either the Midwest or the Eastern Establishment. All he had was the phenomenal support from the faceless Republican masses, who perceived him dimly as the proper heir to that other vague popular hero, Dwight D. Eisenhower. Lodge's only chance for the nomination, miniscule though it was, depended upon two things: (1) victory in both New Hampshire and Oregon and (2) first place in the national polls. The two went hand in hand. Once he lost a primary election, that not entirely rational support from the faceless masses would begin to drift away.

Actually, the Gallup Poll showed that Lodge was slipping a bit even before Oregon. His defeat turned the slip into a plunge. Gallup Poll percentages showed:

	April	May (pre-Oregon)	May (post-Oregon)
Lodge	42	36	28
Nixon	26	27	29
Goldwater	14	15	16
Rockefeller	6	7	17
Scranton	4	5	4
Romney	4	4	2

But Dr. Gallup was not needed to tell the Lodge people that the jig was up.

Assuming that Lodge would finish first in Oregon (but apprehensive that his winning total might fall well below the hoped-for 40 percent of the vote), the two old Lodge aides who were directing the Draft Lodge campaign—Max Rabb and Bob Mullen—were set to fly from Washington to Los Angeles on May 16. At the Ambassador Hotel there, they would huddle with New Hampshire–Oregon campaign managers Paul Grindle and Dave Goldberg to plan their next step: help for Rockefeller in his California showdown against Goldwater—a two-man race with no write-ins permitted. Their logic was correct. Goldwater would have to be stopped in California if Lodge were to have any chance at the nomination.

But the Lodge captains met in Los Angeles as the vanquished, not as beneficent victors. They agreed that the Lodge campaign had ended. They would stay on in California to help beat Goldwater in the interests of liberal Republicanism, but not in any hopes of winning the nomination for Henry Cabot Lodge. From back in Boston, George Lodge sent a telegram to Rockefeller: "I wish you the very best of luck in California."

The Oregon primary had finished Lodge. For the others, however, its only real impact was to be found in how it affected the California showdown on June 2.

This was particularly true of *Rockefeller*. Euphoric over a victory at last after so many months of defeat, Rockefeller's aides were dreaming long dreams now. They pointed to the Oregon results as proof that the marriage issue had been eradicated. Why not, then, the nomination itself, if he could only win in California? This was sheer nonsense, of course. Rockefeller had no chance whatever to be nominated. But his victory in Oregon did rehabilitate Rockefeller as a serious candidate in the eyes of Californians. And, as if by magic, Rockefeller pushed ahead of Goldwater in the California polls for the first time.

Similarly, the poor Oregon showing by *Goldwater* was of significance only in relation to California. Actually, his showing in Oregon was not a great deal worse than his performance in the other in-between primaries, and it was perhaps a shade better than had been expected. What hurt was the fact that he had been beaten—and beaten quite badly—by Rockefeller. It was no great injury to get trounced by the phantom Lodge candidacy, but it was quite another to be routed by the flesh-and-blood foe whom he would face again in California.[24]

Nixon's dismal showing in Oregon, badly disappointing

[24] Certain Goldwater supporters believed, however, that Rockefeller's win in Oregon was a godsend. For what it's worth, their logic went like this: if Lodge had won in Oregon, a Goldwater victory in California would have proved only that he could beat Rockefeller, which was beating next to nothing. By winning in Oregon, according to this argument, Rockefeller greatly enlarged the importance of the California primary.

his managers there, put him in a far less advantageous spot for the wide-open convention in San Francisco that would result from a Rockefeller win in California over Goldwater. The party leaders who would dominate a wide-open convention of maneuver duly noted that Nixon had carried not a single county in Oregon, despite a professional campaign in his behalf.

It was not Nixon but *Scranton* who was best placed strategically for a wide-open convention. Much to the humiliation of his aides in Harrisburg, Scranton had tallied less than 2 percent of the vote in the Oregon primary and barely half as much as Margaret Chase Smith. But in the curious code of professional politicians, this was less damaging than Nixon's fourth-place finish, because Nixon had waged an absentee campaign and Scranton hadn't. Unwittingly, perhaps, Scranton's instinct to remain a noncandidate had paid off. Assuming that Rockefeller won in California, Scranton was favored to be nominated.

Yet, Scranton was entirely the creature of California. If Rockefeller won there, the odds were that Scranton would be nominated without half trying. If Rockefeller lost there, Scranton's aides had no alternative battle plan. Too much time had been wasted. Nothing had been done since those early January days of the Scranton boomlet when powerful party figures had been literally begging to put together a Scranton-for-President campaign. Now, as the climax in San Francisco neared, Scranton's Presidential hopes hinged entirely on the California primary—a contest that he had absolutely no power to affect.

XXI

★ ★

California

The greatest Presidential primary of 1964 was to be fought in an arena of heroic proportions. This was not vest-pocket New Hampshire, where the campaigners collided with each other if they didn't watch their step. This was California, the nation's largest state in population and third biggest in size (surpassed only by Alaska and Texas), a nation more than a state, with the varied topography and peoples befitting a nation. It posed a formidable problem for the politicians.

The strain on the bankroll and the energy needed in getting around the state are enough to make a politician wince. It is as if a wide band running from Boston, Massachusetts, to Charleston, South Carolina, were superimposed on the West Coast and called one state—running from the sparsely settled cow counties in the north, to naturally air-conditioned and cosmopolitan San Francisco, to the irrigated cotton country, to that stupendous bit of megalopolis called Los Angeles (complete with freeways and suburban housing tracts), to the exurban sprawl of Orange County, to the luxurious Southern California desert dotted with golf courses and swimming pools, to the climatic paradise of San Diego, and finally to the Mexican border.

But what concerned the politician was the people—the more than two million of them expected to vote in the Cali-

fornia primary. To begin with, the Californian thinks of his
state as two states, "The North" and "The South." And beyond that are ethnic subdivisions: the few old Californians,
the wave of Midwesterners who came steadily for a generation after World War I, the later and still continuing wave of
Arkies and Okies. And there are the ethnic groups: a prosperous Jewish minority, a rising Mexican-American minority,
the angry Negro minority.

Then, mix them well. The mobility of the Californian is
breathtaking. In sprawling Los Angeles County (where reside 40 percent of the state's population), one out of every
four persons moves each year. With such a wanderlust afflicting the populace, it is impossible to build the permanent
precinct organization as conceived by East Coast politicians.

Finally, add to this big, dynamic, heterogeneous state the
nation's most volatile Republican politics in the 1960's. This
was the setting for the final showdown between Nelson
Rockefeller and Barry Goldwater.

California politics had been dominated for forty years by
two liberal Republicans, Hiram Johnson and Earl Warren,
and their lieutenants. In a state with Democrats nominally
in a three to two numerical advantage, Johnson and Warren
successfully tried to blur partisan distinctions—even to the
point of the notorious cross-filing device by which a well-
known personality could seek the nomination in both parties
without revealing his true party preference on the ballot.
Republican hegemony over the state scarcely seemed weakened when Governor Earl Warren left the state in 1953 to
become Chief Justice of the United States. In fact, however,
it was the beginning of the end.

The end came in 1958, when the Republican Party split
into right and left factions, led by two former Warren lieutenants, William F. Knowland and Goodwin Knight, respectively. Knowland, giving up his seat as Republican Floor
Leader in the U.S. Senate, insisted on running for the Gov-

ernor's chair held by Knight—and on an antiunion platform that drove organized labor into the open arms of the Democrats. Knight, unsuccessfully trying to stand clear of the Knowland wreckage, ran for the Senate. Both were inundated by a Democratic landslide that took over both houses of the State Legislature in Sacramento. In 1961, this Democrat-controlled Legislature gerrymandered the state's Congressional districts to give the Democrats top-heavy control of California representation in Washington for the foreseeable future. What had once been the Republican bastion of the West was now just another Democrat-controlled state.

Out of the ashes of the 1958 defeat came not a newly united Republican Party, but a party so schizophrenic as to really be two separate parties. In his 1962 race for Governor, Richard Nixon was plagued by this ideological factionalism in his own party.[1] A new breed of militant conservative, led by former University of Southern California football star Joe Shell, had emerged and multiplied since 1958—giving Shell 33 percent of the vote against Nixon in the Governor's primary of 1962 and then sitting on their hands in the general election to ensure the reelection of Democratic Governor Pat Brown. Opposing the new-breed conservatives were the remnants of the Warren tradition, led by Senator Thomas Kuchel, the last of Warren's political protégés. In 1962, Kuchel won reelection to the Senate by landslide proportions against an inept Democratic foe, but played the role of the lone wolf, keeping Nixon at arm's length.

Nixon had tried to bridge the widening gap between the party's two factions and had fallen into the chasm. Other Nixon Republicans also tried to stave off the Armageddon. The state's Republican Congressmen tried to put together a unity delegation to the National Convention, thereby ruling out a Presidential primary.[2] Joseph Martin, Jr., a suave and

[1] See Chapter VII.
[2] When Rockefeller was leading Goldwater prior to the remarriage, a compromise California delegation that would give Goldwater approximately

urbane San Francisco lawyer who had been named to the Republican National Committee in 1960 as Nixon's personal choice, pleaded with both the Rockefeller and the Goldwater camps to stay out of the California Presidential primary and thereby save the state party from a bloodbath.

But there was to be no such peace. The California situation was a bigger-than-life version of the Republican turmoil nationally, with conservative and moderate factions at each other's throats for party control primarily and the Presidential nomination only incidentally.

William F. Knowland, isolated from the political wars while running the family newspaper in Oakland since his 1958 debacle, was returning to active political combat and making it clear he wanted no part of a compromise delegation. A front-page editorial in Knowland's *Oakland Tribune* ended any chance for that late in 1963. But plodding, respectable Bill Knowland was really only the front man for a militant grass roots movement unequaled anywhere else in the country. In both zeal and numbers, the Goldwater Movement reached its full flowering in the big and balmy Southern California counties of Los Angeles, Orange, and San Diego.

From the beginning, a few California moderates perceived two salient facts: (1) the Goldwater movement would parlay the Goldwater candidacy into conservative control of the California Republican Party unless it were opposed in the June 2 primary; (2) with a March 8 deadline for filing the candidate's petitions, Nelson Rockefeller was the only possible candidate for the moderates to unite behind. These moderates were more interested in heading off Joe Shell and his conservative militants in California than in actually winning the nomination for Rockefeller, but Rockefeller was their only available candidate. So, as early as December,

one-third of the eighty-six delegates seemed agreeable enough to Draft Goldwater forces. They changed their tune when Goldwater moved far in front after the Rockefeller remarriage.

1963, State Assemblyman Houston Flournoy, a rising young Southern California moderate who wanted desperately to return the Republican Party to a majority status in California by traveling the same ground covered by Earl Warren, made a secret trip to New York to confer with Rockefeller. Impressing Rockefeller with the need for immediate campaign planning in California, Flournoy told him that most California moderates—then fence-sitting—would be on his side if he entered soon.

They were. With the soul of the California party at stake, this was no time for neutralism. Joe Martin, the Nixon man who had called for both sides to keep out of California and let the party bind up its wounds, now jumped off the fence. Early in March, Martin resigned from the National Committee and joined the Rockefeller campaign with this statement:

> The compelling reason for my decision is a desire to do my part to prevent the Republican Party from becoming a branch of the John Birch Society. . . .
>
> While it cannot be denied that Sen. Goldwater is the favorite candidate of many fine Republicans, he is also the only candidate who is vigorously supported by the Birchers and the rightist lunatic fringe.
>
> Inevitably his victory will also be their victory—their mandate to take over the party structure in its entirety.

Martin was overplaying the threat-from-the-right theme. But this statement by a politician heretofore thought of as a moderate compromiser reflects the state of political passions among California Republicans as the exhausting primary campaign began.

Martin was by no means the only big-name California Republican to enlist in the Rockefeller campaign. With Tommy Kuchel serving as his state campaign chairman, Rockefeller enlisted a who's who of the California Republican Establishment: John Krehbiel, the immediate past state chairman;

State Senator Jack McCarthy, minority leader of the State Senate; Edward Shattuck, a former member of the Republican National Committee; George Christopher, former Mayor of San Francisco and nominee for Lieutenant Governor in 1962; movie mogul Jack Warner; industrialist Leonard Firestone; Justin Dart, head of Rexall Drugs.

The announcement in March of this dazzling galaxy, immensely brighter than the collection of conservatives backing Goldwater, made it seem to politicians outside California that Goldwater was headed for still another primary defeat in California. In fact, however, Rockefeller faced deep troubles in California from the beginning.

One was an absolute lack of any grass roots supporters willing to lick a postage stamp or ring a doorbell. Though Establishmentarians like Warner and Dart and Firestone might be willing to give of their time and bank account to ward off the rightward drift, the same sense of alarm did not seep down to the precincts. There was no volunteer army ready to spring to Rockefeller's support.

As an alternative, Rockefeller had to build his own army. As a starter, he hired Spencer-Roberts & Associates of Los Angeles, a political-management firm that was started in 1961 by two young Republican Party campaign workers and had chalked up a remarkable series of successes (including Kuchel's landslide win for the Senate in 1962). Cocky, congenial little Stu Spencer, thirty-nine, and brooding, heavyset Bill Roberts, thirty-seven, were recommended by Kuchel to Rockefeller as the hottest political-management team in California. After a trip to New York, Spencer and Roberts (who in leaner years had been reduced to answering their own phones) signed on the dotted line for a fat fee—and, what was more important, a blank check to build a campaign organization from the ground up.[3]

[3] Clif White was interested in signing Spencer-Roberts for the Goldwater campaign. But Goldwater had not yet announced as a candidate, and the Draft Goldwater organization could not positively make a cash offer to

In cooperation with George Hinman (who virtually abandoned his offices in New York City and Binghamton, New York to become a transplanted Californian), Spencer and Roberts started to work. The suave and debonair Bill Roberts, working with Hinman and Kuchel aide Steve Horn, courted the members of the California Establishment to bring them into Rockefeller's corner. Simultaneously, blunt and earthy Stu Spencer talked rank-and-file Negroes and Mexicans out of their traditional Democratic Party registration and into registering with the Republicans so that they could vote for Rockefeller on June 2.

They also built a model professional organization—professional because volunteer Rockefeller workers were hard to come by. More than twenty paid fieldmen set up Rockefeller offices across the state. Special public-relations firms were hired to deal with Negroes, Mexicans, farmers. It was originally expected that the campaign would cost Rockefeller $2 million. It eventually ran to $3.5 million.

But the glossy organization built for Rockefeller wasn't enough. For all its immensity and peculiar characteristics, California was giving the same results to pollsters that they found elsewhere in the country. In early April, the highly respected poll conducted for newspapers by Marvin Field showed:

	Percent
Lodge	31
Goldwater	25
Nixon	21
Rockefeller	12
Scranton	3
Romney	3
Mrs. Smith	1

A dismal showing for Rockefeller, certainly. But this could not be another New Hampshire. No write-ins are permitted

Spencer-Roberts. Thus, nothing was ever said to Spencer and Roberts by White or anybody else in the Goldwater camp.

on the California ballot, and only three candidates were entered: Rockefeller, Goldwater, and the indefatigable Harold Stassen. Thus, if Rockefeller could cut into the moderate Republican vote, victory was his. But the Field poll showed that Goldwater was picking up almost as much of the Lodge and Nixon vote as Rockefeller, with some of it going to Stassen as a straight protest vote. The Field poll found:

	Percent
Goldwater	43
Rockefeller	31
Stassen	10
Undecided	16

Rockefeller's problem was clear. He must convince Lodge and Nixon supporters that he was the best proxy candidate for their favorites.

Not long after the New Hampshire primary, a close aide told Rockefeller: "Governor, the only way you can win in California is to conceive of yourself in your own mind as a proxy candidate, a stand-in candidate for moderate Republicanism, a substitute for Nixon, Lodge, Scranton, and all the rest." Rockefeller, a proud man, would have none of it. Still enraged at what he considered the Lodge double cross in New Hampshire, he couldn't resist attacking Lodge when he should have been wooing Lodge's California supporters —much to the mortification of Bill Roberts and Stu Spencer in Los Angeles.

That wasn't the only worry for Spencer and Roberts. Rockefeller's candidacy was growing flatter each day. A rebellion of the Republican-dominated New York State Legislature (far worse than the 1963 version) killed his proposed reform of the liquor laws and forced him back to Albany in late April to convene a special session to try again, thereby canceling out a heavy California speaking schedule. Moreover, his California managers were worried what impact a disastrous showing in Oregon on May 15—say a third or fourth finish, as now seemed quite possible—would have on his meager prestige in California. Finally, Rockefeller's own campaigning was flat, cliché-ridden, repetitious. Only the enormous crowds at Rockefeller's receptions, drummed up by Stu Spencer's special invitations, gave any cause at all for cheer in the Rockefeller camp.

Goldwater had problems of his own in California, but problems directly opposite to Rockefeller's.

He had no lack of grass roots support, but instead a plethora of militant, often fanatic workers competing with one another. While Rockefeller's paid petition circulators took a solid month, beginning March 4, to collect the necessary 13,702 signatures and filed the petitions just under the April 3 deadline, Goldwater volunteers (in what was called "Operation Q") picked up more than 50,000 signatures on the first day.[4]

There was no end to Goldwater groups at the grass roots. The California Republican Assembly, founded by Earl Warren a generation earlier as a grass roots sounding board of liberal Republican sentiment, now was dominated by Goldwater men nearly everywhere in the state. The newer and far more militant United Republicans of California was devoted entirely to the cause of making Goldwater the next President. The California Young Republicans was dominated by conservative zealots who were willing to work around the clock for Goldwater. And behind them all was the well-financed, well-disciplined John Birch Society, willing to stay out of the limelight, but infiltrating the other party organizations in Goldwater's behalf.

And there was plenty of money in California to finance

---

[4] Stu Spencer insisted that the close shave in meeting the April 3 deadline was caused not so much by lack of Rockefeller popularity at the grass roots as by the fact that the professional petition circulators had other clients to serve and did not really start the big Rockefeller push until well after the March 4 opening date.

Goldwater. Some of the ultraconservative businessmen—
many of them oil producers—who had originally backed
Dick Nixon but later became disenchanted with him over
what they considered his leftward drift were enthusiastically
for Goldwater. Among them was oil magnate Henry Salvatori,
who a few years earlier had seemed to be drawing away from
support of Republican politics and instead was backing right-
wing anti-Communist causes. Now he was doling out gen-
erously to Goldwater and had a seat on his proposed National
Convention delegation to show for it.

On the top level, there were big names, though something
less than the all-star team rounded up by Rockefeller. A
hero to the state's conservative Republicans despite his
humiliating loss for the Governorship in 1958, Knowland
was state chairman—and not content to be just a figurehead.
The operating campaign manager in Los Angeles was Bern-
ard Brennan, a savvy veteran who had managed Nixon's
successful California campaign in the 1960 Presidential election.

But somehow the Goldwater operation seemed all confusion and wasted effort. Nobody could get the myriad of
volunteer groups to work in lockstep. Against the policy of the
state leaders, right-wing radicals were taking control of the
campaign in certain local areas. Brennan in the south and
Knowland in the north were often at swordpoint. Baus
& Ross, a Los Angeles political public-relations firm, was
not satisfying the Goldwater chieftains back in Washington.
Dick Kleindienst, popping into California periodically as
Goldwater's emissary, couldn't cope with the massive confusion in this enormous state.

Worst of all from Goldwater's standpoint were ominous
echoes of the New Hampshire nightmare. Knowland, an old-
fashioned newspaper editor and an old-fashioned politician,
believed in an old-fashioned campaign—lots of traveling,
lots of speeches, lots of press conferences. In San Diego in

March, Goldwater was shocked to find that Knowland had scheduled twenty-four separate appearances (including four press conferences) on one day. Goldwater fulfilled his commitment in a state of exhaustion, but he vowed that it wouldn't happen again. It was then that he and Kitchel firmly determined to assume control over their own campaign to avoid another New Hampshire.[5]

Goldwater laid down the law on the night of April 4 at a secret meeting with Knowland and his other lieutenants at the Hilton Inn, just outside San Francisco International Airport. He told Knowland flatly that he could not tolerate any more schedules even faintly resembling that long day in San Diego. He was cutting Knowland's schedule to the bone, reducing both the number of days in California and the number of stops each day. Finally, he set forth this preview of his new California campaign style:

1. Hold down press conferences and question-and-answer sessions to an absolute minimum.

2. Hold down total appearances to three or four a day.

3. Limit these appearances to speeches before mass rallies or chats with campaign workers—that is, audiences guaranteed to be friendly.

4. Secure a maximum audience by televising these speeches before rallies—either through live TV or video tape.

Knowland, his face taking on the deepest shade of crimson, argued indignantly. He indicated that he might just quit entirely. He didn't, and Goldwater was at last campaigning in a way that conserved his energy, kept control of the subject matter in his own hands (rather than the hands of reporters), and used television to the maximum.

Consider one of his trips to California late in April. Arriving in Los Angeles in late afternoon, he drove in a motorcade to Long Beach for a quiet talk with his leaders there.

[5] See page 334.

Then followed a fund-raising dinner attended mainly by campaign workers, a brief talk at the dinner, and finally a speech to a rally in the Long Beach Sports Arena (which was taped for telecasting around the state that night). He was back at his suite at the Ambassador Hotel in Los Angeles in plenty of time to relax and watch the taped speech over television. The next day started with a midmorning flight to San Francisco, featuring a friendly, on-the-record bull session with reporters—an informal atmosphere that usually found Goldwater at his best, while the tension-ridden formal press conference often found him at his worst. It was the only press conference of the two-day swing. In the San Francisco Bay area, Goldwater was strictly in friendly territory on visits to three gatherings of party workers. He returned to Washington by plane in early evening. In contrast, Knowland originally had scheduled three full days, with plenty of formal press conferences each day.

Along with the reduced schedule went a totally new speech format cooked up by Goldwater and speech writer Karl Hess.[6] "They've got Goldwater under wraps," bemoaned Rockefeller manager Stu Spencer. Indeed, Spencer and the other Rockefeller strategists had expected Goldwater to trip over Social Security, the United Nations, nuclear weapons, and all the rest of the touchy stumbling blocks that had tripped him in New Hampshire. It wasn't really a matter of being under wraps. He was, a bit belatedly, trading the harsh invective of the Chautauqua circuit for the bland homilies of the partisan campaign trail. By nature, both Goldwater and Hess were political preachers. But in the interests of victory, they had decided to give up preaching. Furthermore, Hess's workmanlike set speeches gave Goldwater a confidence in California that he had lacked in New Hampshire.

The devoted Goldwaterites who poured into California arenas to hear their idol denounce the United Nations or call

[6] See page 335.

for an end to the Social Security system were badly disappointed. But Goldwater wasn't talking to them. He was talking over their heads to the television tape machine, recording his words for later transmission through the whole giant state.

For instance, facing a rally of fire-eating Young Republicans at the Casino Ballroom on Catalina Island on May 16, Goldwater delivered a set speech scarcely calculated to set them roaring. It was a sobersided plea for peace through strength that might well have been delivered by Richard M. Nixon in 1960—particularly in its peroration:

> When will America turn again to the sort of leadership, the sort of Republican leadership that has always kept the peace in the past?
>
> I say that America is ready for that change today—and that in November we will know it!
>
> And on that very day, if we have that change, we will move closer to the greatest day of all—the day an American President tells Nikita Khrushchev or his successor:
>
> You are wrong.
>
> Our children will not live under socialism or communism.
>
> Your children will live under freedom.

It was not the most inspiring or exciting of campaigns, but Goldwater seemed to be safely ahead of Rockefeller— that is, he was until the Oregon primary on May 15.

Even before Oregon, Rockefeller had inched up from his rock-bottom position of mid-April. Back home in Albany, he had recovered some face by ramming another liquor reform bill through the Legislature. In California, the courts had ruled enough of Harold Stassen's petition signatures invalid to force him off the ballot and thereby removed the threat of a 10 percent protest vote for Stassen by the Lodge-Nixon supporters. Rockefeller's own campaigning was getting firmer and stronger, no longer just some vague mumblings of "keeping in the Republican mainstream away from side eddies," but direct, sharp attacks on Goldwater.[7]

What really lengthened the stride in Rockefeller's step and put new authority in his voice was the May 15 victory in Oregon. In California as elsewhere, Oregon cut deeply into the Lodge strength, with much of it going to Rockefeller. Moreover, Nixon backers and the remaining Lodge supporters now could vote for Rockefeller without being afraid that they were throwing away their vote on somebody who didn't have a chance. The polls showed that Rockefeller suddenly had forged ahead. This was Lou Harris' finding in the *Washington Post*:

	Percent
Rockefeller	47
Goldwater	36
Undecided	17

But it was an uneasy lead—partly because of the heavy "undecided" total, partly because the first-choice preference of California Republicans was split almost evenly in four different directions. The Harris poll showed:

	Percent
Rockefeller	26
Lodge	24
Goldwater	21
Nixon	21
Scranton	2
Mrs. Smith	2
Undecided	4

But in the next few days, Rockefeller was much more successful in identifying himself with the non-Goldwater Republicans. The Lodge forces, led by the Grindle-Goldberg

---

[7] However, some members of Rockefeller's campaign staff were dead set against the Governor himself personally attacking Goldwater. They felt that the hatchet work should be left strictly to subordinates. They later claimed that this had cost him the election. It is a questionable thesis, however.

duo, were actively supporting Rockefeller in California. With Lodge no longer a rival, Rockefeller was naturally willing to forgive and forget what he considered the double cross of New Hampshire. The most effective Rockefeller campaign pamphlet for the California primary, distributed on a mass-mailing basis, sought to identify Rockefeller as the candidate of the other leading Republicans. Asking this question:

WHICH DO YOU WANT—
A LEADER? OR A LONER?

the pamphlet showed Rockefeller's photograph and a smaller picture of Lodge, Nixon, Romney, and Scranton, adding:

THESE MEN STAND TOGETHER
ON THE PARTY'S PRINCIPLES

Lodge, Nixon, Rockefeller, Romney, Scranton, Stassen.

These men stood together solidly and proudly on the up to date platforms of 1952, 1956 and 1960. . . .

In the California Primary Rockefeller represents them—in the kind of Republicanism that they and the overwhelming majority of Republicans believe in.

Opposite this united array of united Republicans was a picture of Goldwater alone, with this text:

THIS MAN STANDS OUTSIDE

By himself.

Not a single other nationally known Republican would substitute a mere statement of principles for the 1964 platform. . . .[8]

Goldwater has voted against all major issues proudly cited by the Republican platform—and has been in the distinct Senate Republican minority on 23 of them![9]

---

[8] Actually, by this time, Goldwater no longer was insisting on a statement of principles in substitution for the regular party platform.

[9] But other parts of the pamphlet were much more incendiary. For example: "Whom do you want in the room with the H-Bomb button?" and, "The very life of your Republican Party—and, perhaps, our nation's—is up to you."

But the major Rockefeller coup in the closing days of the California primary concerned Dwight D. Eisenhower.

All that winter and spring, the General was the unknown factor in Republican Presidential politics. The Republican moderates hoped against hope that he would be stirred to come out openly against Goldwater in public, denouncing him as antithetical to Eisenhower-style Republicanism. With Eisenhower a winter resident of California in a desert home near Palm Springs, a word or two for Rockefeller—or against Goldwater—would be invaluable. In the days before the Oregon primary, when Goldwater seemed well in front in California and almost certain to win the primary *and* the nomination, Eisenhower was besieged by old associates asking him to intervene. Goldwater was well aware of the danger. No longer referring to the Eisenhower Administration as the "Dime Store New Deal," he (and Rockefeller as well, of course) made the pilgrimage to Eisenhower in the desert.[10] More important, George Humphrey, the Cleveland steel magnate who as Secretary of the Treasury was strong man in the first Eisenhower Cabinet, was now an ardent Goldwater booster. His major assignment: keep Eisenhower neutral. He worked hard at it. So did Bryce Harlow, former White House aide and now a Procter & Gamble representative in Washington. Harlow, who had handled most of the General's speech writing since he had left the White House, felt that Eisenhower's only proper role was as healer of wounds after the San Francisco convention. Remembering the clumsy and unsuccessful efforts to sway the Democratic conventions of 1956 and 1960 by Harry Truman, Harlow wanted his old chief to suffer no such indignity.

[10] Some of Goldwater's more militant supporters in California hadn't quite gotten the message yet, however. At the state convention of the super-conservative United Republicans of California at the Bakersfield Civic Auditorium on May 2, the organization's founder and leader—Bruce Reagan, former militantly conservative State Assemblyman—launched a bitter attack against both Dwight and Milton Eisenhower. This sort of thing made the Goldwater managers understandably uneasy.

All this gave the old General a tense, uneasy winter, when he just wanted to be left in peace. He had never cared at all for this side of politics—the clash of personalities, the intrigue, the maneuver. Anyone who had the slightest idea of Eisenhower's point of view could hardly believe that he would intervene. Indeed, to get out of the maelstrom of the California campaign, Eisenhower took the long train ride back to Gettysburg, Pennsylvania, in early May—a month ahead of time.

But the anti-Goldwater friends of Eisenhower had not given up on the General. Certainly not Walter Thayer, the urbane president of the *New York Herald Tribune*. No great lover of Rockefeller, Thayer was nevertheless aware of the need for Rockefeller to win in California if Goldwater was to be stopped short of the nomination. Like Harlow, he had no desire to see Eisenhower suffer the indignities that Truman had at Democratic conventions. Thayer's answer was ingenious: a *Herald Tribune* article signed by Eisenhower, describing the kind of candidate that ought to be nominated for President, but not naming any names—a description that tacitly would embrace Rockefeller and reject Goldwater. The selling job to the General was made by Milton Eisenhower (who always had been a firm anti-Goldwater man); Elmer Anderson, the former Governor of Minnesota and a close friend of Eisenhower; and, of course, Thayer.

The resulting article appeared on the front page of the *Herald Tribune* on Monday, May 25. Not only was it distributed to the client papers receiving the *Herald Tribune's* news service, but also, in an unprecedented move, was given away by Thayer to the Associated Press, United Press International, and the rival *New York Times* (which also used it on the front page).

The article was more than Rockefeller had a right to hope for. Eisenhower backed the 1956 and 1960 national platforms (much criticized by Goldwater) and pointed to his adminis-

tration's record in Social Security, urban renewal, depressed-
areas aid, medical care for the aged, aid to low-income
farmers, and Federal highway building—all programs either
criticized or opposed by Goldwater. The General continued:

> I cite these examples not to applaud a past record but to
> illustrate the positive nature of true Republicanism—spotting
> new needs, sizing them up, and acting decisively when their
> national nature and scope requires it.

Next came the subject of civil rights, with Eisenhower
taking this strong stand:

> As the party of Lincoln, we Republicans have a particular
> obligation to be vigorous in the furtherance of civil rights. In
> this critical area, I have been especially proud of the dramatic
> leadership given by Republicans in Congress these past two
> years. . . .

After calling for "loyal support for the United Nations,"
Eisenhower concluded:

> I earnestly hope the party will select a nominee who skillfully
> and wholeheartedly would apply to our principles, both do-
> mestic and foreign, those principles which I have noted here.

It's doubtful that Eisenhower had any idea of how hard
he was hitting Goldwater and his positions. In fact, the General was boiling mad when the *Herald Tribune* accompanied
his story with a front-page column by Roscoe Drummond
interpreting the article as an anti-Goldwater tome. But Drummond's interpretation was the universal one. Naturally, Rockefeller and his supporters crowed to high heaven about it.
Goldwater tried to put the best possible face on it, calling it
a "forthright restatement of the basic Republican principles
upon which I proudly stand." This was nonsense, and everybody knew it. Goldwater and his staff were shocked and hurt
by the Eisenhower bombshell. That night, Goldwater could
not dissemble his true feelings. Appearing at Shasta College

in Redding, California, Goldwater produced an arrow, stuck
it under his arm, and then turned so that it looked like he
had been shot in the back. It made a hilarious news photo.
The Goldwater campaign had moved into another slump.
To reporters following it, it had the smell of defeat about it.
In a May 28 dispatch from Los Angeles, veteran political
correspondent Jack Steele of the Scripps-Howard newspapers
wrote:

> Stridence and confusion are the twin notes now dominating
> Sen. Barry M. Goldwater's campaign in California.
> They inescapably hint at the growing fear of the Senator
> and his campaign directors that he may lose this state's crucial
> Presidential primary next Tuesday. . . .
> The Senator has been hit by almost every conceivable brick-
> bat in the 10 days since the Oregon Primary put the brakes on
> his pre-convention bandwagon.
> And the new note of stridency stems chiefly from his effort
> to counter-attack. He has zeroed in on the press, which he
> accuses of distorting his views, on Gov. Rockefeller's alleged
> "lies" about his record, and on the "mysterious clique" of
> Easterners he claims inspired former President Eisenhower's
> weekend statement—which even Sen. Goldwater now says
> has enabled Rocky to "ride Ike's coattails."

Steele added that Goldwater "was unable to restrain his
penchant for shooting from the hip on any subject—including nuclear weapons." In fact, Goldwater had backslid from
his cool control of late April and early May into another
siege of foot-in-mouth disease. The worst came on ABC's
"Issues and Answers" televised interview on May 24. Goldwater proposed interdicting supply lines in North Vietnam.
There then followed this exchange between ABC commentator Howard K. Smith and the Senator:

> SMITH: Now a lot of supply lines seem to run in on the
> Laotian border, in any case, through jungles and along trails.
> How could you interdict those, with no good—

GOLDWATER: Well, it is not as easy as it sounds, because these are not trails that are out in the open. . . . There have been several suggestions made. I don't think we would use any of them. But defoliation of the forests by low yield atomic weapons could well be done. When you remove the foliage, you remove the cover. . . .

As he had done before and as he would do again, Goldwater had forgotten that he was running for President and had reverted to the easy, bull-session tone of a reserve major general talking things over with his fellow officers.[11] Goldwater was perfectly justified in protesting when the Associated Press and other news media reported that he had *advocated* using nuclear weapons in Vietnam. He had merely discussed the possibility. But his aides had been pleading and begging with him not to mention anything at all about nuclear weapons.

Goldwater just missed getting into worse trouble at an informal press conference in San Diego. Ironically, only friendly newspaper correspondents had been invited to the informal session at the *San Diego Union* offices in which the Senator would give them his real thinking about issues on which he claimed unfriendly reporters had misquoted him. But he again reverted to the barracks bull-session technique, suggesting that it might be wise to make an air strike against Red China. A reporter asked the Senator whether he really meant that, and Goldwater quickly withdrew the statement.

The polls reflected all this. The Harris poll showed that Rockefeller had a clear lead on May 26, going above the 50 percent mark for the first time. The Field poll showed the same big Rockefeller lead, though it gave him less than 50 percent:

	Harris	Field
Rockefeller	51	46
Goldwater	41	33
Undecided	8	21

[11] See page 237.

Rockefeller men were in a state of euphoria, predicting to reporters that they now were counting not just on a victory, but on a two-to-one victory that would rehabilitate Rockefeller as a national contender. In private chats with reporters, Goldwater conceded the real possibility of defeat. It was reflected in his campaigning. Writing in the *New York Herald Tribune* of May 29, Richard Dougherty said of the Senator: "He goes through the motions, but it is apparent that his heart is not in the game."

The party's leaders were getting the same impression. They had buried Goldwater early in the year, resurrected him about mid-April, and now were preparing to bury him again.

The second premature burial of Barry Goldwater took place May 24–26 at a preconvention meeting of the Republican National Committee at the Marriott Twin Bridges Motor Hotel in Arlington Virginia, just across the Potomac from Washington.

It was a repeat performance of Goldwater's first burial at the National Committee meeting at the Mayflower in January. Again there was a sense of emancipation, a feeling that they would not have to put up with Goldwater as a candidate after all, thanks to—of all people—none other than Nelson Rockefeller, the winner in Oregon and now apparently the certain winner in California. But the failure of Goldwater to unify the party, or even try to unify it, as front-runner these past weeks made this sense of emancipation even deeper than it had been before. They deeply feared the divisive impact on the party of Goldwater as nominee.

While suitably thankful to *Rockefeller* for serving as the Goldwater-slayer, nobody at the National Committee meeting thought that he had a chance for the nomination—no matter how big his victory margin in California.

Lodge was completely forgotten.

Nixon had a good deal of second- and third-ballot strength from his old Midwestern strongholds such as Ohio, Indiana, and perhaps Illinois. Moreover, he was most definitely interested in the nomination. Fred Seaton, who had run the Nebraska write-in campaign, appeared to be the *de facto* campaign manager for the unannounced Nixon national campaign, and he flew into New York City in the last week of May for secret conferences with his chief. On May 30, as much of the old Nixon team as it was possible to reassemble (including many old Eisenhower Administration officials) gathered in Seaton's suite at the Waldorf Towers for a day-long Memorial Day strategy session, with Seaton presiding and Nixon attending. Debate centered around what course Nixon should take after Goldwater's expected defeat in California: should he become a more-or-less open candidate, or should he continue to play the waiting game? No decision was reached. Perhaps the most significant fact of the meeting was that Leonard Hall, the faithful old Nixon lieutenant, was not present.

The absence of Hall reflected the general party opinion evidenced at the National Committe meeting earlier in the week: by and large, party leaders just didn't want another Nixon campaign. The tone of Nixon's heavy speaking schedule in the past six weeks hadn't helped either. In an attempt to cultivate the Goldwater Movement, Nixon was casting off his reputation as a civil rights crusader and attacking Negro demonstrations and boycotts. It was a maladroit move that failed to win over the Goldwaterites and repelled much of his old following. There was not the slightest sign that Goldwater, who had not seen Nixon since Nixon's Phoenix speech in October, 1960, would throw his delegate strength to Nixon if he were stopped in the California primary. In the closing days of the California campaign, Nixon tried his best to ingratiate himself with Goldwater—even making a personal telephone call to Goldwater on the campaign trail to give his regrets for not being able to attend the wedding of nineteen-year-old Peggy Goldwater in Phoenix the next month.

But it became increasingly clear that the Goldwater mantle was most likely to fall on *Scranton*. They had become good friends during Scranton's Congressional stint in 1961–1962, when he served in Capitol Hill's 9999th Air Force Reserve Squadron, commanded by Major General Barry Goldwater. Just as he had personally liked Rockefeller before their break, so now did Goldwater personally like Scranton. Just as he had been willing to gloss over his ideological differences with Rockefeller, so now was he willing to gloss over them with Scranton. He was telling reporters that there was no real gulf between them. He was telling close friends a good bit more—that he would swing his support to Scranton if he himself were stopped. Taking note of this, Scranton's aides were as careful about maintaining warm relations with the Goldwater camp as was Nixon. Craig Truax was particularly industrious in this effort, quietly informing both Clif White and John Grenier that they would have big, important slots in the Scranton-for-President drive if Scranton took top prize.

This unofficial and indefinite dropping of Goldwater's mantle about Scranton's shoulders certainly helped, but it wasn't what really made him the Presidential choice—indeed, the overwhelming Presidential choice—of the Republican National Committee as it gathered at Twin Bridges in late May. His great asset was an absence of defects, an absence of political wounds. Because he had not really turned himself into a national figure during the preceding five months, Scranton was still fundamentally the dim, hazy, and unknown figure that he had been in January. His campaign organization was still so amateurish and chaotic that two separate and rival Scranton volunteer groups opened competing hospitality rooms at Twin Bridges. But to a party sick of three and a half years of intermittent and five months of incessant squabbling,

Scranton looked good—not because he was the most popular candidate, but because he was the least unpopular.

There were even some signs that die-hard Goldwaterites would not insist on manning the barricades to the bitter end, that 1964 would not be the great year of decision in the Republican Party between left and right, and that Scranton might be accepted as the centrist compromise candidate.

During the National Committee meeting, Senator John Tower of Texas wandered by mistake into one of the Scranton hospitality suites (located next door to the Goldwater suite).

"I'm afraid you're in the wrong place, Senator," said one of the Scranton men.

"Oh, this isn't such a bad place to be," replied Tower, one of Goldwater's closest political advisers, with a knowing wink.

More concrete evidence came from one deep South supporter of Goldwater. Asked by a reporter at Twin Bridges where his state's delegation would go if Goldwater were stopped, this Southerner noticed John Grenier of Alabama, the Goldwater Southern chieftain, standing not far away. "Well, man," the Southerner bellowed in reply, "I suppose you're talking about the hundred and first ballot, because we'll stay with Barry Goldwater for a hundred ballots." When Grenier walked away a few minutes later, the Southerner pulled the reporter close to him and whispered a totally different story into his ear: "To be perfectly honest, we'll stay with Barry as long as he has a *reasonable* chance. But that won't be more than three ballots. This may surprise you, but I'm sure we'll go for Scranton after that."

This was the story of Twin Bridges—all based on the assumption that Goldwater was a sure loser in California. This assumption was strengthened by some telltale signs that National Chairman William Miller, a nimble political operator, was moving ever so slightly away from Goldwater.

Nominally neutral, Miller had been edging over into Goldwater territory in the last few months. He was, for instance,

Goldwater's choice to keynote the San Francisco convention —and get it off to a conservative start. Miller was agreeable, and so was the National Committee. Senator Thruston Morton of Kentucky, like Miller a moderate conservative, was to be permanent chairman. The only convention plum to be tossed to the liberals was to be the totally meaningless job of temporary chairman, which would go to Governor Mark Hatfield of Oregon.

But as the National Committee met at Twin Bridges on Sunday night, May 24, Miller suddenly announced that he couldn't handle the national chairman's job at the convention and still have time to prepare the keynote address. He bowed out—without a word of advance warning to Clif White, who was handling convention arrangements for Goldwater. That meant that the party's anti-Goldwater wing could boost Hatfield for the combined job of temporary chairman and keynoter, interpreted widely in the press as a setback for Goldwater.[12] It was much too late for a conservative alternative to Hatfield to be found.[13]

Rightly or wrongly, the Goldwater staff suspected Miller's motives in handling the keynoter's job to Hatfield. They became all the more suspicious when two largely symbolic convention jobs went to Rockefeller men without clearance from the Goldwater camp. Art Richardson, a New York Young Republicans leader, was named chief doorkeeper. Sandy Lankler, the Rockefeller coordinator in New Hampshire and now working in the California campaign, was named assistant chief sergeant at arms.

The mood of impending disaster for Goldwater was in-

[12] However, Goldwater himself was not at all upset by this. Miller had informed Goldwater of his decision not to be the keynoter, but Goldwater did not relay the news to White. While Goldwater would have preferred Miller, he did not object to Hatfield.

[13] Governor Tim Babcock of Montana, a Goldwater man, actually ran against Hatfield for the keynoter's post but did not have the support of either the Goldwater organization or the full Goldwater strength on the National Committee.

advertently heightened on Friday, May 29, when Clif White summoned Washington correspondents to his office in the Duryea Building for a background briefing. "California is not a conservative state," White began. He then launched into a discussion of how Goldwater could be nominated even if he lost in California.

White really meant it. The trouble was that Goldwater and Kitchel didn't. They were convinced that defeat in California was the end of the road. Even if Goldwater brought four hundred firm delegates into San Francisco, he could scarcely hope to add to that total in his defeatist mood. But what was happening in California made all this academic.

Louis Harris' pollsters were finding strange things in California as election day neared. These were the results of his last three soundings (the figures are percentages):

	May 26	May 30	June 1
Rockefeller	51	49	42
Goldwater	41	40	40
Undecided	8	11	18

The California primary was breaking the political rules. The "undecided" vote was increasing rather than decreasing as election day neared. Goldwater's support was more or less firm, but Rockefeller's following was falling into the "undecided" column. In one of his articles for the *Washington Post*, Harris asserted that "the vote for Rockefeller remains soft and even mushy."[14] Why it was falling away from him— and why it eventually ended up in Goldwater's corner—can be explained in large part by a brilliantly executed couterattack.

In the first place, the slump in Goldwater's California campaign after the Oregon loss was largely confined to Goldwater

[14] In the wake of the know-nothing reaction against pollsters, Harris was accused of trying to hedge his bets. Actually, the fluid state of affairs right up to election day described by Harris can be attested to by top managers in both the Goldwater and the Rockefeller camps.

himself. Actually, statewide coordination had improved a hundredfold because of one change: Dean Burch had been sent West from Washington to take charge. As assistant to Kitchel, young Burch had proved a quietly competent administrator in the running of Goldwater headquarters in Washington. He did the same kind of efficient job in Los Angeles, bringing a degree of coordination to the campaign for the first time.

Moreover, Goldwater strategists were launching mammoth couterattacks on Rockefeller's every attack in the last days. Take the case of the Rockefeller pamphlet seeking to represent the Governor as the proxy candidate for Lodge, Nixon, Romney, and Scranton. With the Draft Lodge movement actively working for Rockefeller in California and with Lodge privately telling visitors in Saigon that his one great political desire was to see Goldwater beaten, the Senator could scarcely hope to get Lodge to repudiate the pamphlet. But he could—and did—try with the others. His "Dear Bill" telegram to Scranton is representative. After describing the Rockefeller pamphlet as "a shabby misstatement of my views," Goldwater gets to the point:

> But there is one aspect of the campaign folder I'm sending which will interest you . . . it says the Governor represents you in the California primary, with the obvious implication that you are opposed to my candidacy and in favor of his in the June 2nd election.
>
> The reason I intrude on your busy schedule with all this is to let you know that I have instructed my California managers to contact you in the next few days. They will ask your public comment on whether you oppose my candidacy and support Governor Rockefeller in the California primary. Also whether the Governor, as his campaign literature claims, does in fact represent you in California.
>
> With warm personal regards, and hope to see you soon.
>
> Barry Goldwater

Scranton didn't even wait for Goldwater's managers to contact him. This was no time to be anything but chummy with Goldwater. On May 26, he mailed a special-delivery "Dear Barry" letter to Washington (received in Washington the next day and telephoned to Burch in Los Angeles by Kitchel). Asserting that "I want to answer your inquiry immediately," Scranton wrote what could only be interpreted as a repudiation of Rockefeller:

> I have not been asked by anyone for permission to include my name or picture in this literature. Since I am not a candidate, no one "represents" me in California or anywhere else. That I subscribe to a modern, pragmatic, positive approach to politics in government is well known.
>
> My one overriding interest is for unity within the Republican Party. Consequently, I have refused to join "Stop Goldwater, Stop Rockefeller, or Stop Anybody" movements.
>
> I believe that a unified Republican Party can score a resounding victory this Fall. . . . We cannot do this, however, unless we are unified and strong.
>
> With warm personal regards,
>   Most sincerely,
>   Bill /s/
>   William W. Scranton

In much more formal language, Romney telegraphed Knowland in Los Angeles that "I am neither supporting nor opposing any candidate" in the California primary. So frantic was Nixon to stay chummy with Goldwater that he didn't even wait for Goldwater to ask him.[15] When he heard about the Rockefeller pamphlet, he issued a disavowal to the wire services, then sent a copy of the press release to Goldwater.[16]

[15] But Nixon's mother, still living in California, got the wrong idea and accepted an invitation to attend a Goldwater rally just before election day. Nixon didn't want to be that friendly. Hannah Nixon was on the next plane for a vacation with her son in New York.

[16] During the California campaign, Rockefeller was philosophic about the conduct of his fellow moderate Republicans. On May 28, he told reporters: "They are all ambitious and hoping lightning will strike. What other position could they take?" As we shall see in the next chapter, his attitude toward them changed after June 2.

Much more significant was the manner in which Goldwater neutralized the Eisenhower article of May 25.

One-half of this neutralization ironically involved Dr. Milton Eisenhower, the most liberal of the Eisenhowers and the one Eisenhower openly and decidedly against Goldwater. Milton Eisenhower, president of Johns Hopkins University in Baltimore, served as head of the Critical Issues Council— a subsidiary of the National Republican Citizens Committee, whose formation Goldwater had opposed so bitterly.[17] As California election day neared, Goldwater asked Dr. Eisenhower whether they could meet to discuss the affairs of the Critical Issues Council. Incredibly enough, Dr. Eisenhower accepted. The private meeting was set for breakfast at Goldwater's hideaway in the Capital at eight o'clock Monday morning, June 1—just one day before the California balloting, Goldwater forces promptly leaked the news of the meeting to the press.[18]

The other half of the Eisenhower neutralization was executed for Goldwater by George Humphrey, the General's old Secretary of the Treasury, in Cleveland. When he read the Eisenhower article of May 25, the short-tempered Humphrey was outraged. He phoned Kitchel in Washington to ask whether he could read the riot act to his old chief. Kitchel told him to go ahead. Humphrey then phoned Gettysburg, telling the General that the *Herald Tribune* article compromised his avowed position of neutrality.

The Humphrey conversation paid off a week later. In New York City for a Republican meeting on Monday, June 1, General Eisenhower made a clear effort to knock down his own article as an anti-Goldwater device. "You people tried to read Goldwater out of the party, I didn't," he told reporters.

[17] See page 75.
[18] Goldwater spokesmen never misrepresented the meeting as implying that Dr. Eisenhower was supporting the Senator. The spokesman said only that the Critical Issues Council was discussed, which was the truth. The fact that Milton Eisenhower and Goldwater were breakfasting together was sufficient for the Senator's purpose, however.

The result was two headlines in election-day newspapers of June 2. In one headline, Milton Eisenhower and Goldwater were reported breakfasting together. In the other headline, Dwight D. Eisenhower was welcoming Goldwater back into the party. Goldwater had knocked Rockefeller aside to join him on the Eisenhower coattails.

The other big event of the last days of the campaign was not an act of Goldwater but an act of God. At 4:15 P.M. on May 30, just three days before the vote, a seven-pound ten-ounce boy named Nelson Rockefeller, Jr., was born in New York Hospital—to the great joy of Nelson and Happy Rockefeller and to the despair of his aides.[19] The old remarriage issue was opened again with this first child of the fifty-six-year-old Governor and his thirty-seven-year-old bride. The remarriage issue had been hinted at three days earlier, when Loyola University of Los Angeles, a Catholic college, canceled a Rockefeller speech there on May 27 after pressure from Goldwater supporters. This raised in some minds the question of his divorce and remarriage. The birth of his son brought the question home to many more minds.

The election results were close enough so that the combined impact of events—the Scranton-Romney-Nixon repudiation, the Eisenhower neutralization, the birth of the Rockefeller baby—may have made the difference.

But what perhaps was the most meaningful development of those last few days was the curious attitude taken by the Rockefeller high command. Once Rockefeller's post-Oregon spurt had put him ahead of Goldwater in the California polls, his top advisers acted as though the California primary were as good as won and the next job was to build delegate strength for an uphill fight at San Francisco. George Hinman, who had spent so many weeks in California preparing

[19] Some aides felt that the Rockefeller camp should have made the most of the birth of the baby, hailing it as a great and joyous event. According to this theory, the adverse political impact of the event was aggravated by the dead silence in the Rockefeller camp.

for June 2, left for the National Committee meeting in Washington on May 24—and never returned to California for those last crucial weeks. It was typical of the mood in the Rockefeller high command.

However, one faction of the Rockefeller staff—headed by Charley Moore, the ex-Ford vice-president who was heading Rockefeller's public relations, and Sandy Lankler—argued that this was madness. They pointed out that Rockefeller had never pulled more than 20 to 25 percent of the vote in statewide polls of all Republican possibilities, that the "undecided" vote was uncomfortably large, that Rockefeller's new post-Oregon support in California was not at all firm, that his California political base was insubstantial, that Goldwater had a bedrock strength that would go to the polls come what may. Their plea: fight hard right up to the last minute; fight as if you were behind. But most of Rockefeller's managers disagreed—including Dr. William Ronan, the Governor's personal secretary and probably his most influential adviser. Now in California with the Governor, Ronan argued that Rockefeller should take a don't-rock-the-boat attitude. Now that he was ahead, he shouldn't do anything to endanger that lead—slim though it might be. Rockefeller agreed.

The focus of this debate was a half-hour documentary film on the dangers of the far right wing (narrated by Dave Garroway) that had been prepared for possible last-minute use if needed in California. Actually, it had been prepared, against heavy opposition, at the insistence of Charley Moore. Skillfully prepared, it at no time mentioned Goldwater by name, but instead played on the menaces of the far right, replete with the beating of hollow drums and other dramatic effects. Dr. Ronan argued forcefully that the film could kill Rockefeller by stirring up unneeded controversy at a time when he was ahead. Moore and Lankler argued that the election was far from won and that a last dramatic effort was needed.

The showdown came on May 28 in a meeting at the Warner

Brothers Studio in Hollywood. The film was shown to a select group of Rockefeller leaders. Industrialist Harvey Firestone, Rockefeller's Southern California chairman, gave the verdict: it's the best thing of its kind we've seen, but it's too controversial and too dangerous to be shown. Rockefeller accepted the advice. It never was shown.

With the Rockefeller campaign apparently becalmed in the final days, Charley Moore went back to New York. He wasn't needed. While full-page advertisements for Goldwater blossomed in California newspapers and a blitz advertising campaign poured over radios and television sets, Rockefeller's campaign—perhaps the most lavishly financed primary-election campaign in American political history—fell silent, with practically no newspaper ads and no radio-TV commercials. While Goldwater field offices purred with activity on the Sunday before election day, Rockefeller's were either padlocked or virtually padlocked (with one girl to answer the telephone). They were playing don't-rock-the-boat until the bitter end.

On June 2, just twenty-two minutes after the polls in Southern California closed (and while Rockefeller workers were still trying to get the vote out in the Governor's Northern California stronghold, where the polls stayed open an hour later), CBS (with the aid of computers) declared Goldwater the winner, with 53 percent, on the basis of the returns from forty-two model precincts. When more returns came in, Lou Harris—manning the computers for CBS—called it 51 percent. He was right.[20] The results:

		Percent
Goldwater	1,089,133	51.3
Rockefeller	1,030,180	48.7

[20] But everybody concerned was forced to spend a long, unnecessarily suspenseful evening. Because it was far behind CBS and the other networks in tabulating, the Associated Press reported at 6 A.M. that Rockefeller had forged ahead with 40,000 votes. The AP simply hadn't counted the Southern California precincts, where Goldwater was strongest.

Populous, clamorous Southern California—the national capital of the Goldwater Movement—had given Goldwater his great victory. Goldwater carried Los Angeles County (with immense pluralities in the middle-to-upper-class suburban areas) by a surprisingly large 158,000 votes, Orange County by a surprisingly large 49,000 votes, and San Diego County by a surprisingly small 16,000 votes. Rockefeller carried every other county in the state, coming through with big victory margins in San Francisco County and the rest of the north. It cut away all but 59,000 votes of the Senator's Southern California bulge.

By just 59,000 votes, out of more than 2,000,000 cast, Goldwater had won the California primary—and with it the nomination. California was the first and last line of defense for the moderates. They had no alternative or fallback strategy. Like the British, Goldwater had lost every battle but the last. But the last battle was enough. Now, aside from one slight obstacle—the Conference of Governors in Cleveland during the week of June 7—Goldwater's road to San Francisco was an open one.

XXII

★ ★

Cleveland

For a half century, the annual Conference of Governors was a routine, good-natured affair—the nation's governors exchanging ideas about state government, getting to know one another better, and having a fine time. Governor Thomas E. Dewey of New York changed that at the 1952 conference in Houston's Shamrock Hotel. The regular agenda at Houston was forgotten when Tom Dewey led thirty-two Republican Governors into signing a statement urging adoption of a "fair play" amendment at the Republican National Convention—an amendment that supported the seating of Eisenhower delegations instead of Taft delegations in three contested states (Texas, Louisiana, Georgia), thereby ensuring the nomination for General Eisenhower. It was a coup of historic significance. The Governors, representing then most of the power and a generous portion of the talent of the Republican Party, had really stopped the front-running Taft. From that point on, it was Eisenhower's bandwagon all the way.

The Dewey coup transformed the Conference of Governors into an annual political circus, attended by an ever-growing delegation of newsmen. The stories these newsmen got from the conference usually had some political overtones, but nothing to compare with Houston in 1952. Thus, the press looked to Cleveland in 1964 as another great political

416

story. Indeed, the moderates looked to it as their last, best chance to stop Barry Goldwater.

However, there were at least four good reasons why the Governors Conference at the Sheraton-Cleveland in 1964 would not be a carbon copy of the Governors Conference at the Shamrock in 1952.

1. *There were only sixteen Republican Governors in 1964.* In the intervening twelve years, the real party power had passed from the Governors' mansions to Congress.[1]

2. *There was no Tom Dewey in 1964.* No one Republican Governor could lead his colleagues. Nelson Rockefeller of New York and Mark Hatfield of Oregon, each elected for the first time in 1958, had shown the most leadership qualities in past Governors Conferences. But now Rockefeller was an embittered, exhausted loser. Hatfield, believing that the Goldwater nomination was a certainty, felt that the party's liberals should try to make friends with the Senator in order to bring him closer to the middle of the road. He was not about to lead a stop-Goldwater movement.

3. *The Republican Governors were badly divided in 1964.* At least four of the sixteen were Goldwater men. Others— James Rhodes of Ohio, Robert Smylie of Idaho, Hatfield— had no love for Goldwater, but were about ready to throw in the towel. George Romney of Michigan was a lone wolf, not liked by his fellow Governors and not likely to join in any concerted effort with them. Other than William W. Scranton of Pennsylvania, the number of Governors who might be apt to join a stop-Goldwater movement could be counted on one hand—John Love of Colorado, John Chafee of Rhode Island, John Reed of Maine, and John Anderson of Kansas.[2] It was not what could be called an awesome collection.

[1] This was later apparent at the San Francisco convention when House members almost completely dominated the platform fight.

[2] Anderson, it should be remembered, was a leading political casualty of the Goldwater Movement. He had been badly beaten in a drive to lead a non-Goldwater Kansas delegation to San Francisco. See page 351.

4. *There was no groundwork laid prior to the conference in 1964.* In sharp contrast with Dewey's careful planning in 1952, nothing had been done prior to the Cleveland conference. As had been the case with the moderates all year, there seemed to be a feeling that last-minute help would fall from heaven.

Apart from the obvious inability of sixteen badly divided Governors to change the fate of the Republican Party, the basic difference between 1964 and 1952 was immense. In 1952, Taft and Eisenhower were neck and neck when the Governors convened in Houston. In 1964, Goldwater was far, far in front of the field when the Governors convened in Cleveland. With 655 votes needed to nominate, he had in excess of six-hundred sure delegates and perhaps two-hundred probables. Besides, why should the moderates be able to pull themselves together in a few days at Cleveland when they had frittered away three and a half years?

And yet, there was that long shot—call it 1 in 25—that something might be put together at Cleveland for Bill Scranton. It would have to be done perfectly, smoothly, producing that sense of momentum that means everything in politics. There would have to be the verisimilitude of the old Dewey juggernaut at work. The odds were long. But with the stakes so high, 25 to 1 odds were worth betting on.

At any rate, the Goldwater forces weren't taking any chances. Both Clif White and Dick Kleindienst would be on hand to smell out in advance anything that had the odor of the Shamrock Hotel in 1952.

The one therapeutic effect of the California primary from the standpoint of the moderates was to thin the ranks of their candidates. Now *Rockefeller* was out. Eliminated earlier were *Romney* and *Lodge*. Nobody thought at all of *Nixon* as a Presidential contender any longer. The field had narrowed

to one man: *Scranton*. It was now either Scranton or Goldwater.

But Scranton was scarcely surefooted in moving into the
vacancy left by Rockefeller. One June 3, the telephone lines
hummed into the Governor's office. Anti-Goldwater forces
from throughout the country pleaded with him to enter the
race. In addition, there was one call from a neutral—Charles
M. Percy, the Republican candidate for Governor of Illinois.
Hemmed in by a primary-campaign commitment not to
oppose Goldwater, Percy nevertheless made it clear that
Scranton would be most welcome at the top of the ticket in
Illinois.

Thus, there was then a sense of expectancy when Scranton
called a press conference in Harrisburg on June 4. But
Scranton was not about to move an inch from his old
position. Consider this exchange, for example:

> LEONARD LINDGREN (*Pittsburgh Press*): Governor, have you
> reassessed your own personal position in view of the result in
> California?
>
> SCRANTON: No, I haven't reassessed anything. I feel exactly
> the way I did before California, and as of last April, when I
> made what I hoped was the final statement on this matter.[3]

Worse yet from Scranton's standpoint was this exchange
about Goldwater:

> DUKE KAMINSKI (*Philadelphia Bulletin*): Governor, why is
> it that people who say Goldwater won't do, think you will.
> What is your difference in political philosophy?
>
> SCRANTON: Between Sen. Goldwater and me? I don't know
> of any extremely basic difference. Both of us believe in a strong
> foreign policy, at least I gather that from statements of his;
> we both believe in governmental levels of action being as
> strong as possible on the local level, and then on the state, and
> last on the Federal. We might differ, and I'm sure we do, on

[3] This was the statement that very nearly took Scranton out of the race
completely. See page 341.

the methods of implementing those two general theses, but again I say there's little difference between Republican leaders in comparison to that between various Democratic leaders.

From Scranton's standpoint, it would have been better if he had never held the June 4 conference. At an hour when time was running out, a good many political reporters got the erroneous impression that he was definitely trying to remove himself from the Presidential race and was instead angling for the Vice-Presidential nomination with Goldwater.

Yet, beneath the surface, strong forces were moving in Harrisburg.

In the first place, Mary Scranton was changing her mind. The Governor's lady, so strong that past winter against the idea of her husband undergoing the ordeal of a Presidential race, had begun to feel that a mission against Goldwater was a matter of duty.

In the second place, Scranton's friends and staff were putting more and more pressure on him during that first week of June. Thomas McCabe of Scott Paper Co., who previously had contributed no money to Scranton-for-President efforts in deference to the Governor's wishes, telephoned Scranton aide Bill Keisling to pledge a hefty sum for any Presidential activity. Keisling was constantly prodding Scranton. After the dreary Harrisburg press conference of June 4, Keisling pointed to the bust of Abraham Lincoln on Scranton's desk and asked: "Governor, what would he think of you if you didn't run?"

And, despite the unhappy experience of Rockefeller in California, the Scranton camp was determined to get some help from General Eisenhower. They still believed that the General looked upon Scranton as a protégé of sorts and would give him the kind of help that he couldn't find it in his heart to give Rockefeller. Working feverishly after the California primary, friends of the General urged him to see Scranton to ask the Governor to make himself more available to the nomination. This would not violate Eisenhower's pledge of neutrality, but it would enhance the prospects for the open convention that he desired. Eisenhower agreed.

The invitation came on Friday, June 5. There was a bit of a mix-up. At first, Eisenhower was to come to Harrisburg. Then that was changed. Scranton was going to Gettysburg on Saturday morning. He understood the purpose of the visit.

Bill Keisling and Craig Truax arrived in Cleveland on Friday night as Scranton's advance guard, with a new bounce in their step, a lilt in their voice, and a secret that they intended to disclose presently. Keisling was wearing an $8 gold-plated SCRANTON lapel button that he had worn in both the 1960 and the 1962 campaigns. "I only wear this when I got a candidate," he chortled. "Believe me, I've got a candidate now." A few Washington correspondents for afternoon newspapers were invited to the Scranton suite in the Sheraton-Cleveland; they were served drinks by Keisling and Truax and then were told the news of the Saturday pilgrimage to Gettysburg.

On Saturday, press secretary Jack Conmy was putting out the news in Harrisburg. The old General and the young Governor had met in Gettysburg for one hour and thirty-five minutes on Saturday morning. Eisenhower asked Scranton to be more positive in his position about the Presidency, to make it clear that he would accept the nomination if a majority of the delegates wanted him—a marginally more positive stand than his past position that he would succumb only to a genuine, spontaneous draft.

To an amazing degree, the press interpretation (or rather, misinterpretation) of the Gettysburg meeting was that Eisenhower at long last was casting off his cloak of neutrality— a misinterpretation that the Scranton staff did nothing to discourage. Rather, they were walking on air. Scranton had informed them that he now was ready to make a statement of availability that, if not a true statement of candidacy, was the next thing to it and was certain to be followed in short order by an active campaign. What's more, there was a ready-made opportunity for Scranton to make his announcement before a nationwide television audience. The Governor was scheduled to appear on "Face the Nation," the CBS interview program, at 12:30 P.M. Sunday afternoon from Cleveland. Keisling was assigned to prepare a brief statement of availability for the broadcast, to be ready for the Governor when he flew in from Harrisburg early Sunday.

There was an unusual guest in the Scranton suite at the Sheraton-Cleveland Saturday night: Clif White. He tried to impress on Keisling, Truax, and William Murphy (Scranton's secretary) that it was too late to stop Goldwater. He pleaded with them not to have the Governor blast Goldwater over "Face the Nation" the next day. White wanted Scranton to be Goldwater's running mate, and he assumed that the Scranton aides were willing to settle for the same thing. In an effort to keep Scranton in line, White had started a rumor on Saturday that the Goldwater forces now were most interested in Governor James Rhodes for Vice-President—assuming that the threat of a Vice-Presidential rival would exorcise all errant thoughts of challenging Barry Goldwater. But White had misjudged what Truax and Keisling were after. They wanted the big prize only.

As a professional politician, Truax realized that the odds were long against Scranton. But he felt that there was a real chance. One necessary first step was to bring in a familiar Republican face as campaign manager or executive director —probably Fred Scribner of Maine—so that party leaders would not have the feeling that they were dealing with a bunch of amateurs. From there, he felt that it was necessary to start chipping away at Goldwater's delegate strength—in Goldwater's heartland, if possible, for maximum psychological impact. A likely point of attack: Florida, where State Republican Chairman Tom Fairfield Brown was still seething over the unsuccessful attempt of the Goldwater forces to take the state party away from him in the May 26 primary.[4]

In such a frame of mind, Truax was not about to heed White's words of caution. When White left the Scranton suite, he really had no idea whether or not he had impressed the young Scranton aides. In fact, he had not. As soon as White left (about three o'clock in the morning), Keisling set to work writing the Scranton statement for the next morning.

It was a night without sleep for Bill Keisling. But he didn't mind it really. The Scranton-for-President campaign he had dreamed about for months was just about eight hours from fruition. But in this case, things looked brightest before the dawn. Bill Scranton, Bill Keisling, and the Republican Party were about to embark on a Black Sunday that they never would forget.

It is worth chronicling Black Sunday in some little detail, partly because the events of the day sealed the doom of the Republican moderates and ensured the nomination of Barry Goldwater. Perhaps if all had gone well for the moderates that Sunday, June 7, that 1 in 25 long shot for Scranton might have come in. Most likely not. Yet, the utter confusion and bickering inside the moderate ranks help to explain why Goldwater had moved into his mightly lead in the first place. This is the real reason for looking at Black Sunday. When faced with their last real chance to unite or perish, the anti-Goldwater forces in the party simply could not unite.

At around nine o'clock on Sunday morning, the Scranton suite at the Sheraton-Cleveland was empty except for a cleaning woman. Keisling had finished the Governor's statement for "Face the Nation" and had driven to the airport to meet Scranton. At about the same time, two Scranton aides— Bill Murphy and Jack Stark, a Washington, D.C., lawyer and experienced political manager who had been asked by Truax

---

[4] See page 368.

to come to Cleveland to "help out"—returned to the suite at about the same time.[5] Stark had been in his own room shaving. Murphy had gone down to the lobby to buy some newspapers. No sooner had they entered the suite than the telephone rang. Murphy answered. It was General Eisenhower calling from Gettysburg for the Governor.

When Scranton arrived at the hotel from the airport, he immediately placed the call to Eisenhower, after ushering his aides out of his private bedroom. The General's words were sobering. He told Scranton that he didn't want their conversation of yesterday to be interpreted as meaning that he was encouraging or supporting a "cabal" to stop Goldwater for the nomination. He wanted no part of anything like that, Eisenhower made abundantly clear.

What Scranton did not then know was that George Humphrey had been busy on the telephone again. When they first heard the news of the Scranton-Eisenhower meeting, Goldwater staffers on hand in Cleveland called Humphrey at his suburban home just outside the city to ask whether he would try to neutralize Eisenhower for the second time.[6]

Humphrey was glad to lend a hand. Blunt, salty George Humphrey could talk to Dwight David Eisenhower as few men had ever dared. He phoned the General Saturday night to tell him that his presence as a houseguest at the Humphrey home on Monday night (the night that Eisenhower was to address a banquet session of the Governors Conference) might prove embarrassing if Eisenhower were masterminding a sinister plot to stop Barry Goldwater with Bill Scranton. Eisenhower, who had been mightily displeased by the scare headlines produced by what he thought was an innocent little chat with Scranton, was receptive to Hum-

---

[5] Stark had sat in on that January, 1964, plea by moderate Republican Congressmen for a green light from Scranton. See page 299.
[6] See page 411.

phrey's criticism. The call to Scranton the next morning was the result. Eisenhower had been neutralized again.

Without mentioning the unsettling conversation with Eisenhower to his aides, Scranton immediately set off for another unsettling experience—a closed-door breakfast meeting of the Republican Governors downstairs in the Sheraton-Cleveland.

The breakfast meeting probably would have been a routine affair had not George Romney suddenly picked that moment to set off on a crusade to save the soul of the Republican Party.

Arthur Elliott, the Michigan state party chairman and a longtime Romney adviser, had been urging the Governor to stay scrupulously neutral in the Presidential contest. Clif White, in continuous contact with Elliott, had told him that the Goldwater forces would not try to pry Michigan delegates loose from Romney's favorite son candidacy if the Governor maintained that position of neutrality. But John B. Martin, Jr., Michigan's national committeeman, and Romney's bright, young aides felt quite differently. Since the California primary on June 2, they had been urging the Governor to come out strongly against Goldwater, thereby disassociating himself completely from the Senator. The Michigan polls showed that such a disassociation was absolutely essential. If it were not made, they felt, Romney would be tied to Goldwater so closely that he would be defeated for reelection in November.

Arriving in Cleveland on Saturday night after settling a strike back in Michigan, Romney suddenly made up his mind —without consulting Elliott, who was back in Michigan. He would lead an attack against Goldwater. On Sunday morning, he called surprised aides together in his Cleveland hotel suite. So concerned was he about the Goldwater menace to the party, Mormon Romney announced, that he was for the first time in his career about to break his flat prohibition against politics on Sunday by calling a press conference to announce his crusade against Goldwater. Moreover, he would attend the breakfast meeting of Republican Governors to try to achieve the same purpose. He then proceeded to dictate a statement for the press conference.

George Romney was the last Republican Governor who should have tried to lead his colleagues in a stop-Goldwater movement. He was a loner who didn't mix well with his colleagues. When Romney refused to attend an important Sunday caucus of Republican Governors during the 1963 Governors Conference in Miami Beach, the other Governors believed that he was taking a holier-than-thou attitude. They were miffed later in the summer of 1963 when he sent an aide, instead of attending himself, to the first meeting of the newly formed Republican Governors Association in Denver. Now Romney surprised them all by purposefully striding into the Sunday breakfast—obviously a man with something to say.

What Romney said might have made some impact had Nelson Rockefeller, well respected among his fellow Governors, backed him up. But this was not the Nelson Rockefeller who had fought for civil rights resolutions at the two previous Governors Conferences. Nor was it the Nelson Rockefeller who had tirelessly campaigned from one end of the country to the other. It was a Rockefeller never exhibited in public before: tired, bitter, cynical.[7] He talked privately of his contempt for Nixon, Scranton, and Romney for sending their avowals of neutrality to Goldwater in the closing days of the California primary.[8] If the Republican Party had not helped him when he had tried to save it from Goldwater, he was not about to help the party now—when it was too late anyway. Governors closely allied with Rockefeller, such as

[7] It is a commentary of sorts on the national political press corps that the correspondents suddenly took an immense liking to Rockefeller for the first time. They much preferred the hard-bitten cynic to the Eagle Scout.

[8] See page 410.

Mark Hatfield of Oregon and Robert Smylie of Idaho, felt the same way.

In this less than congenial atmosphere, Romney stepped in to announce his determination to lead a drive against Goldwater and to get the Senator to "clarify" his views.

Governor Paul Fannin of Arizona, a ranking member of the Arizona Mafia, bridled. What right did Romney have to ask the party's probable nominee to submit to cross-examination? This kind of attitude from a Goldwater intimate was expected. What was not so expected was the aid and support that Fannin got from liberal Mark Hatfield.

"George," Hatfield told Romney coolly, "the war's over. You remind me of the French generals who wanted to attack after the Maginot Line had been snapped and the Germans were entering Paris. It's too late."

Romney insisted that it was never too late. That only gave Hatfield another chance to sink his hooks in a little deeper.

"Where were you, George," Hatfield asked, "when Nelson here was trying to stop Goldwater? Were you helping him then?"[9]

Rockefeller, silent through it all, put his hands to his face to cover a sardonic little smile.

In the middle of this, Scranton entered. Siding with Romney, Scranton declared that Goldwater should be asked to explain his views to a breakfast meeting of Governors on Tuesday morning. He met with a reaction no more favorable than the one received by Romney.

When this somber meeting ended, Romney strode directly to the Sheraton-Cleveland's press-conference room, where hundreds of reporters were waiting. He declared:

---

[9] Romney could well have replied (but didn't): "Where were *you*, Mark?" Hatfield had given his status as host Governor of a Presidential primary state as the reason for his neutrality in the Presidential race. Actually, there is no precedent one way or another covering the question of neutrality by the Governor of a Presidential primary state.

Ordinarily, I undertake nothing of a political character on Sunday. This is the first time I have done it, and I do it now because of what I consider to be the importance of the situation that exists. . . .

It is my conviction that the Republican Party in its 1964 convention will either take actions that will enable the party to provide the leadership the nation needs, or commence the suicidal destruction of the Republican Party as an effective instrument in meeting the nation's needs.

Our situation today is in some respects similar to the situations in the 1850's, when the fundamental underlying trends were leading clearly to crisis, and the nation was beset by a multiplicity of views, including those of an extreme and reactionary character.

After a great deal more of such comment, Romney unleashed a totally unexpected frontal assault on Goldwater. Contending that Goldwater's publicly stated views "do not square with the principles for which the Republican Party stands on the basis of its past record and heritage," Romney declared that he had been unable to get a private audience with the Senator for discussion of these views.

He then made this thinly qualified pledge to try to keep Goldwater from the nomination:

. . . if his [Goldwater's] views are in fact as clearly in variance with the nation's needs and the Republican Party's needs, and if his views deviate as indicated from the heritage of our party, I will do everything within my power to keep him from becoming the party's Presidential candidate, and I fully realize what the odds are on that score too.

In other words, I will devote all of the time I can to persuading Republicans generally and convention delegates to keep from committing themselves irrevocably to particular candidates before the convention opens, so that the Republican Party can put first things first. . . .

Was this at last the sleeping giant of the Republican Party's progressive wing stirring itself, the ghost of Willkie-Dewey-Eisenhower returning?

Hardly. Romney was not equipped by temperament or desire to lead the kind of well-organized campaign of political infighting that would be needed to stop Goldwater. For all the rhetoric contained in his Sunday attack against Goldwater, it should be noted that at no time did he endorse or urge the candidacy of the one man left as an alternative to Goldwater: William W. Scranton. He never did. In fact, his pledge of June 7 to fight Goldwater on the barricades was the last heard from Romney on the national scene until the San Francisco convention. At no time did he give real support to those frantic eleventh-hour efforts to chop away at Goldwater's lead. Once he had clearly disassociated himself from Goldwater, he fell mute.

Meanwhile, while Romney was making his debut as a Sunday politician, Scranton and aides were on their way to a downtown Cleveland television studio for the "Face the Nation" program. It had been a troubled morning. The telephone call showed that he couldn't count on any help from Eisenhower. The breakfast showed that he couldn't count on much help from his fellow Governors. In his pocket was the statement of availability—and the attack on Goldwater—written for him by Keisling. He carried it with him as he sat down in front of the cameras.

The questioning began, and to the amazement of Scranton's aides, the Governor did not read the statement. Instead, he was coming out with rambling, equivocal statements only slightly stronger than the Harrisburg press conference of the previous Thursday:

PAUL NIVEN (CBS correspondent): Gov. Scranton, what is your position with regard to the Republican Presidential nomination?

SCRANTON: Well, I would— I feel very strongly that we should have the type of reaction in this country to the Republican Party that we have had under Lincoln and under Theodore Roosevelt and under Dwight David Eisenhower. And I feel very strongly that in having that image and that reaction that

we can go on and win the election. And I am concerned about
the next six weeks, because I want to make sure that we do
that, and as such I have said that I am available for the nomination, as I gather a number of other people are, and that if
the majority of the delegates at the convention want me, that
I would serve.

ALAN OTTEN (*Wall Street Journal*): Are you saying that
Sen. Goldwater does not fit that image of Lincoln and Eisenhower?

SCRANTON: No, I am not saying that. I am simply saying that
in the last few days particularly there has come to my attention,
by a great number of people, the feeling that perhaps the party
is wedging itself away from those principles—the principles
of equal rights and unlimited opportunity for people; the idea
that this should be fostered and abetted around the world.
And I want to make sure that this does not happen.

Later in the program, when asked by Niven whether he
agreed with the sentiments in Romney's just completed
press conference back at the Sheraton-Cleveland, Scranton
said:

No, I don't think I do. I don't plan to go out and try and
defeat Goldwater. I have no such intention.

Time and again, the interviewers tried to lead Scranton
into an overtly anti-Goldwater statement, but they were
unsuccessful. At the break in the program for a commercial,
Scranton summoned Jack Conmy, his press secretary. He
then gave Conmy the Keisling-written statement—unread.
The ambivalent tone of the program was typified at the end
in one exchange with Otten:

OTTEN: Do you think that as a result of your meeting here
Tuesday morning Sen. Goldwater may satisfy you enough that
you will emerge from that and declare you are now—you are
less available than today?

SCRANTON: I would doubt that—but how would I know until
I am there? My feeling is quite strong on these principles and

on these issues, and also I represent, I hope, the Republican
Party in Pennsylvania, and I think this is my job.

OTTEN: Well, aren't you saying right there that you know
that Sen. Goldwater is not the type of Republican you want?

SCRANTON: No, I am not saying that. And I think you are
putting words in my mouth, sir.

Certainly, Scranton had not possibly embarrased General
Eisenhower as George Humphrey's houseguest. Nobody
could possibly have interpreted his "Face the Nation" performance as the surfacing of an anti-Goldwater cabal led by
Scranton and Eisenhower.

But Black Sunday was not yet over. Back at the Sheraton-
Cleveland, Nelson Rockefeller was up next on the press-
conference line. Bemused, embittered, and practically
conceding the nomination to Goldwater, he swiped at nearly
everybody in the party—but hardest at Scranton:

QUESTION: Gov. Scranton said today that he is available for
the nomination. Would you support Gov. Scranton?

ROCKEFELLER: Gov. Scranton said that he was waiting to see
where Sen. Goldwater stood. And after listening to his press
conference ["Face the Nation"], I think I've got to wait to see
where *he* stands. . . .

QUESTION: If Gov. Romney's rather vigorous position comes
too late, what can be done here that isn't too late?

ROCKEFELLER: Well—

QUESTION: Specifically.

ROCKEFELLER: More *Romneys*.

QUESTION: Are you unsatisfied with Gov. Scranton's presentation today?

ROCKEFELLER: I have no reason to judge. I just watched the
program.

Of course, he and everybody else were "unsatisfied." But
Scranton actually repeated the whole dismal performance.
A 4:30 P.M. press conference had been scheduled for the
hotel in which Scranton would enlarge on his supposedly

strong statement on "Face the Nation." After the fiasco over
television, Scranton and Keisling toyed with the idea of
canceling the press conference, but decided that the reaction
would be worse if they ran away from it. It was a mistake.
Scranton struggled through more than forty-five minutes of
the same mushy, confused, and uncommunicative prose that
he had displayed on nationwide television a few hours
earlier.

Warren Sinsheimer, a young New York lawyer who had
started a national Scranton-for-President movement out of
his own funds in 1963 and had been remarkably successful
in founding Scranton clubs around the country, was broken-
hearted. "I thought I had found another Wendell Willkie,"
he said. "Now I don't know what I have." Scranton's own
aides, usually loyal to a fault, were in the same frame of
mind. At the 4:30 P.M. press conference, the usually ebullient
Craig Truax sat at the rear of the room, a study in blackness.
When the Governor and his staff returned to the suite, Truax
and other aides led a torrent of criticism against the Governor. Then Scranton explained to them for the first time
why he had not read the statement over television. He told
them about the call from Eisenhower.[10]

It was only Sunday night, and the formal opening of the
Governors Conference was not scheduled until Monday
morning. But from the standpoint of Republican Presidential
politics, everyone might just as well have gone home. There
would be no stop-Goldwater movements formed in Cleveland—or anywhere else.

Goldwater himself arrived as the conquering hero to hear
General Eisenhower's speech at the Monday-night banquet.[11]

[10] This story was leaked to the press by the Scranton staff on Sunday
night and appeared in afternoon newspapers on Monday.

[11] Although the invitation to Goldwater to attend the Governors Conference had been arranged by Arizona's Governor Fannin with host Governor
Rhodes of Ohio on Friday, June 5, Goldwater had no desire to attend.
Aides convinced him, however, that he had to go once the invitation had
been announced publicly.

After all the stumbling, feuding liberal Governors, Mr. Conservative—smiling, bronzed, self-assured after his California victory—was a welcome relief. Quite properly, Goldwater flatly rejected Scranton's suggestion that he appear before the sixteenth Republican Governors on Tuesday morning to be grilled by them. Instead, he was whisked in and out of the Sheraton-Cleveland for the banquet—chatting, pleasantly and easily, with Eisenhower, Rockefeller, and Scranton in full view of the public.

There was one faintly ludicrous postscript to the conference. His timing off as it had been all year, Nixon arrived in Cleveland on Tuesday, June 9, after all the fireworks had been fired. He had spent Monday traveling in Michigan as part of a whirlwind pre-San Francisco nationwide tour that was supposed to put him in the public eye as convention time approached. Arriving in Cleveland Monday with Romney (who had returned to Michigan to accompany Nixon), Nixon suddenly changed his tactics. After months of trying to cultivate Goldwater in an effort to get his blessing when the San Francisco convention deadlocked, Nixon now volunteered to lead a stop-Goldwater movement.

After years of silence about Goldwater's views, Nixon fired a broadside attack at the Senator's stands on foreign policy, Social Security, the TVA, "right to work" laws, and civil rights. "Looking to the future of the party," he said, "it would be a tragedy if Senator Goldwater's views as previously stated were not challenged—and repudiated."

How to do it? Even more surprisingly, Nixon now urged Romney to enter as an active candidate. For five months, Nixon had been waiting for a natural deadlock, after which Nixon would be tapped as the natural unity candidate. Now he was trying to rush that process in the span of six weeks. With Rockefeller's chances dead and Scranton apparently uninterested, Romney was the only man to play the role of Nixon's stalking-horse. But Romney refused.

There was one other course: Nixon himself as the candidate. In his chats with the other Governors at Cleveland, Nixon gave the impression that he was exceedingly available. From Cleveland, he placed phone calls all over the country, giving the same impression. The reaction, in Cleveland and over the telephone, was a fat zero.

Dick Nixon had come to the end of the line. After the 1960 Presidential defeat, the loss for the Governorship of California in 1962 (and the postelection diatribe against the press), the move back to New York, and the inability to get a boom going for the Presidential nomination in 1964, it was all over. Cleveland was the dismal last chapter. The cliché of Republican politicians became: "I never knew what they meant when they used to say those things about Nixon. Now I know."

The confusion and ineptitude in Cleveland convinced a good many disbelievers that Mark Hatfield was right: the war *was* over. Hatfield and others who wanted to maintain a semblance of party unity believed that all resistance to Goldwater should cease immediately if the party's moderates were to have any influence at all in Goldwater's campaign— and, if elected, in his administration. Their fear was that continued criticism and opposition to Goldwater would not stop him at this late date, but would strengthen the hand of the more militantly conservative elements in the party who saw Goldwater's nomination not merely as a victory by a conservative, but as a true revolution within the party.

That's why the Hatfield school of thought didn't even want the last disorganized effort that was made in Cleveland. The abortive Cleveland drive certainly did cool off the warm Goldwater-Scranton relationship a bit. At one point during the Cleveland conference, when Scranton aides were complaining that a Goldwater candidacy would turn Pennsylvania over to the Democrats, Dick Kleindienst asked belligerently: "And who needs Pennsylvania?" Other Goldwater aides were telling the Senator that he ought to forget Scranton as a Vice-Presidential possibility and turn to somebody more acceptable to the Goldwater Movement—say, William Miller, who could make as conservative a stump speech as Goldwater if necessary. Goldwater himself reacted with surprising heat to the laughable attempts made against him in Cleveland. On Wednesday, June 10, he told an impromptu press conference just outside the Senate chamber in Washington: "They [the moderate Republicans] seem to be more intent on wrecking the party than on helping to win some elections."[12]

But Goldwater wasn't really all that angry. He had felt out Scranton (without success) as a Vice-Presidential possibility as early as their January meeting in the Senator's apartment.[13] Now, even after Cleveland, Scranton was still his top choice for the Vice-Presidency. Moreover, Goldwater wanted to offer the defeated moderates other olive branches in order to show that his nomination was not the signal for revolution. At this stage of the game, for instance, he had no intention of giving the national party chairmanship to a Goldwater staff man. He would either keep Miller on the job or give it to Ray Bliss, the Ohio state party chairman who was still pointedly staying off the Goldwater bandwagon while Ohio's big delegation remained pledged to Governor Rhodes. At the Governors Conference in Cleveland, Kleindienst implicitly offered Bliss the national chairmanship in return for the Ohio delegation, but no deal was consummated. Goldwater planned to bring old pro Len Hall in for a key campaign job. He was willing to give a little in regard to the party platform. But most important was the Goldwater-Scranton ticket. Just

---

[12] Goldwater devoted most of his fire in that press conference to Nixon, whom he had never cared for much anyway and now had a good excuse to blister. Said Goldwater of Nixon: "He is sounding more and more like Harold Stassen every day."

[13] See page 275.

as John F. Kennedy had instantly achieved party unity by
picking Lyndon B. Johnson in 1960, so Barry Goldwater
could do the same by picking William W. Scranton in 1964.

Considering the facts of life, it is incredible that the
moderates did not throw down their arms after Cleveland
and try to infiltrate—and moderate—the Goldwater camp,
just as Hatfield proposed. They probably would have, save
for one factor: William Scranton suddenly and inexplicably
decided to run—now that all was lost and all was hopeless.
It was not a decision made by the moderates in council assembled, but a personal decision by the Governor of Pennsylvania.

Why? Or, more properly, why *now?* In the five days between Black Sunday in Cleveland and Scranton's announcement of candidacy, the only event of interest was Goldwater's
vote against closing off debate on the civil rights bill. But
Scranton had said flatly in Cleveland that Goldwater's vote
on the bill would not be enough to change his mind about
running.[14]

Actually, he began to change his mind that Sunday night.
Mary Scranton, sitting in their suite at the Sheraton-Cleve-
land with a highball and a bag of knitting, was boiling mad.
Now she wanted him to run and to win. Moreover, the
Governor himself had faced humiliation for probably the
first time in his life. He didn't like playing the fool.

In a June 17 dispatch in the *New York Times,* Joseph A.
Luftus gave this play-by-play account (based largely on interviews with Governor and Mrs. Scranton) of what happened in Cleveland later—on Tuesday night, June 9:

> The Governor, wearing shorts and a towel, appeared in the
> doorway and light-heartedly called:
> "Hey, I have an idea. Why don't I run?" . . .

[14] On the "Face the Nation" show of June 7, Scranton said: "I don't
think one bill makes the difference between how a man stands on a whole
issue."

Alone in their room that night, Mrs. Scranton said to her husband:

"Bill, I think you better run."

But no decision was made then and there. Scranton was still brooding over the matter when they returned to Harrisburg on Wednesday. At one point, an aide told him: "There are two things you can do, Governor. You can live with it the rest of your life. Or you can run for President."

There were two more calls from General Eisenhower, trying to clear up the confusion of the previous weekend. The General was not at all discouraging this time, but neither Scranton nor his aides were about to make any announcement of it. But no decision had been made by Thursday, June 11. According to Loftus' account in the *Times:*

> "Mary came to see me in the office on Thursday," [Scranton] said. The visit was brief. "We don't have to converse at length. I know when something is bothering her."
>
> Mrs. Scranton recalled that she went to her husband's office to clarify some things that were on her mind.
>
> "I wanted to be sure his decision was made on the basis of the actual situation and not wishful thinking," she said, continuing:
>
> "It appeared to me he had done a great deal of thinking and was ready to move."

The move came at 2 P.M. on Thursday. Scranton ordered Craig Truax to make a quick telephone check of all Pennsylvania counties to get their assessment of the political impact of a Goldwater candidacy and to have it ready for a 5 P.M. meeting at the Governor's mansion in Indiantown Gap, Pennsylvania, to be attended by all state party leaders. The county reports spelled out disaster in state and local elections if Goldwater were the candidate. By 8 P.M., the decision was firm. Scranton would run.

The announcement was made Friday, June 12, in Baltimore, during a hastily arranged appearance by Scranton be-

fore the Maryland State Republican Convention. Gone were
the mushy phrases of Cleveland. Contending that "we are going to San Francisco to hold a convention, not a coronation,"
Scranton declared to the cheering Marylanders (and some
booing Goldwaterites in the balcony):

> The Republican Party is in danger. And some say our country
> may be too. We could send down to defeat good men and good
> women who stand ready to carry our banner in the several
> states. We could take the responsibility, the reason, the Lincoln,
> the heart and the soul—all of these things we could take out of
> our party. We will do so if we let an exclusion-minded minority
> dominate our platform and choose our candidates.
>
> But we have a choice. And that is why I come here today. I
> have come to offer our party a choice. I reject the echo we have
> thus far been handed—the echo of fear, of reaction—the echo
> from the never-never land that puts our nation on the road
> backward to a lesser place in the world of free men.
>
> I come here to announce I am a candidate for the Presidency
> of the United States.

At long last (and pathetically late), the deed was done.
Now there would be a contested—at least, nominally contested—convention—the first in twelve years. But all hopes
for party unity were gone.

XXIII

★ ★ ★ ★ ★ ★ ★ ★ ★ ★ ★ ★ ★ ★ ★ ★ ★ ★ ★ ★

San Francisco

The first (and supposedly routine) session of the 1964 Republican National Convention was gaveled to order at 10:35 A.M. on Monday, July 13, at the San Francisco Cow Palace. Less than two hours later, the convention had its first fight—not a very good fight, but a typical one for this convention. Newton Steers, the new Maryland party chairman and a Scranton man, rose to offer a resolution that would bar any delegations that had denied anybody a seat on the delegation for reasons of race—a move that would effectively exclude Goldwater's lily-white delegations from the South.

The rule was the brainchild of the Scranton staff. They hoped that the Republican National Convention might be loath to vote for racial segregation and would thereby give Scranton a quick opening victory, possibly turning the tide against Goldwater. Considerably less naïve, Rockefeller's staff—now working in tandem with the Scranton staff—advised against the move and suggested that all emphasis should be placed on the Tuesday-night platform fight. But the Scranton forces persisted in the hope that the resolution might split Goldwater forces.

As soon as Steers mounted the rostrum to argue for his resolution, there was activity in an unmarked—but well-guarded—trailer parked just outside the Cow Palace. This was the nerve center for the Goldwater convention operations, under the command of F. Clifton White. Admission

439

to the Goldwater trailer was strictly limited to men wearing a special golden eagle in the coat lapel (in contrast to the Scranton trailer not far away, where a Goldwater agent was usually wandering inside). Inside the Goldwater trailer were Clif White and his regional directors—each regional director seated at a telephone console hooked up with key delegations in their region, White seated at a master console hooked into some thirty telephones on the convention floor. Besides this, White had at his disposal an elaborate walkie-talkie system of radio communications—with three separate bands of communications to guard against jamming. Television technicians wondered how Goldwater's walkie-talkies could wander so far from the Cow Palace and still maintain contact with the convention floor. The reason was simple: White had somehow managed to stick an aerial on the very top of the Cow Palace roof, an advantage denied to the television stations—and to Scranton, for that matter. White, a master and a veteran of convention warfare, had arranged all this during a week-long trip to San Francisco back in April, when Scranton was debating with himself whether to make a Sherman-like statement about the Presidency.

White's communications system was geared to a tough, close convention floor fight. Considering the amount of artillery that the Scranton forces could bring up, it was a classic case of overkill—certainly overkill considering the pitiful strength behind the Steers resolution. White quickly flashed the word on the Steers resolution: "Vote no." Senator Carl Curtis of Nebraska, Goldwater's floor manager (with Dean Burch sitting by his side in the Nebraska delegation), was assigned to make the speech opposing the Steers resolution.

After a thirteen-minute speech by Steers, Curtis took the rostrum with the benevolent smile of a man who has the votes. He told the delegates: "You are the salt of the earth. You are the hope of mankind." The delegates cheered. He next said that "there is no need" for the Steers amendment. Six minutes later, he sat down.

The Steers resolution was defeated by an overwhelmingly unfavorable voice vote. In the Pennsylvania delegation, Walter Alessandroni was shouting frantically in an effort to get a roll-call vote. William Miller, presiding over the convention's first session as Republican national chairman, overlooked him. Alessandroni had failed to check in advance to make sure that he could get a roll call. It didn't make much difference, though. The Steers resolution would have been badly beaten on a roll call anyway.

The incident was the first, soon-to-be-forgotten skirmish of the convention. But it tells the full story. Goldwater outnumbered, outorganized, and outmaneuvered Scranton. The Goldwater camp was resolute, disciplined, and monolithic. The Scranton camp was divided, vague, and disorganized. The issue never was in doubt.

Of course, the issue never really was in doubt before San Francisco. If that last month of frantic cross-country campaigning by Scranton changed anything, it made Goldwater's lead a little larger—by showing clearly to party leaders that Scranton was going nowhere.

Soon after announcing his availability, Scranton got a pleasant surprise. The polls showed that Bill Scranton, struggling around the 5 percent point in the national ratings all year, now was getting about as many votes in the Gallup Poll as anybody else. The Gallup Poll of June 28 (here compared with the June 6 poll) showed a virtual dead heat between the four leading candidates (the figures are percentages):

	June 28	June 6
Goldwater	22	21
Nixon	22	25
Lodge	19	26
Scranton	18	9
Rockefeller	8	10
Others, no position	11	9

But that same June 28 Gallup Poll showed a startling result when it paired Scranton against Goldwater in a head-on race. The result:

	Percent
Scranton	55
Goldwater	34
Undecided	11

In other words, Scranton seemed able to do what Rockefeller had been unable to do in California: coalesce that stubborn Lodge and Nixon vote into a winning moderate Republican total.

Indeed, as Scranton's whirlwind campaign began on June 12, the moderate Republicans were better unified than they had been at any other time during the year. On June 15, Rockefeller pulled out of the long, exhausting, expensive race for the Presidency and endorsed Scranton. It was much more than just an endorsement. With the bitterness and cynicism that he had displayed at Cleveland apparently worked out of his system, Rockefeller donated his entire nationwide professional organization to Scranton for the balance of the campaign—with Rockefeller still picking up the tab. It was an act of unselfishness not often seen in politics. Eight days later, Lodge resigned as Ambassador to South Vietnam to return to the United States to campaign for Scranton. Here and there, members of the old Eisenhower team were lining up for Scranton—including Dr. Milton Eisenhower, who agreed to place Scranton's name in nomination at San Francisco (and was hurriedly given a seat on the pro-Scranton delegation).[1]

But even in the face of certain Goldwater victory (or perhaps *because* of its certainty), the non-Goldwater wing of

[1] The Goldwater Movement's diehards in Maryland were ready to challenge the unquestionably irregular procedures used to give Milton Eisenhower a seat on the delegation, but were stopped by Goldwater headquarters in Washington. Goldwater strategists wanted no floor fight over the seating of a man named Eisenhower.

the party was not really united. General Eisenhower was doggedly neutral (withstanding entreaties from his old lieutenant Henry Cabot Lodge to try to get him to make the nominating speech for Scranton). His dreams of a second shot at the Presidency shattered, Nixon was primly neutral once more. In Michigan, Romney was back in lone-wolf obscurity after his blazing performance in Cleveland.

Moreover, the old pros from the Eastern Establishment who had been so anxious to work for Scranton in January— the political trio of Len Hall, Meade Alcorn, and Fred Scribner—had other fish to fry in June. Hall said that he had promised Goldwater that he would back no candidate prior to the nomination. Alcorn said that he was busy as a special political commentator for CBS. Scribner said that he scarcely could manage the campaign of a candidate while still serving as general counsel of the Republican National Committee. It just proved that nobody loves a loser.

The fact is that the Scranton campaign badly needed a general manager. Walter Alessandroni acted more or less as Scranton's chief of staff, but lines of command in that confused campaign were indistinct. Senator Hugh Scott of Pennsylvania, for instance, was out of the regular chain of command in his dual role as convention floor manager and Scranton's representative on the platform committee, ranking neither above nor below Alessandroni. Nor did the marriage of the Scranton and Rockefeller staffs mesh too well. Scranton staffers feared that Rockefeller veterans George Hinman and Jack Wells were trying to take over the whole show. The Rockefeller staffers looked down on Alessandroni, Keisling, Truax, and company as a bunch of neophytes unskilled in running a national political campaign.

But the lack of an old pro field general and the internal disarray were only incidental problems for the Scranton campaign. Its real problem was much more serious.

Goldwater had more than the 655 votes needed to get

nominated. Moreover, there seemed to be no way to get enough delegates away from him to push him below the 655 mark. About four hundred of his delegates came straight out of the Goldwater Movement and were cemented to their leader in a manner that no human force could break. Another three hundred to four hundred delegates were by no means so solidly for Goldwater, but took the position that, at this late date, after the win in California, to stop Goldwater would be to risk a mass revolution of workers at the grass roots of the Republican Party. This is the year of the conservative, they reasoned. Why not let him have it and get on the bandwagon?

The full details were spelled out in a secret meeting at Rockefeller's New York City campaign headquarters on June 16, the day after Rockefeller endorsed Scranton. Rockefeller fieldmen were called in from all parts of the country. Representing Scranton were Bill Murphy, his secretary; and George Bloom, former Pennsylvania state chairman and now Secretary of the Commonwealth in Scranton's cabinet.

The bad news for Scranton: Goldwater had better than six hundred delegates and was picking up more every day. Of these six hundred plus, no more than one hundred offered even the most remote chance of being pulled away from Goldwater. That wasn't the half of it. The only thing that was keeping Goldwater from hitting the eight-hundred mark was the favorite sons. If Governor James Rhodes of Ohio and Representative John Byrnes of Wisconsin were to drop out, Goldwater would be the winner by some 200 votes over the 655 needed. In fact, if Rockefeller released his own delegates in New York and Oregon, a good many of them would go to Goldwater. Hence, it was decided that Rockefeller's name would be placed before the convention after all, just to keep votes away from Goldwater.

It was just now becoming clear to the moderates that hundreds of these Goldwater delegates had fought their way to San Francisco through precinct mass meetings, through county conventions, through state conventions—and all for one purpose. "They came here to vote for Barry Goldwater," Clif White was fond of saying.

More die-hard delegates were picked in June as the convention neared. Washington, twenty-one of twenty-four; Colorado, fourteen out of eighteen; New Mexico, fourteen out of fourteen; Montana, fourteen out of fourteen; Texas, fifty-six out of fifty-six.

Only the Minnesota state convention on June 12 broke the chain of Goldwater victories. Here, by a slender margin of 60 votes, the Goldwater slate of at-large delegates was defeated. But Scranton had nothing to do with it. The non-Goldwater delegates were pledged to former Representative Walter Judd, keynoter of the 1960 Republican National Convention, as Minnesota's favorite son. It was a clever move by the anti-Goldwater forces in Minnesota, helped by the failure of the national Goldwater strategists to come to some agreement with Dr. Judd (a thoroughgoing conservative and friend of Goldwater). The truth is that Goldwater would have beaten Scranton or anybody else but Judd on June 12 on that convention floor in St. Paul.[2] Minnesota conservatives just didn't like the idea of voting against Walter Judd.

Faced with the fact that Goldwater's delegate total grew a little every day and that attempting to chisel away Goldwater delegates one at a time was an exercise in futility, Scranton drifted into what amounted to a three-part strategy:

1. Concentrate on cracking one strategic Goldwater state that would have a psychological impact of nationwide proportions. The state: Illinois (fifty-eight delegates).

[2] In fact, the anti-Goldwater forces in Minnesota were afraid that the announcement of Scranton's candidacy in Baltimore just before the balloting in St. Paul might upset their strategy. They had been urging Goldwater delegates at St. Paul to back Judd on the grounds that Goldwater was a cinch to be nominated anyway without any real competition.

2. Keep the favorite son delegations—notably Ohio (fifty-eight delegates) and Wisconsin (thirty delegates).

3. Try for some kind of national "incident" that would transform the mood of the San Francisco convention.

Making Illinois a target was natural enough. This was the keystone of Goldwater strength north of the Mason-Dixon Line. The most conservative estimate gave Goldwater forty of the fifty-eight delegates, and he probably would wind up with closer to fifty-two. Consequently, Scranton reasoned that if the Illinois delegation could be neutralized, it might mean the beginning of the end for Goldwater.

He had two causes for hope in Illinois. One was Charles M. Percy, the liberal-leaning young candidate for Governor who had talked politics on the warmest of terms with Scranton on June 2, when the Governor was in Chicago for a speech. The other was Senator Everett McKinley Dirksen, hero of the civil rights fight and a principal author of the civil rights bill that Goldwater had opposed and denounced as unconstitutional.

Actually, neither Percy nor Dirksen was much cause for hope. Percy was powerless in the Illinois delegation. Militant Goldwaterites, still fighting their April 14 primary battle against Percy, blocked a move to make him delegation cochairman with Dirksen (despite Dirksen's support for the cochairman plan).[3] Moreover, state party leaders warned Percy that they would emasculate him in the general-election campaign if they caught him flirting with Scranton. Dirksen was more the master of his own fate than Percy, but he was far less inclined toward Scranton. The flexible old fox of the Senate had survived for twenty-five years by never becoming too closely identified with any single faction or any single cause. Of late, he had been under heavy attack from the Goldwater Movement, the *Chicago Tribune*, and party workers for his support of the United Nations, civil rights, the

[3] See page 360.

test-ban treaty, and foreign aid—on the opposite side from Goldwater on each issue. It was time to move a bit rightward, and Goldwater was the proper vehicle. Dirksen might have preferred Nixon, but he most certainly could live with Goldwater—civil rights bill or no civil rights bill. Goldwater was under no illusions. "That old boy's got an antenna three feet long," Goldwater told friends. "He knows where the winner is."

But, like so many other eager young men, Scranton completely misunderstood crafty old Dirksen. On a June 22 visit to Washington, the Governor asked Dirksen to become a favorite son candidate—to hold Illinois in check as Rhodes was holding Ohio and Byrnes was holding Wisconsin. Scranton and his staff really thought they had a fair chance of getting a yes from Dirksen. They didn't understand that Dirksen could not control the Illinois delegation. They didn't understand that Dirksen had no particular affection for Scranton (whom he privately considered an upstart and an unknown). And they didn't understand that Dirksen felt no particular contempt for Goldwater (though no particular admiration either). Dirksen's answer to Scranton was a grunt.

The climax in Illinois came on Tuesday, June 30. The fifty-eight Illinois delegates assembled in Chicago at O'Hare Inn —the scene of many secret national Goldwater huddles over the past two years. Both Barry Goldwater and Bill Scranton were on hand to address the delegation. It was face-to-face combat, with an immediate prize—and immense publicity— to the winner. The delegation would be polled as soon as the two candidates left. Apparent to almost everybody but Scranton and his staff, Scranton had walked into a trap. The vote was forty-eight delegates for Goldwater (including Dirksen and Percy), eight uncommitted, and two refusing to disclose their preference.[4] It was a disastrous whitewash for Scranton

[4] A good many of the people around Scranton considered this a double cross by Percy, but Percy actually had no choice. He had promised during his primary campaign to abide by the wishes of a majority of the Illinois delegation.

and a splendid preconvention gift for Goldwater. Dirksen put the frosting on the cake in Washington the next day by announcing that he would place Goldwater's name in nomination at the convention (climaxing a quiet but earnest courtship of Dirksen by Goldwater).[5]

Still, optimists in the Scranton camp grasped at a shred of hope as long as the favorite sons from Ohio and Wisconsin kept their delegations away from Goldwater. If they did, Scranton still had a chance, they argued. During the maneuvers within the platform committee the week before the convention, Senator Hugh Scott (acting as Scranton's agent) deferred to the wishes of Representative Melvin Laird of Wisconsin, the committee chairman, on more than one occasion in an effort to keep Wisconsin away from Goldwater.

The bombshell fell on Thursday, July 9, just four days before the convening of the convention. In Columbus, Ohio, Governor Rhodes released the delegation from its favorite son commitment—with 42 of Ohio's 58 votes immediately going to Goldwater. What's more, Goldwater had a fighting chance at grabbing every Ohio delegate except one, a Negro. Craig Truax, an incurable optimist, admitted now to friends that it was hopeless.[6]

It was a surprise to Truax and Scranton, but also to Ray Bliss, the Ohio state chairman. Rhodes had not given the prestigious Bliss the slightest advance warning of his move. Indeed, Rhodes was declaring to Bliss that James Rhodes was now Mr. Republican of Ohio. When Rhodes arrived in San Francisco the next night, Scranton asked to have a chat with him.

---

[5] However, the Scranton campaign still couldn't get out of its mind the idea that Illinois was fertile country. Scranton made another visit to the state just before the convention, leading to the ridiculous situation in which Scranton was shaking hands in Chicago suburban shopping centers while the Illinois delegation was on its way to San Francisco. This did not raise the general confidence in the Scranton campaign within the party.

[6] When Ohio fell, it was assumed that Byrnes would then deliver Wisconsin to Goldwater. He did, but it wasn't announced until July 15, the day of the balloting.

They met alone in Scranton's suite at the Mark Hopkins Hotel. In view of Rhodes' past position that Goldwater on the ticket would mean Republican disaster in Ohio, why did he now make the move that washed away the last practical island of anti-Goldwater resistance? Rhodes replied that he had changed his mind, that he now was convinced that Goldwater would run well in Ohio—partly because of the white backlash against the Negro revolution in such industrial centers as Youngstown and Cleveland.[7]

There was a bit more to Rhodes' conversion than this. While Dick Kleindienst had been wooing Bliss without success for six months, Clif White had been somewhat more successful in sweet-talking Rhodes. More important, some of Rhodes's sources of campaign funds had been prodding him about Goldwater. Never a man to buck a tide or swim upstream, Rhodes decided to go along with the man who was the sure winner anyway.

The loss of Illinois and Ohio opened the flood gates. Just before the convention opened, Clif White coaxed Tom Fairfield Brown, the Florida state party chairman, and Florida's 34 votes back into the Goldwater fold—even though Brown still wouldn't talk to John Grenier, Goldwater's Southern director, who had tried to beat Brown's slate in the May 26 Florida primary but failed.

All that now was left for Scranton was his third tactic: some kind of "incident" that would miraculously change the mood in San Francisco. He was game to try it.

Just what kind of "incident" the Scranton camp wanted to create is murky. They wistfully looked back to the disputed Southern-delegation fight of 1952 that ensured the nomination for Eisenhower, though, of course, the situation in 1964 was not even roughly similar. The mood was brilliantly cap-

[7] Rhodes was furious when he found out that Scranton had related this conversation to a well-attended Scranton strategy session.

tured by Murray Kempton in an article for *The New Republic* comparing the convention with Anton Chekhov's *The Cherry Orchard*.[8] Kempton wrote:

> . . . before the play had opened in San Francisco, Lopahin, the practical man, played by Senator Scott of Pennsylvania, had protested: ". . . Such odd, unbusinesslike people I never saw. You are told in plain Russian that your estate is about to be sold up and you just don't seem to take it in."
>
> Gayeff, the hereditary proprietor, played perforce by William Scranton, speaks:
>
> "Tomorrow I must go to town. They have promised to introduce me to a certain general who might make us a loan."
>
> Lyuboff Andreevna, his sister, in her one line by Nelson Rockefeller:
>
> "He's just raving. There aren't such generals."

Incredible though it may seem, the Scranton camp was still praying and hoping for help from "a certain general." Though Eisenhower had made it clear that he would not deviate an inch from neutrality, there was still hope that he might lend a helping hand.

If he couldn't actually endorse Scranton, at least Eisenhower's help would be useful in the platform fight. A group of anti-Goldwater members of the platform committee visited the General in his suite at the St. Francis Hotel in San Francisco in hopes of getting his support for some platform planks that would be offered on the convention floor. When they left, they had the impression that Eisenhower would back the changes if asked about them at his press conference the next day. But Mel Laird of Wisconsin, the platform committee chairman, saw the General next and talked him into backing the platform without change. Watching the Eisenhower press conference over television, the anti-Goldwater platform committee members who had visited the General were amazed to

[8] Murray Kempton, "They Got Him," *The New Republic*, July 25, 1964.

hear him oppose any changes in the platform as written by Laird's committee.

If not help from the General, Scranton's hoped-for "incident" seemed to be one dramatic event that would reverse the existing trend. Most of the talk centered around the platform. If only Scranton forces could win a fight on one plank, then that just might be the "incident" that was needed.

Senator Scott had gotten nowhere inside the platform committee. The tough, imperturbable Laird was not exactly an original Goldwater man (though not an anti-Goldwater man either). But he was going to make sure that the convention adopted a platform that Barry Goldwater, the certain nominee, could run on. That meant a platform far to the right of recent ones. In full control of the committee, Laird smashed all attempts by the Scranton forces to put anti-Goldwater material in the platform. Representing Goldwater in the closed-door fight was pint-size, shrewd Senator John Tower, shuttling back and forth from the all-night platform sessions in the St. Francis Hotel up Nob Hill to Goldwater headquarters in the Mark Hopkins. At one point when it seemed that the committee was about to adopt a plank pledging immediate "enforcement" of the civil rights act, Tower quietly demurred. The word "enforcement" had unfortunate connotations in the South and ought to be avoided, Tower said quietly. Not wanting to put any roadblocks in the way of Goldwater's Southern strategy, the committee quickly changed "enforcement" to "faithful execution" (lifted right from the President's oath prescribed in the Constitution). Most of the time, however, Tower did not have to intervene.

The real fight came after the Goldwater-style platform, the party's most conservative since 1936, came out of committee. After innumerable strategy sessions, the Scranton forces decided to make a floor fight on three points: (1) a plank condemning extremist groups, with the Communist, Ku Klux Klan, and John Birch Society mentioned by name;

(2) a tougher civil rights plank; and (3) a plank asserting that only the President could prescribe the use of nuclear weapons (a direct slap at Goldwater).

There was an air of unreality about it all. Anybody who could and bothered to count knew that there was not a chance for any of these planks to be approved. But there pervaded a crazy sort of optimism in the anti-Goldwater camp. Take the case of Henry Cabot Lodge, who participated in most of the Scranton strategy sessions at San Francisco. "I can assure you that a Republican National Convention could never vote against a strong civil rights plank on a roll-call vote, particularly not on television," he would say. His time had past. The Goldwater convention could and did.

Besides the air of unreality in Scranton's platform strategy, there was a divided camp. At the last minute, Romney—ever the lone wolf—pulled out of the moderate coalition and offered his own planks on extremism and civil rights (delivering an antiextremist speech that constituted the only memorable public speaking of the entire convention).

Tuesday night, July 14, was platform night—an endless evening interspersing utter boredom with moments close to high drama. It was a marathon session lasting eight hours and eight minutes. The convention officials had insisted that General Eisenhower deliver his speech before the platform was debated. Then Laird insisted that the platform be read in full, a procedure requiring some two hours. By the time that the platform was read and Nelson Rockefeller stepped to the rostrum to begin the platform fight, it was 8:54 P.M. in San Francisco—11:54 P.M. for East Coast viewers, most of whom missed the next four hours of internal Republican warfare.

Rockefeller's speech not only was the dramatic high point of the convention, but also brought forth the truest distillation of this convention's spirit: tough, intransigent, abrasive. Rockefeller had barely started denouncing the John Birch

Society, in his speech calling for adoption of the antiextremist plank, when the booing began. Rockefeller could scarcely complete a sentence without being interrupted by a volley of boos. In the Goldwater command post outside the Cow Palace, Clif White hurriedly notified all points to stop the booing. However, only a tiny fraction of the booing was coming from the Goldwater delegates on the floor. Almost all of it was from the spectator galleries. Here were the rank and file of the Goldwater Movement. This was their day, and they weren't going to let Nelson Rockefeller spoil it for them.

But there was an affinity on the part of some Goldwater delegates on the floor for the Goldwater supporters in the balconies. One alternate delegate from Louisiana nudged his neighbor, pointed to the spectators booing Nelson Rockefeller, and said approvingly, "Look at that; it's America up there."

It was a part of America that was tired of the welfare state, of high taxes, of big government, of Communist successes abroad, and—most of all, or so it seemed—of the East Coast. These were the political have-nots (though by no means were they economic have-nots) in revolt against the political haves. Even before they booed Rockefeller, there was a strong smell of the mood earlier that Tuesday night when General Eisenhower denounced "sensation-seeking columnists and commentators." The General was amazed to hear the animal-like roar of approval from both the floor and the galleries. Delegate and spectator alike shook their fists in a spirit of revolt against the broadcast booths and press stands, symbols to them of the Eastern Establishment yoke that they were throwing off at the Cow Palace.

In fact, the East was an ideological island in this convention. Goldwater forces and pro-Goldwater forces were in command almost everywhere else. Of course, all the platform proposals were defeated—the Scranton civil rights plank in an 897 to 409 roll-call vote, the rest by voice votes.

The discipline of the Goldwater forces was impressive. Clif White recognized that to concede on any of these issues would be immediately interpreted as an admission of Goldwater's weakness and a great victory for Scranton. It was therefore necessary to apply the full force of the Goldwater strength against all of them, even though Romney's anti-extremist plank (which merely condemned extremists without mentioning the Birchers or any other group) probably would have passed the convention in a free vote.

Just before the vote was to be taken on the Romney plank, W. Y. (Billy) Walter, Republican state chairman of Washington and chairman of the pro-Goldwater Washington delegation, motioned a Goldwater walkie-talkie man to come over. "Hey," said Walter, "ask Steve Shadegg why we can't vote for this thing. We want to." The message was duly relayed to Steve Shadegg, the Western states regional director, who was manning his regional telephone console in the Goldwater command trailer. The cryptic reply from Shadegg: "The Senator has his own good reasons for opposing this." The Washington delegation went along.

The platform fight was not Scranton's only search for an "incident." Both Scranton and Lodge made much of the flood of mail and telegrams backing Scranton, feeling that it would help him as it had Willkie in 1940 and Eisenhower in 1952. In fact, it made no impact whatever.

Scranton really believed that his hour-long appearance on "Meet the Press" (Goldwater had accepted an invitation, then canceled his appearance) on the Sunday before the convention began might be the catalytic agent. In fact, it wasn't.

Scranton strategists thought that a nationwide reaction might result from a June 30 Goldwater interview with *Der Spiegel*, a German news magazine, in which the Senator went back to his old barracks bull-session habits of talking about nuclear weapons. In fact, the interview was but a passing flurry for a few days before the convention.

The search for the "incident" was becoming desperate. After conferring with Lodge and Rockefeller, Scranton decided upon a final gimmick: a challenge to debate Goldwater before the convention itself. It was unprecedented and a trifle absurd. Anyway, there was not the slightest chance of an acceptance by Goldwater, who had spent all year rejecting challenges for conventional debates from Rockefeller and later from Scranton. But Scranton seemed to take this final challenge seriously. On Sunday, July 12, the eve of the convention, he ordered his staff to send a letter to Goldwater goading him into the debate. It was a fateful move that removed the possibility of any reconciliation in San Francisco.

From a powder-puff start on June 12 in Baltimore, when he didn't even mention Goldwater by name, Scranton had steadily escalated his attacks on Goldwater as his own condition became more desperate. At first, he had even held back some polls that showed that Goldwater would be beaten badly by President Johnson in traditionally Republican heartland, but soon he released them to the press. By the last week of June, he was attacking the Senator without restraint.

On Goldwater's vote against the civil rights bill: "When you arouse emotions in that very vital and human field, it can create disruptive disorders, even violence, which we all want to avoid."

On Goldwater's foreign-policy positions: ". . . isn't he playing the warmongers' game when he proposes authorizing field commanders to use tactical nuclear weapons on their own initiative, when he suggests sending the Marines to capture Guantanamo water supply? These are reckless proposals. . . ."

On the sale of TVA: "I cannot ascribe these views of my opponent, all placed firmly on record, to malice. He is not that kind of man. I think ignorance must be the explanation."

But that letter of July 12 established a new level of vituperation. A bone-tired Bill Keisling banged it out on his typewriter. A weary Walter Alessandroni hastily approved it. A busy Bill Scranton never even saw it.[9] The letter's tone was aptly described by another Scranton staffer as "more bellicose than moral." It is the kind of political letter that ought never to be written. It began on a note of shrill outrage:

> . . . Will the convention choose the candidate overwhelmingly favored by the Republican voters, or will it choose you?
>
> Your organization does not even argue the merits of the question. They admit that you are a minority candidate, but they feel they have bought, beaten and compromised enough delegate support to make the result a foregone conclusion.
>
> With open contempt for the dignity, integrity and common sense of the convention, your managers say in effect that the delegates are little more than a flock of chickens whose necks will be wrung at will. . . .

Next, the letter picks up steam with this indictment of Goldwater:

> You have too often casually prescribed nuclear war as a solution to a troubled world.
>
> You have too often allowed the radical extremists to use you.
>
> You have too often stood for irresponsibility in the serious question of racial holocaust.
>
> You have too often read Taft and Eisenhower and Lincoln out of the Republican Party.

The letter then moves on to talk of "ill-advised efforts to make us stand for Goldwaterism instead of Republicanism," adding:

> Goldwaterism has come to stand for nuclear irresponsibility.

[9] Scranton broke the politicians' code when, during a CBS interview the next day, he disclosed that he had neither seen nor signed the famous letter and that he regarded its contents as "too strong." The fact that in this same interview he assumed "full responsibility" for the contents of the letter did not atone for his failure to play the game as it should be played among big-league politicians.

Goldwaterism has come to stand for keeping the name of Eisenhower out of our platform.[10]

Goldwaterism has come to stand for being afraid to forthrightly condemn right-wing extremists.

Goldwaterism has come to stand for refusing to stand for law and order in maintaining racial peace.

In short, Goldwaterism has come to stand for a whole crazy-quilt collection of absurd and dangerous positions that would be soundly repudiated by the American people in November.

Finally, the letter got around to challenging Goldwater to debate before the convention.

Reading the letter with unbelieving eyes, Goldwater was understandably enraged. He returned it to Scranton without an answer, but first copied it and sent a copy to every delegate to the convention—accompanied by this letter: "I am attaching a copy of a letter I received today from Governor Scranton. I consider it an insult to every Republican in San Francisco."

The last hope for a Goldwater-Scranton *rapprochement* was gone.

The long road stretching from the Chicago convention in 1960 entered its final turn at the Cow Palace on Wednesday night, July 15. After nearly seven hours of insanely long nominating and seconding speeches for no less than eight candidates, the balloting began at 10:14 P.M. (1:14 A.M. Thursday on the East Coast). Just twenty-four minutes later, Barry Goldwater received vote 655—fittingly from South Carolina. Six minutes later, the roll call was over, with these results:

Alabama (20)—Goldwater, 20

Alaska (12)—Scranton, 8; Mrs. Smith, 2; Senator Hiram Fong of Hawaii, 1; former Representative Walter Judd of Minnesota, 1

Arizona (16)—Goldwater, 16

[10] This refers to an abortive effort by Southern Goldwater diehards inside the platform committee to keep Eisenhower's name out of the platform.

Arkansas (12)—Goldwater, 9; Scranton, 2; Rockefeller, 1
California (86)—Goldwater, 86
Colorado (18)—Goldwater, 15; Scranton, 3
Connecticut (16)—Goldwater, 4; Scranton, 12
Delaware (12)—Goldwater, 7; Scranton, 5
Florida (34)—Goldwater, 32; Scranton, 2
Georgia (24)—Goldwater, 22; Scranton, 2
Hawaii (8)—Goldwater, 4; Fong, 4
Idaho (14)—Goldwater, 14
Illinois (58)—Goldwater, 56; Rockefeller, 2
Indiana (32)—Goldwater, 32
Iowa (24)—Goldwater, 14; Scranton, 10
Kansas (20)—Goldwater, 18; Scranton, 1; Romney, 1
Kentucky (24)—Goldwater, 21; Scranton, 3
Louisiana (20)—Goldwater, 20
Maine (14)—Mrs. Smith, 14
Maryland (20)—Goldwater, 6; Scranton, 13; Rockefeller, 1
Massachusetts (34)—Goldwater, 5; Scranton, 26; Mrs. Smith,
    1; Lodge, 2
Michigan (48)—Goldwater, 8; Romney, 40
Minnesota (26)—Goldwater, 8; Judd, 18
Mississippi (13)—Goldwater, 13
Missouri (24)—Goldwater, 23; Scranton, 1
Montana (14)—Goldwater, 14
Nebraska (16)—Goldwater, 16
Nevada (6)—Goldwater, 6
New Hampshire (14)—Scranton, 14
New Jersey (40)—Goldwater, 20; Scranton, 20[11]
New Mexico (14)—Goldwater, 14
New York (92)—Goldwater, 5; Rockefeller 87
North Carolina (26)—Goldwater, 26
North Dakota (14)—Goldwater, 7; Rockefeller, 1; Mrs. Smith,
    3; Judd, 3
Ohio (58)—Goldwater, 57; Mrs. Smith, 1
Oklahoma (22)—Goldwater, 22

[11] Actually, Goldwater had only about 10 sure votes in New Jersey. However, Scranton forces agreed to record the delegation 20 to 20 on the Presidential tally Wednesday night in return for a 40 to 0 vote in favor of the Scranton civil rights plank on Tuesday night.

Oregon (18)—Rockefeller, 18
Pennsylvania (64)—Goldwater, 4; Scranton, 60
Rhode Island (14)—Goldwater, 3; Scranton, 11
South Carolina (16)—Goldwater, 16
South Dakota (14)—Goldwater, 12; Scranton, 2
Tennessee (28)—Goldwater, 28
Texas (56)—Goldwater, 56
Utah (14)—Goldwater, 14
Vermont (12)—Goldwater, 3; Scranton, 2; Rockefeller, 2; Mrs. Smith, 5
Virginia (30)—Goldwater, 29; Scranton, 1
Washington (24)—Goldwater, 22; Scranton, 1; Mrs. Smith, 1
West Virginia (14)—Goldwater, 10; Scranton, 2; Rockefeller, 2
Wisconsin (30)—Goldwater, 30
Wyoming (12)—Goldwater, 12
District of Columbia (9)—Goldwater, 4; Scranton, 5
Puerto Rico (5)—Scranton, 5
Virgin Islands (3)—Scranton, 3
Total (1,308)—Goldwater, 883; Scranton, 214; Rockefeller, 114; Romney, 41; Mrs. Smith, 27; Judd, 22; Fong, 5; Lodge, 2[12]

Scranton had arrived at the Cow Palace at nine o'clock, more than an hour before the balloting started, with the intent of offering a motion to make the nomination unanimous—plus delivering a unanimity speech. It was a graceful, well-done job under difficult circumstances. He called attention to Goldwater's speech at Chicago in 1960, when he quelled the anti-Nixon conservative revolt and paraphrased Goldwater's words:

> Some of us did not prevail at this convention, but let it be clearly understood that this great Republican Party is our historic home. This is our home. We have no intention of deserting it. We are still Republicans—and not very still ones, either. And let the Democratic Party find no comfort in the spirited campaign we have just waged within our own party.[13]

[12] Clif White's preballoting tally sheet missed the Goldwater-Scranton outcome by only one vote.
[13] See page 44.

Scranton had warm words and warm congratulations for Goldwater. But Goldwater was not reciprocating—not then, anyway. He would make the effort at conciliation weeks later, when it was too late to undo the damage of San Francisco.

The only true impact of the Scranton campaign was to force Goldwater deeper and deeper into his own coterie. Goldwater's nomination had become a true revolution, with no soothing words for the defeated. He broke the rule of Machiavelli, which says the defeated must be either destroyed or embraced.

Hit harder and harder by the desperate Scranton campaign, Goldwater grew angrier and more truculent—and less likely to make conciliatory gestures. He would not give an inch on the platform fight. Though he had once planned to name Ray Bliss as Republican national chairman, Goldwater now felt that Bliss had waited far too long to support him. Instead of naming a familiar party figure, Goldwater tapped Dean Burch—one of the most able members of the Arizona Mafia, but unknown nationally—as chairman.

But most important of all was Goldwater's attitude toward the Vice-Presidency. Just as he had regarded Rockefeller's attack against him in the summer of 1963 as a betrayal, so now was he deeply hurt by Scranton's attacks of late June. Now there was no question in his mind of putting Scranton on the ticket. Goldwater felt that Scranton had gone beyond the pale. The Senator's attitude came over clearly when he was asked about a Goldwater-Scranton ticket in the *Der Spiegel* interview of June 30:

> I would say he has completely ruled that out. At one time, there was a very strong possibility for it. But when he has turned to attacking personally a man that I always thought he considered a friend . . . well, the old *et tu* Brutus. I think probably if I get the nomination I will have to seek elsewhere.

The jarring, insulting Scranton letter of June 12 reinforced this sentiment. Now whatever remote possibility of putting

Scranton, or somebody else from the Scranton-Rockefeller camp, on the ticket was gone. The easy way beckoned for Goldwater. The Goldwater Movement wanted Bill Miller for Vice-President. They knew him to be a tough conservative (if occasionally a bit more pliable in his Congressional voting record than was Goldwater), a good political hatchet man, and a hard party worker who had traveled the country from one end to the other as national chairman. But Miller added no diversity to the ticket. Though a New Yorker, he was a conservative upstate New Yorker—more closely allied in spirit with the Midwest than with Gotham. Certainly, Miller was not the bridge to the moderates that Goldwater so desperately needed.

But Goldwater was in no mood for conciliation as his moment of victory approached. He didn't even go through the little ritual of calling in party graybeards after his nomination to "confer" with them about the choice of a running mate. Nor did he actually seek out the advice of respected party leaders, either inside or outside his own wing of the party. His choice of Miller was his own, decided finally on Wednesday morning. Seated with some of his staff in his suite at the Mark Hopkins, Goldwater picked up a phone and said: "Well, I guess I'll let Bill know." That was the first anybody knew for certain that the choice was absolutely final.

Goldwater had passed up three opportunities for conciliation—the platform, the Vice-Presidency, the national chairmanship. All that was left was the acceptance on Thursday. Surely here, Goldwater would go through the motions of holding out the olive branch—particularly since Scranton had made the first conciliatory gesture with his unity speech of Wednesday night.

But Goldwater did not. For the first time in memory at a contested convention, the victor had no words of kindness or of praise for the vanquished. Nor were there any words indicating a drift toward the middle of the road. It was all conservatism—anticommunism, antiterror in the streets, fiscal and governmental integrity. The tone was set early in the address with these words of ringing conservatism:

> . . . the tide has been running against freedom. Our people have followed false prophets. We must, and we shall, return to the proven ways—not because they are old, but because they are true.

There was no direct reference to the cause of civil rights (though the unusual emphasis on the need for better police protection on city streets had anti-Negro implications).

But the words that will always be most remembered from Goldwater's acceptance speech were the words that most disturbed the vanquished at San Francisco:

> I would remind you that extremism in the defense of liberty is no vice.
>
> And let me remind you also that moderation in the pursuit of justice is no virtue.

These words shattered the last flickering hope that party unity would come out of San Francisco. Until they were spoken, Clif White hoped against hope that Goldwater would make some gesture of conciliation toward the Republican left. Scranton had been White's choice for Vice-President until the end. White had wanted Goldwater to take a walk into Scranton's suite in the Mark Hopkins to shake hands on the Thurday morning after the nomination. When he didn't, White still hoped that the acceptance speech might provide the answer.

But while White preoccupied himself with the details of pinning down the nomination at the Cow Palace, he lost real control over the campaign itself. In command now was the mysterious Bill Baroody, moving ever so slightly out of the tax-exempt shadows of his American Enterprise Institute into Goldwater's suite at the Mark Hopkins (where NBC cameras picked up a shirt-sleeved Baroody, who usually denied anything more than a social friendship with Goldwater, seated among Goldwater's inner circle). Baroody was later described by a rival Goldwater adviser as "a combination of Svengali and Dave Powers [companion and storyteller for John F. Kennedy] as far as the Senator is concerned." Starting with San Francisco, Baroody was in full command of Goldwater's increasingly important brain trust and with Denison Kitchel and Karl Hess composed the troika that was to run the Goldwater campaign right down to November 3.

Hess, with some help from Baroody and Kitchel, had written the basic draft of the acceptance speech two weeks earlier. A few finishing touches were applied at the Mark Hopkins during convention week. But up to the very moment that Goldwater arrived at the Cow Palace to accept his nomination, no working politician either inside or outside the Goldwater staff (including Clif White) saw a draft of the speech. Hess maintained such extraordinary security, even to the point of posting Pinkerton men to guard copies of the speech at the Mark Hopkins, that only a few copies got out to the Cow Palace in time to do the press much good.

On the floor of the Cow Palace early during that final Thurday-night session, Rockefeller aide Carl Spad approached Clif White to talk about the possibilities of future party unity. White was agreeable. But Rockefeller's intentions, whatever they might have been, were obliterated a few minutes later by Goldwater's memorable acceptance speech.

The nonpoliticians—Baroody, Kitchel, Hess—were "in," and the politicians were "out." Even Dean Burch, Goldwater's surprise choice as Republican national chairman, was essentially a nonpolitician with deep personal loyalties to the Senator, and he had not much more regard for party unity than did the Baroody-Kitchel-Hess troika.

The fate of Clif White is illustrative. Though widely supported by conservative Republican politicians to replace

Miller as national chairman, White was ignored by Goldwater after the nomination on Wednesday night. Waiting in vain to be summoned for a meeting with the Senator, a despondent White left San Francisco the following Monday for a vacation in Hawaii with his family. It was more than two weeks later before he finally saw Goldwater and got his assignment for the campaign: national director of the Citizens for Goldwater-Miller, a secondary assignment at best.

Indeed, as the convention ended, even the Goldwater camp was divided. Overall, the party was preoccupied with internal party strife.

The victorious Goldwaterites talked about extending their rule into the last Eastern holdouts of the moderates. The vanquished moderates talked about the need to prevent the conservative capture of the national party machinery from enduring. The talk was not nearly so much about the contest against Lyndon Johnson in November as about the future struggle for party control.

Against frightening odds, the conservative movement of Barry Goldwater had won at least temporary possession of the Republican Party—but a party split more deeply than at any time since the great schism of 1912.

XXIV

★ ★

"Where Pragmatism Ends"

How did it happen?

This was the question asked incessantly after Barry Goldwater had astounded so many to become his party's nominee. It was asked by laymen, by disconsolate Republican liberals, by conservatives who could not quite believe that they had finally succeeded after so long in the wilderness.

The answer usually given was a wrong answer, which in turn led rapidly to the propagation of a Goldwater myth. The trouble is that the answer was usually given by people who had seen what happened in San Francisco and nothing before. It was akin to analyzing a winning football team based on watching it in the last quarter of a game, after its opponent has been ground down to impotence. Watching the Goldwater juggernaut crush the feeble opposition in San Francisco and forgetting all that came before led to this answer:

"Goldwater was nominated because behind him was a smooth-working, well-disciplined, well-led political organization that had so dominated state conventions that Goldwater had enough delegates at San Francisco to win no matter what happened in the primaries. Therefore, for the future, primaries are obsolete and Goldwater-style organizations are absolutely essential." This is the Goldwater myth.

In the first place, this book has tried to show that all the confusion, the indecision, and the blunders that are inherent in political-campaign organizations were to be found in abundance within the Goldwater organization. These were scarcely robot-like supermen running Barry Goldwater's campaign.

In the second place, it is almost certain that Goldwater could not have been nominated if he had lost to Rockefeller in the California primary on June 2. And if Goldwater had won his earlier primary tests in New Hampshire, Oregon, and elsewhere, he would have been the certain nominee, without much opposition—quite probably by acclamation. So primaries *do* count. Despite their limitations, they are the only way (other than the much abused polls), that a candidate's popular appeal can be tested prior to the convention.

The truth is that the Goldwater organization really picked up no more than four hundred absolutely hard-core delegates (not counting California's eighty-six). The remaining delegates had to come from delegations whose support for Goldwater was something less inviolate than a sacred vow. If Goldwater had lost to Rockefeller in California, he would have lost more than eighty-six delegates. He would have lost much of Ohio, Colorado, Florida, Wisconsin, and parts of Illinois, Georgia, and Washington. In other words, Goldwater would have had an extremely difficult time being nominated—*if* thirty thousand voters in California had voted for Rockefeller instead of Goldwater. This is just the first of many such *ifs*. They are worth recording only to show that the Goldwater nomination was something a good deal less than inevitable:

If Nelson Rockefeller had not remarried in May, 1963, he would have been difficult to beat, if not unbeatable, for the nomination—particularly if Goldwater campaigned no better than he actually did in 1964.

If Rockefeller had been realistic enough to withdraw from the Presidential race after his remarriage, the gap probably would have been quickly filled (particularly after the Kennedy assassination). That would have meant Lodge, Nixon, or Scranton as Goldwater's principal contender. It is questionable whether Goldwater could have won in California against any of these three.

If Lodge or Nixon or Scranton had actively entered the race even though Rockefeller stayed in it, it is likely that one of these three would have won in Oregon and California.

If Nixon had either been elected Governor of California in 1962 or had not entered that race at all, he would have been difficult to stop for the 1964 Presidential nomination after the assassination—whether an active candidate or not.

The point here is that the Goldwater organization and the Goldwater campaign were not invincible. But it was different. From a strictly organizational standpoint, its distinctiveness was a matter of its insinuating itself so early in the delegate-selection process—right down to the precinct mass meetings. It meant that hundreds of delegates went to San Francisco who were Goldwater men from the beginning, their progress from precinct to county to district to state conventions carefully followed by national tacticians in the Goldwater campaign.

This was the great contribution of F. Clifton White, Goldwater's chief delegate hunter. From the time that White put together the Draft Goldwater nucleus, not long after the 1960 election, he exercised a degree of personal control and personal observation of the delegation-selection process not seen before in American politics.

But the organization that Clif White built was not the invincible machine that some of the postnomination newspaper accounts portrayed it to be. Not long after the nomination, the Goldwater organization was put in proper perspective by one of the originals in the Draft Goldwater group —Representative John Ashbrook, thirty-five, a militant and attractive conservative Congressman from Ohio. "I get a kick out of all this praise heaped on us," said Ashbrook. "We booted a lot of them. We almost lost Florida by backing the wrong people down there. We could have lost Ohio. We *did* lose Minnesota by not coming to an agreement with Walter Judd. We made a lot more bobbles. The only reason we came out all right is the people at the grass roots."

Ashbrook's "people at the grass roots" are the warriors of the Goldwater Movement—the real heroes and the real winners of the Republican fight of 1964. These were the foot troops who swarmed into precinct meetings from Seattle to Atlanta to take over the Republican Party. Often, their sleeping foes didn't oppose them. But even when opposed, the Goldwaterites proved hard to outnumber. The Minnesota Republican Party fought a year-long war to prevent the Goldwater onslaught in the precincts, but only partially succeeded and then only through the gimmick of using Walter Judd as a Presidential candidate to oppose Goldwater.

The real question of the 1964 Republican fight should be not "How did it happen?" but "How does the Goldwater Movement manage to flood the precinct meetings in every part of the country?" The Movement cannot outpull a Lodge in New Hampshire or a Rockefeller in Oregon, but it can find more people who care enough to sit through a precinct meeting.

Why?

The answer to this is the real answer to the nomination of Barry Goldwater in 1964 and the sudden dominance in the Republican Party of the new conservatives. For without the Movement, Goldwater would have been finished after New Hampshire.

It is not enough to dismiss the Goldwaterites as kooks. A more penetrating answer is suggested by a senior staff member in the organization of one of the unsuccessful contenders for the 1964 nomination. In a brief unsigned monograph on the 1964 campaign called "Where Pragmatism Ends," this staff member blames the hold of pragmatism—the test of

"Does it work?"—on what used to be called the progressive wing of the Republican Party. The paper depicts Rockefeller as the archetype of the political pragmatic:

> . . . he tends to shy publicly from discussions of political doctrine, arguing the pragmatic line that government is a matter of "problem solving" rather than of adherence to abstract political philosophies. He gave currency to the rather mealy-mouthed label "moderate" to describe his own position.

After quickly tracing the dismal course of the party's non-Goldwater wing in 1964, the monograph comes to this conclusion:

> Pragmatism failed the moderates and the progressives in the Republican Party in 1964, not only because it prevented them from developing a positive alternative to . . . "Goldwaterism," but also because it prevented their leaders from giving free rein in crucial moments to those moral checks or moral impulses which might have enabled them to maintain their supremacy within the party. The argument against Goldwater was based too much on his "electability," too much on the damage that his presence might do to other candidates running on state or local tickets. . . .

For all the *ifs* that show how many different ways Goldwater could have been stopped, this monograph points to the true weakness of his opposition. It is true that the anti-Goldwater forces were victims of an unlucky chain of events, beginning with the Rockefeller remarriage. But if they had had some nonpragmatic moral philosophy to oppose Goldwater and his conservatism, they might have survived the bad breaks.

In the final analysis, then, Rockefeller and Scranton lost because they had nothing to offer the people but themselves. Goldwater had a moral philosophy that stirred enough people to the heights of enthusiasm so that the nomination was his. Indeed, this attraction was so strong that the Goldwaterites could not see disaster looming ahead in November.